ADO 2.1
Programmer's Reference

David Sussman

Wrox Press Ltd. ®

ADO 2.1 Programmer's Reference

Published by Wrox Press Ltd
Arden House, 1102 Warwick Road, Acock's Green, Birmingham B27 6BH, UK
Printed in USA
ISBN 1-861002-68-8

Trademark Acknowledgements

Wrox has endeavored to provide trademark information about all the companies and products mentioned in this book by the appropriate use of capitals. However, Wrox cannot guarantee the accuracy of this information.

Credits

Author
David Sussman

Additional Material
Alex Homer

Editors
Chris Goode
Ian Nutt

Index
Martin Brooks

Technical Reviewers
Michael Corning
David Elmqvist
Dan Hollacher
Todd Lewis
Rob Macdonald
Sophie McQueen
Eric Wilson

Design/Layout
Mark Burdett

Cover
Andrew Guillaume
Image by Rita Ruban

About the Author

David Sussman is a developer, trainer and author, living in a quiet country village in Oxfordshire, surrounded by nothing but fields and trees. One day soon he intends to stop working so hard and get some form of social life.

A.V. Ramelli.

Table of Contents

Table of Contents

Table of Contents

Table of Contents

Table of Contents

Table of Contents

Table of Contents

Table of Contents

Introduction

This book provides a concise and comprehensive guide to the ways in which ADO 2.1 can be used in all kinds of applications. It demonstrates the use of ADO both in Web applications written using ASP, and in compiled applications written using Visual Basic and other languages. It also includes a reference section for fast access to detailed lists of the properties, methods and events available in ADO.

What Is ADO?

If you are new to data access programming with Microsoft technologies, you may not yet be aware of ADO, although it's hard not to have come across it if you've had anything at all to do with the Internet. ADO stands for **ActiveX Data Objects** (although it's sometimes – mistakenly – called **Active Data Objects**).

ADO is a set of ActiveX components that provide programmatic access to Microsoft's latest underlying data access technologies. You can use ADO through almost any programming or scripting language, as long as it can instantiate and use ActiveX controls. An ActiveX control is effectively a COM object.

ADO is based on an underlying data access technology called **OLE-DB**. This is a defined set of COM interfaces that all data sources can implement through special drivers (or **providers**), and thereby expose their data content in a uniform way. OLE-DB relies on a COM Application Programming Interface (API), which is designed for use with languages like C++. ADO makes these same interfaces available in a far wider range of languages.

In other words, ADO gives us a standard way of managing data from all kinds of data stores, not just relational databases. In Chapter 1, we'll expand on these concepts to show you just how useful this whole approach is when building data management applications.

The design of ADO has also been driven by the ever-increasing role and importance of the Internet in application development. ADO provides a range of techniques with which remote data access can be achieved over the Internet, using a Web browser or through custom applications written in a range of programming languages.

What Is This Book About?

This book covers the broad outlines and purpose of ADO as the Microsoft data access technology of the future. It also describes the new features that are included in version 2.1 of ADO.

It covers the advanced ADO topics, as well as acting as a vital reference on syntax and semantics for working with ADO. In addition, it covers the new ADO Extensions for Data Definition and Security (ADOX), as well as introducing ADO for Multi-Dimensional (OLAP) data and the Jet and Replication Objects.

In addition, the book explains how ADO fits into **Windows Distributed interNet Applications** (DNA) – Microsoft's picture for distributed data-oriented applications – and describes the advantages of ADO over other existing Microsoft data access technologies.

Finally, it shows how ADO interfaces with the core OLE-DB data access driver model to provide connectivity with a whole range of data stores. This can include messaging systems, text files and specific non-standard data formats, as well as the more usual relational databases.

Who Is This Book For?

This book is a reference guide for the ADO programmer; it's primarily aimed at demonstrating and explaining the features of ADO 2.1 and the ways that they can be used. As such, it isn't a beginner's guide – though if you have programmed any data-access applications in the past, you'll be able to use it to get up-to-speed with ADO.

In particular, the book is aimed at application developers who already use Microsoft's data access methods in their applications, but want to take full advantage of the new features of ADO 2.1. It includes all the information required for any reasonably experienced developer to start using ADO within their Web pages and distributed applications. Finally, it is ideal for existing ADO users, to bring them quickly up-to-date with version 2.1.

What Does It Cover?

In this book, we've avoided discussion of ASP and data-handling programming in components – with the exception of the techniques directly connected with using ADO. As a result, the examples are concise, and designed to demonstrate ADO techniques rather than to build entire applications. However, we do provide pointers to other sources of information to indicate the kind of things that can be achieved.

The book offers users an easy-to-follow tutorial and reference to ADO, by splitting the whole topic into neat and intuitive segments. This also makes it easier to find specific information later as you come to use ADO in real-world applications. To help out, a comprehensive quick reference section is also included. It lists the properties, methods and events of each of the objects found in ADO, ADOX, RDS, JRO and ADOMD, together with other useful information.

The segmentation of the book looks like this:

- ❏ Introduction to ADO, and what's new in ADO 2.1
- ❏ Connecting to data stores, with or without the `Connection` object (includes a discussion of driver technologies)
- ❏ The `Command` object, and techniques for executing queries against a data store
- ❏ Using the `Recordset` object to control recordsets and cursors, and how they are used to retrieve data from a data store
- ❏ Collections of objects – including the `Fields` and `Errors` collections
- ❏ Remote data access, showing how ADO can be used in Web-based applications
- ❏ Using ADOX for data definition and security
- ❏ Using ADOMD for multi-dimensional representation of data
- ❏ Using JRO for compaction, replication and refreshing of data
- ❏ Data shaping, events, and offline usage
- ❏ Examination of ADO performance, comparing cursor and locking types

What Do I Need To Use This Book?

ADO has been available for some time, and it is installed with a whole range of other applications and development environments. The shipping of ADO has followed this path:

Version	...was released with
1.5	Windows NT 4.0 Option Pack
2.0	Visual Studio 6.0
	Windows NT4 Service Pack 4 (full install)
	Microsoft Data Access Components 2.0 (MDAC 2.0)
2.1	Office 2000
	MDAC 2.1
	SQL Server 7

The official release of ADO 2.1 is with Office 2000 and MDAC 2.1, and any other versions are deemed to be beta versions. This includes the version shipped with SQL Server 7.

In the meantime, if you don't have version 2.1 of ADO, you can download it from the Microsoft Data Access site, at http://www.microsoft.com/data/. The official 2.1 release is MDAC 2.1.1.3711.11 (GA).

Introduction

We provide the source code for the samples that you'll see in this book on our Web site, and you can even run some of them directly from there – to save you the trouble of installing them on your own machine. The main samples menu page for this book is at http://webdev.wrox.co.uk/books/2688/. This site also contains a range of other resources and reference material that you might find useful, including other books that demonstrate ADO applications.

To run the samples yourself, and build applications that use ADO 2.1, you will require only your usual preferred development tools – you should check your development tool for its compatibility with ADO 2.1. To build Web-based or Intranet-based applications that use ASP, this will be just a Web server that supports ASP and a client browser. The Web server will need to have ADO 2.1 installed, and will probably be running Internet Information Server 4 from the NT4 Option Pack. For the remote data access examples in Chapter 7, the browser should be Internet Explorer 4 or higher.

To build compiled applications that don't use the Internet or your own Intranet, but rely on communication over a traditional LAN, you'll need just your own choice of programming language development tool. This will also be required if you want to build custom business components for Internet- or Intranet-based applications.

Which Programming Language Do I Use?

Because ADO is COM based, it is language-neutral – in other words, it can be used in any programming language that supports the instantiation of ActiveX/COM objects. This includes Visual Basic, C++, Delphi, Java and J++, and scripting languages such as JavaScript, JScript and VBScript – as used in client-side browser and server-side ASP programming.

As such, we've provided some guidance as to how the ADO objects can be accessed in various languages in Chapter 1. We then use a Visual Basic-like syntax for each part of the ADO object model. We decided against including samples in each language because this really breaks up the flow of text. However, we've put together a package of samples that demonstrate ADO usage in a number of languages: Visual Basic, ASP/VBScript, ASP/JScript, Visual C++ and Visual J++. You'll find these samples, and supporting documentation, on our web site at http://webdev.wrox.co.uk/books/2688.

Conventions

We have used a number of different styles of text and layout in the book to help differentiate between the different kinds of information. Here are examples of the styles we use and an explanation of what they mean:

Bullets appear indented, with each new bullet marked as follows:

- ❑ **Important Words** are in a bold type font
- ❑ Words that appear on the screen in menus like the File or Window are in a similar font to the one that you see on screen
- ❑ Keys that you press on the keyboard, like *Ctrl* and *Enter*, are in italics

Code has several fonts. If it's a word that we're talking about in the text, for example, when discussing the For...Next loop, it's in this font. If it's a block of code that you can type in as a program and run, then it's also in a gray box:

```
objRec.Open "authors", objConn, adOpenKeyset, adLockOptimistic, _
            (adCmdTable OR adAsyncFetch)
```

Sometimes you'll see code in a mixture of styles, like this:

```
<OBJECT CLASSID="clsid:BD96C556-65A3-11D0-983A-00C04FC29E33"
                        ID="dsoBookList" HEIGHT=0 WIDTH=0>
    <PARAM NAME="Server" VALUE="http://www.yourserver.com">
    <PARAM NAME="Connect" VALUE="SERVER=http://dataserver.com;
                        DRIVER={SQL Server};DATABASE=yourdb;
                        UID=anon;PWD=">
    <PARAM NAME="SQL" VALUE="SELECT * FROM BookList">
</OBJECT>
```

The code with a white background is code we've already looked at and that we don't wish to examine further.

Advice, hints, and background information come in an italicized, indented font like this.

> **Important pieces of information come in boxes like this.**

We demonstrate the syntactical usage of methods, properties (and so on) using the following format:

> *Recordset*.**Find**(*Criteria*, [*SkipRecords*], [*SearchDirection*], [*Start*])

Here, the italicized parts indicate object references, variables or parameter values to be inserted; the square braces indicate optional parameters.

Customer Support

We've tried to make this book as accurate and useful as possible, but what really matters is what the book actually does for you. Please let us know your views, either by returning the reply card at the back of the book, or by writing to us at feedback@wrox.com.

The **source code** for this book – including ADO samples in C++, Visual Basic, J++ and scripting languages – is available for download at http://www.wrox.com. You can also run many of the samples directly from our Web Developer site, at http://webdev.wrox.co.uk.

We've made every effort to ensure there are no errors in this book. However, to err is human, and we recognize the need to keep you informed of errors as they're spotted and corrected. **Errata sheets** are available for all our books, at http://www.wrox.com. If you find an error that hasn't already been reported, please let us know. Appendix Q gives more information about how to submit errata.

Our web site acts as a focus for other information and support, including the code from all our books, sample chapters and previews of forthcoming titles.

1

What Is ADO?

ActiveX Data Objects (ADO) and OLEDB, its underlying technology, are going to play a big part in the future of data access. Microsoft has unequivocally committed its future to it, and quite rightly so. The paperless office has yet to appear, but the amount of data being stored on computer systems is increasing every day. This is shown quite clearly in the rate at which the Web is expanding – and that's just the public face of data. There's much more data that is hidden from general view.

In this chapter we are going to look at the terms and technology behind ADO. If you need to start coding straight away then you could skip to the relevant chapters, but – like any form of learning – your understanding will be better if you have a good foundation.

So, to give you that good grounding, there are several important topics we will discuss in this chapter:

- ❑ What we mean by 'data'
- ❑ What we mean by a 'data store'
- ❑ How ADO fits with existing data access strategies
- ❑ Data access in the client/server world

ADO is central to Microsoft's data access strategy, so it's important to understand why it came about and what sort of a future it's got. We'll be looking at these issues too.

What is Data?

If you've got a few spare minutes sometime, open up Windows Explorer and have a look around your hard disk. Make a little note of how many separate pieces of information you've got: databases, documents, spreadsheets, email messages, HTML and ASP documents, etc. Quite a lot, eh? They are all pockets of data, albeit stored in different forms. This might seem obvious, but traditionally data has really only been thought of as being stored in a database: to build a business application the data had to be in a database. While a large proportion of existing data may be contained in databases, why should the remaining data be excluded from our grasp? In fact, as computers get more powerful, the term 'data' is starting to include multimedia items such as music and video, as well as objects, and the more normal document-based data.

So, by 'data' we mean any piece of information, whatever its contents. Whether it's your address book, your monthly expenses spreadsheet, or a pleading letter to the taxman, it's all data.

What are Data Stores?

Now we've established what we consider data to be, the definition of a Data Store might be fairly obvious – it's somewhere where data is kept. However, there is much more to Data Stores than you might think. Instead of looking at your hard disk, let's look at mine this time, and see what I've got installed:

❑ **Databases**: We consider these the traditional store of data – I've got both SQL Server and Access databases, which I use to store everything from accounts and invoicing to sample databases for books.

❑ **Spreadsheets**: Financial data with year end figures for my tax returns and bills.

❑ **Mail and News**: I use Outlook and Outlook Express to handle my mail and Internet news.

❑ **Documents**: This is the largest proportion of data on my machine, containing all of my personal letters and documents, and chapters for books (including this one).

❑ **Graphics**: Screen dumps and pictures for books.

❑ **Internet**: HTML and ASP pages, containing samples and applications.

❑ **Reference Material**: Including MSDN and encyclopedias.

So that's the actual data, but how is it stored? Well, the databases are self-contained, so they are their own data store. The reference material is, by and large, stored in its own format, so that could also be considered a data store. The mail and news hold data on their own as well, so they are a data store. Everything else is stored as files – therefore the file system itself becomes a data store (OK, the data it stores is in a myriad of formats, but it's all stored in the same way – folders and documents).

You could even include my CD-ROM drive and tape backup unit. The CD-ROM uses the standard documents and folders format, so this could be considered part of the file system data store, but the tape backup has its own format, and could therefore be considered a data store too.

There are numerous other data stores, from mainframe file systems to databases and mail. As the enterprise gets bigger we also need to include user account databases, and other machines attached to the network, such as printers and scanners. They might not all be data stores themselves, but as items of data they'll be contained in a data store somewhere.

About Universal Data Access

Universal Data Access (UDA) is Microsoft's strategy for dealing with all of this data. It's aimed at providing high-performance access to a variety of data sources. The cynical amongst you might suspect this to be an attempt to shoehorn another Microsoft technology onto the scene – but let's look at the modern business.

To be a successful business you have to be flexible, to adapt to change. How do you know when to change? There's no simple rule here, but most companies make decisions by asking a few questions. How much can we sell? How much *are* we selling? How much are our competitors selling? What does research show about what customers want? Questions like these can be answered using statistical analysis, and where do the statistics come from? That's right, data. But we've already seen that data is stored in many different ways, and there is no central way of accessing them all.

So with UDA we are looking at an easy-to-use methodology, that allows access to multiple sources of data in a single way. Build in high performance and support for existing data access methods, and you're on your way to something that could make a real difference. This means that you don't have to bundle all of your data together into a single data source. Let's have a look at how this could work.

When building an application you can make sure it uses ADO for its data access, and ADO will talk to all of the data sources required. This means that programming is made easier, since only one technology needs to be learned. Because ADO gives fast, transparent access to different types of data, there's no reason to use any other method.

You can clearly see what Microsoft is intending when you look at the three main design goals for the Data Access Components:

- ❑ Meeting the key customer requirements, such as performance, reliability and broad industry support.
- ❑ Giving access to the widest range of data sources, through a common interface.
- ❑ Providing an easy migration path for existing data access technologies.

So far they seem to be meeting these admirably.

This method contrasts with Oracle who, naturally, are pushing Universal Server, in which all of the data will be stored under one central data store. The ultimate aim is the same – broader access to data. The Oracle approach involves a bigger initial investment in data conversion and translation, as the data is imported to the store. But once that investment has been made, the data is easy to access. Of course, ADO can be used to access Oracle databases.

In terms of superiority, it's difficult to choose between the two methods – the best method for you will be dependent upon your business needs and current computer systems.

Existing Technologies

Before we explain why ADO came about, let's take a quick look at some existing technologies and see how they fit into the picture.

❑ **DBLib:** This is the underlying technology for connecting to SQL Server. It is primarily designed for C, but is often used in Visual Basic. Because it is specific to SQL Server, it is extremely fast and functional. For this very reason, however, it doesn't allow access to any other source of data. Other databases, such as Oracle and Sybase, have similar native communication libraries.

❑ **ODBC:** Open DataBase Connectivity (ODBC) was the first step on the road to a universal data access strategy. ODBC was designed (by Microsoft and other DBMS vendors) as a cross-platform, database-independent method, using API calls. It was designed for multi-database use; however, it was often used on only single databases, and from a programmer's point of view was complex to use, much like DBLib, because it was a low-level library ODBC is also restricted to data sources that support SQL, and is therefore not suitable for non-SQL based repositories.

❑ **DAO:** The Data Access Objects (DAO) were introduced with Microsoft Access, and provided a strict hierarchical set of objects for manipulating data in Jet, other ISAM and SQL databases. These objects were available with Visual Basic and quickly became the most commonly-used data access method for Visual Basic programs. DAO also had the advantage of being able to sit on top of ODBC – this allowed it to communicate with many different databases.

❑ **RDO:** Aimed as the successor to DAO for Visual Basic programmers, Remote Data Objects (RDO) is a thin layer that sits on top ODBC, allowing better access to server databases, such as SQL Server. This brought the flexibility of ODBC with a much easier programming model, but like DAO it has a strictly hierarchical programming model. RDO also brought the world of remote database servers to the world of many programmers.

❑ **ODBCDirect:** An extension to DAO, and combined portions of DAO and RDO. It allows programmers to use the DAO programming model, and also allows access to ODBC data sources without having the Jet database loaded.

❑ **JDBC:** Java Database Connectivity (JDBC) was designed by Microsoft as another DBMS-neutral API, especially for use in Java applications.

The problems with these technologies are very simple. DBLib and ODBC are low-level APIs and therefore, for many programmers, are complex to use. DAO and RDO offer the user another interface to ODBC, but this introduces another layer of code to go through and performance can drop. Moreover, all of these technologies suffer from a very strict and hierarchical model, which adds extra overhead to both programming and execution.

They are also more or less constrained by providing access to relational databases, although Microsoft Excel and simple text documents could also be used as data sources when using ODBC. ODBC drivers have also been produced for object oriented and hierarchical databases, which allow the data to be accessed in a way similar to a relational databases.

What is OLEDB?

OLEDB is designed to be the successor to ODBC. You might be asking, why do we need a successor? Well, there are three main trends at the moment. The first, fairly obviously, is the Internet. The second is an increasing amount of data being stored in a non-relational form, such as Exchange Server and file systems. The third is Microsoft's desire for a COM world, where all object usage is handled through their Component Object Model. In fact OLE DB encourages the use of componentization, allowing database functionality and data handling to be encapsulated into components.

The Internet brings a different aspect to standard data access because of its distributed nature. Applications are now being written on a truly global scale, and you can no longer guarantee that the data you are accessing is stored on your local network. This means that you need to give careful consideration to the *way* you access data, as well as the *type* of data you access. The new business opportunity of e-commerce has meant that selling becomes a whole new ball game – you can now have an application that shows pictures of your products, plays music, and even videos, all running over the Web. The Web is also more distributed (and often less reliable) than conventional networks, so your data access method has to take this into account. You can't, for example, assume that your client and server remain connected at all times during an application – in the stateless nature of the Web this doesn't make sense.

So OLEDB is a technology designed to solve some of these problems, and over time it will gradually replace ODBC as the central data access method. Even so, new versions of ODBC are supplied with ADO 2, and ODBC will continue to be developed and supported. OLEDB is the guts of the new data access strategy, and from version 3.5 of ODBC, OLEDB is now a core part.

Why ADO?

OLEDB is a COM-based set of object-oriented interfaces, and thus for a large proportion of the programming community it is too complex to use, or is not suitable because they use programming languages which don't have access to custom COM interfaces. ADO is the higher-level model that most people will use, because it provides a dual-interface, allowing access from Visual Basic and scripting languages. It equates fairly well to the DAO level, where you create an object, and call its methods and properties. Being an ActiveX component means it can be used from any language that supports COM – including Visual Basic, VBA, scripting languages, VC++ and VJ++.

So now our diagram looks even more enticing:

We have various languages, all with the ability to use a central data access strategy. Some languages (like Java and Visual C++) can talk directly to OLEDB, as well as talking to the easier ADO – although we'll only be looking at the ADO layer here.

ADO also addresses the speed and ease of development by introducing an **object model** that allows data to be retrieved from a data source with as little as one line of code. And this line of code can be switched between languages (such as between Visual Basic and ASP Scripting) with minimal changes.

ADO addresses another pressing need, which is created by the increasing use of the Web as an application medium. Conventional applications are generally connected via a Local Area Network to their data store. They can open a connection to the data, and keep that connection open throughout the life of the program. Consequently, the data store knows who is connecting. Many applications also process data on the client – perhaps a set of records that the user is browsing through or updating. Since the client is connected to the server, or source of the data, there's no trouble updating the data.

On the Web however, the native mechanism is stateless. There's no permanent connection between client and server. If you think about the way the Web works for a second, you'll realize why this is a problem:

❑ First, you request a web page in your browser;

❑ Then, the web server receives the request, runs any server-side script, and sends the page back to you.

That's it. As soon as this is over the web server forgets about you. Admittedly with ASP you can store some sort of session state, but it's not very sophisticated. How then, with this disconnected network, do you provide a system that allows data to be updated on the client and sent back to the server? This is where ADO comes in, with **disconnected recordsets**. This technology allows the recordset to be disassociated from the server, and then re-associated at a later date. Add this to the fact that you can save these disconnected recordsets locally, and you can have an application that allows the user to save updates to records in a client copy of the recordset, and update the central set of records (the server) at a later date. In fact, disconnected recordsets don't have to be associated with a database at all – they can be manually created and used as a data store, in much the same way as collections.

The use of client-side data manipulation also allows you to sort data, find records, and generally manage recordsets without resorting to additional trips to the server. Although his idea primarily fits with the nature of the Web, it can work just as well for the standard type of applications running on a LAN, and can reduce network traffic.

Data Providers and Data Consumers

OLEDB introduces two new terms that help to explain how OLEDB and ADO fit together:

❑ A **Data Consumer** is something that uses (or consumes) data. Strictly speaking, ADO is actually a consumer, because it uses data provided by OLEDB.

❑ A **Data Provider** is (unsurprisingly) something that provides data. This isn't the physical source of the data, but the mechanism that connects us to the physical data store. The provider may get the data directly from the data store, or it may go through a third party product (such as ODBC) to get to the data store. It can even use other data sources and provide added value along the way – the MSDataShape provider is an example of this. This means that you can immediately start using ADO to access existing data stores that support ODBC, even if there isn't an OLEDB provider available for them yet.

The initial set of OLEDB providers supplied with ADO 2.1 are:

❑ **Jet 4.0**, for Microsoft Access databases. This allows access to standard Access databases, including linked tables. ADO 2.0 shipped with the Jet 3.5 Provider.

❑ **Directory Services**, for resource data stored, such as Active Directory. This will become more important when Windows 2000 is available, as the Directory Service will allow access to user information, as well as network devices.

❑ **Index Server**, for Microsoft Index Server. This will be particularly useful as web sites grow, as the indexed data will be available.

❑ **Site Server Search**, for Microsoft Site Server. Again for use with web sites, especially large complex sites, where Site Server is used to maintain them.

❑ **ODBC Drivers**, for existing ODBC Drivers. This ensures that legacy data is not omitted as part of the drive forward.

❑ **Oracle**, for Oracle databases. Connection to Oracle has never been particularly easy with Microsoft products in the past, but a native driver will simplify access to existing Oracle data stores.

❑ **SQL Server**, for Microsoft SQL Server, to allow access to data stored in SQL Server.

❑ **Data Shape**, for hierarchical recordsets. This allows creation of master/detail type recordsets, which allow drilling down into detailed data.

❑ **Persisted Recordset**, for locally saved recordsets, and recordset marshalling

❑ **OLAP**, for accessing On Line Analytical Processing data stores.

❑ **Internet Publishing**, for accessing web resources that support Microsoft FrontPage Server Extensions or Distributed Authoring and Versioning (DAV). For more information on DAV check out the WebDAV Working Group home page at http://www.ics.uci.edu/~ejw/authoring/.

❑ **Remoting Provider**, for connecting to data providers on remote machines.

This is just the list of standard providers supplied by Microsoft; other vendors are actively creating their own. For example, a company called ISG provide an OLEDB provider that allows connection to multiple data stores at the same time. Oracle provide an OLEDB provider, which they claim is better than Microsoft's Oracle provider, and most other database suppliers have OLEDB providers for their databases.

OLEDB also provides a few other services, such as a query processor and a cursor engine, so these can be used at the client. There are two reasons for this. First, it frees the actual provider from providing the service – thus the service can be smaller. Second, it makes it available as a client service. This means that cursor handling can be provided locally, which is an important function of disconnected recordsets and Remote Data Services. The cursor engine is enhanced in ADO 2.1 with a more visible Cursor Service, exposing features such as better client-side indexing and the control of updating multi-table recordsets. Another advantage of the Cursor Service is that, as a client-based service, it can provide a more uniform set of features across all providers.

Providers and Drivers

It's important to understand how OLE DB Providers relate to ODBC Drivers, especially since there is an OLE DB Provider for ODBC, which seems somehow confusing. Take a look at the following diagram:

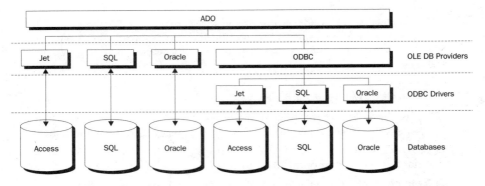

This distinctly shows the two layers. OLE DB Providers can be used to access data sources, including ODBC data sources. This allows OLE DB to access data for which there is an ODBC Driver, but no native OLE DB Provider. So, Providers are for OLE DB and Drivers are for ODBC.

Distributed Internet Applications

Distributed interNet Applications (DNA) is the architectural strategy that Microsoft is defining as the ideal way to write distributed, n-tier, client–server applications. One of the interesting things about this strategy is that it's really just a set of ideas and suggestions, rather than a complex, locked-in solution. It's not a new idea, but there are now some really good tools that make creating this type of application not just a reality, but a relatively easy reality.

The basic premise is to partition your application into at least **three tiers**. The first tier is the **user interface tier** – this is what the user sees, and could be a Web page or another type of application, written in any language. The second tier is where the **business rules** or processes lie – these determine where the data comes from, what rules apply to the data, and how it should be returned to the user interface. The third tier is the **data layer** – the actual source of the data:

The great thing about DNA is that it aims to be language-independent, since it all hinges around COM (and COM+ when we see it come to fruition in Windows 2000). COM is the Component Object Model, which allows easy object creation and re-use. Any component that supports COM will fit into this picture, so you can write your application in ASP and JavaScript, Visual Basic, VC++, VJ++, Delphi, or any language that supports COM. Likewise, your business components can be in any language, so you can program in whatever environment you feel happy in. There's no need to learn a new language.

In the diagram above, you can see that IIS and MTS are mentioned in the Business Processes tier. IIS supplies the connection from Web applications to components, which could be stand-alone components or MTS components. The great advantage of MTS is that it makes your middle tier suddenly very easy to manage – you can just create a component and install it into MTS. Once you've done that, it becomes available to all applications that can call COM. You can access the components on remote machines using DCOM. You also get the added advantage of transaction processing and easy scalability, without having to program it in yourself. The user interface can then be built in any language that supports COM.

> *If you want to learn more about MTS and its use in DNA applications, take a look at* Professional MTS MSMQ with Visual Basic and ASP *(Wrox Press, ISBN 1-861001-46-0).*

ADO 2.1 Availability

The Microsoft Data Access Components (MDAC) are available as a separate download from the Microsoft Web site, at http://www.microsoft.com/data, as well as being supplied with Internet Explorer 5 and Microsoft Office 2000. A future version of ADO (version 2.5) will ship with Windows 2000.

If you're at all unsure of what version of ADO, or any of its components, you've got installed, then download CLSIDVIEW from http://support.microsoft.com/support/kb/articles/q176/5/62.asp. This utility will give you a complete list of ADO DLLs and their version numbers. You can also use the `Version` property of the `Connection` object (see Chapter 3).

ADO 2.1 New Features

ADO 2.1 has a host of new features that make programming easier. This section is not going to cover them thoroughly – we'll deal with in more detail in the later chapters – but serve to provide a summary.

Extensions for DDL and Security

The **ADO Extensions for DDL and Security** (commonly known as ADOX) are a big new feature of ADO 2.1 – because in previous versions of ADO, these DDL commands had to be made using SQL statements. This means that you might have to use code specific to a certain data store (such as using Access SQL), which partly goes against the grain of UDA.

The ADO Extensions are designed to access the Data Definition Language (DDL) of the data store, abstracting these features into a simple set of components. This allows you to access metadata, create tables and procedures, set permissions, etc. without knowing the specific language that the data store uses.

The ADOX library is covered in Chapter 8, and the object model is introduced in Chapter 2.

Jet 4.0 Provider

An OLEDB Provider for Jet 4.0 and DAO 3.6 is included, for connection to Access 2000 databases, as well as previous access database versions.

Jet and Replication Objects

The Jet and Replication Objects (JRO) allow access to the replication functionality of Jet. In particular it allows:

- ❑ The creation of new design masters and replicas.
- ❑ The synchronization of replicas.
- ❑ The population of partial replicas.
- ❑ Viewing the conflict table.
- ❑ Creation of replica filters.

We'll touch on JRO in Chapter 10, but check out the ADO documentation if you want to find out more. This documentation is including within the Office 2000 documentation, or is available on MSDN Online at http://msdn.microsoft.com.

SQL Server 7.0 Provider

An OLEDB Provider for SQL Server 7.0 (and earlier) is included, giving better performance.

Shaping

As an extension to the existing data shaping service, ADO 2.1 will allow local reshaping of hierarchies. This is covered in Chapter 11.

ADO Examples

Since this is primarily a reference book, it seems sensible to give you a few documented samples of code, so that you can see what's possible and how some of the components fit together. You can use this as a sort of "table of contents" to the rest of the book, where the various aspects are covered in more detail. The next chapter goes into the language specifics in more detail, so we'll use Visual Basic here because it's easy to read and understand. Versions for other languages, such as JScript, C++, and Java will be available from the supporting Web site – http://webdev.wrox.co.uk/books/2688.

Example 1

The following section of Visual Basic code creates a connection to SQL Server, opens a recordset, and then adds some details from the recordset to a listbox:

```
' Define two object variables
' The object model is discussed in Chapter 2
Dim objConn     As New ADODB.Connection
Dim objRec      As New ADODB.Recordset

' Open a connection to the pubs database using the SQL Server OLEDB Provider
' Connection strings are discussed in Chapter 2
' The Connection object is discussed in Chapter 3
objConn.Open "Provider=SQLOLEDB; Data Source=Tigger; " & _
             "Initial Catalog=pubs; User Id=sa; Password="

' Open a recordset on the 'authors' table
' The Recordset is discussed in Chapter 5
objRec.Open "authors", objConn, adOpenForwardOnly, adLockReadOnly, adCmdTable

' Loop whilst we haven't reached the end of the recordset
' The EOF property is set to True when we reach the end
While Not objRec.EOF
    ' Add the names to the listbox, using the default Fields collection
    ' The Fields collection is discussed in Chapter 6
    List1.AddItem objRec("au_fname") & " " & objRec("au_lname")
    ' Move to the next record
    objRec.MoveNext
Wend

' Close the objects
objRec.Close
objConn.Close

' Release the memory associated with the objects
Set objRec = Nothing
Set objConn = Nothing
```

Example 2

This example runs a SQL statement and doesn't expect a set of records to be returned. It also uses an ODBC Data Source Name called `pubs`, that has previously been set up.

```
' Define the object variable
Dim objConn      As New ADODB.Connection

' Open a connection to the pubs database using the OLEDB Provider for ODBC
objConn.Open "DSN=pubs"

' Run a SQL UPDATE statement to update book prices by 10%
objConn.Execute "UPDATE titles SET price = price * 1.10" _
        , , adExecuteNoRecords

' Close the connection
objConn.Close

' Release the memory associated with the objects
Set objConn = Nothing
```

Example 3

This example runs a stored query in Access, passing in some parameters.

```
' Declare the object variables
' The Command object is discussed in Chapter 4
' The Parameter object is discussed in Chapter 6
Dim objConn      As New ADODB.Connection
Dim objCmd       As New ADODB.Command
Dim objRec       As ADODB.Recordset
Dim objParam     As ADODB.Parameter

' Open a connection to an Access pubs database,
' using the Access OLEDB provider
objConn.Open "Provider=Microsoft.Jet.OLEDB.4.0; " & _
            "Data Source=C:\temp\pubs.mdb"

' Create a new Parameter, called RequiredState
Set objParam = objCmd.CreateParameter("RequiredState", adChar, _
                                    adParamInput, 2, "CA")

' Add the parameter to the Parameters collection of the Command object
objCmd.Parameters.Append objParam

' Set the active connection of the command to the open connection object
objCmd.ActiveConnection = objConn

' Set the name of the stored query that is to be run
objCmd.CommandText = "qryAuthorsBooksByState"

' Set the type of command
objCmd.CommandType = adCmdStoredProc

' Run the stored query and set the recordset which it returns
Set objRec = objCmd.Execute

' Loop through the recordset, adding the items to a listbox
While Not objRec.EOF
    List1.AddItem objRec("au_fname") & " " & objRec("au_lname") & _
            ": " & objRec("title")
    objRec.MoveNext
Wend

' Close the recordset and connection
objRec.Close
objConn.Close
```

```
' Reclaim the memory from the objects
Set objRec = Nothing
Set objCmd = Nothing
Set objParam = Nothing
Set objConn = Nothing
```

Example 4

This example uses the `Fields` collection of the recordset to loop through all of the fields in a recordset, printing out the details in the debug window:

```
' Declare the object variables
Dim objRec      As New ADODB.Recordset
Dim objFld      As ADODB.Field

' Open a recordset on the 'authors' table using the OLEDB Driver for ODBC
' without using a connection
objRec.Open "authors", "DSN=pubs", _
            adOpenForwardOnly, adLockReadOnly, adCmdTable

' Loop through the Fields collection printing the name of each Field
' The Fields collection is discussed in Chapter 6
For Each objFld In objRec.Fields
    Debug.Print objFld.Name; vbTab;
Next
Debug.Print

' Loop through the records in the recordset
While Not objRec.EOF
    ' Loop through the fields, this time printing out the Value of each field
    For Each objFld In objRec.Fields
        Debug.Print objFld.Value; vbTab;
    Next
    Debug.Print
    objRec.MoveNext
Wend

' Close the recordset and release the memory
objRec.Close
Set objRec = Nothing
Set objFld = Nothing
```

Example 5

This example uses a `Catalog` and its associated `Tables` collection to list the tables in a data store:

```
' Declare the object variables
Dim objCat    As New ADOX.Catalog
Dim objTable  As ADOX.Table
Dim strConn   As String

' set the connection string
strConn="Provider=Microsoft.Jet.OLEDB.4.0; Data Source=C:\temp\pubs.mdb"

' point the catalog at a data store
objCat.ActiveConnection = strConn

' loop through the tables collection
For Each objTable In objCat.Tables
    Debug.Print objTable.Name
Next

' clean up
Set objTable = Nothing
Set objCat = Nothing
```

Example 6

This examples uses a `Catalog`, its `Tables` collection, and the `Indexes` and `Columns` collections for a table, to print out a list of columns for the index:

```
Dim objCat      As New ADOX.Catalog
Dim objTbl      As ADOX.Table
Dim objIdx      As ADOX.Index
Dim objCol      As ADOX.Column
Dim strConn     As String

' set the connection string
strConn="Provider=Microsoft.Jet.OLEDB.4.0; Data Source=C:\temp\pubs.mdb"
' point the catalog at a data store
objCat.ActiveConnection = strConn

' loop through the tables
For Each objTbl In objCat.Tables

    ' has the table got indexes
    If objTbl.Indexes.Count > 0 Then
        Debug.Print objTbl.Name

        ' loop through the indexes
        For Each objIdx In objTbl.Indexes
            Debug.Print vbTab; objIdx.Name; vbTab; objIdx.PrimaryKey

            'loop through the columns in the index
            For Each objCol In objIdx.Columns
                Debug.Print vbTab; vbTab; objCol.Name
            Next
        Next
    End If
Next

' clean up
Set objCol = Nothing
Set objTbl = Nothing
Set objIdx = Nothing
Set objCat = Nothing
```

ADO in Visual Basic 6

Although this is an ADO book, it seems a good opportunity to take a quick look at two useful features in Visual Basic 6 which both rely on ADO. We're not going to look at these in detail, but just give you a little glimpse of what's possible.

Data Environment

The data environment makes database programming so much neater within Visual Basic, since you have a central place to keep all of your data store connection details:

This diagram shows three connections – one to the SQL Server pubs database via the OLEDB Provider for ODBC, one to the Access database Biblio.mdb, and one to the pubs database via the SQL Server OLEDB provider. The Biblio connection has two commands added to it – one to the Authors table, and a sub-command, to the TitleAuthors table.

FlexGrid

This sub-command idea is one of the really cool things about the Data Environment, and it goes hand-in-hand with the new Hierarchical FlexGrid:

		Au_ID	Author	Year Born	ISBN	Au_ID
⊟		1	Jacobs, Rus		0-6723050-2	1
⊞		2	Metzger, Ph			
⊟		3	Boddie, Johi		0-1355423-9	3
⊞		4	Sydow, Dan			
⊟		6	Lloyd, John		0-2620822-9	6
					0-2626209-9	6
⊟		8	Thiel, James		0-1335449-9	8
⊟		10	Ingham, Ker		1-8787073-0	10
⊟		12	Wellin, Paul		0-3879443-5	12
⊟		13	Kamin, Sam		0-2010380-4	13
					0-3879443-5	13
					0-6723086-4	13
					1-5659216-3	13
⊟		14	Gaylord, Ric		0-2015652-8	14
					0-3879443-5	14
					0-4710450-7	14

You can see that this grid shows the detail from the AuthorTable and from the TitleAuthor table, and gives you the ability to expand items in the grid, to show the sub-items. Achieving this took less than thirty seconds, as all you have to do is set the data environment, draw the grid on the form and set two properties. Hierarchical recordsets are examined in more detail in Chapter 11.

There are many other features in Visual Basic 6 that greatly increase productivity and make code easier to maintain, including a host of new data-bound controls aimed at use with ADO.

Language Differences

One of the things we've tried to do with this book is make it relatively language-independent. ADO can be used by any programming language that supports COM, so the subject of which language to use for the samples in this book becomes quite a sticky one. Therefore, to give this the widest possible audience, we've stuck with a pseudo-code type style. For example, in the examples that show something being printed we've just used `Print`. You can then substitute the command for your language of choice. The different methods for languages are shown below:

Language	Method	Notes
Visual Basic	`Debug.Print "message"`	Prints the text to the debug window
	`MsgBox "message"`	Pops up a window with the text
ASP & VBScript	`Response.Write "message"`	Returns the text to the browser
ASP & JavaScript	`Response.Write ("message");`	Returns the text to the browser
VBScript	`document.write "message"`	Inserts message into the html document
	`MsgBox "message"`	Pops up a window with the text
JavaScript	`document.write ("message");`	Inserts message into the html document
	`alert ("message");`	Pops up a window with the text

Although we've tried to make our samples as language-independent as possible, you'll notice that most of the samples in the book use a Visual Basic/VBScript style – because we see this to be the greatest market for ADO usage. However, the samples should be easily translatable into your favorite language.

If you want to use ADO in a variety of languages then have a look at the document entitled *Implementing ADO with Various Development Languages*. This can be found at http://msdn.microsoft.com/library/sdkdoc/dasdk/ador895x.htm.

There is also a set of samples in a variety of languages, available from the supporting web site, at http://webdev.wrox.co.uk/books/2688.

Creating Objects

Creating the ADO objects is one area where pseudo-code doesn't really work too well. There are significant differences, even between such apparently similar languages as Visual Basic and VBScript. Therefore, this section is devoted to the act of creating objects – we'll look in some detail at how it's done in each of the five languages where we feel ADO is going to have most impact.

This isn't intended as a full explanation of all of the objects and how they are used in each language, but as a demonstration of the major differences between the languages.

Visual Basic

Before you can create an ADO object in Visual Basic you should ensure that you have a reference to the ADO library set. From the Project menu, select References, and then choose Microsoft ActiveX Data Objects 2.1 Library. The ADO Extensions are in the library labeled Microsoft ADO Ext. 2.1 for DDL and Security. Once selected, there are three ways to create objects. The first is probably the most commonly-used:

```
Dim objRec As New ADODB.Recordset
```

This creates the object reference immediately, but the object is not instantiated until the first property or method is called. This means that the object is not instantiated when declared, but later in the code – which can lead to debugging problems. A better solution is to use this method:

```
Dim objRec As ADODB.Recordset
Set objRec = New ADODB.Recordset
```

This creates a variable of the type Recordset, and then the Set line instantiates the object. The third method is the older style, using late binding, and is less used these days:

```
Dim objRec As Object
Set objRec = CreateObject("ADODB.Recordset")
```

Using the methods and properties is extremely simple. For example:

```
objRec.Cursorlocation = adUseClient
objRec.Open "authors", objConn, adOpenKeyset, _
                    adLockOptimistic, adCmdTable
```

The ad constants are automatically available to you in Visual Basic once you have referenced the ADO library (as described above).

Looping through a recordset is just a question of using the MoveNext method and checking the EOF property:

```
While Not objRec.EOF
  Debug.Print objRec("field_name")
  objRec.MoveNext
Wend
```

ASP/VBScript

Creating the objects in VBScript is different from Visual Basic because VBScript doesn't have variable types or support for a type library (although it does use the Visual Basic syntax for assigning object variables using Set). Therefore there's no need to define the variables, although it's better to define them for completeness:

```
Dim objRec
Set objRec = Server.CreateObject("ADODB.Recordset")
```

This creates a Recordset object in ASP script code.

Using the object follows the same procedure as for Visual Basic:

```
objRec.CursorLocation = adUseClient
objRec.Open "authors", objConn, adOpenKeyset, _
                         adLockOptimistic, adCmdTable
```

The only difference here is that the constants are not automatically available – this is because scripting languages do not have access to the type library and its constants. There are two options available to you. The first is to use the integer values that these constants represent. The problem with this is that your code becomes sprinkled with various numbers whose meaning is not obvious to the reader. For example, without ADO's predefined constants the above statement would read:

```
objRec.CursorLocation = 3
objRec.Open "authors", objConn, 1, 3, 2
```

This makes your code harder to read, and therefore less maintainable.

The second option is to include the constants in your ASP script – this means that you can use the constant names instead of their values. You can include the ADO constants with the following line:

```
<!-- #INCLUDE FILE="adovbs.inc"-->
```

The include file, adovbs.inc, is installed in the default directory of Program Files\Common Files\System\ADO, and can be moved to your local ASP directory or referenced from a central virtual directory.

A better way to use the constants is to create a direct reference to the type library, using some metadata:

```
<!-- METADATA TYPE="typelib"
     FILE="C:\Program Files\Common Files\System\ADO\msado15.dll" -->
```

The advantage of this method is that you use the values from the ADO library itself, rather than those from the include file. This means that you don't have to worry that the location (or even the contents) of the include file might change. Note that the name of the DLL is always msado15.dll, whatever version of ADO you have.

> To learn more about ASP, you could try Beginning Active Server Pages 2.0 (Wrox, ISBN 1-861001-34-7) or Professional Active Server Pages 2.0 (Wrox, ISBN 1-861001-26-6).

Looping through recordsets in VBScript is exactly the same as in Visual Basic:

```
While Not objRec.EOF
  Response.Write objRec("field_name")
  objRec.MoveNext
Wend
```

JScript

JScript has a different syntax to VBScript, although much of the object usage is similar. The major thing to watch for is that JScript is case-sensitive. For example, to create a recordset in JScript you would use:

```
var objRec = Server.CreateObject("ADODB.Recordset");
```

Use of the methods and properties is also very similar:

```
objRec.CursorLocation = adUseClient;
objRec.Open ("authors", objConn, adOpenKeyset, adLockOptimistic, adCmdTable);
```

To loop through a recordset in JScript you would use:

```
while (!objRec.EOF)
{
  Response.Write (objRec("field_name"));
  objRec.MoveNext();
}
```

Visual J++

Visual J++ is Microsoft's version of the Java language. It's a much more object-oriented language than either of the scripting languages, but looks similar in structure to JScript. To use ADO within J++ you must import the ADO library:

```
import com.ms.wfc.data.*;
```

Creating an object follows this syntax:

```
Connection objConn = new Connection();
Recordset objRec = new Recordset();
```

Opening and looping through a recordset is not much different from JScript in layout, although the actual commands are different. The following shows the Java native types feature in ADO 2.1:

```
objConn.open ("DSN=pubs");
objRec.open ("author", objConn,
             AdoEnums.CursorType.DYNAMIC,
             AdoEnums.LockType.OPTIMISTIC,
             AdoEnums.CommandType.TABLE);

while (!objRec.getEOF())
{
    System.out.println (objRec.getFields().getItem(field_number).getString();
    objRec.moveNext();
}
```

Visual C++

To use ADO within C++ you must import the ADO library:

```
#import "c:\program files\common files\system\ado\msado15.dll" \
    no_namespace \
    rename( "EOF", "adoEOF" )
```

You must make sure the filepath points to the location of your version of the ADO DLL. The `no_namespace` keyword is added so that you don't have to scope the ADO names. The `EOF` property has to be renamed due to an unfortunate name collision with the EOF constant defined in the Standard C library.

Creating an object follows this syntax:

```
_ConnectionPtr         pConnection;
pConnection.CreateInstance( __uuidof( Connection ) );
_RecordsetPtr          pRecordSet;
pRecordSet.CreateInstance( __uuidof( Recordset ) );
```

Opening and looping through a recordset is not much different from J++ in layout, although the actual commands are different:

```
pConnection->Open( "DSN=travelDB", "", "", -1 );

pRecordSet->Open( "Packages", pConnection.GetInterfacePtr(),
         adOpenDynamic,
         adLockOptimistic,
         adCmdTable );

_variant_t      theValue;

while ( !pRecordSet->adoEOF )
{
    theValue = pRecordSet->GetFields()->GetItem( fieldNumber )->Value;
    printf( "%s\n", (char *)_bstr_t( theValue ) );

    pRecordSet->MoveNext();
}
```

Summary

So far we've explored the principles of data access, and the range of problems created by the increasing variety and location of data and users. We've taken a bird's eye view of the significance of ADO and its advantages, and briefly looked at the other data access technologies it builds on, replaces or complements. We then moved on to take a closer look at the new features of ADO 2.1. In particular, we've considered:

- ❑ Data and data stores
- ❑ The existing technologies for accessing data, and Microsoft's scheme to streamline data access, UDA.
- ❑ What OLEDB and ADO 2.1 are, and how they tie in with each other.
- ❑ The distinction between data providers and data consumers, and Microsoft's Distributed interNet Applications framework for client/server solutions.
- ❑ The new features of ADO 2.1.
- ❑ How to use the basics of ADO 2.1 in a variety of languages.

In the next chapter we'll be moving on to discuss the ADO and ADOX object models.

2

The ADO Object Model

Like all other data access technologies from Microsoft, ADO has a distinct object model, which defines the objects, their interfaces, and how the objects relate to each other. If you've done any database programming before, you'll probably be familiar with the general layout of these objects, as they lean heavily on the lessons learned from DAO and RDO. ADO has a good object model, but it is not as strict as its ancestors; thus, it gives the programmer a great deal more flexibility and reduces development time. For example, in ADO you can create a recordset of data using just a single line of code.

This has been achieved by flattening the object model. It's still shown in the documentation as a hierarchy (with a single object at the top), but some of the lower objects can exist in your code in their own right – without the need to create higher-level objects explicitly. This means that a programmer can use the object most suitable for a particular task, without having to create a lot of other objects that aren't really required in the program. If ADO requires these objects, then it creates them and uses them behind the scenes; and you need never know that they are there.

The ADO Object Model

There are three main objects within ADO: the **Connection**, the **Command** and the **Recordset**. There is no hierarchy between the three main objects, and you can create them independently of each other.

The objects shown as multiple objects are **collections**. Each collection can comprise zero-or-more instances of its associated object, as shown overleaf:

Collection	Associated Object
Errors	Error
Parameters	Parameter
Fields	Field
Properties	Property

Note that, while the main three objects can all exist independently in our code, the collections must be derived from their parent objects. So (for example) a `Recordset` contains a `Fields` collection, which in turn contains zero-or-more `Field` objects.

Enumerating the objects in a collection is the same for all collections – you just have to use a loop variable of the appropriate type. For example, in Visual Basic the following construct will step through each-and-every object in the `Errors` collection:

```
Dim objErr As ADODB.Error

For Each objErr In objConn.Errors
    Debug.Print objErr.Description
Next
```

The same method can be used in VBScript, although you don't give the object variable a specific type, because VBScript variables are Variants. For example in ASP you could use:

```
Dim objFld

For Each objFld In objRec.Fields
    Response.Write objFld.Name & "<BR>"
Next
```

In JScript you could use the `Enumerator` object. For example, in ASP you could use:

```
for(var objProp = new Enumerator(objConn.Properties);
                          !objProp.atEnd(); objProp.moveNext() )
{
  Response.Write (objProp.item().Name + '<BR>');
}
```

The Main Objects

In this section we'll overview the roles of the three objects that make up the bulk of ADO functionality – `Connection`, `Command` and `Recordset`.

The Connection Object

The **connection** is actually the hub of ADO, because it provides the methods that allow us to connect to a data store. Note that when you create a `Recordset` or `Command` object, it is not necessary to create a connection first – because a `Connection` object is automatically created for you behind the scenes. What this means is that you can actually create a recordset or run a command with just a single line of code. For example:

```
objRec.Open "authors","DSN=pubs",adOpenStatic,adLockReadOnly,adCmdTable
```

This creates a recordset on the `authors` table from the `pubs` database, based on the ODBC Data Source Name `pubs`. Although this example is using a `Recordset` object, it actually creates a connection underneath. In fact, you can create a separate and explicit `Connection` object from the one that ADO created for you:

```
Set objConn = objRec.ActiveConnection
```

This sort of mix-and-match approach to connection creation frees the programmer from a rigid structure and allows the code to be written in a way that is naturally easier.

Although this looks simple, you create a new connection every time you use a connection string to establish a connection to a data store (subject to connection pooling – see Chapter 3). If you are going to be running several commands or creating several recordsets, then it is recommended that you create a `Connection` object directly:

```
objConn.Open "DSN=pubs"
```

or

```
objConn.Open "Provider=SQLOLEDB; Data Source=Piglet; " & _
             "Initial Catalog=pubs; User Id=sa; Password="
```

You can then use this `Connection` throughout your code, without worrying about the number of connections you are creating. Not only is this more efficient but it's faster too – because once a connection to a data store is established, it can be reused. One area where you shouldn't try to use a single connection is in ASP pages, using the `Session` or `Application` scope. Creating an ADO object and storing it in a `Session` or `Application` variable has serious performance penalties if you want your ASP pages to scale.

Once you have decided upon the provider, the properties of the `Connection` object allow you to see what kinds of facilities are available from the data provider. For example, picking the SQL Server provider allows you to see some the properties for that provider, even before the connection is opened:

```
objConn.Provider = "SQLOLEDB"
For Each objProp in objConn.Properties
    Print objProp.Name
Next
```

Since ADO is designed to run against different data stores, it's often worth checking that a particular function is supported, *before* you call it. You do this by examining the `Properties` collection of the `Connection` object. This is particularly useful when using ADO as part of a development or query tool that gives the user the ability to connect to different data stores. You could also, for example, use some of the properties to define a schema if manually creating XML from the data.

The `Connection` object isn't just about connecting to, and holding information about, a data store. You can actually run commands and create recordsets with a `Connection` object too. For example:

```
objConn.Execute "UPDATE titles SET price = price * 1.10"
```

This would run a SQL UPDATE query. Alternatively, to run a command and return a recordset:

```
Set objRec = objConn.Execute ("SELECT * FROM authors")
```

So, not only can you use a Recordset object to connect to a data store, but you can also use a Connection object to create recordsets. It's all part of the 'code as you want' strategy.

The Connection is also where all of the errors are stored, if any occur during your ADO operations. An ADO operation may generate more than one error, and these are stored in the Connection object's Errors collection, which is discussed in more detail in Chapter 6. Although you might think this breaks the flexibility of the object model, it gives a central place to find error information. Since the Recordset and Command objects have a connection underneath, it is extremely simple to get access to this error information without creating a Connection.

The Command Object

The Command object is designed more to run SQL commands (assuming the provider supports the Command object), especially those that require parameters. This is an important point, because the use of stored queries and procedures is a great way to improve speed and segment your application.

Like the Connection object, the Command object can be used to run action queries that don't return a recordset, as well as creating recordsets. Unlike the Connection, however, you'll need a couple more lines of code, because you cannot specify the command text in the same line as the line that specifies the command type:

```
objCmd.CommandText = "UPDATE titles SET price = price * 1.10"
objCmd.CommandType = adCmdText + adExecuteNoRecords
objCmd.Execute
```

To return a Recordset you use a similar style:

```
Set objRec = objCmd.Execute
```

The greatest difference in command execution comes when using the Parameters collection, because this allows you to use stored procedures and queries that are saved on the data store. This removes the SQL code from your program, making it faster and more maintainable. Using stored procedures, you can have SQL statements that are in a compiled form and perform a set of actions using the values you supply as parameters.

With a Command – if the data provider supports this facility – you can also save the command details for execution at a later date. This is known as a **prepared statement**. Once you've finished with your connection, the saved commands are automatically deleted. You can also use a command object more than once, and on different providers if you require. Just change the ActiveConnection property of the command to point to the new connection and re-run the command. If you wish to reuse the command object, it's wise to close any active recordsets that were based on the command first. This ensures that memory is deallocated correctly.

Another feature allows you to turn the command into a method of the `Connection` object, allowing you to build up a `Connection` object that contains many new methods. This is quite useful in client–server scenarios, because you could attach different commands to the connection depending upon the privilege of the user. This is explained in more detail in Chapter 4.

The Recordset Object

The `Recordset` object is probably the most-used object in ADO, and consequently has more properties and methods than the other objects. Like the `Command` object, a `Recordset` can exist on its own or be attached to a `Connection`:

```
objRec.Open "authors", "DSN=pubs", adOpenStatic, adLockReadOnly, adCmdTable
```

This opens a recordset using a new connection. To use an existing connection, you simply substitute the connection string for the existing `Connection` object:

```
objRec.Open "authors", objConn, adOpenStatic, adLockReadOnly, adCmdTable
```

This is the preferred method if you are creating several recordsets, because it means that the connection to the data store doesn't have to be established each time you create a recordset.

Another important point about the `Recordset` object is that it's the only way to specify the recordset's cursor type and lock type. If you use the `Execute` method of the `Connection` or `Command` object, it gives you the default cursor type – which is a read-only, forward-only cursor (often referred to as a **firehose cursor**).

You use recordsets to examine and manipulate data from the data store. The `Recordset` object gives you facilities to move about through the records, find records, sort records in a particular order, and update records. You can do updating in two modes: either directly (where the changes are sent back to the data store as they are made) or in batches (where the changes are saved locally and then sent back to the data store in one go).

In client–server applications, you can also pass recordsets between the business logic tier and the user interface tier, where they can be manipulated locally. This saves database resources, which can be critical on large-scale applications, as well as minimizing network traffic. These recordsets are called **disconnected recordsets**.

The Other ADO Objects

Now, let's take a look at the other objects that play a part in programming with ADO.

The Field Object and the Fields Collection

A `Field` object contains details about a single field (or column) in a recordset. Such information includes the data type of the field, its width, and so on.

The `Fields` collection identifies each field in a recordset, and there are two ways in which this can be used. The first is with existing recordsets, where you can examine each field, see its type, check its name, etc. This is quite useful when you are unsure of exactly what the recordset contains, and can be useful in scripting when showing tables dynamically. Using the `Fields` collection allows you to find the name of each field. For example, in ASP script you could do this:

```
Response.Write "<TABLE>"
For Each objFld In objRec.Fields
   Response.Write "<TR><TD>" & objFld.Name & "</TD></TR>"
Next
Response.Write "</TABLE>"
```

This creates an HTML table showing which fields are in the recordset `objRec`. In fact, using a similar method, you could easily create a simple script routine that accepts any recordset and builds an HTML table from it. You could use the `Fields` collection to supply the table header, showing the column names, and the recordset to fill in the details of the table.

Another use of the `Fields` collection is for recordsets of your own making. In the past, arrays were often used when you needed to store several related items. The trouble with arrays is that you have to manage the array manually – you can't add data to a new array element without first creating room in the array. Then came collections, to which you could add your own objects, but collections are also limited to objects and basic data types. So if you want to store some related items (i.e. records), with each item having different attributes (i.e. fields) then you can use a recordset.

For example, imagine that you need to store details from a questionnaire. You could create a recordset like so:

```
objRec.CursorLocation = adUseClient
objRec.Fields.Append "Name", adVarChar, 50, adFldFixed
objRec.Fields.Append "Age", adInteger, , adFldFixed
objRec.Fields.Append "Question1", adBoolean, , adFldFixed
. . .
objRec.Fields.Append "Comments", adVarChar, 255, adFldFixed
```

The good thing about this method is that you can save the contents of this disconnected recordset to a file, as well as using it as a parameter for functions in business objects.

The Error Object and the Errors Collection

An `Error` object contains details of a single error (or warning) returned from a data provider. Details include a description of the error, an error number and the source object that raised the error. When a provider encounters an error, or wishes to return information to the consumer, the details are placed in an `Error` object, and this is appended to the `Errors` collection.

The `Errors` collection holds all of the errors, when a data provider generates an error or returns warnings in response to some failure. This is provided as a collection because a failure can generate more than one error. For example, the following statement generates two errors because X and Y are unknown columns:

```
objConn.Open "DSN=pubs"
Set objRec = objConn.Execute "SELECT X, Y FROM authors"
```

You could check the errors generated here by looping through the collection:

```
For Each objErr In objConn.Errors
   Print objErr.Description
Next
```

If you haven't got a predefined `Connection` object you can use the `ActiveConnection` property of the `Command` or `Recordset`:

```
objRec.Open "SELECT X, Y FROM authors", "DSN=pubs", _
                        adOpenStatic, adLockReadOnly, adCmdTable
```

```
For Each objErr In objRec.ActiveConnection.Errors
   Print objErr.Description
Next
```

As with the `Fields` collection, you could easily build a simple routine that centralizes error handling.

There is always an `Errors` collection, but it will be empty if no errors have occurred. `Error` objects remain in the collection until the next data access error occurs, where they are cleared and replaced by the new error details.

The Parameter Object and the Parameters Collection

A `Parameter` object contains details of a single parameter for a stored procedure or stored query. Details include the name, the data type, the direction and the value. A parameter can be one of the following types:

❑ An input parameter, which supplies values to a stored procedure
❑ An output parameter, which supplies values from the stored procedure
❑ An input and output parameter
❑ A return value, which supplies the return value from the stored procedure

The usage of the various parameter types is discussed in more detail in Chapter 4.

The `Parameters` collection is unique to the `Command` object and is one way of allowing you to pass parameters into and out from stored queries and procedures. When using parameters you have two options. First, you can ask the data provider to fetch the parameters from the data source, and the `Parameters` collection will be filled in automatically for you:

```
objCmd.Parameters.Refresh
```

The downside of this is that it requires a trip to the server, which may cause your program to perform poorly – especially if you do this often. However, it's a great way of finding out what type and size the provider expects your parameters to be, and is very useful during development and debugging. You should note that not all ODBC Drivers support the `Refresh` method.

The second option is to add the parameters to the collection manually, like so:

```
Set objParam = objCmd.CreateParameter ("ID",adInteger, adParamInput, 8, 147)
```

This creates an input parameter called `ID`, which is an integer (length 8), with a value of 147. Once created, the parameter can be appended to the `Parameters` collection:

```
objCmd.Parameters.Append objParam
```

Another good use of the `Refresh` method is when you first connect to the data store and cache the parameters details locally, perhaps in an array, or in a user collection. This sort of approach allows you to write generic routines that process stored procedures.

The Property Object and the Properties Collection

A `Property` object contains provider-specific information about an object. We know that objects have a fixed set of properties, but one of the fundamentals of OLEDB and ADO is that it can talk to a variety of data providers, and these providers often have different ways of working, or support different items. If all providers had to support a fixed functionality, then OLEDB wouldn't really be very flexible – it would comprise the lowest common denominator of functionality. The solution is to provide a `Property` object and a collection to store all of the provider-specific properties.

The `Properties` collection contains provider-specific information about the object in question. For a `Connection`, it contains a large amount of information about the facilities that the provider supports, such as the maximum number of columns in a `SELECT` statement, and what sort of outer join capabilities are supported. For a `Recordset`, there's just as much information, ranging from the current locking level to the asynchronous capabilities supported by the provider.

You can examine or set the value of an individual property by just using its name to index into the collection. For example:

```
Print objConn.Properties("Max Columns in Select")
```

To examine all of the properties you can use a simple loop:

```
For Each objProp In objConn.Properties
   Print objProp.Name
Next
```

You may well find that you never use this collection, unless you are writing an application that supports multiple data providers, in which case you may need to query the provider to examine what it supports.

The ADOX Object Model

The ADOX (ADO Extensions for DDL and Security) object model observes more of a hierarchy than the ADO object model, but that's because of the nature of the objects it contains. This means there is a parent object and several child objects:

The Catalog Object

The Catalog object is a central repository, and is really just a container for all of the other objects. The Catalog object allows us to connect to a data store and drill-down to the components that it comprises. With the Catalog object we can use the ActiveConnection property to specify the data store that we want to connect to, and then use the collections to obtain more detailed information. It's also possible to obtain and set the owner of various objects without using the collections.

To use a catalog you just point to an existing Connection object, or a Connection string. For example:

```
Dim objCatalog As New ADOX.Catalog

Set objCatalog.ActiveConnection = objConn
```

or

```
objCatalog.ActiveConnection = "Provider=SQLOLEDB; . . ."
```

The Table Object and the Tables Collection

A Table object identifies a single table in a catalog, containing information such as the table name and the last change date. It is also a container for the Columns, Indexes and Keys collections (see below).

The Tables collection contains Table objects, one for each table in the catalog. An example of the Tables and Columns collections is shown in a moment (after we've introduced the Columns collection).

The Index Object and the Indexes Collection

An Index object contains the details for a single index on a table, identifying attributes such as the index name, whether the index is unique, whether the index allows nulls, etc. Using the Index object's Columns collection (see below), you can see which columns comprise the index.

The Indexes collection contains all of the Index objects for a particular Table. For example, the following prints the Indexes on a table, and the columns that make up each Index:

```
Dim objIndex  As ADOX.Index
Dim objColumn As ADOX.Column

For Each objIndex In objTbl.Indexes
  Print objIndex.Name
  For Each objColumn In objIndex.Columns
    Print objColumn.Name
  Next
Next
```

The Key Object and the Keys Collection

A Key object contains information regarding a table key, identifying such items as its name, whether it is a primary or foreign key, the related table, etc. Like the Index object, the Key object contains a collection of Column objects, identifying the columns that make up the key.

The `Keys` collection contains a list of keys for a table. For example, the following prints all of the keys and columns for a table:

```
Dim objKey    As ADOX.Key
Dim objColumn As ADOX.Column

For Each objKey In objTbl.Indexes
   Print objKey.Name
   For Each objColumn In objKey.Columns
      Print objColumn.Name
   Next
Next
```

The Column Object and the Columns Collection

A `Column` object represents an individual column from a `Table`, `Index` or `Key` object. In many respects it is similar to the ADO `Field` object: but rather than storing the details of a recordset, it holds the details of a stored column, such as its name, its data type, etc. For `Key` columns it contains details of the related columns, and for `Index` columns it contains details of the clustering and sorting.

The `Columns` collection contains all of the columns for a particular `Table`, `Key` or `Index` object. For example, to see all of the columns in a particular table you would use this:

```
Dim objTbl As New ADOX.Table
Dim objCol As ADOX.Column

Set objTbl = objCatalog.Tables(0)
For Each objCol In objTbl.Columns
   Print objCol.Name
Next
```

The syntax is exactly the same if you need the columns in an `Index` or a `Key`.

The Group Object and the Groups Collection

A `Group` object identifies a security group, containing a list of users in the catalog. Its main role is to allow the retrieval and setting of permission for a named group, or for allowing access to the `Users` collection, which contains a list of all users belonging to this group.

The `Groups` collection contains a list of `Groups` that belong to a particular catalog, or a list of `Groups` that a particular user belongs to. For example, the following enumerates the `Groups` in a `Catalog`, and then the `Users` in a `Group`:

```
Dim objGroup As ADOX.Group
Dim objUser  As ADOX.User

For Each objGroup In objCatalog.Groups
   Print objGroup.Name
   For Each objUser In objGroup.Users
      Print objUser.Name
   Next
Next
```

Not all providers support the `Group` object and `Groups` collection. At the moment the Jet provider gives the most comprehensive support.

The User Object and the Users Collection

A User object contains details of a single user of the data store and contains the user name, the unique ID of the user, and methods to read and write permissions. The User object also contains a Groups collection, which is a list of groups to which the user belongs. You should be careful about writing recursive procedures that traverse the Users and Groups collections, because they point to each other.

The Users collection contains a list of all users in a catalog. An example of this is shown above, under the Group object.

Not all providers support the User object and Users collection. At the moment the Jet provider gives the most comprehensive support.

The Procedure Object and the Procedures Collection

A Procedure object identifies a stored procedure in a catalog. The Procedure object has very few properties, mainly because one of these properties represents an ADO Command object. The Procedure object identifies the details about the stored procedure (such as its name and when it was last modified), while the Command object identifies the internal details of the procedure (such as the SQL test, etc.).

The Procedures collection contains a Procedure object for each stored procedure in the Catalog. For example, to access a stored procedure and its SQL text you could use the following code:

```
Dim objCmd As ADODB.Command

Set objCmd = objCat.Procedures("proc_name").Command
Print objCmd.CommandText
```

This uses the Command property of the Procedure object, to reference a standard ADO Command object.

The View Object and the Views Collection

A View object identifies a single view in a catalog. A view represents a set of records or a virtual table. Like the Procedure object, the View contains a Command object, allowing access to the view command.

The Views collection contains a list of View objects, one for each view in the catalog.

For example, to obtain all views in a catalog you could do this:

```
Dim objView As ADODB.View

For Each objView In objCat.Views
    Print objView.Name
Next
```

Like the Procedure object, the View also supports an ADO Command as a property. So, to access the details of the command you could use similar code:

```
Dim objCmd As ADODB.Command

Set objCmd = objCat.Views("view_name").Command
Print objCmd.CommandText
```

This is also provider-dependent.

The Property Object and the Properties Collection

The `Property` object and `Properties` collection are identical to their ADO equivalents.

ADOX Supported Features

ADOX is not supported by all providers, even the Microsoft-supplied ones. Currently, only the OLEDB Provider for Microsoft Jet fully supports ADOX. For the other Microsoft OLEDB providers, all features are supported *except* for those listed below:

Microsoft OLE DB Provider for SQL Server	
Object/Collection	**Feature not supported**
Catalog Object	Create method.
Tables Collection	Properties for existing tables are read-only (properties for new tables can be read/write).
Views Collection	Not supported.
Procedures Collection	Append method, Delete method, Command property.
Keys Collection	Append method, Delete method.
Users Collection	Not supported.
Groups Collection	Not supported.

Microsoft OLE DB Provider for ODBC	
Object/Collection	**Feature not supported**
Catalog Object	Create method.
Tables Collection	Append method, Delete method. Properties for existing tables are read-only (properties for new tables can be read/write).
Views Collection	Append method, Delete method, Command property.
Procedures Collection	Append method, Delete method, Command property.
Indexes Collection	Append method, Delete method.
Keys Collection	Append method, Delete method.
Users Collection	Not supported.
Groups Collection	Not supported.

Microsoft OLE DB Provider for Oracle	
Object/Collection	**Feature not supported**
Catalog Object	Create method.
Tables Collection	Append method, Delete method. Properties for existing tables are read-only (properties for new tables can be read/write).
Views Collection	Append method, Delete method, Command property.
Procedures Collection	Append method, Delete method, Command property.
Indexes Collection	Append method, Delete method.
Keys Collection	Append method, Delete method.
Users Collection	Not supported.
Groups Collection	Not supported.

OLEDB Providers

We've already mentioned that ADO can connect to many different data providers, and this is due to OLEDB. Remember that ADO is just a layer that sits on top of OLEDB to hide the complexity, so it seems sensible to look at some of these data providers in more detail. We need to see what differences there are between them, for although most of the ADO usage will be the same, OLEDB providers don't always support the same facilities. This is natural, because some of them are fundamentally very different. Most of the relational database providers, for example, will provide similar facilities, but other providers might not work in the same way.

When you install the data access components you are supplied with the following OLEDB providers:

Provider	Description
MSDASQL	For ODBC which allows connection to existing ODBC data sources, either via a System DSN or from dynamically provided connection details. See Chapter 1 for how ODBC Drivers relate to OLE DB.
Microsoft.Jet.OLEDB.4.0	Jet, for connecting to Microsoft Access databases
SQLOLEDB	SQL Server, for connecting to Microsoft SQL Server.

Table Continued on Following Page

Provider	Description
MSDAORA	Oracle, for connecting to Oracle databases.
MSIDXS	Index Server, for connecting to Microsoft Index Server
ADSDSOObject	Active Directory Services, for connecting to Directory Service agents.
MSDataShape	Data Shape, for hierarchical recordsets.
MSPersist	Persist, for locally saved recordsets.
MSDAOSP	Simple Provider, for creating your own providers for simple text data.
MSDAIPP.DSO.1	Internet Publishing, for connecting to DAV compliant servers, to aid publishing data on the Internet.

These are just the defaults supplied, some of which may not appear – depending upon your installation options. For example, Index Server does not act as a remote provider, and you can only connect to local Index Servers. Therefore, if you do not have Index Server on your machine, the MSIDXS may not get installed.

You can find out which providers are available on your system by creating a new Data Link. This is similar to an ODBC DSN, but for OLEDB connections. You can create one in any directory using Windows Explorer, simply by right mouse-clicking (or selecting the File menu), picking New, and selecting Microsoft Data Link. This creates a file with a .udl extension, and you can then view its properties. From the Provider tab you can see the available providers:

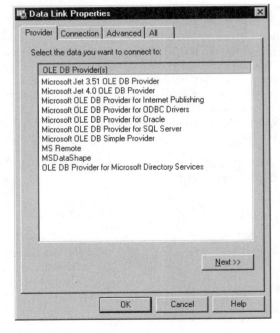

In fact, using the Data Link is a good way to create connection strings if you are unfamiliar with them – you can even use them instead of a DSN within connection strings (see the next section). You can create a Data Link file, filling in the details on screen, and then examine the .udl file (which is what the data link file is stored as) in notepad.

Connection Strings

One of the major differences between providers is in the connection string: different providers require different information in order to make the connection to the data store.

ADO recognizes only four of the arguments in the connection string; the remaining arguments are passed onto the provider. The main argument you are interested in is `Provider`, which identifies the OLEDB provider to be used. The second argument is `File Name`, which can be used to point to an existing Data Link file. If you use a Data Link file then you can omit the `Provider` argument, because the Data Link file contains this information. The other two arguments (`Remote Provider` and `Remote Server`) relate to Remote Data Services, and are covered in detail in Chapter 7.

OLEDB Provider for the ODBC Drivers

The OLEDB Provider for ODBC is the default provider, so if you don't specify which one to use, this is what you'll get. If you *do* specify this provider explicitly in your connection string, you have to give the rather obscure name `MSDASQL`. When using the OLEDB Provider for ODBC, you have three choices: to use an existing ODBC Data Source Name (DSN), a DSN-less connection string, or an ODBC File DSN

For a DSN-based connection, simply specify the data source name:

```
Provider=MSDASQL;DSN=data_source_name
```

For a DSN-less connection, the connection string varies with the database you are connecting to. It follows the same conventions as an ODBC connection string – you can see the parameters in the ODBC applet in the Control Panel. There is one important option which is the same for all ODBC connections, as it specifies the ODBC driver to use:

```
Provider=MSDASQL;Driver=
```

The name of the driver, which you should specify here, will be one of those shown on the **Drivers** tab of the **ODBC Control Panel** applet. Your list of drivers may differ from this:

You should enclose the driver name in curly braces. Let's look at some examples.

Microsoft Access

To connect to Microsoft Access, your connect string would start like this:

```
Provider=MSDASQL;Driver={Microsoft Access Driver (*.mdb)}
```

You then have to specify the Access database:

```
Provider=MSDASQL;Driver={Microsoft Access Driver (*.mdb)};
DBQ=C:\mdb_name.mdb
```

Note: An interesting fact has recently come to light that causes the following error with the OLEDB Provider for ODBC:

Microsoft OLE DB Provider for ODBC Drivers error '80004005'
[Microsoft][ODBC Driver Manager] Data source name not found and no default driver specified

This seems to occur of you leave a space after the first semi-colon in the connection string shown above, just before the `Driver`. So, this works:

```
Provider=MSDASQL;Driver={Microsoft Access Driver (*.mdb)};
DBQ=C:\mdb_name.mdb
```

But this doesn't:

```
Provider=MSDASQL; Driver={Microsoft Access Driver (*.mdb)};
DBQ=C:\mdb_name.mdb
```

Notice the space – it's hard to spot.

Of course, since this is the default OLE DB Provider, you can use the following string (without specifying the `Provider`) perfectly well:

```
Driver={Microsoft Access Driver (*.mdb)}; DBQ=C:\mdb_name.mdb
```

Microsoft SQL Server

To connect to SQL Server you need to supply a little more information:

- ❑ `Server` is the name of the SQL Server
- ❑ `Database` is the database name
- ❑ `UID` is the SQL Server user ID
- ❑ `PWD` is the password for the SQL Server user ID

For example:

```
Provider=MSDASQL;Driver={SQL Server}; Server=Tigger; Database=pubs; UID=sa;
PWD=
```

Microsoft Excel

To connect to a Microsoft Excel (any version) spreadsheet you must first make sure that a range has been specified in the spreadsheet. This range should enclose all of the data that you wish to select, and equates to the recordset. You can have any number of ranges in a spreadsheet. To create a range you select the cells in the spreadsheet and enter the name in the range box, like so:

Range name goes here

The connect string is:

```
Provider=MSDASQL;Driver={Microsoft Excel Driver (*.xls)}; DBQ=C:\xls_name.xls
```

You then specify the range as the name of the recordset to open:

```
objRec.Open "Authors", objConn
```

Text Files

Text files are slightly different from Excel files, in the following respect: in the connect string, you specify the directory where the text file resides, rather than the text file itself:

```
Provider=MSDASQL;Driver={Microsoft Text Driver (*.txt; *.csv)};
DBQ=C:\directory_name
```

You then specify the text file as the name of the recordset to open:

```
objRec.Open "TextFile.txt", objConn
```

OLEDB Provider for Jet

When using the provider for Jet you only need to specify the database name:

```
Provider=Microsoft.Jet.OLEDB.4.0; Data Source=C:\mdb_name.mdb
```

If you have a system database you can use the `Properties` collection to set this before opening the connection, but you must specify the provider first:

```
objConn.Provider = "Microsoft.Jet.OLEDB.4.0"
objConn.Properties("Jet OLEDB:System database") = "C:\system_db_name"
objConn.Open "Data Source=C:\pubs\pubs.mdb"
```

A database password is also set in this way:

```
objConn.Properties("Jet OLEDB:Database Password") = "LetMeIn"
```

OLEDB Provider for SQL Server

As SQL Server can contain multiple databases, you need an extra parameter here:

```
Provider=SQLOLEDB; Data Source=server_name; Initial Catalog=database_name;
User Id=user_id; Password=user_password
```

For example:

```
Provider=SQLOLEDB; Data Source=Tigger; Initial Catalog=pubs; User Id=sa;
Password=
```

OLEDB Provider for Index Server

For Index Server you only need to specify the provider name, unless you have multiple catalogs in use under Index Server. In this case you use the Data Source to specify the required catalog:

```
Provider=MSIDXS; Data Source=catalog_name
```

OLEDB Provider for Internet Publishing

The Internet Publishing provider allows you to connect to Web Servers that support either the Microsoft FrontPage Server Extensions or the Distributed Authoring and Versioning protocol. This allows you to use ADO to query the web server for directory contents, resources etc., as well as being able to update these resources. You use the Data Source to specify the web server:

```
Provider=MSDAIPP.DSO.1; Data Source=http://web.server.name
```

Data Link Files (. udl)

A data link file can contain connection details for any OLE DB Provider. Data Link files have a suffix of .udl, and allow the connection details to be stored in a file, rather than being embedded within an application.

To use a Data Link file as a connection string you simple set the File Name option to point to the .udl file:

```
objConn.Open "File Name=C:\temp\pubs.UDL"
```

Asynchronous Processing

Asynchronous processing was one of the new features in ADO 2, and allows commands to be executed at the same time as other commands. This is particularly useful when creating very large recordsets, or running a query that may take a long time, as you can continue with another task and allow ADO to tell you when the command has finished. You can also cancel a long running command if you wish. Events can also be used when certain actions are about to happen or when they have happened.

Note that ASP scripting languages do not support events.

Events

Only the `Recordset` and `Connection` objects support events. There are generally two types of events:

❏   `Will...` events – those that are called before an operation starts

❏   `...Complete` events – those that are called after it has completed

There are a few other events that are called after an event has completed, but they are not part of the `Will...` and `...Complete` event pairs.

A `Will...` event is called just before the action starts. It gives you the chance to examine the details of the action, and to cancel the action if you decide that you do not want it to run. The `...Complete` event is called just after the action completes, whether or not it was cancelled. If it was cancelled then the `Errors` collection is filled with details of why it was cancelled.

The `Will...` events generally have an argument, `adStatus`, indicating the status of the event. You can set this argument to `adStatusCancel` before the method ends, to cancel the action that caused the event. For example, suppose a connection generated a `WillConnect` event; setting `adStatus` to `adStatusCancel` will cancel the connection. The `ConnectComplete` event will then be called, with a status indicating that the connection failed.

The nature of events means that there can be several `Will...` events that could result from a single action. Although all of these will be called, there is no guaranteed order in which this will happen.

Event Pairings

The way the `Will...` and `...Complete` events are generated can often be confusing, especially in terms of what happens when you wish to cancel an event. The action triggers the `Will...` event, which has its own event procedure. This code runs, and then the action itself is run. After the action is finished, the `...Complete` event is triggered, which runs its event procedure. Once that has completed, execution will continue at the line after the action. The following diagram shows this using `Connection` events, when opening a connection:

In the `WillConnect` event procedure we can decide whether we want this action (that is, the `objConn.Open`) to take place or not. The event procedure has a parameter called *adStatus*, which we can use. If we set this to `adStatusCancel` before the event procedure finishes, then the action is cancelled. The `ConnectComplete` event will still run, but with its parameters indicating an error. For example:

The important thing to note is that the `ConnectComplete` event is still generated, but the connection does not actually take place.

Some actions may generate more than one event, so what happens here? Well, the `Will...` event is always generated before its associated `...Complete` event; but where there are two `Will...` events, the order in which they are generated is not guaranteed. If you cancel the action from within an event procedure, and this happens to run as the first event procedure, then the second set of event procedures (both the `Will...` and the `...Complete`) are never generated. For example, imagine a recordset, where you have events to detect when fields and records change:

Here the action has been canceled in the `WillChangeField` event procedure. The `FieldChangeComplete` event procedure runs, but indicates that an error occurred, and the actual action, that of setting the field value is not executed. The `WillChangeRecord` and `RecordChangeComplete` event procedures are not run.

While these diagrams use Visual Basic, the choice of language is not crucial: it's the order of events that's important.

Events in Visual Basic

To use events within Visual Basic you declare a variable using the `WithEvents` keyword. This must be a module level, or global variable, as `WithEvents` is invalid within procedures:

```
Private WithEvents objRec As ADODB.Recordset
```

Note that the `New` keyword is omitted when using this syntax, because you can't instantiate objects at the same time as declaring the variable with events. You have to do this separately:

```
Set objRec = New ADODB.Recordset
```

Once you have declared the variable, the object will appear in the objects list in the code combo, and a list of events in the event combo:

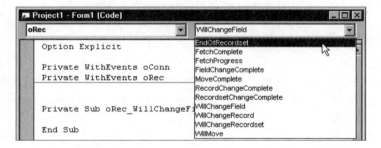

Events in Visual J++

The procedure is a little more complex in J++, but it's still pretty easy. First you must declare an event handler variable – this one's for a connection:

```
ConnectionEventHandler evtConnHandler =
    new ConnectionEventHandler(this, "onConnectComplete")
```

The handler variable is called `evtConnHandler`, and the procedure we are creating is `"onConnectComplete"`. This can be any name you choose, but it's best to stick to the standard names. Next you need to add that handler to the connection:

```
objConn.add OnConnectComplete (evtConnHandler)
```

This links our piece of handler code to the `ConnectComplete` event. At the end of your program you need to remove the event handler:

```
objConn.remove OnConnectComplete(evtConnHandler)
```

All you have to do now is write the actual handler itself:

```
public void onConnectComplete (Object sender,
                               ConnectionEvent e)
{
    if (e.adStatus = AdoEnums.EventStatus.ERRORSOCCURRED)
        System.out.println("Connection failed");
    else
        System.out.println("Connection succeeded");
    return;
}
```

This is the code that is run when the event is generated. For more details of this you should consult the J++ documentation.

Connection Events

There are nine connection events:

- ❑ BeginTransComplete is called after a BeginTrans method has completed.
- ❑ CommitTransComplete is called after a CommitTrans method has completed.
- ❑ RollbackTransComplete is called after a RollbackTrans method has completed.
- ❑ WillConnect is called just before a connection is established.
- ❑ ConnectComplete is called after a connection is established.
- ❑ Disconnect is called after a connection has disconnected.
- ❑ WillExecute is called before an Execute method is run.
- ❑ ExecuteComplete is called after an Execute method has completed.
- ❑ InfoMessage is called when the provider returns information messages.

An example of the ...Complete events could be to indicate to the user the status of their connection. The individual events for a Connection are discussed in more detail in Chapter 3.

Recordset Events

The recordset has more events than the connection:

- ❑ FetchProgress is called periodically during an asynchronous recordset creation.
- ❑ FetchComplete is called when the recordset has been fully populated with its records.
- ❑ WillChangeField is called before an action causes a field to change.
- ❑ FieldChangeComplete is called after an action caused a field to change.
- ❑ WillMove is called before an action causes the current record to change.

❑ `MoveComplete` is called after an action caused the current record to change.

❑ `EndOfRecordset` is called when there is an attempt to move beyond the end of the recordset.

❑ `WillChangeRecord` is called before an action causes the data in the current record to change.

❑ `RecordChangeComplete` is called after an action caused the data in the current record to change.

❑ `WillChangeRecordset` is called before an action causes a change to an aspect of the recordset (such as a filter).

❑ `RecordsetChangeComplete` is called after an action caused the recordset to change.

The `Will...` events can be used to notify the user that an action may change data, or may change the underlying records in the recordset.

A word of caution when using the new ADO Data Control in Visual Basic 6: this automatically updates records when using the video style buttons to move around the records. This differs from the standard Data Control. If you change a field, then the `WillChangeField` event is called, and if the value is not correct you can cancel the action. However, what gets cancelled is the `Update`, not the move. It's not a major problem, but something to bear in mind.

The individual events for a `Recordset` are discussed in more detail in Chapter 5.

Object Usage

One thing that confuses some people is when to use which object. After all, the `Connection`, `Command` and `Recordset` are all capable of returning a recordset of data. There are only a few hard and fast rules, but in general here's what you should do:

❑ If you only ever need to run queries that don't return a recordset, and those queries are not stored procedures with parameters, then use the `Connection` object and the `Execute` method.

❑ If you need to use stored procedures with output parameters then you must use the `Command` object. You can use the `Connection` object directly to call a stored procedure with parameters, but since this is undocumented, it's probably best to stick to using the `Command` object.If you need to specify the cursor type or lock type, then you must use a `Recordset` object.

❑ If you are creating only one or two recordsets of data, then you can use the `Recordset` directly, passing in a connection string.

❑ If you are creating three or more recordsets, then create a `Connection` object first, then the `Recordset` objects. Remember that each time you connect to a data store with a connection string, a new connection is opened, or retrieved from the connection pool.

Summary

This chapter has introduced the ADO object model, examined at how you go about connecting to data stores, and looked at the connection strings for a variety of OLEDB providers. It has also briefly introduced the asynchronous processing and the use of events, the details of which are covered in the Chapters 3 and 5, which look at the `Connection` and `Recordset` objects in more detail.

Most of the rest of the book is concerned with properties, methods and events of the various ADO objects and related libraries, such as the extensions for DDL and Security, Multi-dimensional Queries, and Jet Replication.

The Connection Object

The Connection object is what connects the consumer to the provider. That is, it's the link between the program and the data. As you've already seen, the flat model of ADO means that Connection objects don't need to be created explicitly – you can pass a connection string directly to a Command or Recordset object. However, creating a Connection object is worthwhile if you are planning to retrieve data from the data source more than once, because you won't have to establish a fresh connection each time.

Connection Pooling

Following the newsgroups in the early days of ADO, there was a lot of talk about connection pooling, and whether the benefits really are worthwhile. One of the most time-consuming operations you can perform is the act of connecting to a data store, so anything that can speed this up is defined as 'a good thing'.

Connection pooling means that ADO will not actually destroy connection objects unless it really needs to. The signal for destroying a Connection object is dictated by a timeout value: if the connection hasn't been reused within the allotted time, it is destroyed. Here's how it works. Suppose you open a connection, perform some data access, and then close the connection; from your point of view, the connection is closed. But underneath, OLEDB keeps the connection in a pool, ready for it to be used again. If you then decide that you need to open the same connection again, you will be given a Connection object from the pool of connections, and ADO *doesn't* have to perform all of the expensive data store stuff again. You may not necessarily get the exact same object back, but you'll get one that matches the same connection details. In fact, existing objects will be given to anyone who requests them, so connection pooling is even more effective in a multi-user system.

One important point to note about connection pooling is that connections will only be reused if they match the exact connection details. So on multi-user systems, if you specify the same data store but different user names and passwords, then you will create a new connection, rather than having one reused from the pool. This may seem a disadvantage, but pooling must be done this way to avoid breaking security – it just wouldn't be right to reuse a connection if the user details differed.

You should also realize that connection pooling is *not* the same as connection sharing. An individual connection is not shared among multiple connection requests. Pooling means that closed connections are re-used, not open ones.

You can test to see whether connection pooling really is working by using a tool to monitor the active connections to a data store. For example, with Microsoft SQL Server you can use SQL Trace. Executing the following code shows only one connection being opened:

```
For iLoop = 1 To 5
    objConn.Open strConn
    objConn.Close
Next
```

However, if you turn off connection pooling, you'll find that the five connections are opened and then immediately closed, one after another.

Although you probably wouldn't want to, you can turn off connection pooling by adding the phrase OLE DB Services = -2 to the end of the connection string:

```
strConn = " . . .; OLE DB Services = -2"
```

Alternatively, you can achieve the same result by setting the Connection object's Properties entry of the same name:

```
objConn.Properties("OLE DB Services") = -2
```

This property takes values from the DBPROPVAL_OS constants (see Appendix B). If you've already flicked to the back to find the constant with a value of -2, you'll notice there isn't one. There is, however, a constant to turn connection pooling on, so to turn it off you have to use some binary arithmetic. Take the value for turning on connection pooling and perform a logical NOT operation on it. DBPROPVAL_OS_RESOURCEPOOLING has a value of 1, so:

```
DBPROPVAL_OS_RESOURCEPOOLING = 00000001
NOT DBPROPVAL_OS_RESOURCEPOOLING = 11111110
```

and this equals -2.

If you're using an include file that contains these constants then you can use this format:

```
objConn.Properties("OLE DB Services") = DBPROPVAL_OS_ENABLEALL AND _
                        (NOT DBPROPVAL_OS_RESOURCEPOOLING)
```

This says we want all services enabled, apart from resource pooling. This sort of bit masking is how many of the Properties are used.

> The Properties collection is discussed in more detail in Chapter 6 and Appendix H.

For ODBC connections, the **ODBC Control Panel** applet controls connection pooling.

Connection State

One important point to note about connection pooling is that the state of the connection is retained when the connection is returned to the pool. This means that if you have set any properties for the connection, the values of these properties will hold their values, and will be the same when the connection is given out from the pool. So, although connection pooling is a useful performance benefit, you cannot rely upon any of the properties being in their default state.

Methods of the Connection Object

Now let's take a look at how we work with the `Connection` object. We'll spend the remainder of this chapter looking at the methods, properties, collections and events that it makes available to us. Let's begin with the methods.

The BeginTrans Method

Begins a new transaction.

*Long = Connection.*BeginTrans

A transaction provides atomicity to a series of data changes to a recordset (or recordsets) within a connection, allowing all of the changes to take place at once, or not at all. Once a transaction has been started, any changes to a recordset attached to the `Connection` are cached until the transaction is either completed or abandoned. At that stage, all of the changes will be either written to the underlying data store (if the transaction is committed) or discarded (if the transaction is aborted).

The return value indicates the level of nested transactions. This will be 1 for a top-level transaction, and will be incremented by 1 for each subsequent contained transaction. You can ignore this value if you don't need to keep track of transaction levels.

Not all providers support transactions, and calling this method against a provider that does not support transactions will generate an error. To check that transactions are supported you can check the `Transaction DDL` property of the connection's `Properties` collection. For example:

```
intSupported = objConn.Properties("Transaction DDL")
If intSupported = DBPROPVAL_TC_ALL Then
    ' transactions are fully supported
    objConn.BeginTrans
End If
```

`DBPROPVAL_TC_ALL` has a value of 8. The constants are explained in more detail in Appendix B, and the `Properties` collection in Appendix C.

For a good description of transactions, check out the MSDN article titled *Microsoft SQL Server: An Overview of Transaction Processing Concepts and the MS DTC*, available at http://msdn.microsoft.com/library/backgrnd/html/msdn_dtcwp.htm.

Nested Transactions

Nested transactions allow you to have transactions within transactions, and allow you to segment your work in a more controlled manner. For example, consider the situation shown opposite:

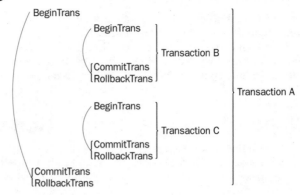

Transaction A starts – this is the first transaction, and no changes made within this transaction will be visible outside of the transaction (unless dirty reads are being used, which allow you to read values before a transaction is committed). Then Transaction B starts, and the nesting level is now 2. While B is running, the changes in B are not visible to Transaction A. When B finishes it either commits or rolls back – at this stage, A can see the changes made in B, but processes outside of A cannot. The same happens with C – its changes will not be visible to A until C commits or rolls back. Once A commits, all of the changes (that is, those in A, B and C) are visible to other processes. Note that if A rolls back its changes, it rolls back transactions B and C, irrespective of whether they have committed or not.

It's possible to use connection attributes to force transactions to start automatically on commit and rollback – and this can have serious consequences when nesting transactions. This is because every time you commit or rollback a transaction, a new one is automatically started. Imagine some code like this:

```
objConn.BeginTrans          ' start first transaction
    objConn.BeginTrans          ' start nested transaction
        ' do some processing
    objConn.CommitTrans         ' commit nested transaction
```

If auto transaction mode is in place, then as soon as this nested transaction is committed, another nested transaction is started. You don't have a way to commit a transaction without it starting another, so you can never get back to the level-1 transaction.

You might never use nested transactions (or be able to for that matter – as some providers, including the Provider for ODBC, don't support them), but it's good to be aware that this problem can arise.

See also the CommitTrans method and the RollbackTrans method.

The Cancel Method

Cancels the execution of a pending, asynchronous Execute or Open operation.

```
Connection.Cancel
```

This is particularly useful when writing applications that allow a user to specify connection details, or when users explicitly log on to a connection. If, after a certain delay, the connection has not been established, you can inform the user and offer the option of canceling the connection attempt. For example, in Visual Basic you could open the connection asynchronously, and offer the user a Cancel button, which would call this method.

Calling `Cancel` will return a run-time error if `adRunAsync` was not used as one of the *Options* on the `Execute` or `Open` operation.

The Close Method

Closes an open connection and any dependent objects.

> *Connection*.**Close**

Closing a connection does not remove it from memory, and you can change its settings and reopen it. In order to free the object from memory (assuming no one else is using the object), you must set the object variable to `Nothing`. For example:

```
objConn.Close
Set objConn = Nothing
```

If you want to ensure you don't get an error when trying to close a connection that is not open, you can check the `Connection` object's `State` property:

```
If objConn.State = adStateOpen Then
  objConn.Close
End If
Set objConn = Nothing
```

When the connection's `Close` method is called, associated recordsets and commands behave differently. Any `Recordset` objects associated with the connection are closed. Any `Command` objects associated with the connection will persist, but the `ActiveConnection` parameter will be cleared, thus disassociating the command from any connection.

When the `Close` method is called, any pending changes in `Recordset` objects associated with the connection will be cancelled. If you call the `Close` method while there is a transaction in progress, an error will be generated. (In comparison, if a `Connection` object falls out of scope then any incomplete transactions will be rolled back, and in this case *no* error is generated.)

The CommitTrans Method

Saves any pending changes and ends the current transaction.

> *Connection*.**CommitTrans**

All changes made since the previous `BeginTrans` will be written to the data store. This only affects the most recently opened transaction, and you must resolve lower-level transactions before resolving higher-level ones. So, if you are nesting transactions, you cannot start two transactions and then `Commit` or `Abort` the outer transaction without first `Committing` or `Aborting` the inner transaction.

If the `Connection` object's `Attributes` property is set to `adXactCommitRetaining` then the provider automatically starts a new transaction after a `CommitTrans` call.

See also the `BeginTrans` method and the `RollbackTrans` method.

The Execute Method

Executes the query, SQL statement, stored procedure, or provider specific text.

> *Set Recordset = Connection.***Execute**(*CommandText, [RecordsAffected], _*
> *[Options]*)

Parameter	Type	Description	Default
CommandText	String	Contains the SQL statement, table name, stored procedure name, or provider specific text to execute.	
RecordsAffected (Optional)	Long	A variable into which the provider returns the number of records that the operation affected.	
Options (Optional)	Long	A value that indicates how the provider should interpret the *CommandText* argument.	`adCmdUnspecified`

Options can be one or more of the `CommandTypeEnum` constants:

- ❏ `adCmdText`, for a SQL string.
- ❏ `adCmdTable`, for a table name.
- ❏ `adCmdTableDirect`, for a table name.
- ❏ `adCmdStoredProc`, for a stored procedure name.
- ❏ `adCmdFile`, for a saved recordset.
- ❏ `adCmdUnknown`, for an unknown command type.
- ❏ `adCmdAsyncExecute`, for asynchronous execution.
- ❏ `adCmdAsyncFetch`, for asynchronous fetching.
- ❏ `adCmdAsyncFetchNonBlocking`, for asynchronous fetching that does not block.
- ❏ `adCmdExecuteNoRecords`, for a non-row returning command.
- ❏ `adCmdUnspecified`, to indicate the command type is unspecified. ADO will work out the command type itself.

More details of these options can be found under the CommandType property (see Chapter 4).

A new Recordset object is returned, even if it is not used. If the command did not return any rows then the recordset will be empty. If you specify the adExecuteNoRecords option, then a null recordset is returned. The Recordset object returned is always a forward-only, read-only cursor (often called a firehose cursor). You can specify different cursor types by using the Open method of the Recordset object.

You can use this method with or without some arguments, and with or without it returning a recordset. For example, to return a recordset you could use this syntax:

```
strCommandText = "SELECT * FROM authors"
Set objRec = objConn.Execute (strCommandText, , adCmdText)
```

If the command specified in the command text does not return any rows, then you should include the adCmdExecuteNoRecords option, as this can improve performance:

```
strCommandText = "UPDATE titles SET price = price * 1.10"
objConn.Execute strCommandText, , adCmdText OR adExecuteNoRecords
```

To supply multiple values you use Boolean logic and OR them together.

If you want to find out how many records were affected by the command then you can use the *RecordsAffected* argument, passing in a variable. This is especially useful for action queries, where a recordset is not returned:

```
strCommandText = "UPDATE titles SET Price = Price * 1.10"
objConn.Execute strCommandText, lngRecs, adCmdText
Print lngRecs & " were updated."
```

If you are using *RecordsAffected* and you find that it always returns –1 when you are expecting a different value, then check that there are no data store options to stop the returning of this information. SQL Server, for example, has a SET NOCOUNT ON statement, which stops the number of rows affected by a command from being returned. Check that this option is not set anywhere in your command (you might not realize it's there if you are using a stored procedure), and check that it's not set as a global database variable.

To have the command executed asynchronously you can also add one of the asynchronous flags to the *Options* argument. For example:

```
objConn.Execute strCommandText, lngRecs, adCmdText OR adAsyncExecute
```

An ExecuteComplete event will be raised when this operation finishes. This happens even if the command is executed synchronously, but is more useful when asynchronous operations are in use.

The Open Method

Opens a connection to a data source, so that commands can be executed against it.

Connection.**Open**(*ConnectionString, UserID, Password, Options*)

Parameter	Type	Description	Default
ConnectionString	String	The connection information.	
UserID	String	The user name to use when connecting.	
Password	String	The user password to use when connecting.	
Options	Long	Extra connection options.	`adConnectUnspecified`

Options can be one of the `ConnectOptionEnum` constants. At the moment the only constants are `adAsyncConnect` (which indicates the connection should be made asynchronously) and `adConnectUnspecified` (the default, which indicates a synchronous connection is to be made).

The `ConnectionString` property takes its value from the *ConnectionString* argument if used.

Values passed in the *UserID* and *Password* arguments override similar values passed in the *ConnectionString* argument – unless the *Password* you supply in the argument is blank, in which case the *ConnectionString* password still seems to take effect.

Some typical connections strings are shown below. For the ODBC Provider connecting to an Access database, you would use:

```
Driver={Microsoft Access Driver (*.mdb)}; DBQ=database_file
```

The DBQ argument points to the physical path name of the Access database. To connect to SQL Server, again using ODBC, you would use:

```
Driver={SQL Server}; Server=server_name; Database=database_name;
UID=user_name; PWD=user_password
```

Switching over to the native OLEDB drivers, connecting to Access would be like this:

```
Provider=Micrsoft.Jet.OLEDB.4.0; Data Source=database_file
```

For SQL Server, using the native driver, it would be:

```
Provider=SQLOLEDB; Data Source=server_name; Initial Catalog=database_name;
User Id=user_name; Password=user_password
```

More details of the different connect strings that can be used can be found under the `ConnectionString` property, as well as in Chapter 2.

The OpenSchema Method

Obtains database schema information from the provider.

> *Recordset = Connection.**OpenSchema**(Schema, [Restrictions], [SchemaID])*

Parameter	Type	Description	Default
Schema	SchemaEnum (Long)	The type of schema query to run.	
Restrictions (Optional)	Variant	An array of query constraints for each Schema option. This is generally the column names and values to filter on.	
SchemaID (Optional)	Variant	The GUID for a provider specific schema query not defined by the OLEDB specification.	

Each value of `SchemaEnum` has a specific set of criteria values. This list is large and is included in Appendix B.

This method is most useful for obtaining table and procedure names from a data store. For example:

```
Set objRec = objConn.OpenSchema(adSchemaTables)
While Not objRec.EOF
   Print objRec("TABLE_NAME")
   Print objRec("TABLE_TYPE")
   objRec.MoveNext
Wend
```

The various Schemas are examined in detail in Appendix D.

For multi-dimensional providers using `adSchemaMembers`, the restrictions can either be the columns in the members schema, or one of the `MDTREEOP` constants, as defined in Appendix L.

An alternative method of obtaining schema information is to use the ADOX library, as discussed in Chapter 8.

The RollbackTrans Method

Cancels any changes made during the current transaction and ends the transaction.

Connection.RollbackTrans

All changes made since the previous `BeginTrans` will be cancelled. This only affects the most recently opened transaction, and like `CommitTrans`, you must resolve lower-level transactions before resolving higher-level ones.

Also, if the `Connection` object's `Attributes` property is set to `adXactCommitAbort` then the provider automatically starts a new transaction after a `RollbackTrans` call.

See also the `BeginTrans` method and the `CommitTrans` method.

Properties of the Connection Object

The Attributes Property

Indicates the transactional facilities of a Connection object.

> *Long = Connection*.**Attributes**
> *Connection*.**Attributes** *= Long*

Its value can be one or more of the adXactAttributeEnum constants:

❑ adXactCommitRetaining, to ensure that a new transaction is started automatically after a CommitTrans

❑ adXactAbortRetaining, to ensure that a new transaction is started automatically after a RollbackTrans

❑ A combination of both, to indicate that new a transaction is started automatically after an existing transaction is finished

Note that not all providers support this property.

You can combine the two by ORing them together:

```
objConn.Attributes = adXactCommitRetaining OR adXactAbortRetaining
```

Beware of automatic transaction enlistment when using nested transactions, as this can lead to problems committing the higher-level transactions. For more details of this see the *Nested Transactions* subsection of the discussion of the BeginTrans method, earlier in this chapter.

The CommandTimeout Property

Indicates how long, in seconds, to wait while executing a command before terminating the command and generating an error. The default is 30.

> *Long = Connection*.**CommandTimeout**
> *Connection*.**CommandTimeout** *= Long*

If the timeout period is reached before the command completes execution, then an error is generated and the command cancelled. Setting this property to 0 will force the provider to wait indefinitely.

For example, the following will ensure that an error is generated if the command doesn't complete within 10 seconds:

```
objConn.CommandTimeout = 10
```

Note that the Command object's CommandTimeout property does *not* inherit the value set here.

The ConnectionString Property

Contains the details used to create a connection to a data source.

> *String = Connection.*ConnectionString
> *Connection.*ConnectionString *= String*

ADO supports only the following four arguments in the connection string (and all other arguments are ignored by ADO and passed directly to the provider):

❑ Provider= identifies the name of the provider

❑ File Name= identifies the name of the provider-specific file containing connection information (for example, a UDL file)

❑ Remote Provider= is the name of a provider that should be used when opening a client-side connection (this only applies to RDS)

❑ Remote Server= is the path name of the server that should be used when opening a client-side connection (this only applies to RDS)

The connection string may be changed by the provider after the connection is established, as it fills in some of its own details.

You cannot pass both the Provider and File Name arguments. Specifying a File Name will cause ADO to load the provider – the provider details will be stored within this file.

Some examples of various connection strings are shown here. For the ODBC provider connecting to Microsoft Access:

```
Driver={Microsoft Access Driver (*.mdb)}; DBQ=database_name
```

For the ODBC provider connecting to Microsoft SQL Server:

```
Driver={SQL Server}; Server=server_name; Database=database_name;
UID=user_name; PWD=password
```

You can also use an existing DSN. To use a DSN called pubs, you would specify this connection string:

```
DSN=pubs
```

The pros and cons of using a DSN versus a full ODBC connect string are discussed in Chapter 12.

When using the OLEDB provider for ODBC, notice that you can omit the Provider option (because it is the default).

For the OLEDB provider for ODBC using an ODBC Data Source Name:

```
DSN=data_source_name
```

For the OLEDB provider connecting to Microsoft Access:

```
Provider=Microsoft.Jet.OLEDB.4.0; Data Source=database_name
```

For the OLEDB provider connecting to Microsoft SQL Server:

```
Provider=SQLOLEDB; Data Source=server_name; Initial Catalog=database_name;
User Id=user_name; Password=user_password
```

For example, to connect to a SQL Server using the OLEDB provider you would do something like this:

```
objConn.ConnectionString = "Provider=SQLOLEDB; Data Source=TIGGER;" & _
                "Initial Catalog=pubs; User Id=davids; Password=letmein"
objConn.Open
```

If, when you open a connection, you pass the connection details into the *ConnectionString* argument, then the `ConnectionString` property will be filled in with these details.

For more information on connection strings, refer to Chapter 2.

The ConnectionTimeout Property

Indicates how long, in seconds, to wait whilst trying to establish a connection before aborting the attempt and generating an error. The default is 15 seconds.

Long = Connection.ConnectionTimeout
Connection.ConnectionTimeout = Long

If the timeout period is reached before the connection opens, then an error is generated and the connection cancelled. Setting this property to 0 will force the provider to wait indefinitely.

You cannot set this property once the connection has been established.

The CursorLocation Property

Sets or returns the location of the cursor engine.

CursorLocationEnum = Connection.CursorLocation
Connection.CursorLocation = CursorLocationEnum

This can be set to one of the following values:

- ❑ `adUseClient`, to use a client side cursor.
- ❑ `adUseClientBatch`, to use a client side cursor. This is included for backward compatibility only, and `adUseClient` should be used instead.
- ❑ `adUseServer`, to use a server side cursor.
- ❑ `adUseNone`, to indicate no cursor services are used. This is included for backward compatibility and should not be used.

A disconnected recordset can only be achieved by setting the `CursorLocation` property to `adUseClient`.

A `Recordset` created against the `Connection` object will inherit the value set here.

Changing this property has no effect on existing connections.

The performance issues surrounding various cursor types are discussed in Chapter 12.

The DefaultDatabase Property

Indicates the default database for a `Connection` object.

> *String = Connection.***DefaultDatabase***
> *Connection.***DefaultDatabase** = *String*

You can access objects in other databases by fully qualifying the objects, if the data source or provider supports this.

For example, using Microsoft SQL Server, you can create two recordsets on different databases:

```
objConn.DefaultDatabase="pubs"

objRec1.Open "authors", objConn, _
             adOpenKeyset, adLockReadOnly, adCmdTable

objRec2.Open "Sales.dbo.Orders", objConn, _
             adOpenKeyset, adLockReadOnly, adCmdTable
```

The first uses the `authors` table from the `pubs` database, and the second uses the `Orders` table in the `Sales` database.

The IsolationLevel Property

Indicates the level of transaction isolation for a `Connection` object.

> *IsolationLevelEnum = Connection.***IsolationLevel***
> *Connection.***IsolationLevel** = *IsolationLevelEnum*

The isolation level allows you to define how other transactions interact with yours, and whether they can see your changes and vice versa.

This value only comes into affect when you call the `BeginTrans` method. The provider may return the next greater level of isolation if the requested level is not available.

The value can be one of the *IsolationLevelEnum* constants:

❑ `adXactUnspecified`, which indicates that the provider is using a different isolation level to the one you specified, but that it cannot determine what this isolation level is.

❑ `adXactChaos`, which indicates that a higher level transaction has control over the records. This means that you cannot overwrite any pending changes from another user.

❑ `adXactBrowse` or `adXactReadUncommitted`, which allows you to view uncommitted changes in another transaction. You should be careful when using this value, as the changes in another transaction have not been committed. They could therefore be rolled back, leaving you with invalid values.

❏ adXactCursorStability or adXactReadCommitted (the default), which indicates that you can only view changes in other transactions once they have been committed. This guarantees the state of the data. However, new records and deleted records will be reflected in your recordset.

❏ adXactRepeatableRead, which doesn't allow you to see changes made from other transactions unless you re-query the recordset. Once you have re-queried the recordset, you can see new records that might have been added by other users to the records that comprise your recordset.

❏ adXactIsolated or adXactSerializable, which indicates that transactions are completely isolated from each other. This means that all concurrent transactions will produce the same effect as if each transaction was executed one after the other.

The Mode Property

Indicates the available permissions for modifying data in a Connection.

```
ConnectModeEnum = Connection.Mode
Connection.Mode = ConnectModeEnum
```

The value can be one of the *ConnectModeEnum* constants:

❏ adModeUnknown, which is the default, to say that permissions cannot be determined, or they haven't been set yet.

❏ adModeRead, for read-only permissions.

❏ adModeWrite, for write-only permissions.

❏ adModeReadWrite, for read/write permissions.

❏ adModeShareDenyRead, for preventing other users from opening a connection with read permissions.

❏ adModeShareDenyWrite, for preventing other users from opening a connection with write permissions.

❏ adModeShareExclusive, for preventing other users from opening a connection.

❏ adModeShareDenyNone, for preventing other users from opening a connection with any permissions.

You can use this to set or return the provider access permission for the current connection.

You cannot set this property on open connections.

The Provider Property

Indicates the name of the provider for a `Connection` object.

> *String = Connection.Provider*
> *Connection.**Provider** = String*

This property can also be set by the contents of the `ConnectionString` property.

Note that specifying the provider in more than one place can have unpredictable results. Microsoft doesn't actually specify what 'unpredictable' means in this case, but it's probably best to only set this in one place.

If no provider is specified then the default is MSDASQL, the Microsoft OLE DB Provider for ODBC. The providers supplied with the data access components are:

❑ **MSDASQL**, for ODBC

❑ **MSIDXS**, for Index Server

❑ **ADSDSOObject**, for Active Directory Services

❑ **Microsoft.Jet.OLEDB.4.0**, for Microsoft Jet databases, both Access 2000 and earlier versions.

❑ **SQLOLEDB**, for SQL Server

❑ **MSDAORA**, for Oracle

❑ **MSDataShape**, for the Microsoft Data Shape with hierarchical recordsets. This provider is discussed in more detail in Chapter 11.

❑ **MSDAIPP.DSO.1**, for Internet Publishing.

❑ **MSPersist**, for locally saved files.

❑ **MSDAOSP**, for simple text files.

The various `Provider` and `ConnectionString` options are discussed in more detail under the `ConnectionString` property, as well as in Chapter 2.

The State Property

Describes whether the `Connection` object is open or closed.

> *Long = Connection.**State***

This will be one of the following *ObjectStateEnum* constants:

❑ `adStateOpen` for an open connection.

❑ `adStateClosed` for a closed connection.

You can use the `State` property to ensure that you don't generate errors when closing a connection. For example:

```
If objConn.State = adStateOpen Then
   objConn.Close
End If
```

The Version Property

Indicates the ADO version number.

> *String = Connection.*Version

The version number of the provider can be obtained from the `Collection` object's `Properties` collection.

Events of the Connection Object

Connection events were a big new feature of ADO 2.0, and they can be quickly summarized as follows:

- ❏ `BeginTransComplete` is raised after a transaction has begun
- ❏ `CommitTransComplete` is raised after a transaction has been committed
- ❏ `ConnectComplete` is raised after the connection has been established
- ❏ `Disconnect` is raised after a connection ends
- ❏ `ExecuteComplete` is raised after an `Execute` command has completed
- ❏ `InfoMessage` is raised when the provider returns extra information
- ❏ `RollbackTransComplete` is raised after a transaction has been rolled back
- ❏ `WillConnect` is raised just before the connection is established
- ❏ `WillExecute` is raised just before a command is executed

These events work in both synchronous and asynchronous modes.

All events will have a bi-directional parameter, *adStatus,* to indicate the status of the event. This is of type *EventStatusEnum* and on entry to the procedure can be one of the following constants:

- ❏ `adStatusOK`, to indicate that the action that caused the event was successful.
- ❏ `adStatusErrorsOccured`, to indicate that errors or warnings occurred, in which case the `Errors` collection should be checked.
- ❏ `adStatusCantDeny`. On a `Will...` event this indicates that you cannot cancel the action that generated the event; on a `...Complete` event it indicates that the action was cancelled.
- ❏ `adStatusUnwantedEvent`, which indicates that the action which generated the event should no longer generate events.

On a `Will...` event (and assuming `adStatusCantDeny` is not set), before the procedure exits you can set *adStatus* to `adStatusCancel` to cancel the action that caused this event. This also generates an error indicating the event has been cancelled. For example, assume that you have moved from one record to the next – this will raise a `WillMove` event on the Recordset. If you decide that you do not wish to move to another record, you can set *adStatus* to `adStatusCancel`, and the `Move` action will be cancelled. This allows you to perhaps cancel actions where the data is incorrect.

When using `Will...` events, one thing to watch for is implicit method calls. Taking the above `Move` as an example; if the current record has been edited, then ADO implicitly calls `Update`. In this case you might get more than one `Will...` event. We discuss this in more detail in Chapter 5.

If you no longer wish to receive events for a particular action, then before the procedure exits you can set `adStatus` to `adStatusUnwantedEvent`, and they will no longer be generated.

The BeginTransComplete Event

Fired after a `BeginTrans` operation finishes executing.

> BeginTransComplete(*TransactionLevel, pError, adStatus, pConnection*)

Parameter	Type	Description
TransactionLevel	Long	Contains the new transaction level of the `BeginTrans` that caused the event.
pError	Error	If *adStatus* is `adStatusErrorsOccurred`, this is an `Error` object that describes the error that occurred. Otherwise it is not set.
adStatus	EventStatusEnum (Long)	Identifies the status of the message.
pConnection	Connection	The `Connection` object upon which the `BeginTrans` was executed.

You can use this to trigger other operations that are dependent upon the transaction having been started. For example, you might like to build a transaction monitoring system, and you could log the start of the transaction in this event.

The CommitTransComplete Event

Fired after a `CommitTrans` operation finishes executing.

> CommitTransComplete(*pError, adStatus, pConnection*)

Parameter	Type	Description
pError	Error	If *adStatus* is `adStatusErrorsOccurred`, this is an `Error` object that describes the error that occurred. Otherwise it is not set.
adStatus	EventStatusEnum (Long)	Identifies the status of the message.
pConnection	Connection	The `Connection` object upon which the `CommitTrans` was executed.

You can use this to trigger other operations that are dependent upon the transaction having been completed successfully, such as updating log files or an audit trail.

The ConnectComplete Event

Fired after a connection starts.

> **ConnectComplete(*pError, adStatus, pConnection*)**

Parameter	Type	Description
pError	Error	If *adStatus* is adStatusErrorsOccurred, this is an Error object that describes the error that occurred. Otherwise it is not set.
adStatus	EventStatusEnum (Long)	Identifies the status of the message.
pConnection	Connection	The Connection object for which this event applies.

You can use the ConnectComplete event to examine the details of the connection and whether it completed successfully. For example, the following Visual Basic example shows how you could use the ConnectComplete event:

```
Private Sub objConn_ConnectComplete(ByVal pError As ADODB.Error, adStatus As
ADODB.EventStatusEnum, ByVal pConnection As ADODB.Connection)
Select Case adStatus
   Case adStatusErrorsOccurred
      Print "Errors occurred whilst attempting to connect."
      Print "Connection String is: " & pConnection.ConnectionString
      Print "Error description: " & pError.Description
   Case adStatusOK
      Print "Connection successful."
End Select
End Sub
```

The text not highlighted is the definition of the event procedure and is automatically created by Visual Basic. (For more on using events with Visual Basic and Visual J++, see Chapter 2.)

The Disconnect Event

Fired after a connection ends.

> **Disconnect(*adStatus, pConnection*)**

Parameter	Type	Description
adStatus	EventStatusEnum (Long)	Identifies the status of the message.
pConnection	Connection	The Connection object for which this event applies.

You can use this to examine whether the disconnection was successful. You can also use it to track users as they log onto and off from data sources. It can also be useful to alert users when a connection drops unexpectedly.

The ExecuteComplete Event

Fired after a command has finished executing.

> ExecuteComplete(*RecordsAffected, pError, adStatus, pCommand, pRecordset, pConnection*)

Parameter	Type	Description
RecordsAffected	Long	A Long variable into which the provider returns the number of records that the operation affected.
pError	Error	If *adStatus* is adStatusErrorsOccurred, then this is an Error object that describes the error that occurred. Otherwise it is not set.
adStatus	EventStatusEnum (Long)	Identifies the status of the message.
pCommand	Command	The Command object for which this event applies. This may not be set if a Command object was not used.
pRecordset	Recordset	The Recordset object upon which the Execute was run. This may be empty if a non-recordset returning command was run, such as an action query.
pConnection	Connection	The Connection object upon which the Execute was run.

This allows you to examine whether the command completed successfully, and how many records it affected. You can use this instead of the *RecordsAffected* argument of the Execute method. For example, the following Visual Basic code shows the use of this event:

```
Private Sub objConn_ExecuteComplete(ByVal RecordsAffected As Long, _
     ByVal pError As ADODB.Error, adStatus As ADODB.EventStatusEnum, _
     ByVal pCommand As ADODB.Command, ByVal pRecordset As ADODB.Recordset, _
     ByVal pConnection As ADODB.Connection)
If adStatus = adStatusOK Then
   Print RecordsAffected & " records were affected by this command."
End If
End Sub
```

The code not highlighted is the Visual Basic generated event procedure.

The InfoMessage Event

Fired whenever a connection event operation completes successfully and additional information is returned by the provider.

> InfoMessage(*pError, adStatus, pConnection*)

Parameter	Type	Description
pError	Error	If *adStatus* is `adStatusErrorsOccurred`, then this is an `Error` object that describes the error that occurred. Otherwise it is not set.
adStatus	EventStatusEnum (Long)	Identifies the status of the message.
pConnection	Connection	The `Connection` object upon which the command was executed.

The parameters define what type of information message this is. This is particularly useful when dealing with ODBC data sources, especially to SQL Server, as it returns informational messages, and could be used to log these in an audit trail.

For example, you could connect to the **pubs** database on SQL server with this connect string:

```
Driver={SQL Server}; Server=Tigger; Database=pubs; UID=sa; PWD=
```

and then put this code into the `InfoMessage` event procedure:

```
Private Sub oConn_InfoMessage(ByVal pError As ADODB.Error, _
        adStatus As ADODB.EventStatusEnum, _
        ByVal pConnection As ADODB.Connection)

    Dim objError As ADODB.Error

    Debug.Print pError.Description

    For Each objError In pConnection.Errors
        Debug.Print vbtab; objError.Description
    Next
End Sub
```

On my server, that gives the following:

```
[Microsoft][ODBC SQL Server Driver][SQL Server]Changed database context to
'master'.
    [Microsoft][ODBC SQL Server Driver][SQL Server]Changed database context
to 'master'.
    [Microsoft][ODBC SQL Server Driver][SQL Server]Changed language setting
to 'us_english'.
    [Microsoft][ODBC SQL Server Driver][SQL Server]Changed database context
to 'pubs'.
```

In general this event can be used to track connection messages, or actions on the connection that return `SQL_SUCCESS_WITH_INFO`.

The RollbackTransComplete Event

Fired after a `RollbackTrans` operation has finished executing.

```
RollbackTransComplete(pError, adStatus, pConnection)
```

Parameter	Type	Description
pError	Error	If adStatus is adStatusErrorsOccurred, then this is an Error object that describes the error that occurred. Otherwise it is not set.
adStatus	EventStatusEnum (Long)	Identifies the status of the message.
pConnection	Connection	The Connection object upon which the RollbackTrans was executed.

You can use this to trigger other operations that depend upon the transaction having failed, such as log files. For example:

```
Private Sub objConn_RollbackTransComplete(ByVal pError As ADODB.Error, _
    adStatus As ADODB.EventStatusEnum, _
    ByVal pConnection As ADODB.Connection)
Print "Transaction was rolled back. Changes have not been saved."
End Sub
```

This could be extremely useful in nightly batch jobs.

The WillConnect Event

Fired before a connection starts, indicating that the connection is about to take place.

WillConnect(*ConnectionString, UserID, Password, Options, adStatus, pConnection*)

Parameter	Type	Description
ConnectionString	String	The connection information.
UserID	String	The user name to use when connecting.
Password	String	The user password to use when connecting.
Options	Long	Extra connection options, as passed into the Connection object's Open method.
adStatus	EventStatusEnum (Long)	Identifies the status of the message.
pConnection	Connection	The Connection object for which this event applies.

The parameters supplied can be changed before the method returns – for instance if the user has specified certain connection attributes, but you wish to change them. As an example, imagine an application that allowed the user to specify connection details. You could prevent them connecting as a certain user, but allow connection as another:

```
Private Sub objConn_WillConnect(ConnectionString As String, _
       UserID As String, Password As String, Options As Long, _
       adStatus As ADODB.EventStatusEnum, _
       ByVal pConnection As ADODB.Connection)
   If adStatus = adStatusOK Then
      Select Case UserID
      Case "sa"
         Print "Connection as system administrator not allowed."
         adStatus = adStatusCancel
      Case "Guest"
         UserID = "GuestUser"
         Password = "GuestPassword"
      End Select
   End If
End Sub
```

This stops the user trying to connect as sa and cancels the connection attempt. If a user tries to connect as Guest then the user id is changed to GuestUser and connection proceeds. This allows you to have a set of real user details that are hidden, whilst exposing a viewable set of user details.

The WillExecute Event

Fired before a pending command executes on the connection.

> **WillExecute(***Source, CursorType, LockType, Options, adStatus, pCommand, pRecordset, pConnection***)**

Name	Type	Description
Source	String	The SQL command or stored procedure name.
CursorType	CursorTypeEnum (Long)	The type of cursor for the recordset that will be opened. If set to adOpenUnspecified the cursor type cannot be changed.
LockType	LockTypeEnum (Long)	The lock type for the recordset that will be opened. If set to adLockUnspecified the lock type cannot be changed.
Options	Long	The options that can be used to execute the command or open the recordset, as passed into the *Options* argument.
adStatus	EventStatusEnum (Long)	Identifies the status of the message.
pCommand	Command	The Command object for which this event applies. This may be empty if a Command object was not being used.
pRecordset	Recordset	The Recordset object for which this event applies. If the Execute command didn't return a recordset, then this will be an empty Recordset object.
pConnection	Connection	The Connection object for which this event applies.

The execution parameters can be modified in this procedure, as it is called before the command executes.

This is particularly useful when building user-query type applications where the user has the ability to set details of the connection, since it allows you to examine the parameters and modify them if necessary. For example:

```
Private Sub objConn_WillExecute(Source As String, _
        CursorType As ADODB.CursorTypeEnum, LockType As ADODB.LockTypeEnum, _
        Options As Long, adStatus As ADODB.EventStatusEnum, _
        ByVal pCommand As ADODB.Command, ByVal pRecordset As ADODB.Recordset, _
        ByVal pConnection As ADODB.Connection)
    If Source = "SalaryDetails" Then
        Print " Nice try, but you're not allowed to look at these'
        adStatus = adStatusCancel
    End If
End Sub
```

This cancels the event if someone tries to connect to the `SalaryDetails` table.

You can also use this to protect against ad-hoc insertions and deletions, and is a good way to build business logic into the connection.

Collections of the Connection Object

The collections are discussed in depth in Chapter 6.

The Errors Collection

Contains all of the `Error` objects created in response to a single failure involving the provider.

Connection.**Errors**

The `Errors` collection is only cleared when another ADO operation generates an error.

Each `Error` object represents a specific provider error, not an ADO error – this is because ADO errors generate run-time errors.

Note that the `Errors` collection often contains warnings as well as errors. For this reason, it's a good idea to use the `Clear` method before certain operations, to ensure that the warnings are relevant to the most recent operation. In particular, you should use the technique for the `Resync`, `UpdateBatch` and `CancelBatch` methods or the `Filter` property on a `Recordset` object, and for the `Open` method on a `Connection` object.

The Properties Collection

Contains all of the `Property` objects for a `Connection` object.

Properties = Connection.**Properties**

The `Properties` collection is discussed in more detail in Chapter 6 and a full list of the properties available is in Appendix C.

The Command Object

Although the Connection object allows the execution of commands against a data store, the Command object has greater functionality and flexibility, and can improve connection performance by avoiding continual reference to default values. It's not actually a requirement that data providers support the Command object; but where the Command object is supported it proves not only useful, but essential in certain areas.

You might be required to pass parameters into stored procedures or stored queries, and as you'll see in this chapter, there's more than one way to do this. One method involves the use of the Parameters collection, which allows complete control over the individual parameters passed to a procedure or query. It's for this reason that the Parameters collection is covered in this chapter (rather than with the other collections in Chapter 6).

> When using stored procedures that have output parameters, you have to use a Command object. The Command object's Parameters collection allows the passing of parameters into and out of stored procedures, as well as allowing a recordset to be passed back to the application.

Methods of the Command Object

The Cancel Method

Cancels execution of a pending Execute method call.

```
Command.Cancel
```

The Cancel method is particularly useful when allowing users to submit their own queries, as these can often have long execution times, and you may wish to provide them with a Cancel button on the screen.

Note that, if you try to cancel an Execute call that was used without the adExecuteAsync option, then a run-time error will be generated. For more information see the Execute method, below.

The CreateParameter Method

Creates a new `Parameter` object.

> Set *Parameter* = *Command*.**CreateParameter**(*[Name], [Type], [Direction], [Size], [Value]*)

The method's arguments are all optional:

Parameter	Type	Description	Default
Name	String	The name of the parameter.	
Type	DataTypeEnum (Long)	The data type of the parameter.	`adEmpty`
Direction	ParameterDirection Enum (Long)	The direction of the parameter.	`AdParam Input`
Size	Long	The maximum length of the parameter value in characters or bytes.	0
Value	Variant	The value for the parameter.	

The ParameterDirectionEnum constants list is as follows:

- ❑ `adParamUnknown`, to indicate that the direction of the parameter is unknown.

- ❑ `adParamInput`, to indicate that the parameter is an input parameter to the command.

- ❑ `adParamOutput`, to indicate that the parameter is an output parameter from the command.

- ❑ `adParamInputOutput`, to indicate that the parameter is both an input to and output from the command.

- ❑ `adParamReturnValue`, to indicate that the parameter is a return value from the command.

The DataTypeEnum list is quite large, and is included in Appendix B.

`CreateParameter` is used to create the parameters that are to be passed to stored procedures and stored queries. There are two ways of using `CreateParameter`: the first is with all of its arguments, and the second is without any arguments. For example, the following two sets of code are logically equivalent ways of assigning specific values to a `Parameter` object's properties:

```
Set objParam = objCmd.CreateParameter("ID", adInteger, adParamInput, 8, 123 )
```

and

```
Set objParam = objCmd.CreateParameter
objParam.Name = "ID"
objParam.Type = adInteger
objParam.Direction = adParamInput
objParam.Size = 8
objParam.Value = 123
```

Note that the code above does not add the parameter to the `Parameters` collection of the command object concerned. For this, you must use the `Append` method. For example:

```
objCmd.Parameters.Append objParam
```

Multiple parameter objects can be appended to the same `Command` object. However, if you attempt to append a `Parameter` object that does not have a specific value assigned to at least one of its properties, an error will be generated. We'll take a look at the `Parameter` object itself, later in this chapter.

Note that the parameters in the `Parameters` collection are matched to those in the stored procedure or query by the order in which they're listed. In particular, this means that the name you assign to a `Parameter` in the collection (via the `CreateParameter` method or the `Name` property) need not be the same as the corresponding parameter name within the procedure or query. It's the *order* of parameters that's important, not the names – although it's best to use similar (or same) names both in the collection and in the procedure or query.

The Execute Method

Executes the query, SQL statement, or stored procedure specified in the `CommandText` property.

> [Set *Recordset* =]*Command*.Execute([*RecordsAffected*], [*Parameters*], [*Options*])

Parameter	Type	Description	Default
RecordsAffected	Long	A Long variable into which the provider returns the number of records that the operation affected.	
Parameters	Variant	An array of parameter values passed with a SQL statement. Output parameters will not return correct values if passed here.	
Options	Long	A value that indicates how the provider should interpret the `CommandText` property of the `Command` object.	-1

RecordsAffected can be used to determine how many records were affected by the command executing. For example:

```
objCmd.CommandText = "UPDATE titles SET royalty = royalty * 1.10"
objCmd.Execute lngRecs
Print "Number of records affected by command: "
Print lngRecs
```

Parameter values passed in the *Parameters* argument will override any values in a command's `Parameters` collection. For example:

```
objCmd.Parameters.Refresh
objCmd.Parameters("@FirstParam") = "abc"
objCmd.Execute , Array("def")
```

This command will use `def` as the value for the `FirstParam` parameter, instead of the value `abc` supplied in the `Parameters` collection.

Options can be one of the following constants:

❑   `adCmdText`, to indicate that the command text is to be interpreted as a text command, such as a SQL statement.

❑   `adCmdTable`, to indicate that the command text is to be interpreted as the name of a table.

❑   `adCmdTableDirect`, to indicate that the command text is to be interpreted directly as a table name. This allows ADO to switch some internal options in order to provide more efficient processing.

❑   `adCmdStoredProc`, to indicate that the command text should be interpreted as the name of a stored procedure or query.

❑   `adCmdUnknown`, to indicate that the nature of the command text is unknown.

For asynchronous operation you can add `adAsyncExecute` to the *Options* argument to make the command execute asynchronously, and `adAsyncFetch` or `adAsyncFetchNonBlocking` to make the recordset be returned asynchronously:

```
objCmd.Execute  , , adCmdTable OR adAsyncExecute OR adAsyncFetch
```

> **Early versions of the ADO documentation state that the asynchronous flags are** adFetchAsync **and** adExecuteAsync. **These are both incorrect.**

Properties of the Command Object

The ActiveConnection Property

Indicates the `Connection` object to which the `Command` object currently belongs.

> Set *Connection* = *Command*.ActiveConnection
> Set *Command*.ActiveConnection = *Connection*
> *Command*.ActiveConnection = *String*
> *String* = *Command*.ActiveConnection

This can be a valid `Connection` object or a connection string, and must be set before the `Execute` method is called – otherwise an error will occur.

There is a subtle difference between using an existing `Connection` object and a connection string when setting the `ActiveConnection`. For example, consider the following lines of code:

```
objConn.Open "Provider=Microsoft.Jet.OLEDB.4.0; " & _
             "Data Source=C:\ADO\ADOTest.mdb"
Set objCmd.ActiveConnection = objConn
```

```
objCmd.ActiveConnection="Provider=Microsoft.Jet.OLEDB.4.0; " & _
                        "Data Source=C:\ADO\ADOTest.mdb"
```

These code fragments both appear to do the same thing; however, the first uses an existing `Connection` object, whereas the second will create a new connection. Connection pooling, however, may reuse an existing connection if it can speed up the connection in this second case.

In Visual Basic, if you set the value of `ActiveConnection` to `Nothing` then the command is disassociated from the connection, but the `Command` object remains active. However, note what happens to the parameters. If the provider supplied the parameters (i.e. via the `Refresh` method of the `Parameters` collection) then the `Parameters` collection will be cleared. On the other hand, if the parameters were created manually then they are left intact. This could be useful if you have several commands with parameters that are the same.

The CommandText Property

Contains the text of a command to be issued against a data provider.

> *String = Command*.CommandText
> *Command*.CommandText = *String*

This can be a SQL statement, a table name, a stored procedure name or a provider-specific command, and the default is an empty string.

For example, to set the command text to a SQL string, you can do the following

```
objCmd.CommandText = "SELECT * FROM authors WHERE state = 'CA'"
```

There are a number of ways to pass parameters into a stored procedure in SQL Server. One way is to use the parameters contained in the `Parameters` collection. Another way is to pass the stored procedure and its arguments as a text command:

```
objCmd.CommandText = "usp_MyProcedure ('abc', 123)"
objCmd.CommandType = adCmdStoredProc
objCmd.Execute
```

This method is sometimes quicker to code than using the `Parameters` collection, although you obviously have no way to use output parameters with this method. Alternatively, you could use the *Parameters* argument of the `Execute` method:

```
objCmd.CommandText = "usp_MyProcedure"
objCmd.CommandType = adCmdStoredProc
objCmd.Execute , Array("abc", 123)
```

If you set the Command object's Prepared property to True, then the command will be compiled and stored by the provider before executing. This prepared statement is retained for the duration of the connection. If you are using the SQL Server provider, this may create a temporary stored procedure for you (if you have the Use Procedure for Prepare property in the Connection object's Properties collection, discussed in Appendix C). This is particularly useful when the same command is to be executed several times, but with different parameters.

The Parameters collection is explained in more detail later in this chapter.

The CommandTimeout Property

Indicates how long, in seconds, to wait while executing a command before terminating the command and generating an error. The default is 30 seconds.

```
Long = Command.CommandTimeout
Command.CommandTimeout = Long
```

An error will be generated if the timeout value is reached before the command completes execution, and the command will be cancelled. If you are using Visual Basic, then the ExecuteComplete event will be fired when the error is generated, and you can check the *pError* argument to detect the error.

This property bears no relation to the Connection object's CommandTimeout property.

The CommandType Property

Indicates the type of Command object.

```
CommandTypeEnum = Command.CommandType
Command.CommandType = CommandTypeEnum
```

You should use this property to optimize the processing of the command. For example, if you know that your command will not return any data, you should use the adExecuteNoRecords in conjunction with adCmdText or adCmdStoredProc:

```
objCmd.CommandType = adCmdStoredProc OR adExecuteNorecords
```

The reason for doing this is that it informs the provider what sort of command you will be executing, in advance of the command being performed. This allows the provider to decide what to do in advance, and this often gives an increase in performance. Using adExecuteNoRecords means that no recordset is created, again giving improved performance.

The distinction between adCmdTable and adCmdTableDirect is quite subtle. Consider the following:

```
objCmd.CommandText = "authors"
objCmd.CommandType = adCmdTable
```

This actually sends SELECT * FROM authors to the provider. Now, in contrast, consider this code:

```
objCmd.CommandText = "authors"
objCmd.CommandType = adCmdTableDirect
```

This only sends `authors` to the provider. Some providers may not support direct table names, and may require explicit SQL code.

The performance implications of these options are discussed in Chapter 12.

The Name Property

Indicates the name of the `Command` object.

> *String* = *Command*.Name
> *Command*.Name = *String*

In many cases you probably won't use this, but it could be used to uniquely identify a `Command` object in a collection of commands. For example, imagine an application that allows users to build up a number of commands. You could store these in a collection and use the `Name` property of the commands to identify them. Think about the query window in SQL Server – you could build quite a good emulation of this using ADO to connect to multiple data sources, and using a collection to store various command objects.

Commands as Connection Methods

There is a rarely-noted feature that goes like this: If you name a `Command` object and then associate the command with a `Connection` object, the `Connection` object inherits a method corresponding to the name of the `Command`. This is a dynamic method, which doesn't show up as part of the object's methods or properties within code editors such as Visual Basic.

Let's consider an example. Suppose you have two types of user – a `Clerk` and a `Manager` – and both types of user need to look at employee details. Managers are allowed to see the salary details, while the humble clerks are not. You have decided to use stored procedures to encapsulate all of your SQL logic, so you have two possibilities. The first is to build a single SQL statement to return the employee details, and have it check whether the user is a manager or a clerk. Your user then calls a business object, which fetches the data:

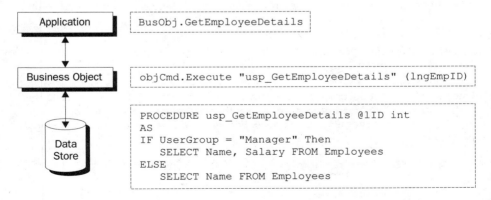

```
Application          BusObj.GetEmployeeDetails

Business Object      objCmd.Execute "usp_GetEmployeeDetails" (lngEmpID)

                     PROCEDURE usp_GetEmployeeDetails @lID int
                     AS
Data                 IF UserGroup = "Manager" Then
Store                    SELECT Name, Salary FROM Employees
                     ELSE
                         SELECT Name FROM Employees
```

One observation to be made here is that you now have a business rule built into the SQL. In many cases this is not a problem (and indeed could be deemed good practice), but this doesn't always fit everyone's needs. You may find that you'd rather not put business rules into your SQL code. For instance, in this example, you also have to work out details such as how to establish which group the user belongs to. That's not a particularly complex problem, but here's a different situation that keeps all the business logic in the same place:

In this situation the application calls a business object first, perhaps when it starts, and the business object establishes the role: clerk or manager. This sets the appropriate stored procedure and attaches the command as a method of the connection. Later on, the application can simply call the business object that calls this new method. Since the method is one of two stored procedures, the correct stored procedure is run. Although this seems like more code, it actually simplifies some of the programming. It puts the business logic in a component where it is easily reused, and it also makes the stored procedures simpler – these will now run faster because there is no run-time decision to make.

> *Using this method you must set the* Name *property before setting the* ActiveConnection, *otherwise an error occurs.*

One thing that's not documented very clearly – or very often – is that when using this method, the newly-named procedure accepts the parameters of the stored procedure, as well as an extra argument – a recordset. For example, imagine the following stored procedure:

```
CREATE PROCEDURE usp_TestProcOne
    @sAuLName varchar(40)
AS
    SELECT * FROM authors
    WHERE  au_lname = @sAuLName
```

You could call this using the following code:

```
strConn = "Provider=SQLOLEDB; Data Source=SQL7Server; " & _
          "Initial Catalog=TestData; User Id=sa; Password="
objConn.Open strConn

objCmd.CommandText = "usp_TestProcOne"
objCmd.CommandType = adCmdStoredProc
objCmd.Name = "TestProc"
Set objCmd.ActiveConnection = objConn

objConn.TestProc "Ringer", objRec
```

This passes `Ringer` into the stored procedure as the parameter, and the results are returned in the recordset `objRec`.

Another shortcut is to just call the stored procedure name directly against the connection:

```
objConn.Open " . . ."
objConn.usp_TestProcOne "Ringer", objRec
```

If ADO doesn't recognize the command, then it passes the command and parameters to the provider to see if it can handle it. If the provider recognizes the command, the command is executed; otherwise an error is generated.

One particularly interesting feature of named commands is that a variation on this allows you to retrieve output parameters of a stored procedure, even when the provider doesn't support it. This is covered in more detail in the section at the end of the chapter.

The Prepared Property

Indicates whether or not to save a compiled version of a command before execution.

> *Boolean = Command.Prepared*
> *Command.Prepared = Boolean*

The default value of the property is `False`. It can be set to `True` when the command is to be repeated several times. Although the compilation process will slow for the first execution of the command, subsequent executions will be quicker since the command text does not have to be parsed and the execution plan can be reused.

If you're using the SQL Server provider, and you set the `Use Procedure for Prepare` dynamic property of the `Connection` object to `True`, then a temporary stored procedure will be created for prepared commands. If you find that you need to prepare a lot of statements, you might want to consider moving the SQL into a stored procedure, since this will be more efficient than preparing statements.

> *`Use Procedure for Prepare` is one of the dynamic properties of the ADO `Connection` object. For more on ADO's dynamic properties, and how to use them see Appendix C.*

If you are creating prepared commands against SQL Server and not disconnecting, then you should ensure that the temporary database (tempdb) has enough space to accommodate the stored procedures.

The State Property

Describes whether the `Command` object is open, closed, or currently processing a command.

> *Command.*State = *Long*

State can be one of the following constants:

❑   `adStateClosed` indicates that the command is closed.

❑   `adStateOpen` indicates that the command is open.

❑   `adStateExecuting` indicates that the command is currently executing.

❑   `adStateFetching` indicates that the command is currently fetching records.

Using the `State` property allows you to detect the current open-state of the command. For example, to detect if the `Command` is still executing an asynchronous query you could use this line:

```
If objCmd.State = adStateExecuting Then
   Print "Command is still executing"
End If
```

Collections of the Command Object

The Parameters Collection

Contains all of the `Parameter` objects for a `Command` object.

> *Parameters = Command.*Parameters

The `Parameters` collection is most often used when passing arguments to stored procedures or queries. `Parameter` objects are appended to this collection by use of the `Append` method:

```
Set objParam = objCmd.CreateParameter("ID", adInteger, adParamInput, 8, 123)
objCmd.Append objParam
```

You can iterate through the objects in this collection by use of the `For Each...Next` command. For example:

```
For Each objParam In objCmd.Parameters
   Print objParam.Name
Next
```

If your provider is capable of describing the parameters of a stored procedure or query, then can use the `Refresh` method to get the provider to fill in the `Parameters` collection for you:

```
objCmd.Parameters.Refresh
```

The `Parameters` collection is discussed more fully later in this chapter.

The Properties Collection

Contains all of the `Property` objects for a `Command` object.

> *Properties = Command*.**Properties**

The Parameter Object

The `Parameter` object comprises all of the information for a single parameter to be used in a stored procedure or query, and is only really used in conjunction with the `Command` object and its associated `Parameters` collection.

Methods of the Parameter Object

The AppendChunk Method

Appends data to a large or binary `Parameter` object.

> *Parameter*.**AppendChunk**(*Data*)

Parameter	Type	Description	Default
Data	Variant	The data to be appended to the parameter.	

The first `AppendChunk` call after editing the parameter details writes data to the parameter, overwriting any existing data. Subsequent calls add to existing data. Although the documentation states that a parameter must support long data for this method to work, this doesn't appear to be compulsory for SQL Server 6.5. You can check the `Attributes` property (see below) to see if it contains `adParamLong`.

This is most often used for putting images into tables. There's a full discussion of using images with `AppendChunk` at the end of Chapter 6.

This is functionally equivalent to the `AppendChunk` method of the `Field` object, and works in the same way. The only difference is you are dealing with a different base object.

Properties of the Parameter Object

The Attributes Property

Indicates one or more characteristics of a `Parameter` object.

> *ParameterAttributesEnum = Parameter.**Attributes***
> *Parameter.**Attributes** = ParameterAttributesEnum*

This can be one of more of the ParameterAttributesEnum values:

❑ `adParamSigned`, to indicate that the parameter will accept signed values. This is the default.

❑ `adParamNullable`, to indicate that the parameter will accept null values.

❑ `adParamLong`, to indicate that the parameter accepts long data, such as binary data.

You can combine these values by using a logical OR statement:

```
objParam.Attributes = adParamNullable OR adParamLong
```

Setting `adParamLong` doesn't appear to be compulsory for binary data. A SQL Server stored procedure with a parameter of type image will accept long data without this set.

The Direction Property

Indicates whether the `Parameter` object represents an input parameter, an output parameter, or an input/output parameter, or if the parameter is a return value from a stored procedure.

> *ParameterDirectionEnum = Parameter.**Direction***
> *Parameter.**Direction** = ParameterDirectionEnum*

ParameterDirectionEnum can be one of the following values:

❑ `adParamUnknown`, to indicate that the direction of the parameter is not known.

❑ `adParamInput`, to indicate that the parameter is to pass information to the stored procedure or query.

❑ `adParamOutput`, to indicate that the parameter is to return information from the stored procedure or query.

❑ `adParamInputOutput`, to indicate that the parameter can be used to pass information to, and return information from, a stored procedure or query.

❑ `adParamReturnValue`, to indicate that the parameter will contain the return value of the stored procedure or query.

In SQL Server you would declare an output parameter by appending OUTPUT to the parameter declaration. For example, the following SQL code creates a stored procedure with input and output parameters, and return values:

```
CREATE PROCEDURE usp_GetValues
    @PubID    char(4),            -- indicates an input parameter
    @Value    integer    OUTPUT   -- indicates an output parameter
AS
BEGIN
    . . . .
RETURN 123                        -- indicates the return value
```

The return value is always the first parameter in the Parameters collection, and is named RETURN_VALUE. If you're creating parameters, you'll need to create the return value first:

```
objCmd.CreateParameter   "RETURN_VALUE", adVarInteger, _
                                adParamReturnValue, 0, lngRetVal
```

The return value should be declared as a long integer. If you use Refresh, then a return value parameter is always created, irrespective of whether the command returns a value.

You can also set this property by using the *Direction* argument of the Command object's CreateParameter method.

> **Microsoft Access does not have output parameters or return values.**

The Name Property

Indicates the name of the Parameter object.

> *String = Parameter.**Name***
> *Parameter.**Name** = String*

This just identifies the parameter name within the Parameters collection, and doesn't have to be the same as the name of the parameter as defined in the stored procedure or query – but it makes sense to keep these the same. This makes the code more readable and easier to maintain.

You can also set this property by using the *Name* argument of the Command object's CreateParameter method.

The NumericScale Property

Indicates the scale of numeric values for the Parameter object.

> *Byte = Parameter.**NumericScale***
> *Parameter.**NumericScale** = Byte*

The numeric scale indicates how many digits are to the right of the decimal point.

Both the NumericScale and Precision properties are required in order to process SQL data of Numeric type correctly. Both Oracle and SQL Server 7.0 support numeric types.

Furthermore, note that the `NumericScale` and `Precision` properties cannot be set via `Command` object's `CreateParameter` method. If you need to set these properties (for example, in the scenario described in the previous paragraph) you must create an explicit `Parameter` object – and set its properties before appending it to the `Parameters` collection.

The Precision Property

Indicates the degree of precision for numeric values in the `Parameter` object.

> *Byte = Parameter.***Precision**
> *Parameter.***Precision** = *Byte*

The precision indicates the maximum number of digits that are used to represent a numeric value.

The `Precision` property, like the `NumericScale` property, is required for the correct processing of SQL data of Numeric type – as supported by both Oracle and SQL Server 7.0. There's more about this in the section on *The NumericScale Property*, above.

The Size Property

Indicates the maximum size, in bytes or characters, of a `Parameter` object.

> *Long = Parameter.***Size**
> *Parameter.***Size** = *Long*

There are a few things to watch out for when using the `Size` property:

❑ For variable-length parameters (such as character strings or binary data), you must always set the `Size`, so that the provider knows how much space to allocate for the parameter. If you don't specify the size an error will be generated.

❑ If you use the `Parameters` collection's `Refresh` method to force the provider to fill in the parameter details, the `Size` for variable-length parameters may be their maximum potential size, and memory may be allocated for these parameters accordingly.

❑ For binary data you have to be quite specific about the size of the parameter. For example, if a SQL Server stored procedure has a parameter of type `image`, and you `Refresh` the parameters, the size of this parameter is returned as `2147483647`. If you create the parameters yourself and use this size, and then use `AppendChunk` to add the data to the parameter, there are no problems – but creating the parameter with the actual size of the binary data doesn't work. That's because `Size` is the *maximum* size of the parameter, not its actual size.

The Type Property

Indicates the data type of the `Parameter` object.

> *DataTypeEnum = Parameter.***Type**
> *Parameter.***Type** = *DataTypeEnum*

A full list of the DataTypeEnum values is shown in Appendix B, but the table below shows the SQL Server provider and Access provider data types and what they map to. The empty table cells indicate that there is no direct mapping between the two database types.

SQL Server 6.5	SQL Server 7.0	Access 97	Access 2000	Enum Value
binary	binary	Binary		adVarBinary
varbinary	varbinary			adVarBinary
char		Text		adVarChar
	char			adChar
varchar	varchar			adVarChar
datetime	datetime			AdDBTimeStamp
Smalldatetime	Smalldatetime			AdDBTimeStamp
float		Single	Single	adSingle
real	real			adSingle
int	int	Long Integer	Long Integer	adInteger
smallint	smallint	Integer	Integer	adSmallInt
tinyint	tinyint	Byte	Byte	AdUnsignedTinyInt
money	money	Currency	Currency	adCurrency
Small money				adCurrency
bit	bit	Yes/No	Yes/No	adBoolean
timestamp				adVarBinary
text		Memo		adVarChar
image		OLE Object		adVarBinary
	float	Double	Double	adDouble
		Date/Time	Date/Time	adDate
	Unique identifier	Replication ID	Replication ID	adGUID
		Value		adEmpty

Table Continued on Following Page

SQL Server 6.5	SQL Server 7.0	Access 97	Access 2000	Enum Value
	nvarchar		Text	adVarWChar
			Memo	AdLongVarWChar
	ntext		Hyperlink	AdLongVarWChar
	decimal		Decimal	adNumeric
	numeric			adNumeric
	image		OLE Object	AdLongVarBinary
	nchar			adWChar
	text			AdLongVarChar
	timestamp			adBinary

There are a few interesting (and often confusing) things to note. For example, date parameters in SQL Server don't map to the obvious adDate datatype, but rather to the adDBTimeStamp data type; and the timestamp maps to adVarBinary for SQL Server 6.5 and adBinary for SQL Server 7.0. You should also note that adInteger maps to a Visual Basic's Long data type – it doesn't fit VB's Integer type. If the parameters are of the wrong type, they can cause your commands to fail.

If you wish to create your parameters using the CreateParameter method, but you're having trouble matching datatypes or sizes, then the simplest fix is to temporarily call the Refresh method and examine the Parameters collection. You can do this in VBScript by looping through the collection, or by using the Locals window in Visual Basic. You can then copy the values that ADO has used and amend your code accordingly. Don't forget to remove the Refresh once you've sorted out your parameters – leaving it in will cause a performance penalty.

You'll find more on data types in Appendix E.

The Value Property

Indicates the value assigned to the Parameter object.

```
Variant = Parameter.Value
Parameter.Value = Variant
```

This is the default property and can be omitted if desired.

The value of a parameter can only be read once, and the recordset should be closed before you read the value. For more details on this, see the section on parameter values at the end of this chapter.

For a parameter holding binary data, you can use this instead of using the AppendChunk method. For example:

```
objRec.Parameters("@Logo").Value = varChunk
```

There's a full description of using binary data at the end of Chapter 6.

The Parameters Collection

When dealing with stored procedures or queries that accept arguments, you have two options:

❑ Use the Command object's Execute method, passing in the parameters as an array of values into the second argument of this method. Not all providers support this.

❑ Use the Command object's Parameters collection.

In many cases the former is acceptable (and is in fact easier to code), but the one restriction of this is that you can't return any values from your stored procedure. For example, suppose you have a stored procedure like this:

```
CREATE PROCEDURE usp_AuthorsByState
    @RequiredState    char(2),
    @ID               integer    OUTPUT
AS
BEGIN
    SELECT *
    FROM   authors
    WHERE  state = @RequiredState

    SELECT @ID=123

    RETURN 456
END
```

This procedure does three things:

❑ It returns a recordset using one of the parameters to restrict the rows that are returned

❑ It sets the output parameter to an arbitrary value (123 in this case)

❑ It returns another arbitrary value (456 in this case)

Whilst the output value and return value are falsely constructed, it illustrates two common techniques for returning information from a stored procedure.

If you wished to call this stored procedure *without* using the Parameters collection, you could do so using code like this:

```
objCmd.CommandText = "usp_AuthorsByState"
objCmd.CommandType = adCmdStoredProc
Set objRec = objCmd.Execute (, Array("CA", lngID))
```

This simply calls the procedure, passing in two arguments – CA to filter the recordset, and lngID (a long integer) to be used as the output parameter. This works fine, as ADO builds a Parameters collection from the values you supply. However, note that the output parameter (lngID) is never populated with the output value, and there's also no way to access the return value. So whilst this method is extremely easy to use, it doesn't give you the functionality that the Parameters collection does.

There's a caveat to this approach: if you reference the parameters collection before calling the Execute method, the Parameters collection is then Refreshed automatically for you. For example:

```
objCmd.CommandText = "usp_AuthorsByState"
objCmd.CommandType = adCmdStoredProc
Print "Parameter Count = " & objCmd.Parameters.Count
```

During the Print statement ADO automatically calls a Refresh and populates the Parameters collection. The key point is that there are *three* parameters, not two: the return value, the input parameter (the required state), and the output parameter (the id value). This means that the next line might fail, because it doesn't use enough parameters:

```
Set objRec = objCmd.Execute (, Array("CA", lngID))
```

However, this line works:

```
Set objRec = objCmd.Execute (, Array(lngRV, "CA", lngID))
```

This shows that if you populate the Parameters collection yourself, or use the Array method, then you don't need to worry about the return parameter. However, if you Refresh the Parameters collection (or if it is refreshed implicitly for you) then you'll find that the return value becomes the first parameter in the collection.

Note that this automatic refresh (and indeed the Refresh method itself) may not supported by all providers, or all versions of SQL Server. If you are using SQL Server 6.5 you should ensure that you have installed the latest Catalog Procedures – see the SQL Books online for more details of this.

Differences from ADO 2.0

The automatic refreshing of parameters in ADO 2.1 is different from what occurred in ADO 2.0. Using an explicit Refresh works for both the OLEDB Provider for ODBC and the OLEDB Provider for SQL, in both versions of ADO. However, using the implicit refresh gives different results.

I've used the following code to test the automatic refresh facility in ADO 2.0 and ADO 2.1:

```
objCmd.CommandText = "usp_AuthorsByState"
objCmd.CommandType = adCmdStoredProc
Print "Parameter Count = " & objCmd.Parameters.Count
```

If you are using SQL Server 6.5 (and you haven't updated your Catalogs) then only the OLEDB Provider for ODBC will return the correct parameter information to the Parameters collection. If you *have* updated your catalogs, or if you're using SQL

Server 7, then there are differences between the way the two versions of ADO handle the parameters. These differences are listed below:

ADO Version	Provider	SQL Server	Supported
2.0	OLEDB for ODBC	6.5	Yes
		7.0	Yes
	OLEDB for SQL	6.5	Yes
		7.0	No
2.1	OLEDB for ODBC	6.5	Yes
		7.0	No
	OLEDB for SQL	6.5	No
		7.0	No

You might think that this removal of functionality is a detrimental step, but in this case it is a deliberate (and documented) move to improve performance and reduce network traffic.

Parameters in ASP

When using the array method in ASP scripting languages you have to make sure that any variables used for output parameters have the correct data type. When you declare variables in scripting languages, they are **variants**, and this may not match the correct parameter type. The output parameter still has to have the correct type, even though you can't actually use it. For example, in VBScript:

```
Dim lngID
Set objRec = objCmd.Execute (, Array(lngRV, "CA", lngID))
```

This produces an error, which indicates that a parameter object has been incorrectly declared. That's because lngID is a variant and the parameter is expecting a Long. However this section of code works:

```
Dim lngID
lngID = 1
Set objRec = objCmd.Execute (, Array(lngRV, "CA", lngID))
```

This forces the variant to hold the correct data type – it gives lngID a sub-type of Integer, which is compatible with the integer type declared in the stored procedure (SQL Server integers map to Longs in Visual Basic and in Scripting languages).

The Parameters collection contains a Parameter object for each parameter in a stored procedure, including the return value if the procedure has one. It only has one property and four methods.

Methods of the Parameters Collection

The Append Method

Appends a `Parameter` object to the `Parameters` collection.

> *Parameters.Append(Object)*

Parameter	Type	Description	Default
Object	Parameter	The `Parameter` object to be appended to the collection.	

Parameters are created using the `CreateParameter` method, and you must set the `Type` property before calling this method. For example:

```
Set objParam = objCmd.CreateParameter
objParam.Name = "Name"
objParam.Type = adVarChar
objParam.Direction = adParamInput
objParam.Size = 25
objParam.Value = "Janine"
objCmd.Parameters.Append objParam
```

Although more cumbersome to use than the `Refresh` method to build a parameter list, this method is much more efficient, as it minimizes the total number of calls made to the provider.

You can combine the `Append` and `CreateParameter` methods into a single statement:

```
objCmd.Parameters.Append
objCmd.CreateParameter("State",adChar,adParamInput,2,"CA")
```

The Delete Method

Deletes a `Parameter` object from the `Parameters` collection.

> *Parameters.Delete(Index)*

Parameter	Type	Description	Default
Index	Variant	The number or name of the `Parameter` object to be removed from the collection.	

You must use the `Parameter` object's index or its `Name` when deleting a parameter. You cannot use an object variable. For example, we can delete the parameter called `ID` using this line:

```
objCmd.Parameters.Delete ("ID")
```

Here's another example. The following line deletes the first parameter in the collection:

```
objCmd.Parameters.Delete (0)
```

The Refresh Method

Updates the `Parameter` objects in the `Parameters` collection.

> *Parameters.***Refresh**

This has the impact of querying the data provider for details of the parameters. You can then access the parameters by name or ordinal number by indexing into the collection. For example:

```
objCmd.Parameters.Refresh
objCmd.Parameters(0).Value = 1
objCmd.Parameters("@FirstName") = "Janine"
```

You should use this method only when you are willing to accept the performance hit of the provider re-querying the data source for the parameter details. This is especially important if the same set of parameters is used frequently.

You can use this method quite effectively by querying the provider for the parameters once – for example, at the start of the program. You could then copy the parameter details into a global variable (perhaps an array or a collection, or even a local, fabricated recordset), where it can be used many times during the program. The advantage with this method is that you don't have to keep repeating `CreateParameter` calls, and you can create a generic piece of code to run a command. In addition, you can change the stored procedure without having to change the code that runs the command. The disadvantage is, of course, the delay as the program starts whilst the parameters are read in. However, you may consider this delay worthwhile, as it gives you a good chance to display that fancy splash screen you've always wanted!

If you do not create your own `Parameters` for a command and access the `Parameters` collection (for example, setting the value of a parameter), then ADO will call `Refresh` automatically, to fill the collection. Not all providers support the `Refresh` method.

The performance issues regarding `Refresh` are discussed in Chapter 12.

Properties of the Parameters Collection

The Count Property

Indicates the number of `Parameter` objects in the `Parameters` collection.

> *Long = Parameters.***Count**

You can use the Visual Basic or VBScript `For Each...Next` command to iterate through the parameters collection without using the `Count` property. For languages that do not support enumeration of collections, you can use this property in a loop.

The Item Property

Allows indexing into the `Parameters` collection to reference a specific `Parameter` object.

> *Parameter = Parameters.Item(Index)*

Name	Type	Description	Default
Index	Variant	The number or name of the parameter within the collection	

This is the default property and can be omitted. For example, the following lines are identical:

```
objRec.Parameters.Item(1)
```

```
objRec.Parameters(1)
```

```
objRec.Parameters("@FirstName")
```

Retrieving Output Parameters

The ability to return information from stored procedures in parameters is extremely useful, but there are some points you should be aware of. The first is whether output parameters are supported at all by the provider – Access doesn't support them. The second is at what stage the output parameters are available, and for this there are two choices:

- ❏ The parameter is available as soon as the command has been executed
- ❏ The parameter is available only after the recordset has been closed

This latter option is the one you have to watch for, because in that case ADO will only read the parameter values from the provider once. This means that if you try and read the parameter before you have closed the recordset, and then you close the recordset, and then you try and read the parameter value again, the value may not be available.

You can check to see which of the modes your provider supports, by examining the `Output Parameter Availability` custom property for the connection. This will return one of the three `DBPROPVAL_OA` constant values:

- ❏ `DBPROPVAL_OA_ATEXECUTE`, which indicates that the parameters are available after the command has been executed. This has a value of 2.
- ❏ `DBPROPVAL_OA_ATROWRELEASE`, which indicates that the parameters are available after the recordset has been closed. This has a value of 4.
- ❏ `DBPROPVAL_OA_NOTSUPPORTED`, which indicates that output parameters are not supported. This has a value of 1.

You could check these values with code like this:

```
Set objCmd.ActiveConnection = objConn

objCmd.CommandText = "usp_ProcedureWithOutputParam"
objCmd.CommandType = adCmdStoredProc
objCmd.Parameters.Append objCmd.CreateParameter("RETURN_VALUE", _
                            adInteger, adParameterReturnValue)
Set objRec = objCmd.Execute

intParamAvail = objConn.Properties("Output Parameter Availability")
    If intParamAvail = DBPROPVAL_OA_ATROWRELEASE Then
    ' parameter not available until recordset is closed
    objRec.Close
End If
intRV = objCmd.Parameters("ReturnValue")
```

This isn't a problem with commands that do not return recordsets, as there is no recordset to close.

The Solution

There is a solution to the problem of parameters not being available until the recordset is closed, and it involves the naming of stored procedures using the Command's Name property. You've already seen that code similar to this is allowable:

```
strConn = "Provider=SQLOLEDB; Data Source=SQL7Server; " & _
            "Initial Catalog=TestData; User Id=sa; Password="
objConn.Open strConn

objCmd.CommandText = "usp_AStoredProcedure"
objCmd.CommandType = adCmdStoredProc
Set objParam = objCmd.CreateParameter("ID", adInteger, adParamInput, 8, 123)
objCmd.Parameters.Append objParam
Set objParam = _
        objCmd.CreateParameter("Name", adVarChar, adParamInput, 25, "Janine")
objCmd.Parameters.Append objCmd.CreateParameter objParam
objCmd.Name = "StoredProcedureName"
Set objCmd.ActiveConnection = objConn

objConn.StoredProcedureName
```

This was never well-documented, but what's even less well documented is that you can pass the arguments to the stored procedure and a recordset object like so:

```
objConn.StoredProcedureName Argument1, Argument2, objRec
```

The arguments are accepted by the stored procedure in the normal way, and the recordset object is filled accordingly. As soon as this command is executed, you can access the return and output parameters, even though the recordset is still open.

As a word of warning, you shouldn't really rely on this procedure. Because it's not documented, we've no way of telling whether this will continue to work in future versions of ADO.

The Recordset Object

The recordset is really all about data, so it's at the very heart of ADO. A recordset contains all of the columns and rows returned from a specific action.

Methods of the Recordset Object

The AddNew Method

Creates a new record for an updateable `Recordset` object.

> *Recordset*.AddNew([*FieldList*], [*Values*])

Parameter	Type	Description	Default
FieldList	Variant	A single name or an array of names or ordinal positions of the fields in the new record.	
Values	Variant	A single value or an array of values for the fields in the new record. If *FieldList* is an array then *Values* must also be an array with the same number of elements.	

You can only use `AddNew` when the recordset supports addition of new records. You can check this by examining the `Supports` method:

```
If objRec.Supports(adAddNew) Then
    ' recordset supports additions
End If
```

You can use AddNew in two ways. The first is without any arguments, and places the current record pointer on the new record. You can then set the details for the new record and save the changes with Update if using immediate update mode, or UpdateBatch if using batch update mode (LockType = adLockBatchOptimistic). When you are adding a new record, and have set the various fields for the record, you can also save the changes by moving off the record. Calling MoveFirst or MoveLast will move to the beginning or end of the recordset respectively. Calling MoveNext will place you at EOF, and calling MovePrevious will move you to the row before the new row.

The second method uses the arguments, allowing you to pass in an array of fields and values. For example, the following line adds a new record filling in one field:

```
objRec.AddNew "author", "Jan Lloyd"
```

The following line adds one record, but fills in two fields:

```
objRec.AddNew Array("author", "year born"), Array("Jan Lloyd", 1969)
```

If you are using arguments to supply both the field names and values, and batch update mode is not being used, then the changes are effective immediately – that is, there is no need to perform the Update method. ADO will automatically call the Update method if you use AddNew whilst editing the current record, or adding a new record. You can check the EditMode property for the value of adEditAdd or adEditInProgress to determine if this is so.

If using batch update mode, however, you must still call the UpdateBatch method to update the data source.

If you're using the array method to add records (as demonstrated above), you must ensure that both arrays contain the same number of arguments, and that the details of the arrays are in the correct order. The array method is also particularly good when you are creating (fabricating) your own recordsets.

AutoNumber and Identity Fields

The following question is probably one of the most frequently-asked questions about ADO, and it's of particular interest to people converting from DAO:

When using AutoNumber and Identity fields, how do you add a new record, and then get the key value for the newly added row?

Unfortunately there's not always a simple answer; it depends on the provider you are using, as well as items like the cursor location, type, locking method, and indexes on the table.

ADO states that when adding a new record, when you then Update that record, the cursor is placed on the newly added record. This is exactly what you need, but the Identity or AutoNumber value may not be available. For example, code such as this may not produce the desired result:

```
objRec.AddNew
objRec("field_name") = "field_value"
objRec.Update

Print objRec("ID")
```

This assumes that ID is an automatically incrementing field.

The table below indicates which schemes support retrieval of auto-incrementing fields.

Provider	Target	Indexed	Cursor Location	Cursor Type	Lock Type
ODBC	Access 97 Access 2000	Yes	Server	Keyset	Pessimistic Optimistic
		No	Server	Keyset	Pessimistic Optimistic
	SQL 6.5	Yes	Server	Keyset	Pessimistic Optimistic
	SQL 7	Yes	Server	Keyset	Pessimistic Optimistic
		Yes	Client	All	Pessimistic Optimistic
		No	Client	All	Pessimistic Optimistic
Jet 4.0	Access 97	Yes	Server	All	All
		No	Server	All	All
	Access 2000	Yes	Server	All	All
		Yes	Client	All	Pessimistic Optimistic
		No	Server	All	All
		No	Client	All	Pessimistic Optimistic
SQLOLEDB	SQL Server 6.5 SQL Server 7.0	Yes	Server	Keyset	Pessimistic Optimistic
		Yes	Client	All	Pessimistic Optimistic
		No	Client	All	Pessimistic Optimistic

Any combination not shown in the list does not support the availability of the auto-number field.

ADO 2.1, with its enhanced client-side cursors, has brought far greater support for this, so converting existing applications should be a little easier than it was previously.

This method only works when adding records directly using AddNew, and will not work if using commands and SQL INSERT statements.

Using @@IDENTITY

If you are using SQL Server and you need to use a combination that does not support the auto-number field, then you can use the global value that represents the latest IDENTITY value added. So using this you can obtain the value you need. For example, in a stored procedure you could do this:

```
CREATE PROCEDURE usp_AddAuthor
    @sAuLName     varchar(25),
    @sAuFName     varchar(25)
AS
BEGIN
    INSERT INTO authors (au_lname, au_fname)
    VALUES (@sAuLName, @sAUFName)

    RETURN @@IDENTITY
END
```

This adds a new record and then returns the IDENTITY field just used. You could then run this stored procedure using a Command object, and access the return value through the first member in the Parameters collection. You can also use this method when running straight SQL queries.

One thing to watch when running this method is that @@IDENTITY is a global variable, and represents the last IDENTITY value updated, irrespective of the table. So if you have an INSERT trigger on a table, and the table the trigger inserts into has an identity field, then @@IDENTITY will reflect this value, rather than the one you intended.

Because the server handles this facility, you can use this with any type of cursor and location.

The Cancel Method

Cancels execution of a pending asynchronous Open operation.

Recordset.**Cancel**

This is particularly useful when allowing users to submit queries, as it gives them an opportunity to cancel the query if they feel it is taking too long.

If you call the Cancel method on a recordset that was not opened asynchronously then an error will be generated.

The CancelBatch Method

Cancels a pending batch update when in batch update mode.

Recordset.**CancelBatch(**[*AffectRecords*]**)**

Name	Type	Description	Default
AffectRecords	AffectEnum	Determines which records will be affected by the batch cancel.	`adAffectAll`

The AffectEnum values can be one of the following constants:

- ❏ `adAffectCurrent`, to only cancel updates for the current record.
- ❏ `adAffectGroup`, to only cancel updates for records that match the current `Filter`, which must be set before using this option.
- ❏ `adAffectAll`, to cancel all pending updates, even those not shown due to a `Filter`.
- ❏ `adAffectAllChapters`, to cancel all pending updates in child (chapter) recordsets, when using shaped data.

You should be careful when using `adAffectGroup`. With this setting, records that do not match the current filter are *not* cancelled: so if your `Filter` is not set as you intend, it's possible you'll fail to cancel all of the pending changes that you wanted to cancel.

You should always check the `Errors` collection after performing this method. It's a good way to catch underlying conflicts, such as a record having been deleted. Conflict resolution is discussed in more detail later in this chapter.

It's always sensible to set the current record position to a known record after this call, as the current record can be left in an unknown position after a `CancelBatch` method call.

The CancelUpdate Method

Cancels any changes made to the current record or to a new record prior to calling the `Update` method.

> *Recordset*.CancelUpdate

This is used when in normal update mode, and cancels changes to the current record only.

You can use this to cancel the addition of a new record, in which case the current record becomes the record you were on before adding the new record.

The Clone Method

Creates a duplicate `Recordset` object from an existing `Recordset` object.

> Set *Recordset_Clone* = *Recordset*.Clone([*LockType*])

Name	Type	Description	Default
LockType	LockTypeEnum	The lock type to create the new recordset with.	`adLockUnspecified`

In this case LockTypeEnum is a subset of the full list of constants, and should be one of:

- ❑ `adLockUnspecified`, to indicate that the cloned recordset should have the same lock type as the original recordset.

- ❑ `adLockReadOnly`, to indicate that the cloned recordset should be read only.

It's important to note that this doesn't create two independent recordsets. Rather, it creates two pointers (which are `Recordset` objects), both pointing to the same recordset. This allows you to have two separate cursors open on the same set of records, allowing you to move the record pointers independently. There is only one set of data, so changes made through either the original recordset pointer or through the clone pointer appear in the other. The important thing to remember is that a `Recordset` object is just a pointer to a set of data. Therefore a `Clone` is just another pointer to the same set of data.

Cloning recordsets is often more efficient than creating a new recordset with the same request criteria, because it avoids a trip to the server.

Cloning is only allowed on bookmarkable recordsets (for more on bookmarkable recordsets see *The Bookmark Property* section, later in this chapter). Bookmarks are valid in all clones. You can use the `Supports` method to determine if bookmarks are supported in the recordset:

```
If objRec.Supports(adBookmark) Then
    Set objRecClone = objRec.Clone
End If
```

If you make any changes to a recordset, then those changes will be visible in all clones until the time you `Requery` the original recordset. At that stage the cloned recordset will no longer be synchronized with the original recordset, and will contain the set of records before the `Requery` took place.

The Close Method

Closes the `Recordset` object and any dependent objects.

> *Recordset*.**Close**

You should beware of closing the recordset when changes are in place, as the following will occur:

- ❑ When in batch update mode, changes will be lost.

- ❑ When in immediate update mode, an error will be generated.

Closing a recordset does not free all of its resources from memory, and you should set its object variable to `Nothing` in VB (or to `Null` in JScript) to achieve this:

```
Set objRec = Nothing
```

To be absolutely sure that you protect against errors, you can also check to see whether the recordset is open before closing it:

```
If objRec.State = adStateOpen Then
    objRec.Close
End If
Set objRec = Nothing
```

The CompareBookmarks Method

Compares two bookmarks and returns an indication of the relative values.

CompareEnum = Recordset.CompareBookmarks(Bookmark1, Bookmark2)

Parameter	Type	Description	Default
Bookmark1	Variant	The bookmark for the first row to be compared.	
Bookmark2	Variant	The bookmark for the second row to be compared.	

CompareEnum will be one of the following constants:

❑ adCompareLessThan, to indicate that the first bookmark is before the second.

❑ adCompareEqual, to indicate that the bookmarks are equal.

❑ adCompareGreaterThan, to indicate that the first bookmark is after the second.

❑ adCompareNotEqual, to indicate that the bookmarks are not equal, and not ordered.

❑ adCompareNotComparable, to indicate that it is not possible to compare the two bookmarks.

For more on setting bookmarks, see *The Bookmark Property* section (later in this chapter). The CompareBookmarks method is only applicable for comparing bookmarks from the same recordset or its clones. Even if two recordsets were created in exactly the same way, their bookmarks are not guaranteed to be the same.

Bookmarks are comparable across sorts and filters.

Note that this compares the actual bookmarks, not the values in the records that the bookmarks point to.

The Delete Method

Deletes the current record or group of records.

> *Recordset.***Delete**([*AffectRecords*])

Parameter	Type	Description	Default
AffectRecords	AffectEnum	A value that determines how many records this method will affect.	adAffectCurrent

The AffectEnum type can be one of the following constants:

- ❑ adAffectAllChapters, to delete all chapters (child recordsets) associated with the record or group of records. For more details on chapters, see Chapter 11.
- ❑ adAffectCurrent, to delete only the current record.
- ❑ adAffectGroup, to delete only records that match the current Filter.
- ❑ adAffectAll, to delete all records.

Remember that when in batch update mode, the records are only *marked* for deletion, and are not removed from the data store itself until UpdateBatch is called.

Once a record has been deleted, the current record remains active until you move away from it. Attempting to access values from a deleted record will result in an error.

An error will be generated if the recordset does not support deletions. You can use the Supports method to determine if the recordset support deletions:

```
If objRec.Supports(adDelete) Then
    objRec.Delete
End If
```

You should also check the Errors collection, as the provider may return errors due to conflicts with the underlying data.

The Find Method

Searches the Recordset for a record that matches the specified criteria.

> *Recordset.***Find**(*Criteria*, [*SkipRecords*], [*SearchDirection*], [*Start*])

Parameter	Type	Description	Default
Criteria	String	The statement that specifies the column name, comparison operator, and value to use for the search. Only one criteria is supported, and multiple values by use of OR or AND will generate an error.	
SkipRecords	Long	The offset (from the current row, or from the bookmark specified by the *Start* parameter) from which point the search should begin.	0
SearchDirection	SearchDirection Enum	Indicates the direction of the search.	`adSearch Forward`
Start	Variant	The bookmark for the record from which the operation should begin.	

SearchDirection can be one of the following SearchDirectionEnum constants:

❑ `adSearchForward`, to search forward in the recordset.

❑ `adSearchBackward`, to search backward in the recordset.

Start can be a valid bookmark, or one of the BookmarkEnum constants:

❑ `adBookmarkCurrent`, to start the search on the current record.

❑ `adBookmarkFirst`, to start the search from the first record.

❑ `adBookmarkLast`, to start the search from the last record.

Criteria follows the basic form of a SQL WHERE clause. For example:

```
state = 'CA'
```

```
age = 13
```

```
au_lname LIKE 'S*'
```

If *Criteria* is met, then the current record is positioned on the found record. If the *Criteria* is not met, then:

❑ If you're searching forward, the current record is set to be the end of the recordset (and EOF is set)

❑ If you're searching backward, the current record is set to be the beginning of the recordset (and BOF is set)

For example:

```
objRec.Find "au_lname = 'Lloyd'"
If objRec.EOF Then
  Print "Record was not found"
End If
```

You can use a *Criteria* to search for values that are less than, equal to, greater than, or like a particular value. For example:

```
objRec.Find "Price < 14.99"
objRec.Find "Price > 14.99"
objRec.Find "au_lname LIKE 'L*'"
```

The latter will find all values of au_lname that start with L.

Only single search values are allowed with Find. Using multiple search values with AND or OR generates an error. For example:

```
objRec.Find "au_lname = 'Lloyd' AND au_fname = 'Janine'"
```

This is invalid and will generate an error. This is one area where the direct migration from DAO to ADO will cause problems.

If you do need to use multiple criteria values, then your only choice is to create a new recordset, or use a Filter, which does accept multiple values.

Not all providers support the Find method, so you can use the Supports method to identify whether this is supported by the recordset:

```
If objRec.Supports(adFind) Then
    objRec.Find "au_lname = 'Lloyd'"
End If
```

The GetRows Method

Retrieves multiple records of a Recordset object into a multi-dimensional array.

Variant = Recordset.GetRows([Rows], [Start], [Fields])

Parameter	Type	Description	Default
Rows	Long	Indicates how many records to retrieve. The default indicates that all remaining rows in the recordset should be fetched.	adGetRowsRest

Parameter	Type	Description	Default
Start	Variant	The bookmark for the record from which the operation should begin.	The current record
Fields	Variant	A single field name, an ordinal position, an array of field names, or an array of ordinal values representing the fields that should be fetched.	All columns

Start can be a valid bookmark, or one of the BookmarkEnum constants:

❑ `adBookmarkCurrent` to start the search on the current record.

❑ `adBookmarkFirst` to start the search from the first record.

❑ `adBookmarkLast` to start the search from the last record.

The array returned by the `GetRows` call is automatically sized to fit the requested columns and rows. The columns are placed into the first dimension of the array, and the rows placed into the second. For example:

```
varRec = objRec.GetRows
intCols = UBound(varRec, 1)
intRows = UBound(varRec, 2)

For intRow = 0 To intRows
  For intCol = 0 To intCols
    Print varRec(intCol, intRow)
  Next
Next
```

Although this is not the obvious way around, this column/row order has been used to allow backward compatibility with DAO and RDO. In fact, the main reason for this is that it's easy to modify the second dimension of an array, to add more data, but it's much harder to modify the first dimension once data is in the array. Any values that do not make sense to store in an array, such as chapters or images, are given empty values.

For *Fields*, you can specify either a single field name, or an array of fields to be returned. Here are a couple of examples:

```
varRec = objRec.GetRows (, , "au_lname")
```

```
varRec = objRec.GetRows (, , Array("au_lname", "au_fname"))
```

If using the latter method, then the order in which the columns are placed in the array dictates the order in which they are returned.

After you call `GetRows`, the next unread record becomes the current record. If there are no more records, `EOF` is set.

When dealing with a large recordset you may find that calling GetRows several times with a smaller number of records is more efficient than calling it once to retrieve all records. For example, if calling GetRows on a table with 1,000 records, it might be quicker to call it 10 times using 100 as the number of rows to retrieve (depending upon the cursor type and location), rather than retrieving all rows at once. This is examined in more detail in Chapter 12.

The GetString Method

Returns a Recordset as a string.

> *String* = *Recordset*.GetString([*StringFormat*], [*NumRows*], [*ColumnDelimiter*], [*RowDelimiter*], [*NullExpr*])

Parameter	Type	Description	Default
StringFormat	StringFormat Enum	The format in which the recordset should be returned.	AdClip String
NumRows	Long	The number of rows to be returned from the recordset. If this is not specified, or if it is greater than the number of rows in the recordset, then all rows will be returned.	-1
ColumnDelimiter	String	The delimiter to use between columns.	TAB character
RowDelimiter	String	The delimiter to use between rows.	CARRIAGE RETURN character
NullExpr	String	Expression to use in place of NULL value.	Empty string

The only valid value for StringFormatEnum is adClipString. You can use this method quite effectively to populate text boxes in Visual Basic, or to quickly create HTML tables in ASP. For example, the code below shows how to fill a text box (named Text1, with its MultiLine property set to True):

```
Dim objConn As New ADODB.Connection
Dim objRec  As New ADODB.Recordset

objConn.Open "Provider=SQLOLEDB; Data Source=Tigger; " & _
             "Initial Catalog=pubs; User ID=sa; Password="

objRec.Open "select au_lname from authors", objConn, _
            adOpenForwardOnly, adLockReadOnly, adCmdText

Text1.Text = objRec.GetString (,,,vbCrLf)

objRec.Close
objConn.Close
Set objRec = Nothing
Set objConn = Nothing
```

The next example shows how to quickly create an HTML table:

```
NBSPACE = chr(160)
Set objConn = Server.CreateObject("ADODB.Connection")
Set objRec = Server.CreateObject("ADODB.Recordset")

objConn.Open "Provider=SQLOLEDB; Data Source=Tigger; " & _
             "Initial Catalog=pubs; User ID=sa; Password="

objRec.Open "authors", objConn, _
            adOpenForwardOnly, adLockReadOnly, adCmdTable

Response.Write "<TABLE BORDER=1><TR><TD>"
Response.Write objRec.GetString (adClipString, -1, _
                                 "</TD><TD>", _
                                 "</TD></TR><TR><TD>", _
                                 NBSPACE)
Response.Write "</TD></TR></TABLE>"

objRec.Close
objConn.Close
Set objRec = Nothing
Set objConn = Nothing
```

This saves having to loop through the `Fields` collection to manually build the table.

Only row data is saved to the string, not schema data. You cannot, therefore, reopen a recordset from this string.

The Move Method

Moves the position of the current record pointer in a `Recordset`.

> *Recordset.***Move**(*NumRecords*, [*Start*])

Parameter	Type	Description	Default
NumRecords	Long	The number of records the current record position moves.	
Start	Variant	The bookmark for the record from which the operation should begin.	`AdBookmark Current`

Start can be a valid bookmark, or one of the BookmarkEnum constants:

- ❑ `adBookmarkCurrent` to start the search on the current record.

- ❑ `adBookmarkFirst` to start the search from the first record.

- ❑ `adBookmarkLast` to start the search from the last record.

You can supply a negative number for *NumRecords* to move backwards in the recordset. For example, to move backwards three records you could do this:

```
objRec.Move -3
```

You should be aware that forward-only recordsets will not allow moving backwards, and may not allow moving forwards by any number other than 1. You can use the `Supports` method to check for this:

```
If objRec.Supports(adMovePrevious) Then
    objRec.Move -3
End If
```

If your recordset has a `CacheSize` other than 1, then you are allowed to move within the records in the cache, but not to records outside of the cache.

If you move past the beginning or end of the recordset, then you will be positioned on `BOF` or `EOF`, and the properties set accordingly. A subsequent call to `Move` beyond the start or end of the recordset will generate an error, as will trying to `Move` in an empty recordset.

If the current record has been changed, and `Update` not called, then a move will implicitly call `Update`. You should call `CancelUpdate` before calling `Move` if you do not wish to keep the changes.

The MoveFirst Method

Moves the position of the current record pointer to the first record in the `Recordset`.

> *Recordset*.**MoveFirst**

This moves to the first non-deleted row in the recordset, and sets `BOF` if all rows are deleted.

You should check to see whether the recordset supports moving to the first row, before issuing a `MoveFirst`. For example:

```
If objRec.Supports(adMoveFirst) Then
    objRec.MoveFirst
End If
```

You should be aware that some providers (for example SQL Server), implement the `MoveFirst` by resubmitting the query to the database server, having the effect of re-opening the recordset, thus placing you back on the first record. This only happens with server-side cursors. This could have serious consequences on performance if the command you are running takes a long time.

If the current record has been changed, but you haven't yet called `Update`, then a `MoveFirst` will implicitly call `Update`. If you do not wish to keep such changes, then you should call `CancelUpdate` before calling `MoveFirst`.

The MoveLast Method

Moves the position of the current record to the last record in the `Recordset`.

> *Recordset*.**MoveLast**

This moves to the last non-deleted row in the recordset, and sets `EOF` if all rows are deleted.

You should check to see whether the recordset supports moving to the last row, before issuing a `MoveLast`. For example:

```
If objRec.Supports(adMoveLast) Then
    objRec.MoveLast
End If
```

One odd problem you may encounter is when using server-based cursors for a read-only, forward-only recordsets. Your provider may say that `MoveLast` is supported, and yet moving to the last row generates the following message:

The rowset does not support fetching backwards

This seems a misleading error, and may be due to the way `MoveLast` is implemented – by using a built-in bookmark on the last row. So this error could result from the fact that forward-only, read-only cursors don't support bookmarks, even though the error message doesn't imply this. I've no confirmation of this, but it seems a sensible reason.

If the current record has been changed, and `Update` not called, then a `MoveLast` will implicitly call `Update`. You should call `CancelUpdate` before calling `MoveLast` if you do not wish to keep the changes.

The MoveNext Method

Moves the position of the current record to the next record in the `Recordset`.

> *Recordset*.**MoveNext**

If you try to move past the last record in a recordset, then the `EOF` property is set. Subsequent calls to `MoveNext` will generate an error.

If the current record has been changed, and `Update` not called, then a `MoveNext` will implicitly call `Update`. You should call `CancelUpdate` before calling `MoveNext` if you do not wish to keep the changes.

The MovePrevious Method

Moves the position of the current record to the previous record in the `Recordset`.

> *Recordset*.**MovePrevious**

If you try to move past the first record in a recordset, then the `BOF` property is set. Subsequent calls to `MovePrevious` will generate an error.

You can use the `Supports` method to check whether `MovePrevious` can be used on the recordset:

```
If objRec.Supports(adMovePrevious) Then
    objRec.MovePrevious
End If
```

If the current record has been changed, and `Update` not called, then a `MovePrevious` will implicitly call `Update`. You should call `CancelUpdate` before calling `MovePrevious` if you do not wish to keep the changes.

The NextRecordset Method

Clears the current `Recordset` object and returns the next `Recordset` by advancing through a series of commands.

> Set *Recordset* = *Recordset*.**NextRecordset**([*RecordsAffected*])

Parameter	Type	Description	Default
RecordsAffected	Variant	A Long variable into which the provider returns the number of records that the operation affected.	

RecordsAffected is only meaningful for a non row-returning recordset.

This can be useful if you only wish to build up a set of SQL statements and send them all to the provider in one go. However, not all of the data may be returned to the client in a single batch, and may require a trip to the server for each recordset. Each SQL command will be executed when the `NextRecordset` command is issued. Issuing a `Close` on the recordset will close the recordset without executing any outstanding commands.

You could use this for returning separate lists to be used in combo boxes. For example, imagine the following code that creates a stored procedure:

```
CREATE PROCEDURE usp_ListBoxes
AS
BEGIN
    SELECT * FROM authors
    SELECT * FROM titles
END
```

Opening a recordset on this stored procedure would return the first command in the series. Once you've finished with the data from that recordset, you could issue a `NextRecordset` command to execute the next command. For example:

```
objRec.Open "usp_ListBoxes", objConn, _
            adOpenForwardOnly, adLockReadOnly, adCmdStoredProc

Set objRecTitles = objRec.NextRecordset
```

Notice that the above example returns the next recordset into a new recordset variable. You can also use the same variable:

```
Set objRec = objRec.NextRecordset
```

The next recordset can be returned in several states:

❑ As a closed recordset, but with records. You can open the recordset and proceed as normal.

❑ As a closed recordset (with no records), for a non row-returning recordset.

❑ As an empty recordset (with no records), where both `BOF` and `EOF` will be set.

You should therefore check the `State` property and the `BOF` and `EOF` properties to determine the status of the recordset. When there are no more recordsets, the recordset object will be set to `Nothing`. There is one problem with this in Visual Basic though, in that testing the recordset object variable for `Nothing` doesn't work. For example:

```
objConn.Open "Provider=SQLOLEDB; Data Source=Tigger;" & _
            " Initial Catalog=pubs; User Id=sa; Password="
objRec.Open "usp_ListBoxes", objConn, adOpenStatic, _
                            adLockOptimistic, adCmdStoredProc

Do
    ' do something with recordset
    Set objRec = objRec.NextRecordset
While Not (objRec Is Nothing)
```

If you step through this routine in Visual Basic and try and look at the Locals Window when there are no more recordsets, you'll see that `objRec` is indeed `Nothing`. However, the test fails, and sets the `objRec` back from `Nothing` back to a variable with a value. The way around this is to check for the `ActiveCommand` property of the `Recordset`. So, change the end of the loop to:

```
Loop While Not (objRec.ActiveCommand Is Nothing)
```

This just seems to be quirk of Visual Basic, and there's a sample on the web site showing this in action.

When using immediate update mode, a call to `NextRecordset` will generate an error if editing is in progress, so you should ensure that you have updated or cancelled the changes.

Closing the recordset will terminate any further pending commands.

Not all providers support multiple recordsets, so you should consult your provider documentation.

The Open Method

Opens a recordset.

> **Recordset.Open**([*Source*], [*ActiveConnection*], [*CursorType*], [*LockType*], [*Options*])

Parameter	Type	Description	Default
Source	Variant	A valid `Command` object, a SQL statement, a table name, a stored procedure, or the file name of a persisted recordset.	
ActiveConnection	Variant	A valid `Connection` object or a connection string, which identifes the connection to be used.	

Table Continued on Following Page

Parameter	Type	Description	Default
CursorType	CursorType Enum	The type of cursor that the provider should use when opening the recordset. If the provider doesn't support the requested cursor type then it may use a different type.	adOpenFor wardOnly
LockType	LockType Enum	The type of locking (concurrency) that the provider should use when opening the recordset.	AdLock ReadOnly
Options	Long	If the *Source* argument represents something other than a Command object or a persisted recordset, then *Options* indicates how the provider should interpret the *Source* argument.	adCmdText

CursorTypeEnum can be one of the following constants (these are covered in more detail under the CursorType property):

- ❑ adOpenForwardOnly, for a recordset that allows forward movement only.
- ❑ adOpenKeyset, for a keyset-type cursor.
- ❑ adOpenDynamic, for a dynamic-type cursor.
- ❑ adOpenStatic for a static-type cursor.

LockTypeEnum can be one of the following constants (these are covered in more detail under the LockType property):

- ❑ adLockReadOnly, for a read-only recordset.
- ❑ adLockPessimistic, for pessimistic locking.
- ❑ adLockOptimisitic, for optimistic locking.
- ❑ adLockBatchOptimistic, for batch optimistic locking.

Options can be one or more of the following constants:

- ❑ adCmdText, to indicate that the command is a textual command.
- ❑ adCmdTable, to indicate that the command is a table name.
- ❑ adCmdStoredProcedure, to indicate that the command is a stored procedure.

❏ adCmdUnknown, to indicate that the command type is unknown.

❏ adCmdTableDirect, to indicate that the command is a table.

❏ adCmdFile, to indicate that the command is a saved recordset.

❏ adAsyncFetch, to fetch the records asynchronously.

❏ adAsyncFetchNonBlocking, to fetch the records asynchronously, but without blocking the return.

The first five of these are discussed in more detail in Chapter 4, under the CommandType property.

You can deal with persisted files in two ways. This first is by setting the Provider to MSPersist:

```
objRec.Open "c:\temp\authors.xml", "Provider=MSPersist"
```

The second is to use the adCmdFile argument:

```
objRec.Open "c:\temp\authors.xml", , , , adCmdFile
```

For asynchronous usage, you use a logical OR to add the asynchronous option. For example:

```
objRec.Open "authors", objConn, adOpenKeyset, adLockOptimistic, _
            (adCmdTable OR adAsyncFetch)
```

You can then use the State property or the FetchComplete event to determine when the recordset has been fully populated.

The difference between adAsyncFetch and adAsyncFetchNonBlocking is what happens when you request a record that has not yet been fetched. If the recordset has been opened using adAsyncFetch and you request a record that hasn't yet been fetched, then the operation will wait until the requested record is available. If the recordset has been opened using adAsyncFetchNonBlocking and you request a record that hasn't yet been fetched, you are placed at the end of the recordset. Note that this is the end of the recordset as it currently exists – because the recordset is being populated asynchronously there may still be more records to be fetched. So in this mode, EOF is the last record that has been fetched, not the physical end of the set of records.

Opening a recordset does not guarantee that there are any records available. If you open a recordset with records then you automatically be placed on the first record. If the recordset doesn't contain any records then both BOF and EOF will be True. Ideally you should check for this before accessing the records:

```
objRec.Open "select * from some_table", objConn
If Not objRec.EOF Then
    ' it is safe to access records
End If
```

The Requery Method

Updates the data in a `Recordset` object by re-executing the query on which the object is based.

> *Recordset.*__Requery__([*Options*])

Name	Type	Description	Default
Options	Long	Indicates the options to use when requerying the recordset.	`adOptionUnspecified` (-1)

This is equivalent to issuing a `Close` and `Open`. Since you cannot change the settings of the recordset, setting *Options* is merely an optimization issue to help ADO. The exception to this is if you add either of the asynchronous flags, `adAsyncFetch` or `adAsyncFetchNonBlocking`, which cause the `Requery` to be executed asynchronously.

If you `Requery` a recordset whilst editing an existing record, or adding a new one, you will generate an error.

When using client-side cursors, you can only issue `Resync` (and not a `Requery`) against a non-read-only recordset.

The Resync Method

Refreshes the data in the current `Recordset` object from the underlying database.

> *Recordset.*__Resync__([*AffectRecords*], [*ResyncValues*])

Name	Type	Description	Default
AffectRecords	AffectEnum	Determines how many records will be affected.	`adAffectAll`
ResyncValues	ResyncEnum	Specifies whether underlying values are overwritten.	`adResyncAllValues`

AffectRecords can be one of the following AffectEnum constants:

- ❏ `adAffectCurrent`, to refresh just the current row.
- ❏ `adAffectGroup`, to refresh all records in the current `Filter`.
- ❏ `adAffectAll` to refresh all records in the recordset.

ResyncValues can be one of the following ResyncEnum constants:

- ❑ adResyncAllValues, to refresh all of the value properties, effectively overwriting any pending updates.

- ❑ adResyncUnderlyingValues, to refresh only the UnderlyingValue property.

Using adResyncUnderlyingValues allows you to repopulate the UnderlyingValue property without discarding any changes or the OriginalValue property. This is particularly useful for investigating optimistic update conflicts, and is discussed in more detail later in this chapter.

Not all providers support resynchronization, so you should use the Supports method before issuing a Resync:

```
If objRec.Supports(adResync) Then
    objRec.Resync
End If
```

Unlike the Requery method the Resync method does not re-execute the underlying command.

The Save Method

Saves the Recordset to a file.

> *Recordset.Save(FileName, [PersistFormat])*

Name	Type	Description	Default
FileName	String	The complete path name of the file where the recordset should be saved.	
PersistFormat	PersistFormatEnum	The format in which the recordset should be saved.	adPersistADTG

PersistFormat can be one of:

- ❑ adPersistADTG, to save the recordset in a proprietary binary format.
- ❑ adPersistXML, to save the recordset as an XML file.

Using Save means the following actions will apply:

- ❑ Only records in the current Filter are saved.
- ❑ If the recordset is being fetched asynchronously then the Save will be blocked until all records are fetched.
- ❑ The first row becomes the current row once the save is complete.

FileName should only be used for the initial save. Subsequent saves on the same recordset will automatically save to the same file, unless another filename is specified. Attempting to save over an existing file will generate an error.

You can only use the `Save` method from a script executed by Microsoft Internet Explorer when the Internet Explorer security settings are low or custom. For more details on this see the article entitled *ADO and RDS Security Issues in Microsoft Internet Explorer*, available at http://msdn.microsoft.com/library/sdkdoc/dasdk/mdse3wj3.htm.

Recordset Persistence

The new `Save` method of recordsets allows data to be saved to a local, binary file, and then re-opened with the `Open` method. The great point about this is that it suddenly opens up the world of roving users. You now have the opportunity to provide the same application to both connected and disconnected users, and an easy way for them to switch states.

Imagine a sales situation where sales people occasionally take their laptops on the road with them. You could provide a Work Offline option that saves their data locally. On the road the application can open these persisted recordsets, and work on them as normal. When the user connects back online, the master copy of the data can be updated with the offline data.

Here's some Visual Basic code that could do this.

```
objRec.CursorLocation = adUseClient
objRec.Save "c:\temp\OfflineData.dat"

' disconnect from connection and close connection
Set objRec.ActiveConnection = Nothing
objRec.Close
objConn.Close

' now re open in offline mode
objRec.Open "c:\temp\OfflineData.dat"
```

This could be executed when the user wishes to work offline. The recordset is saved locally, the connection and recordset closed, and then the local recordset opened. The user would be disconnected from the server and could continue as normal, although only the saved data would be available. Any new information, or information not saved, would only become available once the connection to the server was re-established.

To get back online, you could do this:

```
' reconnect to the data source
strConn = "Provider=SQLOLEDB; Data Source=Tigger; " & _
          " Initial Catalog=pubs; User Id=sa; Password="
objRec.ActiveConnection = strConn

' update the master table with the offline changes
objRec.UpdateBatch
```

This connects the recordset to a connection and then uses `UpdateBatch` to update the master copy of the records with the local copy. See the section on *Conflict Resolution* below for more details of this.

You can see that this makes writing offline applications no different from writing an online application. You could have a simple flag that is set when the application is offline to indicate that the saved copies of the recordset are opened when the application starts.

Conflict Resolution

Using client-side cursors and disconnected recordsets is great, especially since we have the ability to amend records and send them back to the server to update the master copy of the database. One thing you have to consider, however, is how to resolve conflicts between changes to the data you've made, and any changes that might have happened due to other users.

If you think back to the offline code, we used UpdateBatch to update the master records, and this will generate errors if any of the records conflicted with underlying recordset changes. There are two ways to investigate this problem:

❏ Have error trapping in the routine that calls UpdateBatch. You can then filter the recordset using adFilterConflictingRecords to see which records caused the problem.

❏ Use the recordset events, and place some code in the RecordChangeComplete event. If errors are generated by conflicts, then the recordset will already be filtered for you.

If you choose the latter approach, then your code could look like this:

```
Private Sub objRec_RecordChangeComplete( _
      ByVal adReason As ADODB.EventReasonEnum, _
      ByVal cRecords As Long, _
      ByVal pError As ADODB.Error, _
      adStatus As ADODB.EventStatusEnum, _
      ByVal pRecordset As ADODB.Recordset)

    Dim objFld        As ADODB.Field

    If adStatus = adStatusErrorsOccurred Then
        Print cRecords & " caused errors.:"
        For Each objFld In pRecordset.Fields
            Debug.Print "Name"; vbTab; objFld.Name
            Debug.Print "Value"; vbTab; objFld.Value
            Debug.Print "UV"; vbTab; objFld.UnderlyingValue
            Debug.Print "OV"; vbTab; objFld.OriginalValue
        Next
    End If

End Sub
```

Of the event procedure arguments, adStatus indicates that an error occurred, and cRecords identifies the number of records that failed. The recordset, pRecordset, is the recordset filtered to show only those conflicting records.

For more details on the arguments for this event see the RecordChangeComplete event procedure later in this chapter.

A small sample application showing these techniques is available from the Wrox Press web site, at http://webdev.wrox.co.uk/books/2688.

The Seek Method

Uses an `Index` to perform searches to locate specific records.

> *Recordset*.**Seek** *KeyValues, SeekOption*

Parameter	Type	Description	Default
KeyValues	Variant Array	The column values to search for	
SeekOption	SeekEnum	The type of comparison to be made	`adSeekFirstEQ`

SeekOption takes its value from on of the following SeekEnum constants:

- ❏ `adSeekAfter`, to find the key just after the match.
- ❏ `adSeekAfterEQ`, to find the key equal to or just after the match.
- ❏ `adSeekBefore`, to find the key just before the match.
- ❏ `adSeekBeforeEQ`, to find the key equal to or just before the match.
- ❏ `adSeekFirstEQ`, to find the first key equal to the match.
- ❏ `adSeekLastEQ`, to find the last key equal to the match.

KeyValues is a variant array to allow for indexes that contain multiple columns.

If the record being sought is not found, no error is returned, and the current record is placed at `EOF`.

You use the `Seek` method in conjunction with the `Index` property. For example:

```
objRec.Index = "FullName"
objRec.Seek Array("Janine", "Lloyd"), adSeekFirstEQ
If objRec.EOF Then
    Print "Record not found"
End If
```

Not all providers support the `Seek` operation. To check this you should use `adSeek` with the `Supports` method.

The `Seek` operation is only supported by server-based cursors (`CursorLocation = adUseServer`). This is because it uses the cursor service and indexes on the provider, rather than facilities of ADO.

The Supports Method

Determines whether a specified `Recordset` object supports a particular functionality.

> *Boolean = Recordset*.**Supports**(*CursorOptions*)

Parameter	Type	Description	Default
CursorOptions	CursorOption Enum	One or more values to identify what functionality is supported.	

CursorOptions can take one or more of the following CursorOptionEnum constants:

- ❏ adAddNew, to indicate that the recordset supports addition of new records, via the AddNew method

- ❏ adApproxPosition, to indicate that the recordset supports absolute position, via the AbsolutePosition and AbsolutePage properties

- ❏ adBookmark, to indicate that the recordset supports bookmarks, via the Bookmark property

- ❏ adDelete, to indicate that the recordset supports record deletion, via the Delete method

- ❏ adFind, to indicate that the recordset supports the finding of records, via the Find method

- ❏ adHoldRecords, to indicate that changes to the recordset will remain if you fetch more records

- ❏ adIndex, to indicate that you can use the Index property to set the current Index

- ❏ adMovePrevious, to indicate that the recordset supports movement backwards, via the MoveFirst, MovePrevious, Move or GetRows methods

- ❏ adNotify, to indicate that the recordset supports notifications, and will return events

- ❏ adResync, to indicate that the recordset allows the underlying data to be refreshed with the Resync method

- ❏ adSeek, to indicate that you can use the Seek method to find records by an Index

- ❏ adUpdate, to indicate that the recordset allows records to be updated with the Update method

- ❏ adUpdateBatch, to indicate that the recordset allows records to be updated with the UpdateBatch method

You can use the Supports method to find out which features a recordset makes available. For example, the following lines establish whether the recordset is updateable:

```
If objRec.Supports(adUpdate) Then
    ' recordset supports updates
End If
```

You can use Boolean logic to check for multiple values:

```
If objRec.Supports(adDelete Or adAddNew) Then
    ' recordset supports both Delete and AddNew
End If
```

Note that, even if the recordset supports a particular feature, the underlying data may make the feature unavailable – and this may result in errors from the provider. For example, you may have a recordset based on a view where only certain columns are updateable; the recordset will support adUpdate, but certain columns may not allow updating.

The Update Method

Saves any changes made to the current Recordset object.

> *Recordset*.Update([*Fields*], [*Values*])

Parameter	Type	Description	Default
Fields	Variant	A single name or Variant array representing the names or ordinal positions of the fields to be modified.	
Values	Variant	A single name or Variant array representing the values for the fields in the new record.	

You can update fields in three ways. First, by assigning values to fields and then calling the Update method:

```
objRec("au_lname").Value = "Lloyd"
objRec("au_fname").Value = "Janine"
objRec.Update
```

Second, you can pass a single field name with a single value:

```
objRec.Update "au_lname", "Lloyd"
```

Third, you can pass multiple field names and multiple values:

```
objRec.Update Array("au_lname", "au_fname"), Array("Lloyd", "Janine")
```

The three methods are interchangeable. There's little difference between the methods unless updating multiple fields, in which case you should use the first or third methods. Each Update issues a command to the server, so you can make your code more efficient by issuing fewer updates.

Using any of the Move methods when editing a record will implicitly call Update.

The UpdateBatch Method

Writes all pending batch updates to disk.

> *Recordset*.UpdateBatch([*AffectRecords*])

Name	Type	Description	Default
AffectRecords	AffectEnum	Determines how many records will be affected.	adAffectAll

AffectRecords can take any of the following AffectEnum constants:

- ❑ adAffectCurrent, to refresh just the current row.

- ❑ adAffectGroup, to refresh all records in the current Filter.

- ❑ adAffectAll to refresh all records in the recordset.

Using UpdateBatch allows changes to be cached until such time as you request the underlying data store to be updated. Caching starts when opening a recordset with adLockBatchOptimistic.

A failure to update will cause the Errors collection to be populated, and you can use the Filter property to see which records failed. This could be due to a conflict between a change made by you and a change made by another user. There's more on conflicts earlier in this chapter.

Properties of the Recordset Object

The AbsolutePage Property

Specifies in which page the current record resides.

```
PositionEnum = Recordset.AbsolutePage
Long = Recordset.AbsolutePage
Recordset.AbsolutePage = PositionEnum
Recordset.AbsolutePage = Long
```

PositionEnum can be a valid page number, or one of the following constants:

- ❑ adPosBOF, to indicate, or position, the current record pointer at the beginning of the recordset.

- ❑ adPosEOF, to indicate, or position, the current record pointer at the end of the recordset.

- ❑ adPosUnknown, to indicate that the current page is unknown. This could be because the recordset is empty, or because the provider does not support this property, or because the provider cannot identify the current page.

When setting the value of the AbsolutePage property, the record pointer is set to the first record in the specified page. Thus, if you set the AbsolutePage property to 1, this moves to the first page of the recordset, and thus sets the record pointer to the first record in the recordset. This is used in conjunction with the PageSize property.

The AbsolutePosition Property

Specifies the ordinal position of a Recordset object's current cursor position.

```
PositionEnum = Recordset.AbsolutePosition
Recordset.AbsolutePosition = PositionEnum
```

129

PositionEnum can be a valid record number, or one of the following constants:

❑   adPosBOF, to indicate, or position, the current record pointer at the beginning of the recordset.

❑   adPosEOF, to indicate, or position, the current record pointer at the end of the recordset.

❑   adPosUnknown, to indicate that the current position is unknown. This could be because the recordset is empty, the provider does not support this property, or it cannot identify the current position.

You cannot use the absolute position to identify a record uniquely, because this value changes as records are added and deleted. Of course, you could use AbsolutePosition to point to a record through the life of the recordset if your recordset does not allow additions or deletions. However, the AbsolutePosition is affected by the use of Sort and Index, as it points to a record at a particular position in the recordset, and not to an individual record, irrespective of its position. If you need to identify a record throughout sorts and filters, you should use a bookmark.

The ActiveCommand Property

Indicates the Command object that created the associated Recordset object.

> **Set *Command* = *Recordset*.ActiveCommand**

When the recordset was created from a command, you can use this property to access the Command object's properties and parameters. For example:

```
objRec.Open "select * from authors", "DSN=pubs", _
            adOpenForwardOnly, adLockOptimistic, adCmdText
Print objRec.ActiveCommand.CommandText
```

This is particularly useful when you have only been supplied with the recordset, such as in the Visual Basic 6 Data Environment.

If the recordset was not created from a command, then this property will be Null.

The ActiveConnection Property

Indicates to which Connection object the specified Recordset object currently belongs.

> **Set *Variant* = *Recordset*.ActiveConnection**
> **Set *Recordset*.ActiveConnection = *Variant***
> ***Recordset*.ActiveConnection = *String***
> ***String* = *Recordset*.ActiveConnection**

The ActiveConnection can either be set to a pre-existing Connection object, in which case you use the Set form:

```
Set objRec.ActiveConnection = objConn
```

Alternatively you can set the `ActiveConnection` by using a connection string, in which case an implicit `Connection` object is created for you:

```
objRec.ActiveConnection = "DSN=pubs"
```

This property will inherit the value from the `ActiveConnection` argument of an `Open` command, or from the `Source` property of a `Command`. The `ActiveConnection` property may also be modified by the provider, to allow you access to provider-specific connection information.

You can disassociate a client-side recordset from a connection by setting this property to `Nothing`. The recordset remains valid, and can be reconnected to any `Connection` object at a later date.

The BOF Property

Indicates whether the current record pointer is before the first record in a `Recordset` object.

```
Boolean = Recordset.BOF
```

If your recordset is empty, then the `BOF` and `EOF` properties will both be `True`.

The Bookmark Property

Can be used to return a bookmark that uniquely identifies the current record in a `Recordset` object, or to set the current record pointer to the record identified by a valid bookmark.

```
Variant = Recordset.Bookmark
Recordset.Bookmark = Variant
```

Using the `Clone` method on a recordset gives two recordsets with interchangeable bookmarks. This means that bookmarks between cloned recordsets are identical. However, bookmarks from different recordsets are not interchangeable, even if the recordsets were created from the same source or command.

You can use this property to store the position in the recordset temporarily, allowing you to return to that position at a later date. For example:

```
varBkmk = objRec.Bookmark
' ... some processing that changes the current record ...
objRec.Bookmark = varBkmk
```

For example, this is quite useful when using the `Find` method (which positions you at `EOF` if the record you are searching for was not found):

```
varBkmk = objRec.Bookmark

objRec.Find "au_lname = 'Lloyd'"
If objRec.EOF Then
  Print "Record not found - now moving cursor from EOF to bookmarked record"
  objRec.Bkmk = varBkmk
End If
```

Bookmarks are generally only supported on keyset and static cursors and client-side dynamic cursors. Server based dynamic cursors do not support bookmarks because their membership is not fixed. You should check the adBookmark value (using the recordset's Supports method) to verify this.

The CacheSize Property

Indicates the number of records from a Recordset object that are cached locally in memory. This defaults to 1.

```
Long = Recordset.CacheSize
Recordset.CacheSize = Long
```

The cache size affects how many records from the recordset are fetched from the server in one go and held locally, and this can have an effect on performance and memory usage. When a recordset is first opened, only a certain number of records (the number stored in CacheSize) are fetched locally – and the remaining records are not fetched until required. If you move to a record that's not in the current cache, the provider will fetch another cache of records. So, a cache larger than 1 is generally more efficient. Chapter 12 shows the difference in speed between a cache of 1 and a larger value. Changing the size of the cache can have an effect on both client- and server-based cursors.

An important point to note is that records in the cache do not reflect underlying changes made by other users, until Resync is issued, or until recordset navigation options cause those records to be re-read.

You can change the cache size during the life of a recordset, but the new size only becomes effective when the next cache of data is retrieved. A cache size of 0 is not allowed and generates an error.

An undocumented feature, which is not officially supported, is that a negative cache size causes records to be fetched backwards from the current row, rather than forwards.

The CursorLocation Property

Sets or returns the location of the cursor engine.

```
CursorLocationEnum = Recordset.CursorLocation
Recordset.CursorLocation = CursorLocationEnum
```

CursorLocationEnum can be one of the following constants:

- ❏ adUseClient, to specify the Microsoft Client cursor.

- ❏ adUseServer, to specify the cursor support supplied by the data provider, assuming it supports server based cursors.

Server-side cursors often support better concurrency than client-side cursors, because it's the actual provider that is handling the concurrency control.

Client-side cursors must be used when creating disconnected recordsets.

The CursorType Property

Indicates the type of cursor used in a `Recordset` object.

> *CursorTypeEnum = Recordset*.**CursorType**
> *Recordset*.**CursorType** = *CursorTypeEnum*

CursorTypeEnum can be one of the following constants:

- ❏ `adOpenForwardOnly`, for a recordset that only allows forward movement, one record at a time. It is therefore not possible to use anything other than `MoveNext` or `Move` with a value of 1, unless the `CacheSize` is greater than 1. Bookmarks are not supported on this cursor type, since absolute position is not a requirement.

- ❏ `adOpenKeyset`, for a keyset-type cursor. This gives you a set of records for which the data is up-to-date with the underlying data, but the number of records may not be, as additions and deletions may not be visible to the cursor. Keyset cursors work by storing the keys to the row of data, and only fetching the data when it is required. Therefore the set of rows is fixed, but the data is not fixed. Deleted records still remain in the recordset, but as a hole. Insertions by other users are not visible (since they weren't part of the original set of keys), but insertions by you may be visible. Movement is supported both forwards and backwards.

- ❏ `adOpenDynamic`, for a dynamic type cursor, the membership of records in the recordset is not fixed. New records by any user will be visible, deleted records will not be visible, and any data changes will be visible. Movement is supported both forwards and backwards.

- ❏ `adOpenStatic`, for a static type cursor, where the data is fixed at the time the cursor is created. Movement is supported both forwards and backwards.

For keyset cursors you can control the visibility of inserted and deleted records by use of the following dynamic properties:

- ❏ `Remove Deleted Records`, will remove deleted records from the keyset.

- ❏ `Own Inserts Visible`, will ensure that your own inserts into the keyset are visible.

- ❏ `Others' Inserts Visible`, will ensure that inserts by other people are visible in the keyset.

Not all providers support all cursor types, and the actual cursor type used may depend on the cursor location. For this reason you should query the `CursorType` property after the recordset has been opened, to see what type the provider has used. The cursor types requested and supported by the main providers are included in Chapter 12.

The DataMember Property

Specifies the name of the data member to be retrieved from the object referenced by the `DataSource` property.

```
String = Recordset.DataMember
Recordset.DataMember = String
```

Used to create data-bound controls in Visual Basic using the Data Environment.

The `DataMember` identifies the object in the `DataSource` that will supply the recordset.

The DataSource Property

Specifies an object containing data to be represented as a `Recordset` object.

```
Set Object = Recordset.DataSource
Set Recordset.DataSource = Object
```

It is used to create data-bound controls in Visual Basic 6 using the Data Environment.

The `DataSource` identifies the object in the Data Environment to which the `DataMember` belongs.

The EditMode Property

Indicates the editing status of the current record.

```
EditModeEnum = Recordset.EditMode
```

EditModeEnum will be one of the following constants:

- ❑ `adEditNone`, to indicate that the current record has no edits in progress.
- ❑ `adEditInProgress`, to indicate that the current record is being edited.
- ❑ `adEditAdd` to indicate that the current record is being added – that is, it's a new record.
- ❑ `adEditDelete`, to indicate the current record has been deleted.

You could use this in an interactive application that allows users to edit and move around records. Since moving around records intrinsically calls `Update`, you may want to offer the user the option of canceling or saving their changes before moving the record. For example, imagine a section of Visual Basic code that runs when a **Next Record** button is pressed:

```
If objRec.EditMode = adEditInProgress Then
    strMsg = "The current record has changed. " & _
             "Would you like to save the changes?"
    If MsgBox (strMsg, vbYesNo) = vbNo Then
        objRec.CancelUpdate
    End If
End If
objRec.MoveNext
```

This simply checks the edit mode before moving to another record.

The EOF Property

Indicates whether the current record pointer is after the last record in a Recordset object.

> *Boolean = Recordset*.EOF

The Filter Property

Indicates a filter for data in the Recordset.

> *Variant = Recordset*.Filter
> *Recordset*.Filter = *Variant*

The Filter property can be set to a valid filter string, an array of bookmarks, or one of the following FilterGroupEnum constants:

❑ adFilterNone, which removes any current filter, and shows all records.

❑ adFilterPendingRecords, for batch update mode, which shows only records that have been changed but not yet sent to the server.

❑ adFilterAffectedRecords, which shows only records affected by the last Delete, Resync, UpdateBatch or CancelBatch.

❑ adFilterFetchedRecords, which shows records in the current cache.

❑ adFilterPredicate, which shows deleted records.

❑ adFilterConflictingRecords, which shows records that caused a conflict during the last batch update attempt.

You can use an array of Bookmarks to filter with. This small section of Visual Basic code shows an example of this:

```
Dim avarBkmk(5)
avarBkmk(0) = objRec.Bookmark
' ...some more processing...
avarBkmk(1) = objRec.Bookmark
objRec.Filter = Array(avarBkmk(0), avarBkmk(1))
```

This can be quite useful when allowing users to select multiple records from a list.

Using a normal string to filter with follows much the same syntax as a SQL WHERE clause, as the following examples show:

```
objRec.Filter = "au_lname = 'Lloyd'""
objRec.Filter = "au_lname LIKE 'L*'"
objRec.Filter = "Price > 10.99 AND Price < 15.99"
objRec.Filter = "InvoiceDate > #04/04/98#"
```

You'll notice that multiple conditions are allowed here, unlike the Find command. When using date fields, you have to use the VBA syntax, surrounding the date with # symbols.

Once the Filter has been set, the cursor is placed on the first record in the newly filtered recordset.

To cancel a filter, call the `Filter` method again – this time, either use `adFilterNone` or specify an empty string (`" "`):

```
objRec.Filter ""
```

The Index Property

Indicates the name of the index currently in effect.

> *String = Recordset.***Index**
> *Recordset.***Index** = *String*

The `Index` property refers to a previously-defined table index. This can be either an index that was created on the base table, or an ADOX `Index` object.

Changing an `Index` may change the current row position, which may therefore update the current record.

The `Index` property is not related to the indexing used by the dynamic `Optimize` property.

Not all providers support the `Index` property. To check this you should use `adIndex` with the `Supports` method.

The LockType Property

Indicates the type of locks placed on records during editing.

> *LockTypeEnum = Recordset.***LockType**
> *Recordset.***LockType** = *LockTypeEnum*

LockTypeEnum can be one of the following constants:

- ❑ `adLockReadOnly`, for a read-only recordset, where the provider does no locking and the data cannot be changed.

- ❑ `adLockPessimistic`, for pessimistic locking, where the provider attempts to lock edited records at the data source.

- ❑ `adLockOptimistic`, for optimistic locking, where the provider locks records on a row-by-row or page-by-page basis, when `Update` is called.

- ❑ `adLockBatchOptimistic`, for batch update mode, where locking occurs when `UpdateBatch` is called.

Only `adLockBatchOptimistic` or `adLockReadOnly` are supported by client-side cursors. If you attempt to use any other lock type you'll get `adLockBatchOptimistic`.

The locking method you choose is really going to depend upon the application. Since pessimistic locking locks the record at the data source as you start editing, you don't have to worry about a conflict with another user's changes, unless the record is already locked when you try and lock it. However, this implies a permanent connection to the data store, which may be either impractical or impossible.

Optimistic locking gives you better resource management, but you then have to cater for conflicts, as the lock doesn't actually occur until you try to Update the record. This means that someone else might have changed the record between the time you started editing it and the time you went to Update it. Since ADO doesn't know which copy is correct, it deals with this by generating an error, which can be trapped. This error number is -2147217885, however not all providers report error information correctly. To get the best error information you'll need to use the OLE DB Provider for ODBC.

Although batch locking can be used with server-based cursors, it's more useful with client-cursors. This allows changes to multiple records before committing them to the data store in a single batch.

The MarshalOptions Property

Indicates which records are to be marshaled back to the server.

> *MarshalOptionsEnum = Recordset*.MarshalOptions
> *Recordset*.MarshalOptions = *MarshalOptionsEnum*

MarshalOptionsEnum can be one of the following constants:

- ❑ adMarshalAll, to send all rows back to the server, which is the default.

- ❑ adMarshalModifiedOnly, to send back to the server only those rows that have changed.

Marshalling is the term given to transferring a recordset between two processes. This could be between the client and the server in a two-tier system or between the client and a middle-tier in an n-tier system.

This property is only applicable when using disconnected, client-side recordsets. By marshalling only the changed records (as opposed to all records), you can greatly improve performance. If only a few records are modified locally, less data needs to be sent back to the server process.

You can use this quite effectively when using n-tier client/server architecture, using a business object on the server to supply recordsets. These can be modified locally, and only the changed records are sent back to the business processes for updating.

The MaxRecords Property

Indicates the maximum number of records that may be returned to a Recordset object as the result of a query.

> *Long = Recordset*.MaxRecords
> *Recordset*.MaxRecords = *Long*

You can only set this property while the recordset is closed. The MaxRecords property defaults to 0, which indicates that all records should be returned.

Chapter 5

This is quite useful for applications that allow users to submit queries, since you can limit their set of records if it is too big.

While this property is supported, not all providers may implement it.

The PageCount Property

Indicates how many pages of data are contained in the Recordset object.

```
Long = Recordset.PageCount
```

The recordset will consist of a number of pages – each page contains a number of records equal to PageSize, except for the last page, which may contain fewer records. If the PageSize is not set then PageCount will be –1.

The PageCount property allows you to move quickly to the last page in a recordset:

```
objRec.AbsolutePage = objRec.RecordCount/objRec.PageCount
```

This positions your record pointer on the first record of the last page. Note that not all providers support the PageCount property.

The PageSize Property

Indicates how many records constitute one page in the Recordset.

```
Long = Recordset.PageSize
Recordset.PageSize = Long
```

You can use this to change the number of records in a page. For example, imagine a Web application that shows search results from Microsoft Index Server. You could allow the user to page through these records, and to specify how many records should be seen in each page.

The page size doesn't correspond to the cache size. The cache is a way of managing the transfer of a number of records from the server to the client. In comparison, the page size is merely a logical structure that can be used for display purposes. The page size allows you an easy way to access a group of records that are next to each other in the recordset.

Not all providers support PageSize.

The RecordCount Property

Indicates the current number of records in the Recordset object.

```
Long = Recordset.RecordCount
```

The RecordCount will only be accurate for recordsets that support approximate positioning or bookmarks. In practice this is generally all cursor types except server-side, forward-only cursors and server-side, dynamic cursors. If the record count cannot be accurately determined, it is set to -1. You can test to see if the recordset supports approximate positioning or bookmarks by using the Supports method:

```
If objRec.Supports(adBookmark Or adApproxPosition) Then
    ' RecordCount will be accurate
End If
```

If the `Recordset` does not support approximate positioning or bookmarks, it must be fully populated before an accurate `RecordCount` value can be returned. One way to achieve this is by using `MoveLast` to move to the last record in the recordset, assuming the recordset supports `MoveLast`. If `MoveLast` is not supported, then all records will have to be read before an accurate count can be determined.

If the recordset is being fetched asynchronously, the same rules apply. The `RecordCount` will be accurate if approximate position or bookmarks are supported, even if the asynchronous command is still running and the recordset has not been fully populated with records.

The Sort Property

Specifies one or more field names on which to sort the `Recordset`, and the direction of the sort.

> *String = Recordset*.**Sort**
> *Recordset*.**Sort** *= String*

The sort string should be a comma-separated list of columns to dictate the sort order, each optionally followed by the sort direction. The default sort direction is ASC. For example:

```
objRec.Sort = "au_lname ASC, au_fname DESC"
```

If using client-side cursors (`CursorLocation = adUseClient`), then a temporary index will be created for each field in the `Sort`. You can also force the creation of local indexes by setting the `Optimize` property (of the `Field` object's `Properties` collection) to be `True`. For example:

```
objRec("au_lname").Properties("Optimize") = True
```

This will create a local index, which will speed up sorting and searching.

Not all providers support sorting when using server-side cursors.

The Source Property

Indicates the command or SQL command for the data in a `Recordset` object.

> *String = Recordset*.**Source**
> *Recordset*.**Source** *= String*
> **Set** *Recordset*.**Source** *= Variant*

This is useful for identifying the actual command text used to create the recordset, especially if it was created from a `Command` object.

The State Property

Gives the state of the recordset in both synchronous and asynchronous mode. Indicates whether the recordset is open, closed, or whether it is executing an asynchronous operation.

> *ObjectStateEnum = Recordset*.**State**

ObjectStateEnum can be one or more of the following constants:

- ❑ `adStateClosed`, indicating that the recordset is closed.
- ❑ `adStateOpen`, indicating that the recordset is open.
- ❑ `adStateConnecting`, indicating that the recordset is currently connecting to the data store.
- ❑ `adStateExecuting`, indicating that the recordset is currently executing a command.
- ❑ `adStateFetching`, indicating that the recordset is currently fetching records.

When the recordset is opened asynchronously, you should use logical operations to test these values. For example:

```
If (objRec.State And adStateFetching) = adStateFetching Then
   Print "Recordset is still fetching records"
End If
```

A positive test for `adStateExecuting` or `adStateFetching` implies `adStateOpen`, but you cannot test for this alone.

The Status Property

Indicates the status of the current record with respect to batch updates or other bulk operations.

> *RecordStatusEnum = Recordset*.**Status**

RecordStatusEnum can be one or more of the RecordStatusEnum constants shown in Appendix B.

The StayInSync Property

Indicates, in a hierarchical `Recordset` object, whether a reference to the child row should change when the parent record changes.

> *Boolean = Recordset*.**StayInSync**
> *Recordset*.**StayInSync** *= Boolean*

The default for this is `True`; if set to `False`, a reference to a child recordset will remain pointing to the old recordset, even though the parent record may have changed.

Hierarchical recordsets are covered in more detail in Chapter 11, in the discussion of Data Shaping.

Events of the Recordset Object

ADO 2.1 supports notifications, which allows providers to notify the application when certain events occur. Event ordering is covered in Chapter 2, and examples of event usage are available on the supporting web site.

Event Status

All events will have a bi-directional parameter, *adStatus*, to indicate the status of the event. This is of type EventStatusEnum, and can be one of the following constants:

- ❑ adStatusOK, to indicate that the action that caused the event was successful.

- ❑ adStatusErrorsOccured, to indicate that errors or warnings occurred, in which case the Errors collection should be checked.

- ❑ adStatusCantDeny. On a Will... event this indicates that you cannot cancel the action that generated the event; on a ...Complete event it indicates that the action was cancelled.

- ❑ adStatusUnwantedEvent, which indicates that the action which generated the event should no longer generate events.

On a Will... event (and assuming adStatusCantDeny is not set), before the procedure exits you can set *adStatus* to adStatusCancel to cancel the action that caused this event. This also generates an error indicating that the event has been cancelled. For example, assume that you have moved from one record to the next – this will raise a WillMove event on the Recordset. If you decide that you do not wish to move to another record, you can set *adStatus* to adStatusCancel, and the Move action will be cancelled. This allows you to perhaps cancel actions where the data is incorrect.

When using Will... events, one thing to watch for is implicit method calls. Taking the above Move as an example; if the current record has been edited, then ADO implicitly calls Update. In this case you might get more than one Will... event.

If you no longer wish to receive events for a particular action, then before the procedure exits you can set *adStatus* to adStatusUnwantedEvent, and they will no longer be generated.

The EndOfRecordset Event

Fired when there is an attempt to move to a row past the end of the Recordset.

EndOfRecordset(*fMoreData, adStatus, pRecordset*)

Parameter	Type	Description
fMoreData	Boolean	Set to `True` if it is possible to append more data to *pRecordset* while processing this event.
adStatus	EventStatusEnum	Identifies the status of the message.
pRecordset	Recordset	A reference to the `Recordset` object for which this event applies.

While in this event procedure, more records can be retrieved from the data store and appended to the end of the recordset. If you wish to do this, you should set the parameter *fMoreData* to `True`. After returning from this procedure, a subsequent `MoveNext` will allow access to the newly-added records. This can be useful if you wish to provide your own paging scheme, as you can read in the next batch of records when the user attempts to move past the end of the current page of records.

The FetchComplete Event

Fired after all the records in an asynchronous operation have been retrieved into the `Recordset`.

FetchComplete(*pError, adStatus, pRecordset*)

Parameter	Type	Description
pError	Error	If *adStatus* is `adStatusErrorsOccurred`, this is an `Error` object that describes the error that occurred. Otherwise it is not set.
adStatus	EventStatusEnum	Identifies the status of the message.
pRecordset	Recordset	A reference to the `Recordset` object for which the records were retrieved.

This is most useful when the recordset is being fetched asynchronously, as it avoids having to check the state of the recordset periodically.

The FetchProgress Event

Fired periodically by the provider during an asynchronous operation, to report how many rows have been retrieved so far.

FetchProgress(*Progress, MaxProgress, adStatus, pRecordset*)

Parameter	Type	Description
Progress	Long	The number of records that have currently been retrieved.
MaxProgress	Long	The maximum number of records expected to be retrieved.
adStatus	EventStatusEnum	Identifies the status of the message.
pRecordset	Recordset	A reference to the `Recordset` object for which the records are being retrieved.

MaxProgess may not contain the total number of records to be fetched, if the recordset type does not support this.

This would be used for updating status indicators on user screens.

The provider determines when, and why this event is raised.

The FieldChangeComplete Event

Fired after the values of one or more `Field` objects have been changed.

> FieldChangeComplete(*cFields, Fields, pError, adStatus, pRecordset*)

Parameter	Type	Description
cFields	Long	The number of `Field` objects within *Fields*.
Fields	Variant	An array of `Field` objects with completed changes.
pError	Error	If *adStatus* is `adStatusErrorsOccurred`, this describes the error that occurred. Otherwise it is not set.
adStatus	EventStatus Enum	Identifies the status of the message.
pRecordset	Recordset	A reference to the `Recordset` object for which this event applies.

You can use this to update status indicators, or to trigger other actions that are dependent upon some fields being changed.

The MoveComplete Event

Fired after the current position in the `Recordset` changes.

> MoveComplete(*adReason, pError, adStatus, pRecordset*)

Parameter	Type	Description
adReason	EventReasonEnum	The reason for the event.
pError	Error	If *adStatus* is adStatusErrorsOccurred, this is an Error object that describes the error that occurred. Otherwise it is not set.
adStatus	EventStatusEnum	Identifies the status of the message.
pRecordset	Recordset	The Recordset object for which this event applies.

adReason will be one of a subset of the EventReasonEnum constants:

- ❑   adRsnMoveFirst, when a MoveFirst is issued.
- ❑   adRsnMoveLast, when a MoveLast is issued.
- ❑   adRsnMoveNext, when a MoveNext is issued.
- ❑   adRsnMovePrevious, when a MovePrevious is issued.
- ❑   adRsnMove, when a Move is issued
- ❑   adRsnRequery, when a Requery is issued, or a Filter is set.

adReason might also assume the value of adRsnMove when the AbsolutePage or AbsolutePosition property is set, or a Bookmark is set, or a new record is added with AddNew. In addition, this value is generated when the recordset is opened.

These could also be generated when a child recordset has events and the parent recordset moves.

The RecordChangeComplete Event

Fired after one or more records change in the local recordset.

RecordChangeComplete(*adReason, cRecords, pError, adStatus, pRecordset*)

Parameter	Type	Description
adReason	EventReasonEnum	Specifies the reason for the event.
cRecords	Long	The number of records changing.
pError	Error	If *adStatus* is adStatusErrorsOccurred, this is an Error object that describes the error that occurred. Otherwise it is not set.
adStatus	EventStatusEnum	Identifies the status of the message.
pRecordset	Recordset	The Recordset object for which this event applies, containing only the changed rows.

adReason will be one of a subset of the EventReasonEnum constants:

- ❑ adRsnAddNew, when an AddNew is issued.

- ❑ adRsnDelete, when a Delete is issued.

- ❑ adRsnUpdate, when an Update is issued.

- ❑ adRsnUndoUpdate, when an Update is cancelled, with CancelUpdate or CancelBatch.

- ❑ adRsnUndoAddNew, when an AddNew is cancelled, with CancelUpdate or CancelBatch.

- ❑ dRsnUndoDelete, when a Delete is cancelled, with CancelUpdate or CancelBatch.

- ❑ adRsnFirstChange, when the record is changed for the first time.

You could use this event for creation of an audit trail, or triggering other actions that are dependent upon the data having changed.

The RecordsetChangeComplete Event

Fired after the Recordset has changed.

RecordsetChangeComplete(*adReason, pError, adStatus, pRecordset*)

Parameter	Type	Description
adReason	EventReasonEnum	Specifies the reason for the event.
pError	Error	If *adStatus* is adStatusErrorsOccurred, this is an Error object that describes the error that occurred. Otherwise it is not set.
adStatus	EventStatusEnum	Identifies the status of the message.
pRecordset	Recordset	The Recordset object for which this event applies.

adReason will be one of a subset of the EventReasonEnum constants:

- ❑ adRsnRequery, when a Requery is issued.

- ❑ adRsnReSynch, when a Resync is issued.

- ❑ adRsnClose, when a Close is issued.

The WillChangeField Event

Fired before a pending operation changes the value of one or more Field objects.

WillChangeField(*cFields, Fields, adStatus, pRecordset*)

Parameter	Type	Description
cFields	Long	The number of Field objects within Fields.
Fields	Variant	An array of Field objects with pending changes.
adStatus	EventStatusEnum	Identifies the status of the message.
pRecordset	Recordset	The Recordset object for which this event applies.

This can be useful for validating user input.

This can occur due to the following Recordset operations: Value, and Update with field and value array parameters.

The WillChangeRecord Event

Fired before one or more rows in the Recordset change.

WillChangeRecord(*adReason, cRecords, adStatus, pRecordset*)

Parameter	Type	Description
adReason	EventReasonEnum	Specifies the reason for the event.
cRecords	Long	The number of records changing.
adStatus	EventStatusEnum	Identifies the status of the message.
pRecordset	Recordset	The Recordset object for which this event applies.

adReason will be one of a subset of the EventReasonEnum constants:

- ❑ adRsnAddNew, when an AddNew is issued.

- ❑ adRsnDelete, when a Delete is issued.

- ❑ adRsnUpdate, when an Update is issued.

- ❑ adRsnUndoUpdate, when an Update is cancelled, with CancelUpdate or CancelBatch.

- ❑ adRsnUndoAddNew, when an AddNew is cancelled, with CancelUpdate or CancelBatch.

- ❑ dRsnUndoDelete, when a Delete is cancelled, with CancelUpdate or CancelBatch.

- ❑ adRsnFirstChange, when the record is changed for the first time.

You could use this when actions might change the record, and it can be used in parallel with WillChangeField.

The WillChangeRecordset Event

Fired before a pending operation changes the Recordset.

> **WillChangeRecordset(***adReason, adStatus, pRecordset***)**

Parameter	Type	Description
adReason	EventReasonEnum	Specifies the reason for the event.
adStatus	EventStatusEnum	Identifies the status of the message.
pRecordset	Recordset	The Recordset object for which this event applies.

adReason will be one of a subset of the EventReasonEnum constants:

- ❑ adRsnRequery, when a Requery is issued.
- ❑ adRsnReSynch, when a Resync is issued.
- ❑ adRsnClose, when a Close is issued.

You can use this to identify when an action would cause the underlying set of records to change.

The WillMove Event

Fired before a pending operation changes the current position in the Recordset.

> **WillMove(***adReason, adStatus, pRecordset***)**

Parameter	Type	Description
adReason	EventReasonEnum	The reason for the event.
adStatus	EventStatusEnum	Identifies the status of the message.
pRecordset	Recordset	The Recordset object for which this event applies.

adReason will be one of a subset of the EventReasonEnum constants:

- ❑ adRsnMoveFirst, when a MoveFirst is issued.
- ❑ adRsnMoveLast, when a MoveLast is issued.
- ❑ adRsnMoveNext, when a MoveNext is issued.
- ❑ adRsnMovePrevious, when a MovePrevious is issued.
- ❑ adRsnMove, when a Move is issued, or AbsolutePage or AbsolutePosition is set, or the current record is moved by setting the Bookmark, or an AddNew is issued, or the recordset was opened.
- ❑ adRsnRequery, when a Requery is issued, or a Filter is set.

This allows you to identify when an action will cause the current record to change.

Collections of the Recordset Object

The Fields Collection

The `Fields` collection contains zero or more `Field` objects, each representing a field in the recordset.

> *Recordset*.**Fields**

You can iterate though the `Fields` collection to access each `Field` object individually:

```
For Each objField in objRec.Fields
    Print "Field name is " & objField.Name
Next
```

The `Fields` collection and `Field` object are discussed in more detail in Chapter 6.

The Properties Collection

The `Properties` collection contains `Property` objects, each representing an extended property supplied by the provider for the recordset.

> *Recordset*.**Properties**

You can iterate through the `Properties` collection to access each `Property` object individually:

```
For Each objProp in objRec.Properties
    Print "property name is " & objProp.Name
Next
```

The `Properties` collection is discussed in more detail in Appendix C.

New Properties

There are a few dynamic properties new to version 2.1 which are worth covering in a little detail here, rather than in Appendix C, where you might miss them.

The Resync Command Property

The `Resync Command` property specifies a command string that the recordset's `Resync` method will use to refresh data in the `Unique Table`. This allows you to customize what happens when data in the `Unique Table` is resynchronized. For example, imagine that a recordset is created by the following query:

```
SELECT *
FROM    publishers JOIN titles
ON      publishers.pub_id = titles.pub_id
```

Here, the Unique Table property should be set to titles, and its primary key, title_id, is the key that uniquely identifies rows in this recordset. You can specify that only records from the Unique Table that match the non-unique table are resynchronized. This allows you to resynchronize the data for just the Unique Table, rather that data for the whole query.

The Resync Command would therefore be:

```
SELECT  *
FROM    publishers JOIN titles
ON      publishers.pub_id = titles.pub_id
WHERE   titles.title_id = ?
```

The Resync Command should generally be the same as the recordset definition, but with the addition of a WHERE clause parameterizing the primary key of the Unique Table. You add a question mark as the parameter, and ADO handles the matching of this to the non-unique table. In the example above, the result is that only the records that matched the original query are returned.

The rows affected by the Resync are dependent upon the Update Resync property, described below.

The Unique Catalog Property

The Unique Catalog property specifies the catalog (or database name, depending upon your database server terminology) containing the table named in the Unique Table property.

The Update Resync Property

The Update Resync property specifies whether an implicit Resync method is called directly after an UpdateBatch method. This gives you the choice as to what values (if any) are resynchronized. One of the main reasons for the inclusion of these Resync properties is the need for client-cursor based applications to have a better way of handling data changes, especially the insertion of new records.

The values for this property can be one or more of the CEResyncEnum constants:

❑   adResyncNone, to indicate that no Resync is performed.

❑   adResyncAutoIncrement, to indicate that a Resync is performed for all successfully-inserted rows, including values of any auto-incremental columns. This is the default.

❑   adResyncConflicts, to indicate that a Resync is performed for updated or deleted rows that failed because of concurrency conflicts.

❑   adResyncUpdates, to indicate that a Resync is performed for all rows that were updated successfully.

❑   adResyncInserts, to indicate that a Resync is performed for all rows that were successfully inserted, including values of any auto-incremental columns.

❑   adResyncAll, to indicate that a Resync is performed for all rows that have pending changes.

These constants are part of the standard ADO type library.

To set more than one value you should join them together:

```
objRec.Properties("Update Resync") = adResyncUpdates OR adResyncInserts
```

The Unique Schema Property

The Unique Schema property specifies the schema (or owner, depending upon your database server terminology) of the table named in the Unique Table property.

The Unique Table Property

The Unique Table property specifies the name of the base table upon which edits are allowed. This is required when recordsets are created from JOIN statements. For example, consider the following SQL statement:

```
SELECT *
FROM    publishers JOIN titles
ON      publishers.pub_id = titles.pub_id
```

In this example you could set Unique Table to titles, to indicate that titles is the table that contains the unique information. For many-to-one queries, you generally set Unique Table to point to the many table, since this is the table that will contain unique keys for the recordset.

When Unique Table is set, the AddNew, Delete, Resync, Update and UpdateBatch methods of the recordset only affect the table named in this property.

You should generally set the Unique Schema or Unique Catalog properties before setting the Unique Table property, as the table, schema, and catalog names uniquely identify the base table.

The Unique Table is directly related to the Resync Command property.

Collections

Nearly everything you do in ADO uses a collection of some sort. Even the simple task of opening a `Recordset` gives you a collection of fields. When looking at collections you need to look at two things:

❑   The collection itself

❑   The objects of which the collection comprises

You'll find that the ADO collections and objects are named sensibly, where the collection is the plural and the object the singular:

Object	Collection
Error	Errors
Field	Fields
Parameter	Parameters
Property	Properties

In this chapter we'll look at the `Error`, `Field` and `Property` objects, and their associated collections. The `Parameter` object and `Parameters` collection are discussed in Chapter 4.

The Error Object

An `Error` object is used to hold all of the details pertaining to a single error (or warning) from an OLEDB provider, and therefore contains only data access errors. `Error` objects are stored together in the `Errors` collection, which in turn belongs to the `Connection` object. This means that if you want to access the errors, you have to refer to the `Errors` collection of the connection on which they were generated. For example, if you have an explicit connection object called `objConn`, the first error in the collection can be accessed as follows:

```
objConn.Errors(0).Description
```

Here's another example. If you had a `Recordset` object without an explicit connection, then you can use the recordset's `ActiveConnection` property to get access to the errors:

```
objRec.ActiveConnection.Errors(0).Description
```

Since each `Error` object contains a single error, and the provider can return multiple errors, you should really iterate through the entire `Errors` collection to see all of the possible errors. In Visual Basic, for example, you would do this:

```
Dim objErr As ADODB.Error

For Each objErr in objConn.Errors
    Print "Error: " & objErr.Description
Next
```

Methods of the Error Object

The `Error` object has no methods.

Properties of the Error Object

The Description Property

A description string associated with the error.

> *String = Error.**Description***

This is the default property of the `Error` object, so it can be omitted if required. The following two lines of code, for example, are equivalent:

```
Print objConn.Errors(0).Description
```

```
Print objConn.Errors(0)
```

The HelpContext Property

Indicates the ContextID in the help file for the associated error, if one exists.

> *Long = Error.**HelpContext***

You can use this property if you wish to integrate your application with the standard Windows help system. You can do this by calling the Windows API Help functions, then using the `HelpContext` to identify the ID number of the help description.

If no further help is available, this property will have the value 0.

The HelpFile Property

Indicates the name of the help file, if one exists.

> *String = Error.**HelpFile***

Use this in conjunction with the `HelpContext` property when interacting with the Windows help system. If no help file exists, this will be an empty string.

The NativeError Property

Indicates the provider-specific error code for the associated error.

> *Long* = *Error*.NativeError

This is useful for identifying errors produced, say, in stored procedures. The native error will be the *underlying* error code. So, if an error is generated in the data store, it's this error that is returned via the `NativeError` property. This is useful for tracking down the error in the provider documentation, since the `NativeError` is the error code returned by the data provider.

The Number Property

Indicates the number that uniquely identifies an `Error` object.

> *Long* = *Error*.Number

This is a unique ADO number (equivalent to the Windows API `HRESULT`) that corresponds to the error condition. For example, many database-related errors will generate their own error number, which gets stored in the `NativeError` property, and the ADO `Number` property will probably get set to one of the following non-specific errors:

❑　–2147217900 (hex 80040E14) – 'The command contained one or more errors'

❑　–2147467259 (hex 80004005) – 'Unspecified error'

In either case, we can deduce that it was an underlying object that caused the error.

If an `Error` object represents a warning (rather than an error) then its `Number` property will be 0. A full list of the error numbers is included in Appendix P.

The Source Property

Indicates the name of the object or application that originally generated the error.

> *String* = *Error*.Source

This could come from the class name of an object, the provider, or ADO. For example, ADO errors will be in the form:

`ADODB.`*`ObjectName`*

where *`ObjectName`* is the ADO object that generated the error. You'll notice that, in the errors shown in the *Error Examples* section (later in this chapter), the `Source` doesn't follow this form: this is because those errors were generated by the provider.

The SQLState Property

Indicates the SQL state for a given Error object.

> *String = Error*.SQLState

This will contain the 5-character SQL error code if the error occurred during a SQL command. If the error doesn't have a specific state then this may be blank. You should consult your provider's SQL documentation for a list of these error codes.

The SQL State error codes are defined by the SQL Access Group and the X/Open group, and are a standard for SQL error messages. Most database documentation will contain a list of SQL Error messages.

The Errors Collection

The Errors collection contains zero or more Error objects, each representing a single error from the provider. Certain actions may produce more than one piece of information, so each is placed in its own error object, but the collection of errors relates to a single provider error.

Methods of the Errors Collection

The Clear Method

Removes all of the Error objects from the Errors collection.

> *Errors*.Clear

This is called automatically when an error occurs, so the new error information can be entered. It is ADO (rather than the provider) that performs this clearing – this enables the provider to supply multiple errors details in response to a single error condition. There's no way to stop this happening; if you need to keep error information you can store it in a custom data store, such as a collection or recordset.

You might think that this is a bit superfluous if the Errors collection is cleared automatically, but there are some actions that cause the Errors collection to be filled with warning information. This specifically affects the Resync, UpdateBatch and CancelBatch methods of the recordset, where records may have been deleted at the source whilst you were editing them.

Another case of this is miscellaneous warnings from the provider. For example, look at the following lines of code:

```
Dim objRec As New ADODB.Recordset
objRec.Open "authors", "DSN=pubs", _
            adOpenDynamic, adLockOptimistic, adCmdTable
```

This may appear fairly innocuous, but running this may fill in an `Error` in the `Errors` collection of the `ActiveConnection` property of the recordset. For SQL Server you get the following:

```
Description:     [Microsoft][ODBC SQL Server Driver]Cursor concurrency changed
HelpContext:     0
HelpFile:
NativeError:     0
Number:     0
Source:     Microsoft OLE DB Provider for ODBC Drivers
SQLState:     01S02
```

There's nothing wrong here; it's just that when you create a `Recordset` object, the cursor type is initially `adForwardOnly`. But here we have requested a different type, so the provider kindly tells us that it has changed the cursor type. These warnings are dependent upon the provider and data store. You can differentiate between errors and warnings in your `Errors` collection by checking for an error number of 0 (signifying a warning) in your error routines.

The Refresh Method

Updates the `Error` objects with information from the provider.

> *Errors*.**Refresh**

You can use this to ensure that the `Errors` collection contains the latest set of error information from the provider.

Properties of the Errors Collection

The Count Property

Indicates the number of `Error` objects in the `Errors` collection.

> *Long = Errors*.**Count**

You can use the Visual Basic or VBScript `For Each..Next` command to iterate through the `Errors` collection without using the `Count` property. For example:

```
For Each objErr In objConn.Errors
    Print objErr.Number & " " & objErr.Description
Next
```

The Item Property

Allows indexing into the `Errors` collection to reference a specific `Error` object.

> *Error = Errors*.**Item**(*Index*)

Name	Type	Description	Default
Index	Variant	The number of the error in the collection. Zero based.	

This is the default property of the `Errors` collection and can be omitted. For example, both of the following lines are identical:

```
objConn.Errors.Item(1)
```

```
objConn.Errors(1)
```

If you're coding in a scripting language then you should specify the `Item` property – omitting `Item` causes a small performance penalty, because an extra internal call to `IDispatch` is required to query the interface.

Error Examples

The following piece of Visual Basic code shows a good way to list all of the errors in the `Errors` collection:

```
Public Sub ErrorTest()
    ' set the error handling on
    On Error GoTo ShowErrors

    ' declare a new command object and an error object
    Dim objCmd    As New ADODB.Command
    Dim objErr    As ADODB.Error

    ' set the command and run it
    objCmd.ActiveConnection = "DSN=pubs"
    objCmd.CommandText = "UPDATE pub_info SET pub_id='1111' " & _
                         "WHERE pub_id='9999'"
    objCmd.CommandType = adCmdText
    objCmd.Execute

    Exit Sub

ShowErrors:
    ' loop through the errors
    For Each objErr In objCmd.ActiveConnection.Errors
       Debug.Print "Description:"; vbTab; objErr.Description
       Debug.Print "HelpContext:"; vbTab; objErr.HelpContext
       Debug.Print "HelpFile:"; vbTab; objErr.HelpFile
       Debug.Print "NativeError:"; vbTab; objErr.NativeError
       Debug.Print "Number:"; vbTab; objErr.Number
       Debug.Print "Source:"; vbTab; objErr.Source
       Debug.Print "SQLState:"; vbTab; objErr.SQLState
    Next
End Sub
```

This uses the `pubs` databases, and tries to run a SQL statement that violates referential integrity.

If you run this command using different OLEDB providers and data stores, you'll get similar (but not quite the same) results – as the following subsections show.

OLEDB Provider for ODBC to SQL Server

```
Description:    [Microsoft][ODBC SQL Server Driver][SQL Server]UPDATE
statement conflicted with COLUMN FOREIGN KEY constraint
'FK__pub_info__pub_id__2AEA69DC'. The conflict occurred in database 'pubs',
table 'publishers', column 'pub_id'
HelpContext:    0
HelpFile:
NativeError:    547
Number:    -2147217900
Source:    Microsoft OLE DB Provider for ODBC Drivers
SQLState:    23000
```

```
Description:    [Microsoft][ODBC SQL Server Driver][SQL Server]Command has
been aborted.
HelpContext:    0
HelpFile:
NativeError:    3621
Number:    -2147217900
Source:    Microsoft OLE DB Provider for ODBC Drivers
SQLState:    01000
```

Using the OLEDB provider for ODBC connected to SQL Server, you will notice that you get two errors generated. The first is an error indicating the exact nature of the error, and the second indicates that the command has been aborted. You can clearly see the SQL Server error numbers and descriptions.

You can also see that the ADO error number is the same – this corresponds to 'The command contained one or more errors', so it's important you use the `NativeError` property to identify the exact problem.

A full list of ADO error numbers and descriptions is included in Appendix P.

OLEDB Provider for ODBC to Access

```
Description:    [Microsoft][ODBC Microsoft Access Driver] You can't add or
change a record because a related record is required in table 'publishers'.
HelpContext:    0
HelpFile:
NativeError:    -1613
Number:    -2147217900
Source:    Microsoft OLE DB Provider for ODBC Drivers
SQLState:    23000
```

Using the OLEDB provider for ODBC connecting to an Access database with the same structure, you only get one error – the actual error that occurred. The Access ODBC driver doesn't send an extra error back.

SQL Server Provider

```
Description:    UPDATE statement conflicted with COLUMN FOREIGN KEY
constraint 'FK_pub_info_publishers'. The conflict occurred in database
'pubs', table 'publishers', column 'pub_id'.
HelpContext:    0
HepFile:
NativeError:    547
Number:    -2147217900
Source:    Microsoft OLE DB Provider for SQL Server
SQLState:    23000
```

```
Description:    The statement has been aborted.
HelpContext:    0
HepFile:
NativeError:    3621
Number:    -2147217900
Source:    Microsoft OLE DB Provider for SQL Server
SQLState:    01000
```

Using the native OLEDB driver for SQL Server we get two errors – almost identical to the ODBC details.

Jet Provider

```
Description:    You can't add or change a record because a related record is
required in table 'publishers'.  '
HelpContext:    5003000
HelpFile:
NativeError:    -535037517
Number:    -2147467259
Source:    Microsoft JET Database Engine
SQLState:    3201
```

For the OLEDB provider for Jet we only get one error, but we do get a full description of it. Notice that the ADO error number is slightly different – this corresponds to 'Unspecified error'. Also notice that the `NativeError` property returns a different error number than for the ODBC case, although both of these error numbers correspond to 'Application-defined or object defined error'.

The Field Object

A `Field` object represents a single field (or column) in a recordset. When you open a recordset, you'll find a `Fields` collection which contains zero or more `Field` objects. This `Fields` collection will contain a `Field` object for each column in the recordset, and as you move through the records, the `Fields` collection changes its contents to represents the fields of the chosen record.

Although `Field` objects can exist on their own, they are really only useful when used in conjunction with a `Recordset` object. Unless you are creating your own recordsets (with the `Recordset` object's `Append` method), where you create fields, you'll generally be dealing with existing `Field` objects. You can reference these in several ways. The first is by accessing the `Field` directly through the `Fields` collection (as in the following examples, where we print the data types of some `Field` objects):

```
Print objRec.Fields(0).Type
```

```
Print objRec.Fields("FirstName").Type
```

The `Fields` collection is the default collection of a recordset and can therefore be omitted, if desired:

```
Print objRec("FirstName").Type
```

Second, you can use a `Field` object explicitly in your code:

```
Dim objFld As ADODB.Field

Set objFld = objRec.Fields("FirstName")
Print objFld.Type
```

Third, you can use the `Item` property of the `Fields` collection:

```
Print objRec.Fields.Item("FirstName")
```

All of these methods are functionally equivalent, although there may be performance differences. Using the `Item` property is faster in scripting languages, and using a `Field` object will be faster if you plan to reference several properties or methods of a single field.

Methods of the Field Object

The AppendChunk Method

Appends data to a large or binary `Field` object.

> *Field*.**AppendChunk(***Data***)**

Name	Type	Description	Default
Data	Variant	The data to be appended to the object.	

The first call to `AppendChunk` (after an you start editing a field) writes data to the field, overwriting any existing data in the buffer. Subsequent calls add to existing data.

This is most often used when dealing with images or large text fields stored in databases. A full discussion of this is included at the end of this chapter.

The GetChunk Method

Returns all or a portion of the contents of a large or binary `Field` object.

> *Variant = Field*.**GetChunk(***Length***)**

Name	Type	Description	Default
Length	Long	The number of bytes or characters to be retrieved.	

The first call returns data starting from the start of the field. Subsequent calls start where the last call left off.

Like `AppendChunk`, this is most often used with images, and a full discussion is included at the end of the chapter.

Properties of the Field Object

The ActualSize Property

Indicates the actual length, in bytes, of a field's value.

> *Long = Field*.**ActualSize**
> *Field*.**ActualSize** = *Long*

You should use this property when you need to set or find out how long a field actually is (rather than how long it can be – for that, use the `DefinedSize` property). For fixed length data types these two properties will be the same, but they may be different for variable length data.

The Attributes Property

Indicates characteristics of a `Field` object.

> *Long = Field*.**Attributes**

This will be one or more of the following FieldAttributeEnum values:

❑ `adFldMayDefer`, to indicate that the contents of the field are not retrieved from the provider along with the rest of the data, but are only retrieved when they are referenced. This is particularly useful for recordsets that contain large BLOBs, where the BLOB may not be referenced.

❑ `adFldUpdatable`, to indicate that the field can be updated.

❑ `adFldUnknownUpdatable`, to indicate that the provider doesn't know whether the field can be updated.

❑ `adFldFixed`, to indicate that the field contains fixed length data.

❑ `adFldIsNullable`, to indicate that Null values can be used when writing to the field.

❑ `adFldMayBeNull`, to indicate that the field may contain a Null value when you read from the field.

❑ `adFldLong`, to indicate that `AppendChunk` and `GetChunk` can be used on the field, since it contains long binary data.

❑ `adFldRowID`, to indicate that the field contains a RowID that cannot be updated. This doesn't indicate the Access **AutoNumber** or SQL Server **IDENTITY** fields, but rather an internal row number field, which is unique across the database. Oracle has these natively whereas many other data stores don't.

❑ `adFldRowVersion`, to indicate a field that uniquely identifies the version of the row, such as a SQL **Timestamp** field.

❑ `adFldCacheDeferred` to indicate that the values for this field will be cached once it has been read for the first time, and reading the value again will read from the cache.

❑ `adNegativeScale` to indicate that the values for this field have a negative scale.

❑ `adKeyColumn` to indicate that this field is part of the key.

Since this property can be a combination of values, it may not directly match one of the above constants. To check that a value is set you should use a procedure like this:

```
If (Field.Attributes AND ad_constant) = ad_constant Then
  Print "field supports that attribute"
End If
```

For example, to check to see if a field might contain Null values:

```
Set objField = objRec.Fields("field_that_might_be_null")
If (objField.Attributes And adFldMayBeNull) = adFldMayBeNull Then
  Print "Field may contain a null"
End If
```

Note that this field is read/write when fabricating your own recordsets, and becomes read-only once this fabricated recordset is opened.

The DataFormat Property

Identifies the format the data should be displayed in.

> Set *DataFormatObject* = *Field*.**DataFormat**
> Set *Field*.**DataFormat** = *DataFormatObject*

This was new in ADO 2.0 and is only useful when used in conjunction with Visual Basic 6 or Visual J++ 6, which include the `DataFormat` object. This object contains several properties to identify the type of data the object holds, and the way in which it should be displayed. For example, in Visual Basic 6 you could do this:

```
Set txtDate.DataFormat = objRec.Fields("InvoiceDate").DataFormat
```

For more information on this you should consult the Visual Basic 6 or Visual J++ 6 documentation.

The DefinedSize Property

Indicates the defined size of the `Field` object.

> *Long* = *Field*.**DefinedSize**

For variable width fields this indicates the maximum width of the field – as opposed to the `ActualSize` property which identifies the actual size. For example, a SQL Server column declared as `varchar(20)` would have a `DefinedSize` of 20, irrespective of the actual size of the text it contains.

Note that this field is read/write when creating your own recordsets, and becomes read only once the fabricated recordset is opened.

The Name Property

Indicates the name of the `Field` object.

> *String* = *Field*.**Name**

This is a necessary field when creating your own `Field` objects to add to the existing `Fields` collection, or when creating a new recordset.

It is also useful when dynamically creating tables in ASP Script code, or filling grids manually in Visual Basic. For example, in ASP you could create a table header using the `Name` property:

```
Response.Write "<TABLE><THEAD><TR>"
For Each objField In objRec.Fields
   Response.Write "<TH>" & objField.Name & "</TH>"
Next
Response.Write "</TR></THEAD>"
```

You could then go on to create the rest of the table using the values from the recordset.

Note that this field is read/write when creating your own recordsets, and becomes read-only once the fabricated recordset is opened.

The NumericScale Property

Indicates the scale of numeric values for the `Field` object.

> *Byte = Field*.**NumericScale**

This identifies how many digits are stored to the right of the decimal place for numeric data.

Note that this field is read/write when creating your own recordsets, and becomes read-only once the fabricated recordset is opened.

The OriginalValue Property

Indicates the value of a `Field` object that existed in the record before any changes were made.

> *Variant = Field*.**OriginalValue**

The original value is the value stored in the field before any changes were saved to the provider. This is what allows the provider to simply return to the original value when you do a `CancelBatch` or `CancelUpdate` method call. For example:

```
' Assume when read that the field contains a value of 10.99
Set objField = objRec.Fields("Price")
objField.Value = 15.99
Print objField.OriginalValue      ' Prints 10.99
Print objField.Value              ' Prints 15.99
objRec.CancelUpdate
Print objField.Value              ' Prints 10.99
```

For related information see the `UnderlyingValue` and `Value` properties.

The Precision Property

Indicates the degree of precision for numeric values in the `Field` object.

> *Byte = Field*.**Precision**

The precision is the maximum number of digits that will be used. Note that this field is read/write when creating your own recordsets, and becomes read-only once the fabricated recordset is opened.

The Type Property

Indicates the data type of the `Field` object.

> *DataTypeEnum = Field*.**Type**

The data type will be one of the DataTypeEnum values, such as `adInteger` or `adVarChar`. Since this list is quite long, we've included it in Appendix B. Not all providers support all data types, but when creating recordsets you should be able to use all types, and the provider will compensate for any types it doesn't support by converting them into an equivalent supported type. When creating your own recordsets, you should use the data type most appropriate to the type of data you wish to store.

Note that this field is read/write when creating your own recordsets, and becomes read-only once the fabricated recordset is opened.

The UnderlyingValue Property

Indicates a `Field` object's current value in the database.

> *Variant = Field*.UnderlyingValue

The underlying value differs from the original value, as this property holds the current value of the field as stored in the cursor. This would, for example, hold the value if another user changed the value of a field. So if you call the `Resync` method, your fields will get repopulated with values from the `UnderlyingValue` property.

The `UnderlyingValue` is really only useful for those situations where your cursor will not see data changes by other users. In particular this will be:

❑ All client-side updateable cursors.
❑ Server-based keyset cursors, except for the OLE DB Provider for Jet.

Interestingly, there is a difference between server-side keyset and static cursors for the OLE DB Provider for SQL Server – despite the fact they both actually use keyset cursors. When requesting a keyset cursor you get a keyset cursor, and it supports `UnderlyingValue`. *However, when requesting a static cursor, you are returned a keyset cursor, but it doesn't support* `UnderlyingValue`. *If you examine the dynamic properties of the recordset under these two conditions you'll see that the properties are not the same, which seems to indicate that the Properties are not updated when the server changes the cursor type.*

This property is particularly useful when dealing with conflicts between values that you have changed and values that other users have changed. We examine conflict resolution in more detail in Chapter 5.

For related information see the `OriginalValue` and `Value` properties.

The Value Property

Indicates the value assigned to the `Field` object.

> *Variant = Field*.Value
> *Field*.Value = *Variant*

This indicates the current value of the field, and may not reflect the value stored in the database. The difference between the three value fields is quite simple:

❑ `Value` contains the current value of the field in your current recordset. So if you've made any changes to the field, they will be reflected in the `Value`.
❑ `OriginalValue` contains the value of the field as it was before you made any changes.
❑ `UnderlyingValue` contains the value of the field, as stored in the database, which might include changes made by other users.

This is the default property of a field and can be omitted if required. For example, the following lines of code are functionally equivalent:

```
Print objRec("FirstName").Value
```

```
Print objRec("FirstName")
```

```
Print objRec.Fields("FirstName")
```

One place where you might need to specify the `Value` property is when using collections. For example, consider the following Visual Basic code:

```
Dim colNames As New Collection

colNames.Add objRec.("FirstName"), "Name1"
Debug.Print colNames("Name1")
objRec.MoveNext
Debug.Print colNames("Name1")
```

You might expect the same name to be printed twice, since you probably assume that the name was the only thing to be stored in the collection. However, it's actually the `Field` object that gets stored in the collection, and the `Field` object just points to a particular field in the recordset. So, when you move to the next recordset, the `Field` reflects those changes. If you want to store the actual field contents in the collection you need to do this:

```
Dim colNames As New Collection

colNames.Add objRec.("FirstName").Value, "Name1"
```

For related information see the `UnderlyingValue` and `OriginalValue` properties.

Collections of the Field Object

The Properties Collection

Contains all of the `Property` objects for a `Field` object.

> *Field*.Properties

The `Properties` collection contains all of the properties that are associated with a particular field. This is discussed in more detail in Appendix C.

The Fields Collection

The `Fields` collection contains zero or more `Field` objects. In existing recordsets there will be one `Field` object for each column in the recordset. When creating new recordsets, you append `Field` objects to the `Fields` collection.

The `Fields` collection is the default collection of the `Recordset` object, which means that you don't need to specify its name. For example, the following two lines are functionally equivalent:

```
objRec.Fields("FirstName")
```

```
objRec("FirstName")
```

Scripting languages will suffer a slight performance penalty when omitting the default collection name.

Methods of the Fields Collection

The Append Method

Appends a `Field` object to the `Fields` collection.

> Fields.Append(*Name, Type, [DefinedSize], [Attrib]*)

Name	Type	Description	Default
Name	String	The name of a new field object.	
Type	Data TypeEnum	The data type of the new field.	`adEmpty`
Defined Size	Long	The defined size in characters or bytes of the new field. The default value is derived from `Type`.	0
Attrib	Field AttributeEnum	The attributes for the new field.	`adFldUnspecified`

You should set the `CursorLocation` property to `adUseClient` before calling this method, because you cannot append fields to an existing recordset created from a data store.

This is quite useful for those situations where you would like some data to be processed as a recordset, but it is not in a data store, and there is no provider for accessing it. You could create a recordset and append your own fields to it. For example:

```
Dim objRec   As New ADODB.Recordset

objRec.CursorLocation = adUseClient
objRec.Fields.Append "Name", adVarChar, 25, adFldMayBeNull
objRec.Fields.Append "Age", adInteger, 8, adFldFixed
```

Calling this method for an open recordset, or a recordset in which the `ActiveConnection` property has been set, will generate a run-time error. This applies even if the recordset has been disconnected from a data store.

Creating Recordsets

Creating recordsets actually has some very interesting uses, some of which have nothing to do with databases or large stores of data. Consider the following:

❑   You have a source of data for which there is no OLEDB provider, but you want to provide a consistent access to this data for your programmers. You could create a component that reads this data in, and then creates a recordset which is exposed to the caller of the component.

❑   You are creating a multi-tier client/server application that needs to pass data around from tier to tier, but you don't want it to be bound up creating arrays and odd structures. You could create a recordset that contains the data, and have the recordset passed around. This does, however, rely on having ADO installed on the client.

❑   You are using Microsoft Message Queue Server, and need to pass data in the messages. The body of an MSMQ message must be a string of data, or an object that can persist its data, and ADO 2 can do this. It's not actually the object itself that is passed, but its data and state. Suppose you have a group of traveling sales staff, who regularly need to send sales reports back to base: instead of having to connect back to the server to update the data, they could pass their data to-and-fro as a message, which means that the data is available to be processed whenever the server is free.

Creating a recordset is simply a matter of appending fields to an empty recordset that is not connected to a data source. For example, in Visual Basic this could be done with the following code:

```
Dim objRec      As New ADODB.Recordset

objRec.Fields.Append "OrderNumber", adVarChar, 10
objRec.Fields.Append "OrderDate", adVarChar, 20
```

This just creates a recordset with two fields, both holding text data, which can be null. At this stage you have a closed recordset, so you can open it, and then add data as though it were a recordset created from a data source.

The Delete Method

Deletes a `Field` object from the `Fields` collection.

> *Fields.**Delete**(Index)*

Name	Type	Description	Default
Index	Variant	The name or index number of the `Field` object to delete.	

You can use this to delete fields that you have added to your own recordset. For example:

```
objRec.Fields.Delete("Age")
```

You cannot use this method on an open recordset.

The Refresh Method

Updates the `Field` objects in the `Fields` collection.

> *Fields*.**Refresh**

Using this method has no visible effect. You should use the `Recordset` object's `Requery` method to retrieve changes.

Properties of the Fields Collection

The Count Property

Indicates the number of `Field` objects in the `Fields` collection.

> *Long = Fields*.**Count**

In Visual Basic or VBScript you can use the `For Each..Next` command to iterate through the `Fields` collection without referring to the `Count` property. For languages that do not support enumeration of collections you can use this property in a loop.

The Item Property

Allows indexing into the `Fields` collection to reference a specific `Field` object.

> *Field = Fields*.**Item**(*Index*)

Name	Type	Description	Default
Index	Variant	The name or index number of the item in the collection.	

This is the default property of the `Fields` collection and can be omitted. For example, the following lines are equivalent:

```
objRec.Fields.Item(1)
```

```
objRec.Fields(1)
```

```
objRec.Fields("FirstName")
```

```
objRec.Fields.Item("FirstName")
```

Since `Fields` is the default collection, you don't need to specify it in your code:

```
objRec("FirstName")
```

The Property Object

A `Property` object contains the attributes of a single property, for any of the following objects:

- ❏ Connection
- ❏ Command
- ❏ Recordset
- ❏ Field

Each of these objects contains a `Properties` collection, which contains zero or more `Property` objects. It's important to realize that these do not contain the standard properties for an object, but rather the extended, or provider specific properties.

A detailed list of properties is included in Appendix C.

Methods of the Property Object

The `Property` object has no methods.

Properties of the Property Object

The Attributes Property

Indicates characteristics of a `Property` object.

> *Long = Property*.**Attributes**

The `Attributes` can be one or more of the `PropertyAttributesEnum` values:

- ❏ `adPropNotSupported`, to indicate that the provider does not support the property.

- ❏ `adPropRequired`, to indicate that before the data source is initialized, this property must be specified.

- ❏ `adPropOptional`, to indicate that before the data source is initialized, this property does not have to be specified.

- ❏ `adPropRead`, to indicate that the property can be read by the user.

- ❏ `adPropWrite`, to indicate that the property can be set by the user.

For example, before you connect to SQL Server you can examine the `Attributes` of the `User ID` property in the `Properties` collection:

```
Print objConn.Properties("User ID").Attributes
```

This gives a value of **1537**, which is a combination of some of the above constants:

Attribute	Binary Value	Decimal Value
adPropRequired	00000000001	1
adPropRead	01000000000	512
adPropWrite	10000000000	1024
Total	11000000001	1537

You don't have to worry about the numbers because you can test the attributes using the constants:

```
intAttr = objConn.Properties("User ID").Attributes
If (intAttr AND adPropRequired) = adPropRequired Then
  ' Property is required
End If
```

The Name Property

Indicates the name of the Property object.

> *String = Property*.**Name**

This is the name by which the provider knows the property.

The Type Property

Indicates the data type of the Property object.

> *DataTypeEnum = Property*.**Type**

For example, the User ID property of a connection has a value of adBStr, which indicates a string.

The list of constants for DataTypeEnum is quite large, and is included in Appendix B.

The Value Property

Indicates the value assigned to the Property object.

> *Variant = Property*.**Value**
> *Property*.**Value** *= Variant*

Some properties may be read-only, and do not allow you to set the Value, so you should check the Attributes beforehand:

```
intAttr = objConn.Properties("property_name").Attributes
If (intAttr AND adPropWrite) = adPropWrite Then
  objConn.Properties("property_name").Value = some_value
End If
```

This is the default property of the Property object and can be omitted if desired.

The Properties Collection

The `Properties` collection contains zero or more `Property` objects, to indicate the extended properties of the applicable object. You can examine all of the properties by enumerating through the collection. For example:

```
For Each objProp In objConn.Properties
   Print objProp.Name
Next
```

This is a particularly good way to find out which extended properties are supported by a provider.

Methods of the Properties Collection

The Refresh Method

Updates the `Property` objects in the `Properties` collection with the details from the provider.

Properties.**Refresh**

The `Refresh` method is useful for the `Properties` collection because the default provider is the OLEDB Provider for ODBC: if you have set the `Provider` property to point to a different provider, you will need to `Refresh` the properties to ensure that they are applicable to the changed provider.

Properties of the Properties Collection

The Count Property

Indicates the number of `Property` objects in the `Properties` collection.

Long = Properties.**Count**

You can use the Visual Basic or VBScript `For Each..Next` command to iterate through the properties collection without using the `Count` property. For languages that do not support enumeration of collections you can use this property in a loop.

The Item Property

Allows indexing into the `Properties` collection to reference a specific `Property` object.

Property = Properties.**Item(***Index***)**

Name	Type	Description	Default
Index	Variant	The number or name of the property in the collection. Zero-based.	

This is the default property of the `Properties` collection and can be omitted. For example, the following lines are equivalent:

```
object.Properties.Item(1)
```

```
object.Properties(1)
```

```
object.Properties("property_name")
```

Indexing

ADO 2.0 introduced the concept of **local indexing**, for client cursors, and although it's fairly rudimentary at the moment, it can still be quite useful. This is achieved using one of the `Field` object's dynamic properties, called `Optimize`. The way it works is that you decide which field you want to index, and then set the `Optimize` property to `True`. For example:

```
Set objField = objRec("au_lname")
objField.Properties("Optimize") = True
```

You don't have to use a `Field` object, as you can just access the properties directly from the recordset's field:

```
objRec("au_lname").Properties("Optimize") = True
```

This creates a local index, which will improve sorting and finding records. Setting the property to `False` will delete the index.

Future versions of ADO are expected to provide an `Indexes` collection and `Index` objects to help us manage, and give us greater control over, local indexes. Microsoft has yet to finalize plans for this.

Using Images with ADO

This can be one of the most confusing aspects of using databases, as it never seems quite as intuitive as it should be. Many people say that storing images in databases isn't the most efficient use of the storage, and that it can be slow. However, there are times when you need to do this, such as when you have legacy data or if a third party supplies your data to you.

I think a preferable solution is to store the images on disc as files, and just store the file name in the database.

Images and Parameters

There are a few simple rules to follow when using images with parameters:

❑ If reading and writing images from disc, then you should read into, and write from, a Byte array.

❑ The ADO `Parameter` object's `Type` should be `adVarBinary`.

❑ The ADO `Parameter` object's `Length` should be the maximum size of the binary data. For a SQL Server `image` or an Access OLE Object parameter this is 2,147,483,647.

❑ Either set the `Value` property directly, or use `GetChunk` and `AppendChunk` to get the image data into your ADO Parameter.

One thing to watch out for when dealing with images using stored procedures in SQL Server is that your procedure cache might not be big enough to allow the use of large images. In this case you'll get error 701, and you should consult the SQL Server documentation for details of how to increase this cache.

Here are a few examples to show how this works.

Storing Images using Parameters

The following shows how you could read an image from a file and store it in a SQL Server database. We'll use Visual Basic to grab the image file, and a stored procedure to place it in the database. Here's the stored procedure:

```
CREATE PROCEDURE usp_UpdateLogo
    @PubID      char(4),
    @Logo       image
AS
    UPDATE    pub_info
    SET       logo = @Logo
    WHERE     pub_id = @PubID
```

This simply updates the `logo` field for the publisher id supplied.

The code to call this procedure from Visual Basic could look like this:

```
Dim objConn     As New ADODB.Connection
Dim objCmd      As New ADODB.Command
Dim bytChunk()  As Byte
Dim varChunk    As Variant

' open bitmap file
Open "c:\temp\wrox.bmp" For Binary As #1

' resize the byte array, read in the data space, and close it.
ReDim bytChunk(LOF(1))
Get #1, , bytChunk()
varChunk = StrConv(bytChunk, vbUnicode)
Erase bytChunk
Close #1

' connect to data store
objConn.Open "Provider=SQLOLEDB; Data Source=Tigger; " & _
             "Initial Catalog=pubs; User ID=sa; Password="

' set up command
With objCmd
    Set .ActiveConnection = objConn
    .CommandText = "usp_UpdateLogo"
    .CommandType = adCmdStoredProc

    ' create the parameters
    .Parameters.Append .CreateParameter("@PubID", adVarChar, _
                                    adParamInput, 4, "0736")
    .Parameters.Append .CreateParameter("@Logo", adVarBinary, _
                                    adParamInput, 2147483647)

    ' set the parameter value
    ' use either this command, which is commented out
    ' .Parameters("@Logo").Value = varChunk

    ' or this one
    .Parameters("@Logo").AppendChunk varChunk
```

```
        ' now run the command
        .Execute
End With

objConn.Close

Set objCmd = Nothing
Set objConn = Nothing
```

Passing the Image in Smaller Chunks

You may find that reading the whole image file into memory at once is wasteful of resources, especially considering how large images can be. You can break this down into smaller chunks, and use `AppendChunk` to append chunks of the image into the parameter. The Visual Basic code from above would be modified like this:

```
Dim objConn        As New ADODB.Connection
Dim objCmd         As New ADODB.Command
Dim bytChunk(512)  As Byte                   ' Note the size
Dim varChunk       As Variant

' open bitmap file
Open "c:\temp\wrox.bmp" For Binary As #1

' don't read the image file yet

' connect to data store
objConn.Open "Provider=SQLOLEDB; Data Source=Tigger; " & _
             "Initial Catalog=pubs; User ID=sa; Password="

' set up command
With objCmd
    .ActiveConnection = objConn
    .CommandText = "usp_UpdateLogo"
    .CommandType = adCmdStoredProc

    ' create the parameters
    .Parameters.Append .CreateParameter("@PubID", adVarChar, _
                                 adParamInput, 4, "0736")
    .Parameters.Append .CreateParameter("@Logo", adVarBinary, _
                                 adParamInput, 2147483647)

    ' continue reading from file whilst we haven't hit EOF
    While Not EOF(1)
        ' Read in a small chunk. The amount read is determined
        ' by the size of the byte array we are reading into
        Get #1, , bytChunk()

        ' Append the smaller array to the parameter
        .Parameters("@Logo").AppendChunk bytChunk()
    Wend

    ' run the command
    .Execute
End With

objConn.Close
Close #1

Set objCmd = Nothing
Set objConn = Nothing
```

This performs exactly the same action, only using a small chunk of memory to repeatedly read in from the image file. You may find this marginally slower, but it is more efficient on memory and network resources.

Retrieving Images using Parameters

If you want to retrieve images from a database via a stored procedure, the first thing to note is that it's *not* possible to assign an image to a variable (at least, not with SQL Server). This means that you cannot have a stored procedure like this:

```
CREATE PROCEDURE
    @PubID    char(4),
    @Logo     image OUTPUT
AS
    SELECT  @Logo = logo
    FROM    pub_info
    WHERE   pub_id = @PubID
```

Instead, if you need to extract images using a stored procedure, then you must return a recordset.

Images and Fields

Using images with `Recordset` fields is very similar to using `Parameters`.

Storing Images in Fields

To store images directly into fields quite simply requires a call to the `AppendChunk` method. The following Visual Basic code shows this:

```
Dim objConn     As New ADODB.Connection
Dim objCmd      As New ADODB.Command
Dim objRec      As ADODB.Recordset
Dim bytChunk()  As Byte

' open bitmap file
Open "c:\temp\single.bmp" For Binary As #1

' resize the byte array, read in the data, and close it.
ReDim bytChunk(LOF(1))
Get #1, , bytChunk()
Close #1

' open the connection
objConn.Open "Provider=SQLOLEDB; Data Source=Tigger; " & _
             "Initial Catalog=pubs; User ID=sa; Password="

With objCmd
    ' set the commmand properties
    .ActiveConnection = objConn
    .CommandText = "usp_FetchLogo"
    .CommandType = adCmdStoredProc

    ' create the parameters
    .Parameters.Append .CreateParameter("@PubID", adVarChar, _
                                    adParamInput, 4, "0736")

    ' create and open a new recordset
    Set objRec = New ADODB.Recordset
    objRec.Open objCmd, , adOpenDynamic, adLockOptimistic, adCmdStoredProc
End With

' update the logo field, passing in the image
objRec("logo").AppendChunk (bytChunk)
objRec.Update
```

```
objRec.Close
objConn.Close

Set objRec = Nothing
set objCmd = Nothing
Set objConn = Nothing
```

In this case, we've used a stored procedure called `usp_FetchLogo` to fetch
the image from the database. The SQL code for `usp_FetchLogo` is shown
later in this chapter.

Smaller Chunks

To use a smaller chunk size to conserve the memory resources on the client is quite
simple too.

```
Dim objConn          As New ADODB.Connection
Dim objCmd           As New ADODB.Command
Dim objRec           As ADODB.Recordset
Dim bytChunk(512)    As Byte                        ' note the size

' don't read the bitmap file yet

' open the connection
objConn.Open "Provider=SQLOLEDB; Data Source=Tigger; " & _
             "Initial Catalog=pubs; User ID=sa; Password="

With objCmd
    ' set the command properties
    .ActiveConnection = objConn
    .CommandText = "usp_FetchLogo"
    .CommandType = adCmdStoredProc

    ' create the parameters
    .Parameters.Append .CreateParameter("@PubID", adVarChar, _
                                adParamInput, 4, "0736")

    ' create and open the recordset
    Set objRec = New ADODB.Recordset
    objRec.Open objCmd, , adOpenDynamic, adLockOptimistic, adCmdStoredProc
End With

' open bitmap file
Open "c:\temp\chunks.bmp" For Binary As #1

' whilst we haven't reached the end of the image file
While Not EOF(1)
    ' Read in a small chunk. The amount read is determined
    ' by the size of the byte array we are reading into
    Get #1, , bytChunk()

    ' append this small array to the field
    objRec("logo").AppendChunk (bytChunk)
Wend
Close #1

' update the field
objRec.Update

objRec.Close
objConn.Close

Set objRec = Nothing
Set objCmd = Nothing
Set objConn = Nothing
```

Retrieving Images from Fields

Retrieving images from fields is extremely simple, using the `Value` of the field, or the `GetChunk` method. This Visual Basic code shows how it can be done:

```
Dim objConn      As New ADODB.Connection
Dim objCmd       As New ADODB.Command
Dim objRec       As ADODB.Recordset
Dim bytChunk()   As Byte

' open the connection
objConn.Open "Provider=SQLOLEDB; Data Source=Tigger; " & _
             "Initial Catalog=pubs; User ID=sa; Password="

With objCmd
    ' set up the command
    .ActiveConnection = objConn
    .CommandText = "usp_FetchLogo"
    .CommandType = adCmdStoredProc

    ' create the parameters
    .Parameters.Append .CreateParameter("@PubID", adVarChar, _
                                adParamInput, 4, "0736")

    ' now run the command
    Set objRec = objCmd.Execute
End With

' extract the logo into a variable
bytChunk = objRec("logo")

' store the image to a file and load it into a picture box
' Note: Visual Basic has no method to accept the image directly
'       from the variable so you have to save it to disk first
Open "c:\temp\image.bmp" For Binary As #1
Put #1, , bytChunk()
Close #1
Picture1.Picture = LoadPicture("c:\temp\image.bmp")

objRec.Close
objConn.Close

Set objRec = Nothing
Set objCmd = Nothing
Set objConn = Nothing
```

This used a command object and parameters, but you could equally use just a recordset and return a whole set of records with images.

Small Chunks

One of the disadvantages of using the above method is that for a large image it requires a large amount of memory on the client, and is not particularly efficient. If you think about how large images can get, then there seems little point in clogging up the user machine with a large amount of dynamic storage.

To alleviate this problem you can use `GetChunks` and limit the amount it reads. For example, the above Visual Basic code rewritten would be like this:

```
Dim objConn      As New ADODB.Connection
Dim objCmd       As New ADODB.Command
Dim objRec       As ADODB.Recordset
Dim bytChunk()   As Byte
Dim varChunk     As Variant
```

```
' open the connection
objConn.Open "Provider=SQLOLEDB; Data Source=Tigger; " & _
             "Initial Catalog=pubs; User ID=sa; Password="

With objCmd
    ' set up the command
    .ActiveConnection = objConn
    .CommandText = "usp_FetchLogo"
    .CommandType = adCmdStoredProc

    ' create the parameters
    .Parameters.Append .CreateParameter("@PubID", adVarChar, _
                                        adParamInput, 4, "0736")

    ' now run the command
    Set objRec = objCmd.Execute
End With
```

```
' open the output file
Open "c:\temp\barf.bmp" For Binary As #1

' read in the first chunk
varChunk = objRec("logo").GetChunk(512)

' GetChunk returns Null if there is no more data
While Not IsNull(varChunk)
    ' convert the data to a byte array and write it to the file
    bytChunk = varChunk
    Put #1, , bytChunk()

    ' read in the next chunk
    varChunk = objRec("logo").GetChunk(512)
Wend
```

```
' close the file and load the picture
Close #1
Picture1.Picture = LoadPicture("c:\temp\barf.bmp")

objRec.Close
objConn.Close

Set objRec = Nothing
Set objCmd = Nothing
Set objConn = Nothing
```

You might think that this is much slower, but the delay is hardly noticeable.

Images Using ASP

The same sort of procedure is just as simple in ASP, to push an image to the browser. We'll start with a stored procedure to fetch the image:

```
CREATE PROCEDURE usp_FetchLogo
    @lPubID  int
AS
    SELECT    logo
    FROM      pub_info
    WHERE     pub_id = @lPubId
```

Now imagine an ASP page called `GetLogo.asp`:

```
<!--METADATA TYPE="TypeLib" FILE="C:\Program Files\Common
Files\SYSTEM\ADO\MSADO15.DLL"-->
<%
    ' turn on buffering and set the mime type
    Response.Buffer = True
    Response.ContentType = "image/bmp"

    Dim objConn
    Dim objCmd
    Dim objRec
    Dim bytChunk
    Dim sID

    ' get the required id
    sID = Request.QueryString("pub_id")

    Set objConn = Server.CreateObject("ADODB.Connection")
    Set objCmd = Server.CreateObject("ADODB.Command")
    Set objRec = Server.CreateObject("ADODB.Recordset")

    ' open the connection
    objConn.Open "Provider=SQLOLEDB; Data Source=Tigger; " & _
                "Initial Catalog=pubs; User ID=sa; Password="

    ' set the command details
    objCmd.ActiveConnection = objConn
    objCmd.CommandText = "usp_FetchLogo"
    objCmd.CommandType = adCmdStoredProc

    objCmd.Parameters.Append objCmd.CreateParameter("@PubID", adVarChar, _
                                        adParamInput, 4, sID)

    ' run the command and extract the logo
    Set objRec = objCmd.Execute
    bytChunk = objRec("logo")

    ' write image to the browser
    Response.BinaryWrite bytChunk
    Response.End
%>
```

You could use this from another ASP page as the source of the image tag. For example:

```
<IMG SRC="GetLogo.asp?pub_id=0736">
```

7

Remote Data Services

Remote Data Services (RDS) differs from ADO, in that RDS is a set of objects designed to work in the browser, and provide client-side data facilities. This means that RDS must support similar features to ADO, but RDS must work in a stateless HTTP environment.

RDS Object Structure

To understand why RDS must differ from ADO you need to examine the way RDS works. RDS requires support both at the client and at the server. The diagram below shows how this works:

At the server we have the following:

❑ **Data Store**, which is the source of the data.

❑ **Data Factory Object** or **Custom Components**, which supply only the requested data. The custom component can be any COM-compliant component.

❑ **Web Server**, which provides the interface from the server to the client.

This means that you must have certain facilities installed on your web server. The NT4 Option Pack supports RDS version 1.5, and versions 2.0 and 2.1 are available for download. See the section entitled *RDS Support* (later in this chapter) for more details.

At the client side we have the following:

❑ **Data Space Object**, which takes the data from the web server and makes it available to a Data Source object.

❑ **Data Source Object**, which along with the **Client Data Cache** holds the data on the client.

❑ **Data Binding Manager**, which connects the Data Source Object to HTML Tags.

❑ **Client HTML tags**, which display the data.

In the diagram we've just seen, the use of Client and Server is a *logical* separation, and does not have to represent a physical separation of the two items. The web server, for example, can exist on the same machine as the client, which means that RDS based applications can be created and tested on a single machine. Also certain Data Source Objects (such as the Tabular Data Control and the XML Data Control) can work with local data files, and do not always require a server to supply the data.

The Data Binding Manager is only called into action if HTML tags are bound to the Data Source object. This is shown in the Data Binding section later in this chapter.

RDS Support

The use of RDS is browser-dependent – only the Microsoft Internet Explorer browser (version 4 and above) fully supports RDS.

You should also be aware that applications using RDS might have to contend with different versions of RDS at the client. Internet Explorer 4 shipped with RDS version 1.5, while Internet Explorer 5, Office 2000, and Visual Studio 6 shipped with version 2.0. For general compatibility issues you should read the following knowledge-base articles, available from http://support.microsoft.com:

Q216389 – Maintaining Binary Compatibility in Components with ADOR
Q195049 – Maintain Binary Compatibility in Components Exposing ADO
Q201580 – ADO 2.0 and ADO 2.1 Binary Compatibility

You can obtain the latest versions of ADO and RDS at http://www.microsoft.com/data.

Data Source Objects

The simplest way to use RDS is through the use of a Data Source Object (DSO). A DSO is what provides the client interface to the data, allowing the data to be bound to HTML elements, as well as manipulated directly by way of an ADO Recordset.

There are several Data Source Objects available as part of the standard IE4 or IE5 installation, or as a separate download. They are generally created by use of the HTML OBJECT tag:

```
<OBJECT CLASSID="clsid:class id of object"
        ID="id of HTML tag" HEIGHT="0" WIDTH="0">
    <PARAM NAME="parameter name" VALUE="parameter value">
    <PARAM NAME="parameter name" VALUE="parameter value">
</OBJECT>
```

Setting a unique ID allows data binding to take place, and using a Height and Width of 0 ensures that the control doesn't take up any space on the page. You can give a height and width, but since the control doesn't have a visible interface, there's not much to see.

The parameter names correspond to the properties of the object, and are listed below with each object. For example:

```
<OBJECT CLASSID="clsid:BD96C556-65A3-11D0-983A-00C04FC29E33"
        ID="dsoAuthors" HEIGHT="0" WIDTH="0">
    <PARAM NAME="Server" VALUE="http://www.yourserver.com">
    <PARAM NAME="Connect" VALUE="DSN=pubs">
    <PARAM NAME="SQL" VALUE="SELECT * FROM authors">
</OBJECT>
```

You can also set the parameters from within script, by referencing the properties:

```
<SCRIPT Language="JScript">
    dsoAuthors.Server = "http://www.yourserver.com";
    dsoAuthors.Connect = "DSN=pubs";
    dsoAuthors.SQL = "SELECT * FROM authors"
</SCRIPT>
```

There are various security implications when using RDS. See the *Security Issues* section (at the end of this chapter) for more details.

Remote Data Service Data Control

In older versions of RDS, the RDS Data Control was known as the Advanced Data Control (ADC). It is automatically installed with Internet Explorer 4.0 or higher.

Class ID	BD96C556-65A3-11D0-983A-00C04FC29E33
Source	C:\Program Files\Common Files\System\MSADC\msadco.dll
Prog ID	RDS.DataControl

The <OBJECT> Tag

```
<OBJECT CLASSID="clsid:BD96C556-65A3-11D0-983A-00C04FC29E33"
                        ID="DataControl" WIDTH="0" HEIGHT="0">
    <PARAM NAME="Connect" VALUE="ConnectString">
    <PARAM NAME="Server" VALUE="ServerURL">
    <PARAM NAME="SQL" VALUE="SQLQueryString">
    <PARAM NAME="URL" VALUE="URLpath">
</OBJECT>
```

Methods of the RDS Data Control

The Cancel Method

Cancels asynchronous action.

> *datacontrol*.**Cancel**

If data is being fetched asynchronously, such as when the FetchOptions property is set to adcFetchAsync or adcFetchBackground, then calling the Cancel method will cancel the fetching operation.

The CancelUpdate Method

Cancels changes made to the source recordset.

> *datacontrol*.**CancelUpdate**

Any changes made to the recordset since the last Refresh or SubmitChanges method calls will be discarded.

The CreateRecordSet Method

Creates an empty, disconnected recordset.

> *Object = datacontrol*.**CreateRecordSet**(*varColumnInfos*)

Parameter	Type	Description
varColumnInfos	Variant	An array of arrays defining the columns for the recordset.

ColumnInfos should be a variant array, with each column being defined by four array elements:

- ❑ Name, for the name of the column.

- ❑ Type, for the data type of the column.

- ❑ Size, for the size of the column. For fixed length types this should be -1.

- ❑ Nullability, to indicate if the column can contain a null value.

For the data type you should use one of the ADO DataTypeEnum values (except for adChapter, adDBFileTime, adEmpty, adFileTime, adIDispatch, adIUnknown, adLongVarChar, adPropVariant, adUserDefined, adVariant and adVarNumeric, which are not supported). For a full list of these data types and their associated values you should consult Appendix B.

The column arrays should be appended to another array, which becomes the method argument. For example:

```
<SCRIPT LANGUAGE=" JScript">

function cmdCreateNew.onclick()
{
    var aField1 = Array(4);
    var aField2 = Array(4);
    var aField3 = Array(4);
    var aField4 = Array(4);
    var aCols = Array(4);

    // create the individual columns
    aField1[0] = "ID";             // name
    aField1[1] = 3;                // type - adInteger
    aField1[2] = -1;               // size
    aField1[3] = false;            // nullability

    aField2[0] = "FirstName";      // name
    aField2[1] = 202;              // type - adVarWChar
    aField2[2] = -1;               // size
    aField2[3] = false;            // nullability

    aField3[0] = "LastName";       // name
    aField3[1] = 202;              // type - adVarWChar
    aField3[2] = -1;               // size
    aField3[3] = false;            // nullability

    aField4[0] = "DateOfBirth";    // name
    aField4[1] = 7;                // type - adDate
    aField4[2] = -1;               // size
    aField4[3] = false;            // nullability

    // add the columns to an array
    aCols[0] = aField1;
    aCols[1] = aField2;
    aCols[2] = aField3;
    aCols[3] = aField4;

    // create a new recordset
    // dsoNew and dsoTest are data controls on the
    // page as OBJECT tags or created in code
    dsoNew.SourceRecordset = dsoTest.CreateRecordset (aCols);

    // add some data
    dsoNew.AddNew;
    dsoNew.Fields(0) = 1;
    dsoNew.Fields(1) = "Rob";
    dsoNew.Fields(2) = "Smith";
    dsoNew.Fields(3) = 68/03/05;
    dsoNew.Update;
}
</SCRIPT>
```

The Refresh Method

Refreshes the data from the data source.

> *datacontrol*.**Refresh**

The `Refresh` method will discard any unsaved changes, and will position the recordset at the first record.

The Reset Method

Resets the recordset based on filter and sort criteria.

> *datacontrol*.**Reset**(*fRefilter*)

Parameter	Type	Description
fRefilter	Boolean	Setting this to `True` will apply the reset to any records already filtered, whereas setting this to `False` applies the `Filter` to the original set of data. Default is `True`

You should use this method after setting the `FilterColumn`, `FilterCriterion` and `FilterValue` properties to ensure that the filter is applied. This method will fail if there are unsaved changes in the data.

The SubmitChanges Method

Sends pending changes to the data source.

> *datacontrol*.**SubmitChanges**

When sending changes back to the data source, only the changes are sent and one of two actions can occur. The changes will either *all* succeed, or *all* fail – it is not possible for some changes to succeed whilst others fail. For more information on failed changes, see the section *Conflict Resolution* in Chapter 5.

Properties of the RDS Data Control

The Connect Property

Indicates an ADO Connection String to connect to the data source.

> *datacontrol*.**Connect** = *String*
> *String* = *datacontrol*.**Connect**

For locally, persisted files, the connection string can simply be:

```
Provider=MSPersist
```

> If you are using the ODBC Drivers supplied with SQL Server 7.0 then the user credentials in the System DSN will be ignored. You need to explicitly supply the `UID` and `PWD` arguments.

The ExecuteOptions Property

Indicates whether or not to use asynchronous execution.

> *datacontrol*.**ExecuteOptions** = *adcExecuteOptionEnum*
> *adcExecuteOptionEnum* = *datacontrol*.**ExecuteOptions**

The value can be one of the *adcExecuteOptionEnum* constants:

Parameter	Value	Description
adcExecSync	1	Indicates that the command should be executed synchronously. This is the default.
adcExecAsync	2	Indicates that the command should be executed asynchronously.

Synchronous operations mean that control is not returned to the calling program until the data fetching action has been completed. This means that when a data control on a page is running a command to fetch data from a data source, the data control waits until the command has been processed before allowing the data control to continue. Asynchronous operations return control as soon as the command has been sent to the data server.

The FetchOptions Property

Indicates the type of data fetching being used.

```
datacontrol.FetchOptions = adcFetchOptionEnum
adcFetchOptionEnum = datacontrol.FetchOptions
```

The value can be one of the following *adcFetchOptionEnum* constants:

Constant	Value	Description
adcFetchUpFront	1	Indicates that all records are fetched before control is given back to the application. This is the default.
adcFetchBackground	2	Indicates that control is given back to the application as soon as the first batch of records has been fetched.
adcFetchAsync	3	Indicates that control is given back to the application immediately, and that fetching of records continues in the background.

If you are using adcFetchBackground and you try to access a record that has not yet been retrieved, the application will not receive control back until the record has been fetched.

If you are using adcFetchAsync and you try to access a record that has already been fetched, then you will be placed on that record. If the record has not yet been fetched, control is given back to the application immediately, you will be placed on the closest record and EOF will be set for the recordset. This means that when using adcFetchAsync you should really check the ReadyState property before attempting to move to the end of the recordset, because otherwise you will just be moved to the last fetched record, while other records are still being fetched.

The FilterColumn Property

Indicates the column upon which filtering should take place.

```
datacontrol.FilterColumn = String
String = datacontrol.FilterColumn
```

Setting the `FilterColumn` property does not activate the filter. For this you need to use the `Reset` method.

The FilterCriterion Property

Indicates the criteria to be used for filtering.

```
datacontrol.FilterCriterion = String
String = datacontrol.FilterCriterion
```

The value for `FilterCriterion` can be one of the following:

❏   < for less than

❏   <= for less than or equal to

❏   = for equal to

❏   >= for greater than or equal to

❏   > for greater than

❏   <> for not equal to

Setting the `FilterCriterion` property does not activate the filter. For this you need to use the `Reset` method.

The FilterValue Property

Indicates the value to filter for.

```
datacontrol.FilterValue = String
String = datacontrol.FilterValue
```

Setting the `FilterValue` property alone does not activate the filter. To activate the filter, use the `Reset` method.

The Handler Property

Indicates what handler to use.

```
datacontrol.Handler = String
String = datacontrol.Handler
```

The `Handler` enables custom logic to be executed on the server when RDS is used to work directly with remote OLE DB providers. This allows you to build your own custom data handlers, instead of using the default one.

For a detailed explanation of the Customization Handler feature, see the MSDN Online article entitled *Using the Customization Handler Feature in RDS 2.0* – available at http://msdn.microsoft.com/library/sdkdoc/dasdk/usin1x68.htm.

The InternetTimeout Property

Indicates the time in milliseconds to wait for HTTP requests.

> *datacontrol*.InternetTimeout = *Long*
> *Long* = *datacontrol*.InternetTimeout

This property allows you to customize how long to wait before an error is generated. The default value is 300000, which is 5 minutes.

This doesn't override the server timeout facility. Whichever timeout is reached first is used.

The ReadyState Property

Indicates the state of the control.

> *adcReadStateEnum* = *datacontrol*.ReadyState

This property can be one of the *adcReadStateEnum* values:

Constant	Value	Description
adcReadyStateLoaded	2	To indicate that the recordset is open, but no data has been received from the source.
adcReadyStateInteractive	3	To indicate that the recordset is currently receiving data from the source.
adcReadyStateComplete	4	To indicate that the recordset is fully populated, and has received all of its data from the source.

The Recordset Property

Returns the ADO `Recordset` object underlying this data control.

> *Recordset* = *datacontrol*.Recordset

The underlying recordset is a standard ADO `Recordset` object, so you can therefore use the recordset methods to manipulate the records in the data control. For example, if using single table binding you could have several buttons to perform the navigation:

```
<INPUT ID="cmdFirst" TYPE="BUTTON" VALUE="<<"
  onclick="dsoAuthors.Recordset.MoveFirst();">

<INPUT ID="cmdPrevious" TYPE="BUTTON" VALUE="<"
  onclick="dsoAuthors.Recordset.MovePrevious();">

<INPUT ID="cmdNext" TYPE="BUTTON" VALUE=">"
  onclick="dsoAuthors.Recordset.MoveNext();">

<INPUT ID="cmdLast" TYPE="BUTTON" VALUE=">>"
  onclick="dsoAuthors.Recordset.MoveLast();">
```

The Server Property

Indicates the web server URL.

```
datacontrol.Server = String
String = datacontrol.Server
```

The `Server` property can be a standard HTTP or HTTPS URL, the name of a machine (without the leading //) for DCOM use, or empty for local in-process use.

> *If using HTTP, the name of the server must be the same as the name of the machine that the HTML or ASP has been downloaded from. This is a deliberate security restriction – to ensure that only data from data stores on the same server are allowed.*

The SortColumn Property

Indicates the column upon which to perform sorting.

```
datacontrol.SortColumn = String
String = datacontrol.SortColumn
```

The SortDirection Property

Indicates the direction in which to sort.

```
datacontrol.SortDirection = Boolean
Boolean = datacontrol.SortDirection
```

This value is `True` for ascending sorts, and `False` for descending sorts.

The SourceRecordset Property

Sets the ADO `Recordset` to be used for the data control.

```
Set Recordset = datacontrol.SourceRecordset
Set datacontrol.SourceRecordset = Recordset
```

This property allows you to set the source data of a data control to an existing ADO `Recordset`.

The SQL Property

Indicates the SQL query string used to generate the data.

```
datacontrol.SQL = String
String = datacontrol.SQL
```

The SQL string uses the SQL dialect of the server.

Events of the RDS Data Control

The onerror Event

Raised when an event is generated whenever an error occurs during a data operation.

```
onerror(SCode, Description, Source, CancelDisplay)
```

Parameter	Type	Description
SCode	Integer	The status code of the error.
Description	String	The error description.
Source	String	The query or command that caused the error.
CancelDisplay	Boolean	Allows you to prevent an error dialog being shown.

If you set the *CancelDisplay* parameter to `True` in the `onerror` event procedure, then no error dialog box is displayed.

The onreadystatechange Event

Raised when the state of the Data Source Object changes.

> onreadystatechange

The event has no parameters with which to identify the state, but the `this` object refers to the active object. For example, in JScript:

```
<SCRIPT LANGUAGE="JScript" FOR="dsoAuthors"
        EVENT="onreadystatechange">

    if (this.readyState == 'complete')
        // data has been completely read in
</SCRIPT>
```

In VBScript you use the `Me` object:

```
<SCRIPT LANGUAGE="VBScript" FOR="dsoAuthors"
        EVENT="onreadystatechange">

    If Me.readyState == 'complete' Then
        ' data has been completely read in
    End If
</SCRIPT>
```

Values for the `readyState` are:

❑ `uninitialized`, to indicate the object is not initialized with data.

❑ `loading`, to indicate the object is currently loading data.

❑ `interactive`, to indicate the object has not fully loaded its data, although it can be interacted with.

❑ `complete`, to indicate the control is completely loaded.

The Tabular Data Control

The Tabular Data Control is automatically installed with Internet Explorer 4.0 or higher.

Class ID	333C7BC4-460F-11D0-BC04-0080C7055A83
Source	C:\WINNT\System32\tdc.ocx
Prog ID	TDCCtl.TDCCtl

The <OBJECT> Tag

```
<OBJECT CLASSID="clsid:333C7BC4-460F-11D0-BC04-0080C7055A83"
                        ID="DataControl" WIDTH="0" HEIGHT="0">
  <PARAM NAME="DataURL" VALUE="composer.csv">
</OBJECT>
```

Methods of the Tabular Data Control

The Reset Method

Updates the local recordset to reflect current filter and sort criteria.

> *datacontrol*.Reset

Properties of the Tabular Data Control

The AppendData Property

Identifies whether or not the new data replaces the existing recordset or is appended to the existing recordset.

> *datacontrol*.AppendData = *Boolean*
> *Boolean* = *datacontrol*.AppendData

If this is set to `True`, then when the `Reset` method is called, new data is appended to the end of the existing recordset.

The default value is `False`.

The CaseSensitive Property

Indicates whether string comparisons will be case sensitive.

> *datacontrol*.CaseSensitive = *Boolean*
> *Boolean* = *datacontrol*.CaseSensitive

The default value is `True`.

The CharSet Property

Identifies the character set of the data.

> *datacontrol*.CharSet = *String*
> *String* = *datacontrol*.CharSet

The default value is `windows-1252`.

Character sets are particularly important when dealing with data containing non-English characters, such as umlauts, cedillas, and so forth. Identifying the character set of the data correctly ensures that you won't receive errors when the data control tries to load the data. This is particularly important with XML data, as you may receive XML parsing errors if your data contains characters that are not included in your character set.

194

The DataURL Property

Indicates the URL of the data file.

```
datacontrol.DataURL = String
String = datacontrol.DataURL
```

The EscapeChar Property

The escape character used in the source data file.

```
datacontrol.EscapeChar = String
String = datacontrol.EscapeChar
```

The Tabular Data Control is designed to take textual data in a tabular form, with columns and rows being separated by special characters, and a special character to distinguish text data. These characters are defined by the `FieldDelim`, `RowDelim` and `TextQualifier` properties. If your data needs to have one of these characters in it, then the character should be escaped, by placing the `EscapeChar` in front of it. For example, suppose you have some data in the following form:

```
ID,FirstName,LastName,Address
1,Jan,Lloyd,14 Coniston Close, Borden, Hants
2,Nigel,Futter,23a Lemington Road, Risely, Beds
```

There are only four columns, separated by commas, but the fourth column has commas in it. Since the comma is the column delimiter any commas in columns need to be escaped, like so:

```
ID,FirstName,LastName,Address
1,Jan,Lloyd,14 Coniston Close\, Borden\, Hants
2,Nigel,Futter,23a Lemington Road\, Risely\, Beds
```

In this instance we could set the properties of the TDC as follows:

```
dataControl.FieldDelim = ","
dataControl.EscapeChar = "\"
```

The FieldDelim Property

Identifies the character that delimits columns in the data file.

```
datacontrol.FieldDelim = String
String = datacontrol.FieldDelim
```

Only a single character can be used, and it defaults to a comma.

The Filter Property

Indicates the filter that will be applied to data.

```
datacontrol.Filter = String
String = datacontrol.Filter
```

The `Filter` property is a SQL WHERE clause without the WHERE. For example:

```
dataControl.Filter = "LastName=Lloyd"
```

To filter on wildcards you can use the asterisk:

```
dataControl.Filter = "LastName=L*"
```

The Language Property

Specifies the language of the data file.

> *datacontrol.***Language** = *String*
> *String* = *datacontrol.***Language**

The default language is en-us.

The ReadyState Property

Indicates the state of the control as data is received.

> *datacontrol.***ReadyState** = *Long*
> *Long* = *datacontrol.***ReadyState**

ReadyState can be one of the following ADCReadyStateEnum constants:

Constant	Value	Description
adcReadyStateComplete	4	All the available data has arrived, or an error occurred preventing (more) data arriving.
adcReadyStateInteractive	3	Data is still arriving from the server.
adcReadyStateLoaded	2	The control is loaded and waiting to fetch data from the server.

The RowDelim Property

Specifies the character that delimits each row in the data file.

> *datacontrol.***RowDelim** = *String*
> *String* = *datacontrol.***RowDelim**

Only a single character can be used, and it defaults to carriage return.

The Sort Property

Specifies the sort order for the data file.

> *datacontrol.***Sort** = *String* .
> *String* = *datacontrol.***Sort**

For the sort order you specify the column names, as a comma-delimited list. The default order is ascending, but you can insert a minus sign (-) before each column to sort in a descending order. For example:

```
dataControl.Sort = "LastName,FirstName,-Age"
```

The TextQualifier Property

Indicates the character that is used to enclose text fields.

> *datacontrol*.TextQualifier = *String*
> *String* = *datacontrol*.TextQualifier

If some of your columns contain characters that might be column delimiters you can either escape the delimiters (see discussion of the `EscapeChar` property, in this chapter), or use a text qualifier around the column. For example:

```
ID,FirstName,LastName,Address
1,Jan,Lloyd,14 Coniston Close, Borden, Hants
2,Nigel,Futter,23a Lemington Road, Risely, Beds
```

There are only four columns, separated by commas, but the fourth column has commas in it. Using a text qualifier ensures that the commas are not seen as column delimiters:

```
ID,FirstName,LastName,Address
1,Jan,Lloyd,"14 Coniston Close, Borden, Hants"
2,Nigel,Futter,"23a Lemington Road, Risely, Beds"
```

The default is the double quote mark (").

The UseHeader Property

Indicates whether or not the first row of the data file contains column names.

> *datacontrol*.UseHeader = *Boolean*
> *Boolean* = *datacontrol*.UseHeader

The heading row can optionally contain data types for the columns. For example:

```
ID:Int,FirstName:String,LastName:String,Address:String
1,Jan,Lloyd,"14 Coniston Close, Borden, Hants"
2,Nigel,Futter,"23a Lemington Road, Risely, Beds"
```

The data type can be one of the following:

❏ `String`, for textual data. This is the default

❏ `Date`, for dates.

❏ `Boolean`, for Yes/No or True/False

❏ `Int`, for whole numbers

❏ `Float`, for floating point numbers

For `Date` fields, you can add a space and then `D`, `M` or `Y` to indicate the date style. The TDC assumes dates are numbers separated by characters, so any character date separator will work. For example:

```
Name:String, DateOfBirth:Date YMD
Dave,66/06/11
Rob,68.03.05
```

For `Boolean` values, the following applies:

❑ A value of `Yes`, `True`, `1`, `-1`, or any *non-zero number* is interpreted as `True`.

❑ A value of `No`, `False`, or `0` is interpreted as `False`.

Events of the Tabular Data Control

The onreadystatechange Event

This event is triggered when the `ReadyState` property changes. You can use this to detect when the TDC has fully loaded the data into the Data Source Object.

The event has no parameters with which to identify the state, but the `this` object refers to the active object. For example:

```
<SCRIPT LANGUAGE="JScript" FOR="dsoAuthors"
      EVENT="onreadystatechange">

  if (this.readyState == 'complete')
      // data has been completely read in
</SCRIPT>
```

The Java Data Base Control (JDBC)

The Java Data Base Control (also known as the Java DSO) is a Data Source Object written entirely in Java, and is therefore available for browsers other than Microsoft Internet Explorer. All other DSOs use the HTML `OBJECT` tag, but the Java DSO is created with an `APPLET` tag.

The Java DSO is available as either compiled class files or as source, so you can extend it if required. You can get the Java DSO from http://msdn.microsoft.com/downloads/ samples/internet/author/datasrc/jdbcapplet.

If you want to learn more about JDBC, you should consult a specialist book. There's a good discussion of JDBC in Ivor Horton's *Beginning Java 2* (Wrox, ISBN 1-861002-23-8).

The <APPLET> Tag

```
<APPLET CODE="JDC.class" ID="dsoAuthors" WIDTH=0 HEIGHT=0>
  <PARAM NAME=cabbase VALUE= "jdc.cab">
  <PARAM NAME="dbURL" VALUE="jdbc:odbc:pubs">
  <PARAM NAME="showUI" VALUE="false">
  <PARAM NAME="sqlStatement" VALUE="select * from authors">
  <PARAM NAME="allowInsert" VALUE="true">
  <PARAM NAME="allowDelete" VALUE="true">
  <PARAM NAME="allowUpdate" VALUE="false">
  <PARAM NAME="user" VALUE="">
  <PARAM NAME="password" VALUE="">
  <PARAM NAME="filterColumn" VALUE="">
  <PARAM NAME="filterCriterion " VALUE="">
  <PARAM NAME="filterValue " VALUE="">
  <PARAM NAME="driver" VALUE="">
</APPLET>
```

You can obtain the JDC CAB file from MSDN, at http://msdn.microsoft.com/downloads/ c-frame.htm?928521190764#/downloads/samples/internet/default.asp.

Properties of the Java DSO

The allowInsert Property

Indicates whether or not inserts are allowed against the DSO.

```
datacontrol.allowInsert = Boolean
Boolean= datacontrol.allowInsert
```

Inserts only affect the local data and are not sent to the server.

The allowDelete Property

Indicates whether or not deletes are allowed against the DSO.

```
datacontrol.allowDelete = Boolean
Boolean= datacontrol.allowDelete
```

Deletes only affect the local data and are not sent to the server.

The allowUpdate Property

Indicates whether or not updates are allowed against the DSO.

```
datacontrol.allowUpdate = Boolean
Boolean = datacontrol.allowUpdate
```

Updates only affect the local data and are not sent to the server.

The cabbase Property

Specifies the code location of the data control

```
datacontrol.cabbase = String
String = datacontrol.cabbase
```

This is a general APPLET property that identifies the location of the applet code. The applet will be downloaded if it is not already installed on the client.

The dbURL Property

Identifies the ODBC Data Source Name (DSN) that supplies the data.

```
datacontrol.dbURL = String
String = datacontrol.dbURL
```

The connect string takes the following form:

```
jdbc:subprotocol:subname
```

The driver Property

Indicates the JDBC Bridge driver to use.

```
datacontrol.driver = String
String = datacontrol.driver
```

Chapter 7

The JDBC Bridge is what interfaces the JDBC calls to a data source. The Java SDK ships with an ODBC bridge, allowing you to use JDBC to access ODBC data source.

The filterColumn Property

Indicates the column index or name to filter on.

```
datacontrol.filterColumn = String
String = datacontrol.filterColumn
```

The filterCriterion Property

Indicates the filter criteria.

```
datacontrol.filterCriterion = String
String = datacontrol.filterCriterion
```

The value for FilterCriterion can be one of:

❑   < for less than

❑   <= for less than or equal to

❑   = for equal to

❑   >= for greater than or equal to

❑   > for greater than

❑   <> for not equal to

The filterValue Property

Indicates the value to filter on.

```
datacontrol.filterValue = String
String = datacontrol.filterValue
```

The password Property

Indicates the user password to use to connect to the data store.

```
datacontrol.password = String
String= datacontrol.password
```

The preloadRows Property

Indicates the number of rows to preload before loading asynchronously.

```
datacontrol.preloadRows = Long
Long = datacontrol.preloadRows
```

When loading data synchronously, this property indicates the number of rows that are initially loaded before the rest of the rows are loaded asynchronously.

The showUI Property

Indicates whether or not a user interface for the applet should be displayed.

```
datacontrol.showUI = Boolean
Boolean = datacontrol.showUI
```

The Java DSO does not have a User Interface.

The sortColumn Property

Indicates the column number or name upon which to sort.

```
datacontrol.sortColumn = String
String = datacontrol.sortColumn
```

The sortDirection Property

Indicates the direction in which to sort.

```
datacontrol.sortDirection = String
String = datacontrol.sortDirection
```

The sqlStatement Property

Indicates the SQL statement used to return the data.

```
datacontrol.sqlStatement = String
String = datacontrol.sqlStatement
```

The user Property

Indicates the user name to use to connect to the data source.

```
datacontrol.user = String
String = datacontrol.user
```

Methods of the Java DSO

The apply Method

Applies a sort or a filter to the recordset of the DSO.

```
datacontrol.apply
```

The commitChanges Method

The commitChanges method is implemented as a stub and will raise an error if called. Since this method cannot be implemented in a generic way, Microsoft has left this to be implemented by the user if required. In other words, it exists, but doesn't work.

Events of the Java DSO

The Java DSO does not implement any events directly, although some DSO events are available through the `APPLET`. See the section later in this chapter on Events for more details.

The MSHTML DSO

The MSHTML DSO is part of Internet Explorer and allows a DSO to be created based upon HTML tags. To be included in the data the HTML tags must include an `ID` attribute. When parsing an HTML page, unique ID attributes become the columns, and the values within the tags becomes the column values. Separate rows are created by having tags with the same ID attribute. The parser ignores the actual HTML tag type – only the ID and the data are important.

An example of an HTML data file is shown below:

```
<DIV ID="PersonID">101</DIV>
<SPAN ID="FirstName">Jan</SPAN>
<H1 ID="LastName">Lloyd</H1>
<PRE ID="PersonID">104</PRE>
<SPAN ID="FirstName">Rob</SPAN>
<H2 ID="LastName">Smith</H1>
```

Each unique ID field would translate to a column, giving us three columns: `PersonID`, `FirstName` and `LastName`. There would be two rows in the data set because there are two sets of tags with the same ID fields. The actual HTML tag is ignored, as are HTML tags without an `ID` attribute.

The data is taken sequentially from the top down.

Class ID	25336921-03F9-11CF-8FD0-00AA00686F13
DLL	%SystemRoot%\System32\mshtml.dll
Prog ID	htmlfile_FullWindowEmbed

The <OBJECT> Tag

```
<OBJECT ID="dsoAuthors" DATA="HTMLFile.html" HEIGHT="0" WIDTH="0">
</OBJECT>
```

The `DATA` attribute points to the HTML file containing the data.

Methods of the MSHTML DSO

The MSHTML DSO does not have any methods.

Properties of the MSHTML DSO

The Recordset Property

Returns the ADO `Recordset` object underlying this data control.

Recordset = datacontrol.Recordset

The underlying recordset is a standard ADO `Recordset` object, so you can therefore use the `Recordset` methods to manipulate the records in the data control. For example, if using single table binding you could have several buttons to perform the navigation:

```
<INPUT ID="cmdFirst" TYPE="BUTTON" VALUE="<<"
  onclick="dsoAuthors.Recordset.MoveFirst();">

<INPUT ID="cmdPrevious" TYPE="BUTTON" VALUE="<"
  onclick="dsoAuthors.Recordset.MovePrevious();">

<INPUT ID="cmdNext" TYPE="BUTTON" VALUE=">"
  onclick="dsoAuthors.Recordset.MoveNext();">

<INPUT ID="cmdLast" TYPE="BUTTON" VALUE=">>"
  onclick="dsoAuthors.Recordset.MoveLast();">
```

Events of the MSHTML DSO

The MSHTML DSO does not have any distinct events, although it responds to the standard data binding events which are discussed in the Events section of this chapter.

The XML Java Applet in IE4

The XMLDSO Java Applet ships with IE4 and provides read-only access to XML data. It's particularly useful for hierarchical data.

A known problem with the XMLDSO is that when binding hierarchical data to HTML tables, and you have a parent record with different child records, then the second child record doesn't get bound correctly. A way around this is to use the C++ XML DSO, which can be instantiated either in an `OBJECT` tag or from within code. The C++ XML DSO is covered under the IE5 section.

The <APPLET> Tag

```
<APPLET CODE="com.ms.xml.dso.XMLDSO.class" ID="dsoAuthors"
                        HEIGHT="0" WIDTH="0" MAYSCRIPT="True">
  <PARAM NAME="URL" VALUE="XMLDataFile.xml">
  <PARAM NAME="SCHEMA" VALUE="SchemaFile.xml">
</APPLET>
```

The Java Applet has a visible interface, so you can give it a height and width (60 and 400 perhaps). The interface shows trace messages showing successful loading of the XML data or error messages. Rather conveniently, the interface is green when successful and red for errors.

You can also embed XML directly between the `APPLET` tags:

```
<APPLET CODE="com.ms.xml.dso.XMLDSO.class" ID="dsoAuthors"
        HEIGHT="0" WIDTH="0" MAYSCRIPT="True">
<?xml version="1.0"?>
<AUTHORS>
  <AUTHOR>
    <au_id>101</au_id>
    <au_fname>Jan</au_fname>
    <au_lname>Lloyd</au_lname>
  </AUTHOR>
  <AUTHOR>
    <au_id>104</au_id>
    <au_fname>Rob</au_fname>
    <au_lname>Smith</au_lname>
  </AUTHOR>
</AUTHORS>
</APPLET>
```

Methods of the IE4 XMLDSO

The clear Method

Clears the data from the DSO

> *datacontrol*.clear

The getDocument Method

Returns the loaded document.

> *datacontrol*.getDocument

This is synonymous with the `Document` property.

The getError Method

Returns the most recent error encountered by the DSO.

> *datacontrol*.getError

This is synonymous with the `Error` property.

The getSchema Method

Returns the XML schema of the DSO.

> *datacontrol*.getSchema (*Format*)

Parameter	Type	Description
Format	Boolean	`True` to format the schema, `False` to return the schema without formatting.

The getXML Method

Returns the XML data.

> *datacontrol*.getXML (*Format*)

Parameter	Type	Description
Format	Boolean	`True` to format the XML data, `False` to return the XML data without formatting.

Formatted data appears neatly embedded (just like IE5 does when you view an XML file), whereas unformatted means that the XML is just returned as is, with no formatting.

The init Method

Reloads the XML Data

> *datacontrol*.init

If the URL PARAM exists, then the VALUE is used to reload the XML data. If no URL PARAM exists, the XML data is taken to be inline, between the APPLET tags. If no XML exists, then no action is taken.

The load Method
Reloads the XML.

> *datacontrol*.load (*File*)

Parameter	Type	Description
File	String	The URL of the XML Data document.

For local URLs, the load method is dependent upon the security settings of your browser, which may not allow access to the local drives.

The save Method
Saves the XML to a file.

> *datacontrol*.save (*File*)

Parameter	Type	Description
File	String	The name of the file to save the XML into.

For local URLs, the save method is dependent upon the security settings of your browser, which may not allow access to the local drives.

The setRoot Method
Sets the root of the document for the DSO.

> *datacontrol*.setRoot (*elem*)

Parameter	Type	Description
elem	Element	The element to set as the root node of the DSO.

The updateSchema Method
Updates the SCHEMA whenever the document is changed.

> *datacontrol*.updateSchema

This method is automatically called by the clear, load and setRoot methods.

Properties of the IE4 XMLDSO

The Document Property
Returns a DOM document object containing the DSO document.

> *Object = datacontrol*.Document

This is synonymous with the getDocument method.

The Error Property

Returns the most recent error encountered by the DSO.

```
String = datacontrol.Error
```

This is synonymous with the `getError` method.

The URL Property

Identifies the URL of the source of the data.

```
datacontrol.URL = String
String = datacontrol.URL
```

Events of the XMLDSO

The Java XML DSO does not implement any events directly, although DSO events are available through the `APPLET`. See the section on Events later in this chapter for more details.

The XML Tag in IE5

Internet Explorer 5 natively supports XML by way of an `XML` tag. Embedding XML Data into HTML is called using XML Data Islands, and there are two ways to specify the data. The first way is to use the SRC attribute to specify the name of the `XML` data file:

```
<XML ID="dsoAuthors" SRC="authors.xml"></XML>
```

Alternatively, you can also embed the XML data between the `XML` tags:

```
<XML ID="dsoAuthors"
<?xml version="1.0"?>
<AUTHORS>
  <AUTHOR>
    <au_id>101</au_id>
    <au_fname>Jan</au_fname>
    <au_lname>Lloyd</au_lname>
  </AUTHOR>
  <AUTHOR>
    <au_id>104</au_id>
    <au_fname>Rob</au_fname>
    <au_lname>Smith</au_lname>
  </AUTHOR>
</AUTHORS>
</XML>
```

Class ID	550dda30-0541-11d2-9ca9-0060b0ec3d39
DLL	%SystemRoot%\System32\msxml.dll
Prog ID	Microsoft.XMLDSO

The <OBJECT> Tag

Since XML is handled by MSXML, which is a COM object, it can be also created using an HTML OBJECT tab.

```
<OBJECT CLASSID="clsid:550dda30-0541-11d2-9ca9-0060b0ec3d39"
                          ID="dsoAuthors" HEIGHT="0" WIDTH="0">
</OBJECT>
```

This method also works for the XML DSO in IE4.

Code

You can also create and load the XML DSO from code:

```
<SCRIPT LANGUAGE="JavaScript">
function window.onload()
{
  var docAuthors = xmldso.XMLDocument;
  docAuthors.loadXML("authors.xml")
}
</SCRIPT>
```

or

```
<SCRIPT LANGUAGE="JavaScript">
function window.onload()
{
  var docAuthors = new ActiveXDocument("Microsoft.xmldom");
  docAuthors.loadXML("authors.xml")
}
</SCRIPT>
```

Methods of the IE5 XMLDSO

The XML DSO does not implement any methods directly, although the DSO does expose the XML Document object, which allows loading and parsing of XML. For more details on this you should consult an XML DOM reference book, such as *XML IE5 Programmer's Reference* (Wrox, ISBN 1-861001-57-6).

Properties of the IE5 XMLDSO

The JavaDSOCompatible Property

Indicates whether or not the DSO behaves in a way that is compatible with the Java XML DSO supplied with IE4.

> *datacontrol*.JavaDSOCompatible = *Boolean*
> *Boolean* = *datacontrol*.JavaDSOCompatible

A value of True indicates that the same behavior as the IE4 Java DSO is applied when parsing XML. The default value is False, which uses the new parsing mode. See the *Parsing Rules* section for more details on how the XML is parsed into rows and columns.

The readyState Property

Indicates the state of the DSO with regard to its data.

> *String = datacontrol*.**readyState**

Values for the `readyState` are:

- `uninitialized`, to indicate the object is not initialized with data.

- `loading`, to indicate the object is currently loading data.

- `interactive`, to indicate the object has not fully loaded its data, although it can be interacted with.

- `complete`, to indicate the control is completely loaded.

The XMLDocument Property

Returns or sets the XML DOM `Document` for the data control.

> *datacontrol*.**XMLDocument** = *XMLDOMDocument*
> *XMLDOMDocument* = *datacontrol*.**XMLDocument**

This allows you access to the `DOMDocument` object, allowing manipulation of the XML through the DOM. For example:

```
var doc = dsoXMLBooklist.XMLDocument;
var el = doc.getElementsByTagName("CATEGORY").item(0);
alert(el.xml);
```

This searches for XML tags by name and retrieves the first tag that matches.

Events of the XMLDSO

The XML DSO does not implement any events directly, although DSO events are available through the `OBJECT`. See the section on Events later in this chapter for more details.

Parsing Rules

There are set rules for how the XML data is parsed into rows and columns:

- Each sub-element and attribute becomes a column in the same row.

- The column name is the sub-element or attribute name, unless the parent element has an attribute and sub-element of the same name. In this case an exclamation mark (!) is added to the beginning of the column name.

- A column based on an attribute is always a simple-column - that is, it contains normal string or number data.

- If an element has sub-elements or attributes then the column becomes a row column. This corresponds to a Chapter column in a hierarchical recordset.

❏ Multiple instances of sub-elements under different parents use different rules. If any instance implies a row, then all instances become rows. If all instances imply a column, then the element becomes a column.

❏ Each row has an extra column called $Text. This contains the sub-elements of the row concatenated together. This is particularly useful when your XML elements have attributes and you wish to bind data to HTML elements. This is explained in more detail in the Data Binding section.

When in Java Compatibility mode the rules are simpler:

❏ Any element that contains another element is a row.

❏ Text only elements are columns.

❏ Attributes are ignored.

If you want to define your own rules as to how the XML elements are converted into rows or columns then you need to add a DTD to the XML data:

```
<XML ID="dsoAuthors"
<?xml version="1.0" ?>
<!DOCTYPE AUTHORS [
    <!ELEMENT AUTHORS (AUTHOR+)>
    <!ELEMENT AUTHOR (au_id, au_fname, au_lname)>
    <!ELEMENT au_id (#PCDATA)>
    <!ELEMENT au_fname (#PCDATA)>
    <!ELEMENT au_lname (#PCDATA)>
]>

<AUTHORS>
  <AUTHOR>
    <au_id>101</au_id>
    <au_fname>Jan</au_fname>
    <au_lname>Lloyd</au_lname>
  </AUTHOR>
  <AUTHOR>
   . . .
</AUTHORS>
```

RDS DataSpace

The DataSpace object is responsible for creating a client side proxy to communicate with the server, and often goes hand-in-hand with the DataFactory object. When you use a DSO, a DataSpace object is created on the client behind the scenes, connecting to the web server automatically. The DataSpace performs the marshalling of data from the client to server, and vice-versa.

Class ID	BD96C556-65A3-11D0-983A-00C04FC29E36
Source	C:\Program Files\Common Files\System\MSADC\msadco.dll
Prog ID	RDS.DataSpace

The <OBJECT> Tag

```
<OBJECT CLASSID="clsid:BD96C556-65A3-11D0-983A-00C04FC29E36"
                         ID="dspDataSpace" HEIGHT="0" WIDTH="0">
</OBJECT>
```

Methods of the DataSpace Object

The CreateObject Method

Creates a server-side object.

> *variant = dataspace*.CreateObject (*ProgID, Connection*)

Name	Type	Description
ProgID	String	The Program ID of the object to create.
Connection	String	Connection details of the web server or machine name.

The connection details can be a URL for a web server, a UNC name for a machine, or an empty string for a local, in-process business object. For example:

```
dfFactory = dspSpace.CreateObject ("RDSServer.DataFactory",
                                        "http://servername.com");
```

This creates an instance of the `DataFactory` component on the web server servername.com. If you use an ASP file instead of an HTML file you can use the `ServerVariables` method of the `Request` object to extract the name of the web server:

```
dfFactory = dspSpace.CreateObject ("RDSServer.DataFactory",
                "http://<%=Request.ServerVariables("SERVER_NAME")%>");
```

You are not limited to creating the `DataFactory` with this method: you can create any COM object. This is discussed in more detail in the *DataSpace and DataFactory Usage* section, later in this chapter.

Properties of the DataSpace Object

The InternetTimeout Property

Indicates the HTTP timeout in milliseconds.

> *dataspace*.InternetTimeout = *Long*
> *Long* = *dataspace*.InternetTimeout

When creating proxy objects, the `DataSpace` will wait for the amount of time specified in this property. If no response is received from the server, then an error is generated. The default value is 300000, which is 5 minutes.

Events of the DataSpace Object

The `DataSpace` has no events.

RDSServer DataFactory

The `DataFactory` is the server side part of the proxy process, being used to marshal data from the server to the client. You can use the `DataFactory` to execute SQL queries on the server, and return the data back to the client.

As the `DataFactory` is a server-side object you can create it with the `DataSpace` object:

```
dfFactory = dspSpace.CreateObject ("RDSServer.DataFactory",
               "http://servername.com");
```

Class ID	9381D8F5-0288-11d0-9501-00AA00B911A5
Source	C:\Program Files\Common Files\System\MSADC\msadcf.dll
Prog ID	RDSServer.DataFactory

Methods of the DataFactory Object

The ConvertToString Method

Converts a recordset into a MIME64 string.

> *String = DataFactory.**ConvertToString**(Recordset)*

Parameter	Type	Description
Recordset	Recordset	An ADO `Recordset` to convert to a string.

This method was useful in early versions of ADO (pre 2.0) when you needed to transfer a recordset between server and client. Recordsets from ADO 2.0 onwards can now marshal themselves across HTTP, so this method is less used.

The CreateRecordSet Method

Creates and returns an empty recordset.

> *Object = DataFactory.**CreateRecordSet**(ColumnInfos)*

Parameter	Type	Description
ColumnInfos	Variant	An array of arrays containing the column details.

ColumnInfos should be a variant array, with each column being defined by four array elements:

❑   Name, for the name of the column.

❑   Type, for the data type of the column.

❑   Size, for the size of the column. For fixed length types this should be -1.

❑   Nullability, to indicate if the column can contain a null value.

For the data type you should use one of the ADO DataTypeEnum values (except for adChapter, adDBFileTime, adEmpty, adFileTime, adIDispatch, adIUnknown, adLongVarChar, adPropVariant, adUserDefined, adVariant and adVarNumeric, which are not supported). For a full list of these data types and their associated values you should consult Appendix B.

The column arrays should be appended to another array, which becomes the method argument. For example:

```
<SCRIPT LANGUAGE="JavaScript">

function cmdCreateNew.onclick()
{
    var aField1 = Array(4);
    var aField2 = Array(4);
    var aField3 = Array(4);
    var aField4 = Array(4);
    var aCols = Array(4);

    // create the individual columns
    aField1[0] = "ID";              // name
    aField1[1] = 3;                 // type - adInteger
    aField1[2] = -1;                // size
    aField1[3] = false;             // nullability

    aField2[0] = "FirstName";       // name
    aField2[1] = 202;               // type - adVarWChar
    aField2[2] = -1;                // size
    aField2[3] = false;             // nullability

    aField3[0] = "LastName";        // name
    aField3[1] = 202;               // type - adVarWChar
    aField3[2] = -1;                // size
    aField3[3] = false;             // nullability

    aField4[0] = "DateOfBirth";     // name
    aField4[1] = 7;                 // type - adDate
    aField4[2] = -1;                // size
    aField4[3] = false;             // nullability

    // add the columns to an array
    aCols[0] = aField1;
    aCols[1] = aField2;
    aCols[2] = aField3;
    aCols[3] = aField4;

    // create a new recordset
    recNew = dataFactory.CreateRecordset (aCols);
}
</SCRIPT>
```

The Query Method

Execute the request and create a `Recordset`.

> *Recordset = DataFactory.Query(Connection, Query)*

Parameter	Type	Description
Connection	String	The connection details of the data store.
Query	String	The SQL query to run.

The `Query` string should be in the native database format. For example:

```
dfFactory = dspSpace.CreateObject ("RDSServer.DataFactory",
                                   "http://servername.com");
recAuthors = dfDataFactory.Query ("DSN=pubs",
                                  "SELECT * FROM authors");
```

The SubmitChanges Method

Given a recordset with pending changes, this method submits them to the database identified in the connection string

> *DataFactory*.SubmitChanges(*Connection, Recordset*)

Parameter	Type	Description
Connection	String	The connection details of the data store.
Recordset	Recordset	The Recordset containing the changes.

When sending changes back to the data source, only the changes are sent, and one of two actions can occur. Either all of the changes succeed, or all of them fail – it is not possible for some changes to succeed whilst others fail.

Properties of the DataFactory Object

The `DataFactory` has no properties.

Events of the DataFactory Object

The `DataFactory` has no events.

DataSpace and DataFactory Usage

The `DataSpace` and `DataFactory` perform the client and server ends of the data marshalling. Using the two together with a data control, it's easy to get data from a server, allow the user to modify it, and then send those changes back to the server. All this can be performed over HTTP, and therefore allows the creation of genuine Web Applications.

In its simplest form you can use the `DataFactory` on the server to perform your data access:

```
<!-- normal RDS DataControl object, no parameters set -->
<OBJECT ID="dsoDataControl"
            CLASSID="clsid:BD96C556-65A3-11D0-983A-00C04FC29E33">
</OBJECT>

<!-- client-side RDS DataSpace object -->
<OBJECT ID="dspSpace"
            CLASSID="CLSID:BD96C556-65A3-11D0-983A-00C04FC29E36">
</OBJECT>

<SCRIPT LANGUAGE="JavaScript">

   // create a DataFactory object
   dfFactory = dspSpace.CreateObject("RDSServer.DataFactory",
                                     "http://servername.com");

   // create a recordset using the DataFactory
   recAuthors = dfFactory.Query("DSN=pubs",
                                     "SELECT * FROM authors");

   // assign the recordset to the DataControl
   dsoDataControl.SourceRecordset = recAuthors;

</SCRIPT>
```

This does expose one flaw – that of the connection details being visible at the client. A way around this is to use a custom business component. This will be a COM compliant object, perhaps an ActiveX DLL written in Visual Basic.

```
<!-- normal RDS DataControl object, no parameters set -->
<OBJECT ID="dsoDataControl"
            CLASSID="clsid:BD96C556-65A3-11D0-983A-00C04FC29E33">
</OBJECT>

<!-- client-side RDS DataSpace object -->
<OBJECT ID="dspSpace"
            CLASSID="CLSID:BD96C556-65A3-11D0-983A-00C04FC29E36">
</OBJECT>

<SCRIPT LANGUAGE="JavaScript">

   // create a custom business object
   objWroxBooks = dspSpace.CreateObject("Wrox.Books",
                                     "http://servername.com");

   // create a recordset using the business object
   recAuthors = objWroxBooks.GetAuthors();

   // assign the recordset to the DataControl
   dsoDataControl.SourceRecordset = recAuthors;

</SCRIPT>
```

The business object should return a disconnected, client-side recordset.

DHTML Events

When using Data Source Objects in HTML pages, the DSO extends the DHTML event model with events of its own. Although these appear as part of the DSO they are in fact implemented by DHTML, and therefore appear on all HTML Elements that can be sources of data.

The following table lists the events that are generated by the DSO.

Event	Cancelable	Applies to
onbeforeupdate	True	bound elements
onafterupdate	False	bound elements
onrowenter	False	DSO
onrowexit	True	DSO
onbeforeunload	False	window
ondataavailable	False	DSO
ondatasetcomplete	False	DSO
ondatasetchanged	False	DSO
onerrorupdate	True	bound elements
onreadystatechange	False	DSO
oncellchange	False	DSO
onrowsinserted	False	DSO
onrowsdelete	False	DSO

All events bubble to parent objects apart from `onbeforeunload`, which applies to the window object, and therefore has no parent.

The `oncellchange`, `onrowsinserted`, `onrowsdelete` events are new for IE5.

Events that are marked as cancelable allow cancellation of the event, and thus can be used to prevent certain actions taking place. For example, canceling the `onbeforeupdate` event can prevent data changes taking place.

The onbeforeupdate Event

This event is when an element is about to lose focus and the data in that element has been changed.

This event is not fired if the data is changed from within scripting code.

Returning False from the event procedure will cancel the event.

The onafterupdate Event

This event fires after the data has been transferred to the data provider. If the `onbeforeupdate` event is canceled, this event does not fire.

The onrowenter Event

This event fires when a new row of data becomes the current row. You can use this to process the data before it is shown, or to update other elements on the page.

The onrowexit Event

This event fires before the current record pointer moves to a new row. This could happen if you use recordset navigation, if you delete the current record, or if you leave the page.

You can use this event to perform validation at the record level.

The onbeforeunload Event

This event fires before the current page becomes unloaded. This could be caused by navigating to another page, using the browser's Back or Forward buttons, refreshing the page, submitting a request from a FORM element, or selecting from the Favorites folder.

The ondataavailable Event

This event is fired by the DSO when records are available for use. This does not guarantee that all of the records are available, rather that some are available.

This event may fire several times, or may not fire at all. This depends upon the DSO.

The ondatasetcomplete Event

This event fires when all of the data is loaded into the DSO.

This event object has a property, reason, which identifies the download state. The values for this are:

- ❑ 0, to indicate a successful download of data.
- ❑ 1, to indicate the download of data was aborted.
- ❑ 2, to indicate a failure in downloading the data.

For example:

```
function dsoAuthors.ondatasetcomplete()
{
  if (event.reason = 2)
    alert ("Failed to load data");
}
```

The ondatasetchanged Event

This event is fired after a new data set is requested, or when the current set of data is filtered or sorted.

The data might not be available when this event fires, but the metadata (fields, data types, etc.) will be available.

You could use this event to dynamically populate other controls.

The onerrorupdate Event

This event fires when there is an error transferring the data from the server to the client.

If this event is cancelled, system dialog boxes describing the error are not shown.

The onreadystatechange Event

This event fires when the state of the DSO changes. You can examine the `readyState` property of the `this` object (or the `Me` object in VBScript) to identify the state, which will be one of:

❑   `uninitialized`, to indicate that the object is not initialized with data.

❑   `loading`, to indicate that the object is currently loading its data.

❑   `interactive`, to indicate that the object can be interacted with even though it is not fully loaded.

❑   `complete`, to indicate that the control is completely loaded.

The oncellchange Event

This event is fired when data changes in any element. You can use the `dataFld` property to indicate which field changed.

The onrowsdelete Event

This event is fired before rows are deleted. While the event is not cancelable, you can use the `bookmarks` collection to examine the deleted records.

The onrowsinserted Event

This event is fired after rows are added. While the event is not cancelable, you can use the `bookmarks` collection to examine the new records.

Data Binding

There are many HTML fields that can be bound to DSO's. There are four attributes that affect data binding:

❑   DATASRC, indicates the DSO which is supplying the data. You should use the ID of the DSO, with a hash (#) symbol in front of the ID value.

❑   DATAFLD, indicates the field in the DSO to bind to.

❑   DATAFORMATAS, indicates how the bound data is to be formatted.

❑   DATAPAGESIZE, indicates the number of rows to show when using tabular data binding.

The table below shows which elements support data binding.

HTML Element	Bound property	Update data?	Tabular binding?	Display as HTML
A	href	No	No	No
APPLET	PARAM	Yes	No	No
BUTTON	innerText and innerHTML	No	No	Yes
DIV	innerText and innerHTML	No	No	Yes
FRAME	src	No	No	No
IFRAME	src	No	No	No
IMG	src	No	No	No
INPUT TYPE=CHECKBOX	checked	Yes	No	No
INPUT TYPE=HIDDEN	value	Yes	No	No
INPUT TYPE=LABEL	value	Yes	No	No
INPUT TYPE=PASSWORD	value	Yes	No	No
INPUT TYPE=RADIO	checked	Yes	No	No
INPUT TYPE=TEXT	value	Yes	No	No
LABEL	innerText and innerHTML	No	No	Yes
LEGEND	innerText and innerHTML	No	No	No
MARQUEE	innerText and innerHTML	No	No	Yes
OBJECT	param	Yes	No	No
SELECT	text of selected option	Yes	No	No
SPAN	innerText and innerHTML	No	No	Yes
TABLE	none	No	Yes	No
TEXTAREA	value	Yes	No	No

Tabular Binding

Tabular data binding involves the use of TABLE elements. The table is bound to a DSO and the table cells are bound to individual columns. For example:

```
<TABLE DATASRC="#dsoAuthors">
  <TR>
    <TD><SPAN .DATAFLD="au_id"></SPAN></TD>
    <TD><SPAN DATAFLD="au_fname"></SPAN></TD>
    <TD><SPAN DATAFLD="au_lname"></SPAN></TD>
  </TR>
</TABLE>
```

The table is automatically created, with the number of rows being determined by the number of rows in the recordset. To limit the number of rows you can use the DATAPAGESIZE attribute:

```
<TABLE ID="tblAuthors" DATASRC="#dsoAuthors" DATAPAGESIZE="10">
  <TR>
    <TD><SPAN DATAFLD="au_id"></SPAN></TD>
    <TD><SPAN DATAFLD="au_fname"></SPAN></TD>
    <TD><SPAN DATAFLD="au_lname"></SPAN></TD>
  </TR>
</TABLE>
```

You can then add buttons to move through the pages:

```
<INPUT TYPE="BUTTON" ID="cmdNextPage" VALUE=">P"
                           onclick="tblAuthors.nextPage();">
<INPUT TYPE="BUTTON" ID="cmdPreviousPage" VALUE="<P"
                           onclick="tblAuthors.previousPage();">
```

Single Record Binding

Single record binding involves displaying a single record at a time. Each HTML element that is to bind to data specifies both the DATASRC and the DATAFLD attributes. For example:

```
ID: <INPUT TYPE="TEXT" DATASRC="#dsoAuthors"
                           DATAFLD="au_id" SIZE=6><P>
First Name: <INPUT TYPE="TEXT" DATASRC="#dsoAuthors"
                           DATAFLD="au_fname" SIZE=20><P>
Last Name: <INPUT TYPE="TEXT" DATASRC="#dsoAuthors"
                           DATAFLD="au_lname" SIZE=20><P>
Title: <SELECT DATASRC="#dsoAuthors"
                           DATAFLD="au_title" SIZE=4>
          <OPTION>Mr
          <OPTION>Mrs
          <OPTION>Miss
       </SELECT><P>
```

To navigate through the recordset you can add a series of buttons:

```
<INPUT TYPE="BUTTON" ID="cmdFirst" VALUE="<<"
               onclick="dsoAuthors.recordset.MoveFirst();">
<INPUT TYPE="BUTTON" ID="cmdPrevious" VALUE="<"
               onclick="dsoAuthors.recordset.MovePrevious();">
<INPUT TYPE="BUTTON" ID="cmdNext" VALUE=">"
               onclick="dsoAuthors.recordset.MoveNext();">
<INPUT TYPE="BUTTON" ID="cmdLast" VALUE=">>"
               onclick="dsoAuthors.recordset.MoveLast();">
```

Formatting Data

You can use the DATAFORMATAS property to specify how the data from the DSO is to be formatted. A value of HTML means that any HTML elements in the data are applied, and a value of TEXT means that any HTML elements are shown as plain text.

For example:

```
<TABLE DATASRC="#dsoAuthors" DATAPAGESIZE="10">
  <TR>
   <TD><SPAN DATAFLD="au_id"></SPAN></TD>
   <TD><SPAN DATAFLD="au_fname" DATAFORMATAS="HTML"></SPAN></TD>
   <TD><SPAN DATAFLD="au_lname"></SPAN></TD>
  </TR>
</TABLE>
```

This allows formatting, such as <B> or <I> tags to emphasize or italicize text to be embedded with the data.

Updating Data

Many DSO's can update the server with any changes made to the data. This is simply a matter of calling the submitChanges method of the DSO. For example:

```
<INPUT TYPE="BUTTON" ID="cmdSubmit" VALUE="Submit"
       onclick="dsoAuthors.submitChanges();">
```

When using the DataFactory directly, you also use the submitChanges method, but you must also specify the connection information and the recordset as arguments:

```
<SCRIPT LANGAUGE="JavaScript">
function cmdSubmit.onclick()
{
   dfFactory.SubmitChanges("DSN=pubs", dsoAuthors.recordset);
}
</SCRIPT>
```

If you are using a custom business object, then you have to provide a custom method to accept the changed recordset. For example, a Visual Basic component could implement a method like this:

```
Public Sub UpdateRecords (oRec As ADODB.Recordset)
   ' set the connection to the data store
   ' assumes g_sConnect is a global string previously set
   oRec.ActiveConnection = m_sConnect

   ' now update the source data
   oRec.UpdateBatch
End Sub
```

This could be called from the same page that created the custom object:

```
<SCRIPT LANGUAGE="JavaScript">
function cmdUpdate.onclick()
{
   ' get the recordset
   oRec = dsoAuthors.Recordset

   ' marshal only changed records
   oRec.MarshalOptions = 1;   // adMarshalModifiedOnly

   ' call custom component method
   objWroxBooks.UpdateRecords (oRec)
}
</SCRIPT>
```

Security Issues

If you are using MTS as part of your data application then you need to read the article *BUG: MTS Impersonation Returns Incorrect Caller When Using RDS* at http://support.microsoft.com/support/kb/articles/q184/7/02.asp. This details a large security hole in RDS. There is a patch available, for which you must call Microsoft Support.

From version 2.0 of RDS, a new set of security features was added, based around a configuration file. When RDS is installed an INI file called `msdfmap.ini` is placed in your `Windows` (or `WINNT`) folder. This file allows you to completely customize the settings for the `DataFactory` when it is instantiated by a client. You should consult the RDS documentation for full details of this, as well as a series of MSDN articles:

❑ Using the Customization Handler Feature in RDS 2.0

❑ Remote Data Service in MDAC 2.0

❑ Security and Your Web Server

❑ ADO and RDS Security Issues in Microsoft Internet Explorer

Custom Business Objects

Microsoft's Internet Information Server has security settings that restrict which objects can be instantiated by the `CreateObject` method of the `DataSpace` object. If you are using custom business objects then you need to add the details of these objects to the registry. The simplest way is to create a `.reg` file:

```
REGEDIT4
[HKEY_CLASSES_ROOT\CLSID\{your_component_guid}\Implemented
Categories\{7DD95801-9882-11CF-9FA9-00AA006C42C4}]
[HKEY_CLASSES_ROOT\CLSID\{your_component_guid}\Implemented
Categories\{7DD95802-9882-11CF-9FA9-00AA006C42C4}]
[HKEY_LOCAL_MACHINE\System\CurrentControlSet\Services\W3SVC\Parameters\ADCLau
nch\your_component_class_string]
```

The first line tells `regedit` that this is a valid `.reg` file. The next two entries (which should each be on one line, not wrapped like the code above) enable the Safe for Scripting setting, and the third line allows IIS to instantiate the component on the server. Place the file on the server machine, then double-click it to merge the values into the registry. Remember to back up the Registry first before making any changes to it.

ADOX Objects and Collections

This chapter deals with the new ADO Extensions for Data Definition and Security, ADOX. This is the big new feature of ADO 2.1, and allows the manipulation of the data store through ADO objects and methods, thus removing the necessity to learn the explicit syntax of the data provider. Here's a look at the object model again:

The ADOX objects are described individually, but as the handling of collections is the same for each collection, they have been included as a single section at the end of the chapter.

Of the OLE DB Providers currently available, the Jet provider has the fullest support for ADOX. Other providers may not support all properties and methods. The table below shows which features are *not* supported for the SQL Server and Oracle providers:

Provider	Object/ Collection	Feature not supported
SQL Server	Catalog Object	Create method
	Tables Collection	Properties are read only for existing tables
	Views Collection	Not supported
	Procedures Collection	Append method, Delete method, Command property
	Keys Collection	Append method, Delete method
	Users Collection	Not supported
	Groups Collection	Not supported
Oracle	Catalog Object	Create method
	Tables Collection	Append method, Delete method, Properties are read only for existing tables
	Views Collection	Append method, Delete method, Command property
	Procedures Collection	Append method, Delete method, Command property
	Indexes Collection	Append method, Delete method
	Keys Collection	Append method, Delete method
	Users Collection	Not supported
	Groups Collection	Not supported

If you wish to use ADOX against a different provider, you should consult the provider specific documentation for more details on supported properties for ADOX.

The Catalog Object

The `Catalog` object is the parent for all objects as it deals with catalog, or data store information.

Methods of the Catalog Object

The Create Method

Creates a new catalog. In most cases this means the creation of a new database.

> *String* = *Catalog*.**Create**(*ConnectString*)
> Set *Connection* = *Catalog*.**Create**(*ConnectString*)

Name	Type	Description
ConnectString	String	The connection string for the catalog to be created.

The return value is either a connection string or an ADO `Connection` object, depending upon how you call the method. For example, the following line of code sets `strConn` to the connection string of the new database:

```
Dim objCat    As New ADOX.Catalog
Dim strConn   As String

strConn = objCat.Create("Provider=Microsoft.Jet.OLEDB.4.0; Data
Source=C:\temp\newdb.mdb")
```

The following code however, sets `objConn` to a `Connection` object:

```
Dim objCat    As New ADOX.Catalog
Dim objConn   As ADODB.Connection

Set objConn = objCat.Create("Provider=Microsoft.Jet.OLEDB.4.0; Data
Source=C:\temp\newdb.mdb")
```

If using scripting languages, where variables are all Variants, then the use of the `Set` keyword determines what type of variable you receive back from the `Create` method. Without using `Set` you get a string (the connection string), and with the `Set` you get a `Connection` object.

The GetObjectOwner Method

Retrieves the user or group name of the owner of the specified object.

> *String* = *Catalog*.**GetObjectOwner**(*ObjectName*, *ObjectType*,
> [*ObjectTypeId*])

Name	Type	Description
ObjectName	String	The name of the object.
ObjectType	ObjectTypeEnum	The type of the object
ObjectTypeId	Variant	A GUID. If the object type is provider specific and not a standard OLE DB object type, `ObjectType` must be set to `adPermObjProviderSpecific`.

ObjectType can be one of the following:

❑ adPermObjColumn, to specify that the object is a column.

❑ adPermObjDatabase, to specify that the object is a database.

❑ adPermObjProcedure, to specify that the object is a procedure.

❑ adPermObjProviderSpecific, to specify that the object is of a provider specific type.

❑ adPermObjTable, to specify that the object is a table.

❑ adPermObjView, to specify that the object is a view.

For scripting languages, these constants are not in the include files supplied with ADO. They are available in Appendix I, as well as an include file from the supporting web site.

The ADOX documentation mentions adPermObjSchema, adPermObjDomain, adPermObjCollation, adPermObjSchemaRowset, adPermObjCharacterSet, adPermObjTranslation as allowable options for the object type. This is incorrect – these constants are not supported.

Note that to use this method with the Jet Provider you must explicitly set a security database. For example:

```
strConn = "Provider=Microsoft.Jet.OLEDB.4.0; " & _
    "Data Source=C:\temp\pubs.mdb; " & _
    "Jet OLEDB:System Database=" & _
        "c:\Program Files\Microsoft Office\Office\System.mdw"

objCat.ActiveConnection = strConn
Print objCat.GetObjectOwner ("authors", adPermObjTable)
```

The SQL Server provider does not support this method.

The SetObjectOwner Method

Sets the user or group as the owner of the specified object.

> Catalog.SetObjectOwner(*ObjectName, ObjectType, UserName, [ObjectTypeId]*)

Name	Type	Description
ObjectName	String	The name of the object.
ObjectType	ObjectTypeEnum	The type of the object
UserName	String	The name of the User or Group who will be the new owner of the object.
ObjectTypeId	Variant	A GUID. If the object type is provider specific and not a standard OLE DB object type, ObjectType must be set to adPermObjProviderSpecific.

ObjectType can be one of the following:

- ❑ `adPermObjColumn`, to specify that the object is a column.
- ❑ `adPermObjDatabase`, to specify that the object is a database.
- ❑ `adPermObjProcedure`, to specify that the object is a procedure.
- ❑ `adPermObjProviderSpecific`, to specify that the object is of a provider specific type.
- ❑ `adPermObjTable`, to specify that the object is a table.
- ❑ `adPermObjView`, to specify that the object is a view.

The ADOX documentation mentions `adPermObjSchema`, `adPermObjDomain`, `adPermObjCollation`, `adPermObjSchemaRowset`, `adPermObjCharacterSet`, `adPermObjTranslation` as allowable options for the object type. This is incorrect, as these constants are not supported.

To set the new owner of a table you would use this method like so:

```
objCat.SetObjectOwner "authors", adPermObjTable, "Jan"
```

Note that to use this method with the Jet Provider you must explicitly set a security database.

Properties of the Catalog Object

The ActiveConnection Property

Sets or retrieves the information detailing the connection to the data store.

> *String = Catalog*.**ActiveConnection**
> *Catalog*.**ActiveConnection** = *String*
> Set *Connection* = *Catalog*.**ActiveConnection**
> Set *Catalog*.**ActiveConnection** = *Connection*

The connection details can either be a valid ADO connection string, or an ADO `Connection` object. For example, either of the two following syntaxes is valid:

```
strConn = "Provider=Microsoft.Jet.OLEDB.4.0; Data Source=c:\temp\pubs.mdb"
objConn.Open strConn
Set objCat.ActiveConnection = objConn
```

```
strConn = "Provider=Microsoft.Jet.OLEDB.4.0; Data Source=c:\temp\pubs.mdb"
objCat.ActiveConnection strConn
```

Setting the `ActiveConnection` property to `Nothing` will close the `catalog`.

Collections of the Catalog Object

The objects that make up the `Collections` are briefly mentioned here, but are covered in more detail under each object.

The Tables Collection

Returns a collection of the tables that are contained in this catalog.

```
Set Tables = Catalog.Tables
```

This is the default property.

The Groups Collection

Returns a collection of the user group accounts that are contained in this catalog.

```
Set Groups = Catalog.Groups
```

The Users Collection

Returns a collection of the user accounts that are contained in this catalog.

```
Set Users = Catalog.Users
```

The Procedures Collection

Returns a collection of the stored procedures that are contained in this catalog.

```
Set Procedures = Catalog.Procedures
```

The Views Collection

Returns a collection of the views that are contained in this catalog.

```
Set Views = Catalog.Views
```

The Table Object

The `Table` object contains all of the details for a single table.

Methods of the Table Object

The `Table` object has no methods.

Properties of the Table Object

The DateCreated Property

Identifies the date upon which the table was created.

Variant = Table.DateCreated

The DateModified Property

Identifies the date when the table was last modified.

Variant = Table.DateModified

The Name Property

The name of the table.

Table.Name = *String* *String = Table*.Name

The ParentCatalog Property

Identifies the parent catalog for the table.

Set *Catalog = Table*.ParentCatalog Set *Table*.ParentCatalog = *Catalog*

You can use the `ParentCatalog` property to set provider specific properties before the table is added to the catalog. For example:

```
Dim objCat As New ADOX.Catalog
Dim objTbl As New ADOX.Table

objCat.ActiveConnection = "Provider=Microsoft.Jet.OLEDB.4.0; " & _
    "Data Source=c:\temp\pubs.mdb"

objTbl.Name = "tblNewTable"
objTbl.Columns.Append "FirstName", adVarWChar, 25
objTbl.Columns.Append "LastName", adVarWChar, 25
objTbl.Columns.Append "Age", adInteger

Set objTbl.ParentCatalog = objCat
objTbl.Properties("Jet OLEDB:Table Validation Rule") = "[Age]>18"
objTbl.Properties("Jet OLEDB:Table Validation Text") = "Age must be over 18"

objCat.Tables.Append objTbl
```

The Type Property

Identifies the type of table.

> *String = Table.***Type**

This can be one of the following strings:

- ❑ TABLE, for a normal table.
- ❑ SYSTEM TABLE, for a provider system table.
- ❑ GLOBAL TEMPORARY, for a temporary table.

Collections of the Table Object

The Columns Collection

Contains a Column object for each column in the table.

> Set *Columns = Table.***Columns**

You can use the Columns collection to find the details for each Column.

This is the default property.

The Indexes Collection

Contains an Index object for each index associated with the table.

> Set *Indexes = Table.***Indexes**

The Keys Collection

Contains a Key object for each key associated with the table.

> Set *Keys = Table.***Keys**

The Properties Collection

Contains a Property object for each provider specific property of the table.

> Set *Properties = Table.***Properties**

The Properties collection is covered in more detail in Chapter 6, and a full list of ADOX properties is in Appendix J.

The Index Object

The Index object contains all of the details for a single index on a table.

Methods of the Index Object

The Index object has no methods.

Properties of the Index Object

The Clustered Property

Indicates whether or not the Index is clustered.

> *Index*.**Clustered** = *Boolean*
> *Boolean* = *Index*.**Clustered**

By default, indexes are not clustered.

You can only set this property before appending an Index to the Indexes collection.

The IndexNulls Property

Indicates what happens to index entries that contain Null values.

> *Index*.**IndexNulls** = *AllowNullsEnum*
> *AllowNullsEnum* = *Index*.**IndexNulls**

AllowNullsEnum can be one of the following constants:

- ❑ adIndexNullsAllow, ensures that key columns with null values have index values. The index entry will itself be null.

- ❑ adIndexNullsDisallow, ensures that if the key columns are null, Index entries are not allowed. Attempting to insert a record with Null values in a key column will generate an error. This is the default value.

- ❑ adIndexNullsIgnore, allows Null values in key columns, but they are ignored and an index entry is not created.

- ❑ adIndexNullsIgnoreAny, allows Null values in any part of the key (for multiple columns), but they are ignored, and an index entry is not created.

You cannot change this property on Index objects that already exist in the Indexes collection.

The Name Property

Sets or retrieves the name of the Index.

> *Index*.**Name** = *String*
> *String* = *Index*.**Name**

This is the default property.

The PrimaryKey Property

Indicates whether or not the Index is the primary key of the table.

> *Index.*PrimaryKey = *Boolean*
> *Boolean* = *Index.*PrimaryKey

The default value is `False`, and you can only set this value for `Index` objects that have not yet been added to the `Indexes` collection.

The Unique Property

Indicates whether or not the `keys` in the `Index` must be unique.

> *Index.*Unique = *Boolean*
> *Boolean* = *Index.*Unique

The default value is `False`, and you can only set this value for `Index` objects that have not yet been added to the `Indexes` collection.

Collections of the Index Object

The Columns Collection

Contains a `Column` object for each column that exists in the `Index`.

> Set *Columns* = *Index.*Columns

The Properties Collection

Contains a `Property` object for each provider specific property.

> Set *Properties* = *Index.*Properties

The Key Object

The Key object represents a table key, either primary, foreign, or unique.

Methods of the Key Object

The Key object has no methods.

Properties of the Key Object

The DeleteRule Property

Indicates what happens when a primary key is deleted.

```
Key.DeleteRule = RuleEnum
RuleEnum = Key.DeleteRule
```

RuleEnum can be one of the following constants:

❑   adRICascade, to indicate that deletes are cascaded.

❑   adRINone, to indicate that deletes are not cascaded. This is the default value.

❑   adRISetDefault, to indicate that the foreign key should be set to its default value for deletes.

❑   adRISetNull, to indicate that the foreign key should be set to null for deletes.

You can only set this value on keys before you add them to the Keys collection.

The Name Property

Indicates the name of the Key.

```
Key.Name = String
String = Key.Name
```

The RelatedTable Property

If the key is a foreign key, then this represents the name of the foreign table.

```
Key.RelatedTable = String
String = Key.RelatedTable
```

To identify the column in the related table you use the RelatedColumn property of the Column object. For example:

```
objKey.RelatedTable = "sales"
objKey.Columns("store_id").RelatedColumn = "store_id"
```

The Type Property

Indicates the type of the key.

> *Key*.Type = *KeyTypeEnum*
> *KeyTypeEnum* = *Key*.Type

KeyTypeEnum can be one of the following constants:

❑ adKeyForeign, to indicate that the key is a foreign key.

❑ adKeyPrimary, to indicate that the key is a primary key.

❑ adKeyUnique, to indicate that the key is unique.

The UpdateRule Property

Indicates what should happen when primary keys are updated.

> *Key*.UpdateRule = *RuleEnum*
> *RuleEnum* = *Key*.UpdateRule

RuleEnum can be one of the following constants:

❑ adRICascade, to indicate that updates are cascaded.

❑ adRINone, to indicate that updates are not cascaded. This is the default value.

❑ adRISetDefault, to indicate that the foreign key should be set to its default value for updates.

❑ adRISetNull, to indicate that the foreign key should be set to null for updates.

You can only set this value on keys before you add them to the Keys collection.

Collections of the Key Object

The Columns Collection

Contains a Column object for each column in the key.

> *Columns* = *Key*.Columns

The Column Object

The Column object relates to an individual column, or field, in a Key, Table or Index.

Methods of the Column Object

The Column object has no methods.

Properties of the Column Object

The Attributes Property

Retrieves or sets the individual characteristics of a Column.

> *Column*.**Attributes** = *ColumnAttributesEnum*
> *ColumnAttributesEnum* = *Column*.**Attributes**

ColumnAttributesEnum can be either one or both of the following values:

- ❑   adColFixed, to indicate that the column is of a fixed length.
- ❑   adColNullable, to indicate that the column may contain null values.

The default value has neither of these attributes set. You should use bitwise operations to set multiple values, or to retrieve individual attributes. For example, to set both attributes:

```
Set objCol = objTable.Columns("state")
objCol.Attributes = adColFixed Or adColNullable
```

And to check for a single attribute:

```
If (objCol.Attributes And adColFixed) = adColFixed Then
    Print "The column is of a fixed width"
End If
```

The DefinedSize Property

Sets or retrieves the maximum size of a column.

> *Column*.**DefinedSize** = *Long*
> *Long* = *Column*.**DefinedSize**

For variable length columns this indicates the maximum amount of data that the column may contain. It defaults to 0, and a value is not explicitly required for fixed length data types.

You can only set this value on Column objects before they are appended to the Columns collection.

The Name Property

Sets or retrieves the name of a column.

> *Column*.**Name** = *String*
> *String* = *Column*.**Name**

This is the default property.

The NumericScale Property

Sets or retrieves the scale for a numeric column.

> *Column*.**NumericScale** = *Byte*
> *Byte* = *Column*.**NumericScale**

This is only applicable to columns of type `adNumeric` or `adDecimal`, and any value in this property will be ignored for all other column types.

The default value is 0.

The ParentCatalog Property

Sets or retrieves the `Catalog` to which this column belongs.

> Set *Catalog* = *Column*.**ParentCatalog**
> Set *Column*.**ParentCatalog** = *Catalog*

The `ParentCatalog` property allows you to set provider specific properties before the column is appended to the `Columns` collection. For example:

```
strConn = "Provider= Microsoft.Jet.OLEDB.4.0; Data Source=c:\temp\pubs.mdb"
objCat.ActiveConnection = strConn

objTbl.Columns.Append "Name", adVarWChar
objCol.Name = "Age"
objCol.Type = adInteger

Set objCol.ParentCatalog = objCat
objCol.Properties("Jet OLEDB:Column Validation Rule") = ">18"
objCol.Properties("Jet OLEDB:Column Validation Text") = "Age must be over 18"
objTbl.Columns.Append objCol

objCat.Tables.Append objTbl
```

You can only set this value on `Column` objects before they are appended to the `Columns` collection.

The Precision Property

Sets or retrieves the maximum precision of data in the column.

> *Column*.**Precision** = *Long*
> *Long* = *Column*.**Precision**

This is only applicable to columns that are numeric, and is ignored for other column types.

The default value is 0.

The RelatedColumn Property

For key columns, this sets or retrieves the name of the column in the related table.

> *Column*.**RelatedColumn** = *String*
> *String* = *Column*.**RelatedColumn**

You can only set this value on `Column` objects before they are appended to the `Columns` collection.

An error will be generated if you try to read this value for columns which are not part of keys.

The SortOrder Property

For a `Column` in an `Index` this indicates the order in which the `Column` is sorted.

> *Column*.**SortOrder** = *SortOrderEnum*
> *SortOrderEnum* = *Column*.**SortOrder**

SortOrderEnum can be one of the following:

- ❏ `adSortAscending`, to sort in ascending order.

- ❏ `adSortDescending`, to sort in descending order.

The default sort order is ascending.

Accessing this property on a column which is not part of an index will generate an error.

The Type Property

Sets or retrieves the data type for the values that will be held in the column.

> *Column*.**Type** = *DataTypeEnum*
> *DataTypeEnum* = *Column*.**Type**

Because of its size, the listing for `DataTypeEnum` is not shown here, but can be seen in Appendix B.

The default value is `adVarWChar`. Not all providers support all data types, and you should use Appendix E as a guide for picking the correct type for your provider.

You can only set this value on `Column` objects before they are appended to the `Columns` collection.

> *The difference between* `adVarChar` *and* `adVarWChar` *(and indeed other types with a W in them), is that the W types support Unicode, allowing for extended character sets. Jet 4 fully supports Unicode, therefore these W types are now the default over their non-Unicode equivalents.*

Collections of the Column Object

The Properties Collection

Contains all of the Property objects for the Column.

> Set *Properties* = *Column*.**Properties**

The Properties collection contains provider specific properties, and behaves exactly the same as the Properties collection of ADO which is discussed in Chapter 6. A full list of ADOX properties available is in Appendix J.

The Group Object

The group object identifies a security group account.

Methods of the Group Object

The GetPermissions Method

Retrieves the group permissions for an object, or for a class of object.

> *RightsEnum = Group.GetPermissions(Name, ObjectType, [ObjectTypeId])*

Name	Type	Description
Name	Variant	The object name for which to retrieve permissions.
ObjectType	ObjectTypeEnum	The type of object
ObjectTypeId	Variant	A GUID. If the object type is provider specific and not a standard OLE DB object type, `ObjectType` must be set to `adPermObjProviderSpecific`.

ObjectType can be one of the following:

- ❑ `adPermObjColumn`, to specify that the object is a column.

- ❑ `adPermObjDatabase`, to specify that the object is a database.

- ❑ `adPermObjProcedure`, to specify that the object is a procedure.

- ❑ `adPermObjProviderSpecific`, to specify that the object is of a provider specific type.

- ❑ `adPermObjTable`, to specify that the object is a table.

- ❑ `adPermObjView`, to specify that the object is a view.

The ADOX documentation mentions `adPermObjSchema`, `adPermObjDomain`, `adPermObjCollation`, `adPermObjSchemaRowset`, `adPermObjCharacterSet`, `adPermObjTranslation` as allowable options for the object type. This is incorrect, as these constants are not supported.

The return value is a combination of one or more of the `RightsEnum` constants, a list of which is shown in Appendix I. You can test for individual permissions by using bitwise operations:

```
lngPerms = objGroup.GetPermissions ("authors", adPermObjTable)
If (lngPerms And adRightReadDesign)= adRightReadDesign Then
    Print "You have permissions to read the table design"
End If
```

You can also test for multiple permissions:

```
lngPerms = objGroup.GetPermissions ("authors", adPermObjTable)
If (lngPerms And adRightReadDescign = adRightReadDesign) Or
    (lngPerms And adRightWriteDesign = adRightWriteDesign) Then
    Print "You can read from and write to the table design"
End If
```

Substituting `Null` for the `Name` parameter allows you to examine the permissions on the container. For example, the following shows the permissions on the `Tables` container, identifying what permissions the group has for new tables:

```
lngPerms = objGroup.GetPermissions (Null, adPermObjTable)
```

The SetPermissions Method

Sets the group permissions for an object, or for a class of object.

> *Group*.SetPermissions(*Name, ObjectType, Action, Rights, [Inherit],*
> *[ObjectTypeId]*)

Name	Type	Description
Name	Variant	The name of the object for which to set permissions.
ObjectType	ObjectTypeEnum	The object type.
Action	ActionEnum	The type of permission action to set.
Rights	RightsEnum	The individual permissions to set.
Inherit	InheritTypeEnum	Indicates the type of permissions inheritance for containers and objects. Default is `adInheritNone`
ObjectTypeId	Variant	A GUID. If the object type is provider specific and not a standard OLE DB object type, `ObjectType` must be set to `adPermObjProviderSpecific`.

ObjectType can be one of the following `ObjectTypeEnum` constants:

❑ `adPermObjColumn`, to specify that the object is a column.

❑ `adPermObjDatabase`, to specify that the object is a database.

❑ `adPermObjProcedure`, to specify that the object is a procedure.

❑ `adPermObjProviderSpecific`, to specify that the object is of a provider specific type.

❑ `adPermObjTable`, to specify that the object is a table.

❑ `adPermObjView`, to specify that the object is a view.

The ADOX documentation mentions adPermObjSchema, adPermObjDomain, adPermObjCollation, adPermObjSchemaRowset, adPermObjCharacterSet, adPermObjTranslation as allowable options for the object type. This is incorrect, as these constants are not supported.

Action can be one of the following ActionEnum constants:

❑ adAccessDeny, to deny the specific permissions to the Group or User.

❑ adAccessGrant, to grant the specific permissions to the Group or User. This grants an individual permission and will leave other permissions in effect.

❑ adAccessRevoke, to revoke any specific access rights to the Group or User.

❑ adAccessSet, to set the exact permissions for the Group or User. Any existing permissions will be replaced by the new set of permissions.

Rights can be one or more of the RightsEnum constants, a list of which is shown in Appendix I, and indicates the permissions to be set on the object for the group.

Inherit can be one of the InheritTypeEnum constants, and allows you to specify whether containers inherit permissions from the object that you are setting permissions for:

❑ adInheritBoth, to indicate that permissions for the object are inherited by both objects and other containers.

❑ adInheritContainers, to indicate that permissions for the object are inherited by other containers.

❑ adInheritNone, to indicate that no permissions are inherited.

❑ adInheritNoPropogate, to indicate that the adInheritObjects and adInheritContainers permissions are not propagated to child objects.

❑ adInheritObjects, to indicate that permissions are only inherited by objects that are not containers.

To set more than one right you should combine them together:

```
lngRights = adRightInsert Or adRightUpdate
objGroup.SetPermissions "authors", adPermObjTable, adAccessGrant, lngRights
```

If you wish to set the permissions for the container you can supply Null for the name:

```
lngRights = adRightInsert Or adRightUpdate
objGroup.SetPermissions Null, adPermObjTable, adAccessGrant, lngRights
```

This sets the rights on the Tables container to allow inserts and updates.

Properties of the Group Object

The Name Property

Sets or retrieves the name of the group account.

```
Group.Name = String
String = Group.Name
```

This is the default property.

Collections of the Group Object

The Users Collection

Contains all of the User accounts that belong to this group.

```
Set Users = Group.Users
```

To list all of the users in a particular group, you can use the For..Each construct.

The User Object

The User object contains the details of a single user account.

Methods of the User Object

The ChangePassword Method

Allows the user password to be changed.

> *User*.**ChangePassword**(*OldPassword, NewPassword*)

Name	Type	Description
OldPassword	String	The existing user password.
NewPassword	String	The new user password.

To clear a password, or to represent a blank password, you should use an empty string. For example, to clear the password for a user:

```
objUser.ChangePassword "abc123", ""
```

The GetPermissions Method

Retrieves the user permissions on an object.

> *RightsEnum* = *User*.**GetPermissions**(*Name, ObjectType, [ObjectTypeId]*)

Usage of the SetPermission method for a User object is exactly the same as the SetPermissions method for the Group object.

The SetPermissions Method

Sets the user permissions for an object, or for a class of object.

> *User*.**SetPermissions**(*Name, ObjectType, Action, Rights, [Inherit], [ObjectTypeId]*)

Usage of the GetPermission method for a User object is exactly the same as the GetPermissions method for the Group object.

Properties of the User Object

The Name Property

Identifies the name of the user.

> *User*.**Name** = *String*
> *String* = *User*.**Name**

This is the default property.

Collections of the User Object

The Groups Collection

Contains a `Group` object for each group to which the user belongs.

```
Set Groups = User.Groups
```

The Procedure Object

The `Procedure` object contains the details of a stored procedure. It does not directly contain the SQL text associated with the stored procedure, but just identifies the procedure in the catalog. To access the SQL that makes up the procedure you use the `Command` property of the `Procedure` object.

Methods of the Procedure Object

The `Procedure` object has no methods.

Properties of the Procedure Object

The Command Property

Indicates an ADO `Command` object that contains the procedure details.

> Set *Command* = *Procedure*.**Command**
> Set *Procedure*.**Command** = **Command**

The following providers do *not* support the `Command` property and will return an error if you try reference it:

- ❑ OLE DB Provider for SQL Server
- ❑ OLE DB Provider for ODBC
- ❑ OLE DB Provider for Oracle

For providers that support the `Command` interface you can set and retrieve the command details using the ADO `Command` properties:

```
Set objCmd = objCat.Procedures("qryPriceDetails")
Print objCmd.CommandText
```

Or you can update the procedure:

```
objCmd.CommandText = "UPDATE Products SET Price = Price * 1.05"
Set objCat.Procedures("qryUpdatePrices") = objCmd
```

This is the default property.

The DateCreated Property

Indicates the date the procedure was created.

> *Variant* = *Procedure*.**DateCreated**

You will need to `Refresh` the collection to see this value for newly appended procedures.

The DateModified Property

Indicates the date the procedure was last modified.

> *Variant = Procedure.*DateModified

You will need to `Refresh` the collection to see this value for newly appended procedures.

The Name Property

Indicates the name of the procedure.

> *String = Procedure.*Name

The View Object

The View object contains details of views in the catalog. For Microsoft Access, this includes standard select queries.

Methods of the View Object

The View object has no methods.

Properties of the View Object

The Command Property

Indicates an ADO Command object that contains the view details.

> Set *Command* = *View*.**Command**
> Set *View*.**Command** = **Command**

The following providers do *not* support the Command property and will return an error if you try reference it:

❑ OLE DB Provider for SQL Server
❑ OLE DB Provider for ODBC
❑ OLE DB Provider for Oracle

For providers that support the Command interface you can set and retrieve the command details using the ADO Command properties:

```
Set objCmd = objCat.Views("vwTradePriceList")
Print objCmd.CommandText
```

Or you can set the command text:

```
objCmd.CommandText = "SELECT Product, TradePrice From Products"
Set objCat.Views("vwTradePriceList").Command = objCmd
```

This is the default property.

The DateCreated Property

Identifies the date the view was created.

> *Variant* = *View*.**DateCreated**

The DateModified Property

Identifies the date the view was last modified.

> *Variant* = *View*.**DateModified**

The Name Property

Identifies the name of the view.

> *String* = *View*.**Name**

Collections

The handling of ADOX collections is the similar for all ADOX objects, so they have been included here as a single section.

The table below details the objects and their collections.

ADOX Object	Collections
Catalog	Tables, Groups, Users, Procedures, Views
Table	Columns, Indexes, Keys, Properties
Index	Columns, Properties
Key	Columns
Column	Properties
Group	Users
User	Groups
Procedure	
View	

The difference between the collections are:

❏ The Properties collection is a read-only collection, and therefore does not have an Append or Delete method. The Properties collection is the same as the ADO Properties collection, and is detailed in Chapter 6.

❏ The remaining collections have different Append methods. These are detailed below.

Enumerating collections can be achieved with the For Each statement in Visual Basic or VBScript, or the Enumerator object in JScript. C++ and J++ users should use standard loops, using the Item property to access each element in the collection.

Methods of a Collection

The Append Method

The Columns Collection

Adds a new Column to the collection.

```
Columns.Append(Item, [Type], [DefinedSize])
```

Name	Type	Description
Item	Variant	A Column object to append, or the name of the new column to append
Type	DataTypeEnum	The data type of the column. Default is adVarWChar
DefinedSize	Long.	The maximum column size. Default is 0

Because of its size, the listing for DataTypeEnum is not shown here, but can be seen in Appendix B.

The Append method can take one of two forms. The first is to append an existing Column object to the collection:

```
objColumn.Name = "FirstName"
objColumn.Type = adVarWChar
objColumn.DefinedSize = 25
objTable.Columns.Append objColumn
```

The second method is to define the column name:

```
objTable.Columns.Append "FirstName", adVarWChar, 25
```

The Groups Collection

Adds a new group to the collection.

Groups.Append(*Item*)

Name	Type	Description
Item	Variant	A Group object, or the name of the group to be added.

You can specify either a valid Group object, or just the name of a group in this method. For example, the following are equivalent:

```
objGroup.Name = "Finance"
objCat.Groups.Append objGroup
```

```
objCat.Groups.Append "Finance"
```

The Indexes Collection

Adds a new Index to the collection.

Indexes.Append(*Item, [Columns]*)

Name	Type	Description
Item	Variant	An Index object, or the name of the index to append
Columns	Variant	A variant array listing the column names contained in the Index.

You can specify either an existing `Index` object or the name that the new index is to have:

```
objIndex.Name = "NameIndex"
objIndex.Columns.Append "FirstName", adVarWChar, 10
objIndex.Columns.Append "LastName", adVarWChar, 10
objTable.Indexes.Append objIndex
```

```
objTable.Indexes.Append "NameIndex", Array("FirstName", "LastName")
```

If your index consists of only a single column then you can omit the `Array` usage:

```
objTable.Indexes.Append "FirstNameIndex", "FirstName"
```

The Keys Collection

Adds a new key to the collection.

> **Keys.Append(*Item*, [*Type*], [*Column*], [*RelatedTable*], [*RelatedColumn*])**

Name	Type	Description
Item	Variant	A `Key` object or the name of the key to append.
Type	KeyTypeEnum	The type of the key. Default is `adKeyPrimary`
Column	Variant	The column that the key applies to.
RelatedTable	String	For a foreign key, the `Table` that the key points to.
RelatedColumn	String	For a foreign key, the `Column` in the `RelatedTable` that the key points to.

The key *Type* can be one of the `KeyTypeEnum` constants:

❑   `adKeyForeign`, to indicate the key is a foreign key.

❑   `adKeyPrimary`, to indicate the key is a primary key.

❑   `adKeyUnique`, to idicate the key is unique.

The item being appended can either be a valid `Key` object, or the name of the key:

```
objKey.Name = "PKau_id"
objKey.Columns.Append "au_id", adKeyPrimary
objTable("authors").Keys.Append objKey
```

```
objTable("authors").Keys.Append "PKau_id", adKeyPrimary, "au_id"
```

When dealing with foreign keys you should set the *RelatedTable* and *RelatedColumn* arguments accordingly:

```
objTable("authors").Keys.Append "FKpub_id", adKeyForeign, "pub_id", _
                   "publishers", "pub_id"
```

The Procedures Collection

Adds a new procedure to the collection.

> **Procedures.Append(*Name, Command*)**

Name	Type	Description
Name	String	The name of the new procedure.
Command	Object	An ADO Command object containing the procedure details.

Like the Command property, this method is not supported by all providers. For providers that do support this, you can easily create new stored procedures:

```
objCmd.Name.CommandText = "UPDATE . . . ."
objCat.Procedures.Append "UpdateValues", objCmd
```

The Tables Collection

Adds a new Table to the collection.

> **Tables.Append(*Item*)**

Name	Type	Description
Item	Variant	A Table object, or the name of the table to add

The *Item* can be either a valid Table object, or the name of the table to be added:

```
objTable.Name = "Contacts"
objCat.Tables.Append objTable
```

```
objCat.Tables.Append "Contacts"
```

The Users Collection

Adds a new user to a group or to a catalog.

> **Users.Append(*Item, [Password]*)**

Name	Type	Description
Item	Variant	A user object or the name of the user to add.
Password	String	The user password

The *Item* can be either a valid User object or the name of a user:

```
objUser.Name = "Jan"
objCat.Users.Append objUser
```

```
objCat.Users.Append "Jan", "Vouvray"
```

251

You must ensure that a User is added to the Catalog before adding the User to a Group. This is because the User must be valid user account before it can be added to a Group.

The Views Collection

Adds a new view to the catalog.

Views.Append(*Name, Command*)

Name	Type	Description
Name	String	The name of the new procedure.
Command	Object	An ADO Command object containing the procedure details.

Like the Command property, this method is not supported by all providers. For providers that do support this, you can easily create new views:

```
objCmd.Name.CommandText = "SELECT . . ."
objCat.Views.Append "GetValues", objCmd
```

The Delete Method

Deletes an object from the collection.

Collection.**Delete**(*Item*)

Name	Type	Description
Item	Variant	The number or name of the object to be deleted.

Item can either be the number, or the name of the object to delete. For example, to delete a View from the Views collection you could use either of these lines:

```
objCat.Views.Delete(0)
```

```
objCat.Views.Delete("qrySalesByQuarter")
```

The Refresh Method

Refreshes the collection from the provider, ensuring that any deleted objects are no longer shown, and that new objects are available.

Collection.**Refresh**

Using Refresh ensures that any changes taken place by other users of the Catalog are reflected in your collection objects.

Properties of a Collection

The Count Property

Identifies the number of objects within the collection.

> *Long = Collection*.**Count**

For example, to determine the number of tables within a `Catalog` you could use this code:

```
Print objCatalog.Tables.Count
```

The Item Property

Allows indexing into the collection, by either name or number.

> Set *Object = Collection*.**Item**(*Item*)

Name	Type	Description
Item	Variant	The name of the object, or its number

This is the default method and can be omitted. For example, in indexing into the `Columns` collection, both of the following are equivalent:

```
Set objColumn = objTable.Columns ("Name")
```

```
Set objColumn = objTable.Columns.Item("Name")
```

ADO Multi-Dimensional

The ADOMD library is a companion to the standard ADO library, and is specially developed to integrate with On Line Analytical Processing (OLAP) servers. The best way to think about OLAP is to think of spreadsheets. You could compare a normal spreadsheet to a normal database table – you have rows and columns in both. OLAP data also has rows and columns, but is more like the Pivot Table in Microsoft Excel. OLAP is designed for analyzing data, providing calculations, summaries, and so on.

To understand OLAP you really need an example, so let's take the pubs database. Suppose you want to see the book sales for each Publisher, grouped by State and City, and sub-grouped by the period of sale (Year, Quarter, Month, Day). What you are aiming for is something like this:

+ State	- Year	- Quarter	+ Month	All Publishers	Algodata Infosystems	Binnet & Hardley
All Geography	- 1994	- Quarter 3	Quarter 3 Total	163	15	40
			+ September	163	15	40
+ CA	All Dates	All Dates Total		275	65	90
	- 1992		1992 Total	80		80
		- Quarter 2	Quarter 2 Total	80		80
			+ June	80		80
	+ 1993	1993 Total		110	65	10
	- 1994		1994 Total	85		
		- Quarter 3	Quarter 3 Total	85		
			+ September	85		
+ OR	All Dates	All Dates Total		80	65	15
	- 1992		1992 Total			
		- Quarter 2	Quarter 2 Total			
			+ June			
	+ 1993	1993 Total		55	55	
	- 1994		1994 Total	25	10	15
		- Quarter 3	Quarter 3 Total	25	10	15
			+ September	25	10	15

This sort of data analysis is possible with standard SQL queries, or even using the Pivot Table in Excel, but there's a better way – use an OLAP server that can take raw data (from any data source) and transform it into easily accessible structures. That transformation is one of the key points of OLAP – it abstracts the data into more easily accessible features, which can be used to manipulate the data.

These OLAP structures come in two sets. The first set represents how the OLAP server stores the data, and consists of the following objects:

❑ **Catalog**, which is the container for all OLAP objects. This identifies the OLAP server, and the actual data server that supplies the original data.

❑ **CubeDef**, which is a container for a set of data. In the diagram above, the CubeDef is called AllSales and contains the structures that identify the States, Dates (Years, Quarters and Months) and Publishers. A CubeDef doesn't represent how the data is shown – it just represents what the structures are and what they contain.

❑ **Dimension**, which is a distinct set of items. The diagram above shows several Dimensions: Geography (to identify the States and Cities), Dates (to identify the date of the book sales) and Publishers (to identify the book publishers). The Dimensions give us the headings on the axis of the diagram. Moreover, as you can see, Dimensions can be nested.

❑ **Hierarchy**, which identifies the relationship of the items within a Dimension. So, for the Dates dimension we have three Hierarchys; Year, Quarter and Month. The hierarchies give us sub-headings.

❑ **Level**, which identifies the elements in an individual Hierarchy. For the Dates dimension we have a Hierarchy called Year – each year in the Dimension is a Level. Likewise, there is a Level for each Publisher.

❑ **Member**, which represents a unique item in a Level. This is equivalent to the cells in the diagram.

The second set of OLAP structures represent the data as it is actually being displayed. So if you run a query against an OLAP server you get a set of data, which comprises:

❑ **CellSet**, which represents the whole set of data. This would be equivalent to the entire diagram above.

❑ **Axis**, which represents one of the physical axes of the CellSet. For example, the diagram above would require an Axis for the rows (the Y axis) and another Axis for the columns (the X axis).

❑ **Cell**, which is a single cell. In the diagram above, a Cell would represent the quantity sold.

❑ **Position**, which is an individual row or column.

❑ **Measure**, which is a quantitative, numerical column, and is usually the name of the item that is shown in each cell. In the diagram above the Measure is the quantity of books sold.

The object model diagram below illustrates how these objects relate to each other. As you can see, many (although not all) of the objects listed above are contained within collections:

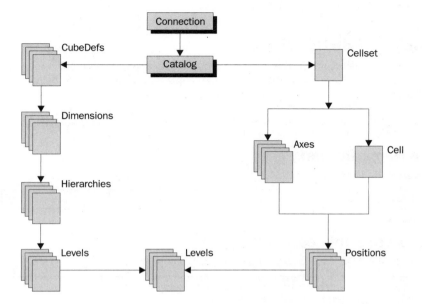

This might all seem to be just another confusing way to represent data. However, OLAP servers give you the ability to manipulate data much more easily than most relational databases. Abstracting the data into known terms (Geography, Sales, Publishers) makes the data more accessible for users – because they are less reliant upon knowing the physical structure of the data.

Multi-Dimension Extensions

SQL Server 7.0 implements MDX, which is a set of SQL extensions that allow processing of OLAP queries. For example, the above set of data could be generated with the following:

```
SELECT     Publishers.Members ON COLUMNS,
CROSSJOIN (Geography.Members, Dates.Members) ON ROWS
FROM       AllSales
```

The MDX extensions allow the use of OLAP names (Members, Levels, and so on) in SQL queries. For more information on MDX you should consults the SQL 7 documentation.

OLAP Servers

To use ADOMD you'll need access to an OLAP server – Microsoft SQL Server comes with an OLAP server, so check out the documentation. The OLAP server for SQL 7.0 is extremely easy to set up and use, and can be obtained (along with SQL 7.0 itself) as a time-limited evaluation. The limit is 120 days, which should give you plenty of time to get to know it.

To use ADO with OLAP you will need to install the Client components when you install the OLAP Services, ensuring that the PivotTable Service is installed. This is the service that provides the interface from ADO into the OLAP Service. The SQL 7.0 installation CD contains a set of ADOMD examples, in a variety of languages.

The Catalog Object

A `Catalog` object contains the `CubeDefs` that make up a multi-dimensional query. The `Catalog` identifies the OLAP server that contains the structures to be used for OLAP queries.

The `Catalog` object has just two properties and one collection (and no methods).

The Name Property

Identifies the name of the catalog.

```
String = Catalog.Name
```

The ActiveConnection Property

Identifies the ADO `Connection` to the OLAP data provider.

```
Set Connection = Catalog.ActiveConnection
Set Catalog.ActiveConnection = Connection
String = Catalog.ActiveConnection
Catalog.ActiveConnection = String
```

This can be an existing ADO `Connection` object or an ADO connection string.

The CubeDefs Collection

Contains a `CubeDef` for each multi-dimensional query in the catalog.

```
CubeDefs = Catalog.CubeDefs
```

You can use the `CubeDefs` collection to access individual `CubeDef` objects:

```
Set objCubeDef = objCatalog.CubeDefs("AllSales")
```

The CubeDef Object

A `CubeDef` object contains the related dimensions from a cube of multi-dimensional data.

The `CubeDef` object has two properties and two collections – and no methods.

The Name Property

Identifies the name of the `CubeDef`.

> *String = CubeDef*.**Name**

You can use the `Name` property to index into the `Catalog` object's `CubeDefs` collection:

```
Set objCubeDef = objCatalog.objCubeDefs("AllSales")
```

The Description Property

Contains descriptive text for the `CubeDef`.

> *String = CubeDef*.**Description**

The Dimensions Collection

Contains a `Dimension` object for each dimension in the `CubeDef`.

> *Dimensions = CubeDef*.**Dimensions**

The Properties Collection

Contains a `Property` object for each provider-specific property.

> *Properties = CubeDef*.**Properties**

The Dimension Object

A `Dimension` object represents a single dimension from a cube in a multi-dimensional query. The `Dimension` object has three properties, two collections and no methods.

The Name Property

Identifies the name of the `Dimension`.

> *String = Dimension*.**Name**

You can use the `Name` property to index into the `Dimensions` collection of the `CubeDef` object:

```
Set objDimension = objCubeDef.Dimensions("Geography")
```

The Description Property

Contains descriptive text for the `Dimension`.

> *String = Dimension*.**Description**

The UniqueName Property

Indicates the unique name for the `Dimension`.

> *String = Dimension*.**UniqueName**

Because of the complexity of dimensions, it's possible that you may find yourself using two (or more) Dimension objects with the same Name property. In such cases, UniqueName can be used to provide an unambiguous name for each Dimension object.

The Hierarchies Collection

Contains a Hierarchy object for each hierarchy in the dimension.

Hierarchies = Dimension.**Hierarchies**

The Properties Collection

Contains a Property object for each provider-specific property.

Properties = Dimension.**Properties**

The Hierarchy Object

A Hierarchy object identifies a single way in which data from a Dimension can be represented. This is often called an aggregation or a roll-up.

The Name Property

Identifies the Hierarchy object within the Hierarchies collection of a Dimension.

String = Hierarchy.**Name**

The Description Property

Descriptive text for the Hierarchy.

String = Hierarchy.**Description**

The UniqueName Property

Provides a unique name with which to identify the Hierarchy in the collection.

String = Hierarchy.**UniqueName**

The UniqueName property allows us to uniquely identify a Hierarchy object, and is particularly useful when we have multiple Hierarchy objects possessing the same Name. Thus, it allows us to have multiple Hierarchy objects with the same name, if the situation demands.

The Levels Collection

Contains a Level object for each level in the hierarchy.

Levels = Hierarchy.**Levels**

The Properties Collection

Contains a Property object for each provider-specific property.

Properties = Hierarchy.**Properties**

The Level Object

A `Level` object identifies a single step (or layer of aggregation) in a `Hierarchy`. The `Level` object has five properties, two collections and no methods.

The Name Property

Identifies the name of the `Level`.

> *String = Level*.**Name**

The Description Property

A textual description of the `Level`.

> *String = Level*.**Description**

The Caption Property

Identifies the text to show when the `Level` is displayed.

> *String = Level*.**Caption**

The Depth Property

Identifies how deep in the hierarchy this `Level` is.

> *Integer = Level*.**Depth**

The `Level` object's `Depth` property is the number of levels between the root of the hierarchy and the `Level` object. For example, in the diagram at the beginning of this chapter we have a `Hierarchy` object called `Dates`. The levels of this hierarchy (and their depths) are as follows:

Level Name	Depth
(All)	0
Year	1
Quarter	2
Month	3
Day	4

The UniqueName Property

Provides a unique name for the `Level`.

> *String = Level*.**UniqueName**

The `UniqueName` allows for `Level` objects that have the same `Name`.

The Members Collection

Contains a `Member` object for each unique row or column in the `Level` object.

> *Members = Level.***Members**

The Properties Collection

Contains a `Property` object for each provider-specific property.

> *Properties = Level.***Properties**

The Member Object

A `Member` object represents the data in a `Dimension`. The `Member` object has 12 properties and one collection, and no methods.

The Name Property

Indicates the name of the `Member`.

> *String = Member.***Name**

The Type Property

Identifies the type of the `Member`.

> *MemberTypeEnum = Member.***Type**

MemberTypeEnum can be one of the following constants:

- ❑ `adMemberRegular`, to indicate that the member is data directly from the data source.

- ❑ `adMemberMeasure`, to indicate that the member is a `Measure`, and represents a quantitative attribute.

- ❑ `adMemberFormula`, to indicate the member is calculated from a formula.

- ❑ `adMemberAll`, to indicate that the member represents all members for a given level.

- ❑ `adMemberUnknown`, to indicate the type is unknown.

The default is `adMemberRegular`.

The Caption Property

Identifies the text to that is written to the screen when the `Member` is used in a hierarchical query.

> *String = Member.***Caption**

The ChildCount Property

Identifies how many child members the Member object contains.

> *Long = Member*.ChildCount

The child members can be reached via the Children property.

The Children Property

Identifies the child members of which this Member is the parent.

> *Members = Member*.Children

To make this clearer, look back at the diagram at the beginning of this chapter, and consider the Dates hierarchy again. This has levels for the different types of date measurement (all dates, years, quarters, months and days). OLAP allows you to look at data from a variety of different ways – to implement this, each Member (in the Members collection of each Level) has a collection of Member objects, which are the children of the current Member. You can see this more clearly in the table below:

Level Name	Member	Child Member
(All)	All Dates	1992
		1993
		1994
Year	1992	Quarter 2
	1993	Quarter 1
		Quarter 2
		Quarter 4
	1994	Quarter 3
Quarter	Quarter 2	June
	Quarter 1	February
		March
	Quarter 2	May
Month	June	15
	May	22
		24

The Description Property

The descriptive text for the member.

> *String = Member*.Description

The DrilledDown Property

Indicates whether or not the Level has been drilled down.

```
Boolean = Member.DrilledDown
```

Indicates whether the Member is contained in the deepest level of the hierarchy – that is, whether we have *drilled down* as far as possible. If so, this property returns True. Otherwise (that is, the Member possesses child members) then this property returns False.

The LevelDepth Property

Identifies how deep this Member is, within the Level's hierarchy.

```
Long = Member.LevelDepth
```

The LevelDepth property is the same as the Depth property for the Level, and it is included for a Member because you can access Member objects from their positions in a CellSet, and not just from the Levels collection.

The LevelName Property

Indicates the name of the Level to which the Member belongs.

```
String = Member.LevelName
```

The Parent Property

Indicates the parent object of this Member.

```
Member = Member.Parent
```

In the discussion of the Children property, above, the table illustrates the concept of the parent/child relationship among Member objects.

The ParentSameAsPrev Property

Identifies whether the parent of this member is the same as the parent of the preceding Member in the Members collection.

```
Boolean = Member.ParentSameAsPrev
```

You can use this property to identify siblings, or Member objects that are on the same level.

The UniqueName Property

Indicates the unique name for the Member.

```
String = Member.UniqueName
```

The Properties Collection

Contains a Property object for each provider-specific property.

```
Properties = Member.Properties
```

The Cell Object

This is much like a cell in a spreadsheet, and is uniquely identified by the `Positions` along the Axes.

A cell represents a single item of data, at the intersection of a number of Axes in a `CellSet`. This is much like a cell in a spreadsheet, and is uniquely identified by the Positions along the Axes.

The `Cell` object has three properties, two collections and no methods.

The Value Property

Indicates the value contained within the cell.

```
Cell.Value = Variant
Variant = Cell.Value
```

The FormattedValue Property

Indicates the formatted value of the cell.

```
Cell.FormattedValue = String
String = Cell.FormattedValue
```

The value from this property is the `Value` property formatted according to its type.

The Ordinal Property

The `Ordinal` value uniquely identifies a cell within a `CellSet`.

```
Long = Cell.Ordinal
```

The cellset notionally identifies each cell as though the cellset were a multi-dimensional array, and each array element had a unique number. Cells are numbered starting from 0, and the `Ordinal` can be used in the `Item` property of the `CellSet` to quickly locate a cell.

For the exact formula used to calculate the cell Ordinal you should consult the ADOMD documentation.

The Positions Collection

Contains a collection of `Position` objects.

```
Positions = Cell.Positions
```

Each `CellSet` comprises a number of `Axes`, and each `Axis` contains a number of `Position` objects. Each `Position` object uniquely identifies a row or column in the `Axis`.

You can use the `Positions` collection to iterate through each `Position`:

```
For Each objPos In objCell.Positions
   Print objPos.Name
Next
```

The Properties Collection

Contains an ADO `Property` object for each provider-specific property.

> *Properties = Cell.**Properties***

The CellSet Object

A `CellSet` object contains the results of a multi-dimensional query against an OLAP server. It contains collections of `Cell` objects, a collection of `Axis` objects, and details of the connection and query. The `CellSet` object has two methods, five properties and two collections.

The Open Method

Opens a new `CellSet` based upon a multi-dimensional query.

> *CellSet.**Open**([DataSource], [ActiveConnection])*

Parameter	Type	Description
DataSource	Variant	The multi-dimensional query that will retrieve the data.
ActiveConnection	Variant	Either an ADO `Connection` object or an ADO connection string.

The `DataSource` argument corresponds to the `Source` property of the `CellSet`. Multi-dimensional queries use their own variant of the SQL language. For example:

```
strQuery = "SELECT [Books].MEMBERS ON ROWS," & _
              " [Stores].MEMBERS ON COLUMNS" & _
          " FROM [PubsOLAP]"

objCellSet.Open strQuery, objConn
```

For more information on multi-dimensional queries you should consult the appropriate documentation, such as the SQL Server OLAP documentation, the MDX documentation in the Data Access SDK, or the MDAC web site, at http://www.microsoft.com/data.

The *ActiveConnection* argument corresponds to the `ActiveConnection` property.

The Close Method

Closes an open CellSet.

> *CellSet*.**Close**

Closing a CellSet will release any child collections associated with the CellSet.

The ActiveConnection Property

Identifies the connection to which the CellSet or Catalog belongs.

> **Set** *Connection = CellSet*.**ActiveConnection**
> **Set** *CellSet*.**ActiveConnection** = *Connection*
> *String = CellSet*.**ActiveConnection**
> *CellSet*.**ActiveConnection** = *String*

This can be a valid ADO Connection object or an ADO connection string. Like ADO, if the string method is used then a new connection is made.

If the *ActiveConnection* argument of the Open method was used to specify the connection, then the ActiveConnection property inherits the value from the argument.

The Source Property

Identifies the multi-dimensional query used to return the data.

> *Variant = CellSet*.**Source**
> *CellSet*.**Source** = *Variant*

If the *DataSource* argument of the Open method was used to specify the query, then the Source property inherits its value from the argument.

The State Property

Identifies the current state of the CellSet.

> *Long = CellSet*.**State**

The State can be one of the following ADO ObjectStateEnum constants:

> adStateOpen, to indicate the CellSet is open.

> adStateClosed, to indicate the CellSet is closed.

The FilterAxis Property

Indicates the filtering information for the CellSet.

> *Axis = CellSet*.**FilterAxis**

If filtering has been used to restrict the data returned during the query, then the FilterAxis property will return an Axis object, usually containing one row, with the filter information.

The Item Property

Allows indexing into the Axes collection to reference a specific Axis object.

> Set *Cell* = *CellSet*.Item(*Index*)

Parameter	Type	Description	Default
Index	Variant	The number of the Cell in the collection. Zero-based.	

This is the default property, which means that its name can be omitted when called. For example, the following lines are identical:

```
Set objCell = objCellSet.Item(1)
```

```
Set objCell = objCellSet(1)
```

The Axes Collection

Contains an Axis object for each Axis in the CellSet.

> *Axes* = *CellSet*.Axes

This collection will always contain at least one Axis object. You can iterate through the Axes collection to examine the data in the CellSet. For example, consider the following OLAP query:

```
SELECT Publishers.Members ON COLUMNS,
       Geography.Members  ON ROWS,
       Dates.Members      ON PAGES
FROM   AllSales
```

This creates three Axis objects in the collection, for Publishers, Geography and Dates.

The Properties Collection

Contains an ADO Property object for each provider-specific property.

> *Properties* = *CellSet*.Properties

The Axis Object

An Axis object is an axis from in the Axes collection of a CellSet. It represents the rows and columns of data in a query. The Axis object has two properties and two collections.

The Name Property

Returns the name of the `Axis`.

> *String* = *Axis*.**Name**

The DimensionCount Property

Returns the number of `Dimensions` on this `Axis`.

> *Long* = *Axis*.**DimensionCount**

The Positions Collection

Contains a collection of `Position` objects.

> *Positions* = *Axis*.**Positions**

Using the `Positions` collection allows you to iterate through the unique rows and columns in a query.

The Properties Collection

Contains an ADO `Property` object for each provider-specific property.

> *Properties* = *Axis*.**Properties**

The Position Object

A `Position` object contains the members of those dimensions that identify a point along a specific axis. For example, consider the following OLAP query:

```
SELECT Publishers.Members ON COLUMNS,
       Geography.Members  ON ROWS,
       Dates.Members      ON PAGES
FROM   AllSales
```

Let's suppose you examine just one set of members – `Geography`, for example. In this case, the `Positions` collection will contain an entry for each unique column:

```
[Geography].[All Geography]
[Geography].[All Geography].[CA]
[Geography].[All Geography].[CA].[Fremont]
[Geography].[All Geography].[CA].[Los Gatos]
[Geography].[All Geography].[CA].[Tustin]
[Geography].[All Geography].[OR]
[Geography].[All Geography].[OR].[Portland]
[Geography].[All Geography].[WA]
[Geography].[All Geography].[WA].[Remulade]
[Geography].[All Geography].[WA].[Seattle]
```

A `Position` contains the members and levels that allow a row or column to be uniquely identified.

The `Position` object contains one property and one collection.

The Ordinal Property

Identifies a position along an axis.

> *Long = Position*.Ordinal

The Ordinal is a unique identifier for a position and corresponds to the Index of the position in the Positions collection.

The Members Collection

Contains a Member object for each member in the Position.

> *Members = Position*.Members

The ADOMD Collections

All collections in ADOMD have the same properties and work in the same way. The objects and collections are shown below:

Object	...contains collections
Catalog	CubeDefs
CubeDef	Dimensions, Properties
Dimension	Hierarchies, Properties
Hierarchy	Levels, Properties
Level	Members, Properties
Member	Children, Properties
CellSet	Axes, Properties
Axis	Positions, Properties
Cell	Positions, Properties
Position	Members

Note that these collections do not offer any events or collections of their own.

The Refresh Method

Updates the collection from the provider to ensure that it contains the latest objects.

> *Collection*.Refresh

The Count Property

Indicates the number of objects in the collection.

> *Long = Collection*.**Count**

The Item Property

Allows indexing into the collection to reference a specific object.

> Set *Object = Collection*.**Item**(*Index*)

Parameter	Type	Description	Default
Index	Variant	The number or name of the object in the collection. Zero-based.	

This is the default property, which means that its name may be omitted when called. For example, the following lines (which use the `Positions` collection) are identical:

```
Set objPosition = objPositions.Item(1)
```

```
Set objPosition = objPositions(1)
```

10

Jet and Replication Objects

The Jet and Replication Objects (JRO, in `msjro.dll`) allow you to manipulate the replication features of a database through a simple set of objects. Although JRO is part of ADO, it only applies to Access databases.

With the JRO you can:

❑   Compact databases

❑   Set passwords and encryption on databases

❑   Create replica databases

❑   Synchronize replica sets

❑   Control the memory cache

Replication allows you to create copies of a database in which changes (both to objects and to data) may be shared between the copies. These copies are called the **replica set**, and you can replicate between any members in a replica set.

One replicated database is the **design master**. Changes to objects (tables, queries and so on) can only be done in the **design master**. Any replica in the replica set can be the design master (by default it's the first replica created), but you can only have one design master at any time.

A database may be defined as replicable, but not actually be replicated. This just means that the database can be replicated if desired, but it isn't at the moment.

If replication is used with Access 2000 and SQL Server 7.0, then you can get full, bi-directional data replication between the Access and SQL Server databases. For more details on this, and other areas of replication, you should consult the documentation of Microsoft Office 2000, Microsoft SQL Server, and Microsoft Office Developer Edition. The object model looks like this:

The Replica Object

The `Replica` object represents a copy of a replicated database.

Methods of the Replica Object

The CreateReplica Method

Creates a replica of any database that is replicable (i.e. allows replicas of itself to be created).

> **Replica.CreateReplica**(*replicaName, description, [ReplicaType], _*
> *[Visibility], [Priority], [updatability]*)

Parameter	Type	Description
replicaName	String	The name and path of the replica to be created.
description	String	A description of the newly replicated database
ReplicaType	ReplicaTypeEnum	Indicates the type of the replica database to create. Default is `jrRepTypeFull`
Visibility	VisibilityEnum	Indicates the visibility of the new replica database. For more details see the `Visibility` property. Default is `jrRepVisibilityGlobal`
Priority	Long	The priority of the database for use in conflict resolution. For more details see the `Priority` property. Default is `-1`
updatability	UpdatabilityEnum	Indicates the type of updates allowed in the new replica database. Default is `jrRepUpdFull`

ReplicaType can be one of the following `ReplicaTypeEnum` constants:

- ❑ `jrRepTypeFull`, to indicate a full replica.
- ❑ `jrRepTypePartial`, to indicate a partial replica.
- ❑ `jrRepTypeDesignMaster`, to indicate the replica is a design master.
- ❑ `jrRepTypeNotReplicable`, to indicate the database is not replicable. This is the default.

Visibility can be one of the following `VisibilityEnum` constants:

- ❑ `jrRepVisibilityGlobal`, to indicate a global replica.
- ❑ `jrRepVisibilityLocal`, to indicate a local replica.
- ❑ `jrRepVisibilityAnon`, to indicate an anonymous replica.

Updatability can be one of the following `UpdatabilityEnum` constants:

- ❑ `jrRepUpdFull`, to indicate that the new replica allows changes to the schema and records.
- ❑ `jrRepUpdReadOnly`, to indicate that the new replica does not allow changes to the schema and records.

For example:

```
objDB.ActiveConnection = _
    "Provider=Microsoft.Jet.OLEDB.4.0; Data Source=C:\Temp\pubs.mdb"
objDB.CreateReplica _
    "C:\Temp\NewReplica.mdb", "A new replica", jrRepTypePartial
```

You can only create a replica of the source database if the source database is replicable – that is, its `ReplicaType` property must not be `jrRepTypeNotReplicable`.

The GetObjectReplicability Method

Identifies whether or not the object is replicated, or has been marked to be replicated the next time sychronization between replicas takes place.

> *Boolean = Replica.GetObjectReplicability(objectName, objectType)*

Parameter	Type	Description
objectName	String	The name of the object
objectType	String	The type of the object

objectName identifies the object that is to be tested for replicability, and *objectType* gives the object type. The object type is the container name in Access, so this will be one of `Tables`, `Queries`, `Forms`, `Reports`, `Macros` or `Modules`.

If *objectName* is contained in a non-replicable database, then the
GetObjectReplicability method will return True – because the object will be
replicable if the database is made replicable.

A value of False indicates that the database is replicable, but that the object itself is
not replicable.

For example:

```
If objDB.GetObjectReplicability("authors", "tables") = True Then
    Print "The authors table may be replicated in the future"
End If
```

The MakeReplicable Method

Adjusts the properties of the database to allow it to be replicated.

> *Replica*.**MakeReplicable([**connectionString], [columnTracking])

Parameter	Type	Description
connectionString	String	The full path of the database that is to be made replicable.
columnTracking	Boolean	Indicates whether changes are tracked by row or column. Default is True, indicating column tracking.

The source database must be opened exclusively before it can be made replicable.

The PopulatePartial Method

Populates a partial replica.

> *Replica*.**PopulatePartial(**FullReplica**)**

Parameter	Type	Description
FullReplica	String	The full path of the replica database to be populated with data.

You can only replicate a database if it is replicable – that is, its ReplicaType property
must not be jrRepTypeNotReplicable.

For full details on the implications of replication, including conflict resolution and
orphaned records, you should consult the Jet documentation.

The SetObjectReplicability Method

Sets whether or not an object will be replicated (in the event of a call to the
CreateReplica method).

Replica.**SetObjectReplicability**(*objectName, objectType, replicability*)

Parameter	Type	Description
objectName	String	The name of the object to replicate
objectType	String	The type of the object
replicability	Boolean	Set to `True` to make this a replicable object, and `False` to keep the object local.

Note that, if the database has not been marked for replication, then all of its objects are replicable by default – unless `SetObjectReplicability` is used to mark them otherwise. For example:

```
objDB.SetObjectReplicability "authors", "tables", False
```

The object type is the container name in Access, so this will be one of `Tables`, `Queries`, `Forms`, `Reports`, `Macros` or `Modules`.

The Synchronize Method

Synchronizes two replica databases.

Replica.**Synchronize**(*target, [syncType], [syncMode]*)

Parameter	Type	Description
target	String	The full path of the target replica database with which the current database will synchronize, or the name of a Synchronizer to manage the target replica database, or the Internet server on which the target replica is located.
syncType	SyncTypeEnum	The type of synchronization to be performed. Default is `jrSyncTypeImpExp`
syncMode	SyncModeEnum	The synchronization method to be used. Default is `jrSyncModeIndirect`

syncType can be one of the following SyncTypeEnum constants:

❑ `jrSyncTypeExport`, to export changes from the current database to the target database.

❑ `jrSyncTypeImport`, to import changes from the target database into the current database.

❑ `jrSyncTypeImpExp`, to exchange changes between the current database and the target database.

syncMode can be one of the following SyncModeEnum constants:

❑ jrSyncModeIndirect, to indicate that indirect synchronization is to take place. This is where the *target* parameter contains the name of the Synchronizer that will perform the remote synchronization, and is best used over poor or inconsistent lines, such as WANs or modem lines.

❑ jrSyncModeDirect, to indicate that direct synchronization is to take place. Here, both databases are opened together and the appropriate changes made.

❑ jrSyncModeInternet, to indicate that synchronization will take place over the Internet. Here, the *target* parameter will contain the URL of the Internet server on which the target database is located.

Properties of the Replica Object

The ActiveConnection Property

Indicates the ADO Connection string or object.

> Set *Object* = *Replica*.**ActiveConnection**
> Set *Replica*.**ActiveConnection** = *Object*
> *String* = *Replica*.**ActiveConnection**
> *Replica*.**ActiveConnection** = *String*

You can use the standard ADO formats for this. Here are a couple of examples:

```
objDB.ActiveConnection = "Provider=Microsoft.Jet.OLEDB.4.0; " & _
                         "Data Source=C:\temp\pubs.mdb"
```

```
Set objDB.ActiveConnection = objConn
```

The ConflictFunction Property

Points to the name of a function that will be used to perform conflict resolution.

> *Replica*.**ConflictFunction** = *String*
> *String* = *Replica*.**ConflictFunction**

This function allows you to specify your own method for resolving conflicts. The default action is for Access to call its built-in Conflict Resolver.

The ConflictTables Property

Identifies the list of tables that contain conflict information.

> *Recordset* = *Replica*.**ConflictTables**

If conflict errors are generated during synchronization, the ConflictTables property will contain a recordset made up of two columns. The first column, TableName, indicates the first table; the second column, ConflictTableName, indicates the table with the conflicts.

The DesignMasterId Property

The unique ID of the design master database.

> Replica.DesignMasterId = *Variant*
> *Variant* = Replica.DesignMasterId

This property is created automatically at the time a database is set to be the design master. The `DesignMasterID` is a GUID value.

The Priority Property

Identifies the relative priority of a replica during conflict resolution.

> *Long* = Replica.Priority

During conflict resolution the following applies:

❑ The replica with the highest `Priority` value wins. Priorities range from 0 to 100.

❑ If the `Priority` values are equal, the replica with the highest `ReplicaID` wins.

The default priority for global replicas is 90% of the priority of the parent replica. The value for local and anonymous replicas is 0.

The ReplicaId Property

A unique identifier for a replica database.

> *Variant* = Replica.ReplicaId

This value is a GUID value, and is automatically generated at the time the replica is created.

The ReplicaType Property

Identifies the type of the replica database.

> *ReplicaTypeEnum* = Replica.ReplicaType

ReplicaTypeEnum can be one of the following constants:

❑ `jrRepTypeNotReplicable`, to identify that the database is not replicable. This is the default

❑ `jrRepTypeDesignMaster`, to indicate that the database is the design master.

❑ `jrRepTypeFull`, to indicate that the database is a full replica.

❑ `jrRepTypePartial`, to indicate that the database is a partial replica.

A value of `jrRepTypeNotReplicable` does not mean that the database cannot ever be replicated, but that it has not yet been made replicable. You can use the `MakeReplicable` method to make the database replicable.

The RetentionPeriod Property

Identifies the number of days for which replica histories should be kept.

> *Replica*.RetentionPeriod = *Long*
> *Long* = *Replica*.RetentionPeriod

A replica set retains details of changes for the number of days (from 5 to 32,000) specified in this property.

The default value is dependent on how the database was made replicable. If the database was made replicable with the Replication Manager, RDO or ADO, the `RetentionPeriod` value defaults to 60. If the database was made replicable with Access, the `RetentionPeriod` value defaults to 1000.

You can only set this property on a design master database.

The Visibility Property

Indicates the visibility of the database.

> *VisibilityEnum* = *Replica*.Visibility

VisibilityEnum can be one of the following constants:

❑   `jrRepVisibilityGlobal`, to indicate a global replica.

❑   `jrRepVisibilityLocal`, to indicate a local replica.

❑   `jrRepVisibilityAnon`, to indicate an anonymous replica.

A global replica is typically the design master, and is allowed to synchronize with any replica in the replica set. A local or anonymous replica can only synchronize with a global replica.

For more information on replica schemes you should consult the Access documentation.

Collections of the Replica Object

The Filters Collection

Contains a `Filter` object for each filter specifying replication information.

> Set *Filters* = *Replica*.Filters

There's more on the `Filters` collection later in this chapter. Before we look at that, we'll take a look at what an individual `Filter` object can do.

The Filter Object

A `Filter` object specifies the details of a filter that limits the records transferred during replication. This allows you to create partial replicas containing a subset of the main database.

Don't confuse the `Filter` object with the `Filter` property of the ADO `Recordset` object – the two are not related. `Filter` objects are created by adding them to the `Filters` collection of the `Replica` object.

Methods of the Filter Object

There are no methods for the `Filter` object.

Properties of the Filter Object

The FilterCriteria Property

Sets or returns the string that controls the filter.

```
String = Filter.FilterCriteria
Filter.FilterCriteria = String
```

The filter string is a standard SQL WHERE clause, without the WHERE keyword.

The filter criteria is set in the `Append` method of the `Filters` collection.

The FilterType Property

Indicates the type of the filter.

```
FilterTypeEnum = Filter.FilterType
```

FilterTypeEnum can be one of the following constants:

❏ `jrFilterTypeRelationship`, to indicate that the filter is based on a relationship.

❏ `jrFilterTypeTable`, to indicate that the filter is based on a table.

The filter type is set in the `Append` method of the `Filters` collection.

The TableName Property

Identifies the table to which the `Filter` applies.

```
String = Filter.TableName
```

When the filter is based on a one-to-many relationship, the table name is the table on the many side of a join.

The filter table name is set in the `Append` method of the `Filters` collection.

The Filters Collection

The `Filters` collection contains a `Filter` object for each filter applicable to the replication process.

Methods of the Filters Collection

The Append Method

Adds a new filter to the collection.

> Filters.Append(*TableName, FilterType, FilterCriteria*)

Parameter	Type	Description
TableName	String	The name of the table to which the filter applies, or (if the filter is based on a relationship) the name of the table on the many side of a join.
FilterType	FilterTypeEnum	The type of filter.
FilterCriteria	String	The SQL clause that makes up the filter.

The *FilterType* can be one of the following constants:

❑ `jrFilterTypeRelationship`, to indicate that the filter is based on a relationship.

❑ `jrFilterTypeTable`, to indicate that the filter is based on a table.

Using the filter types specified above, you can create filters that apply either to tables or to relationships. For example, the following creates a filter based upon a table:

```
objDB.Filters.Append "authors", jrFilterTypeTable, "state='CA'"
```

The second example creates a filter based upon a join:

```
objDB.Filters.Append "authors", _
                jrFilterTypeRelationship, "qryPublishersAuthors"
```

For the *FilterCriteria* you specify the query that makes up the relationship, and for the `TableName` you specify the table that is on the many side of the relationship.

The Delete Method

Deletes a `Filter` object from the collection.

> Filters.Delete(*Item*)

Parameter	Type	Description
Item	Variant	The index number or name of the `Filter` object to be deleted.

The Refresh Method

Refreshes the collection so that changes are visible.

> *Filters*.**Refresh**

This is particularly useful when adding and deleting members of the collection, as they may not always be visible until the collection has been refreshed.

Properties of the Filters Collection

The Count Property

Returns the number of `Filter` objects in the collection.

> *Long = Filters*.**Count**

The Item Property

Allows indexing into the collection, by either name or number.

> *Filter = Filters*.**Item**(*Item*)

Parameter	Type	Description
Item	Variant	The name of the `Filter`, or its index number.

This is the default method, which means that the method name can be omitted when the method is called. For example, the following expressions are equivalent:

```
objReplica.Filters("Name")
```

```
objReplica.Filters.Item("Name")
```

The JetEngine Object

The `JetEngine` object gives you control of the Jet Database Engine.

Methods of the JetEngine Object

The CompactDatabase Method

Copies and compacts a database into a new database.

> *JetEngine*.**CompactDatabase**(*SourceConnection, DestConnection*)

Parameter	Type	Description
SourceConnection	String	An ADO Connection string identifying the database that is to be compacted.
DestConnection	String	An ADO Connection string identifying the new database that is to be created from the compaction.

Using this method you cannot compact in-place – that is, you cannot compact a database into itself. You must specify a new database name or location, otherwise an error will be generated. For example:

```
objJE.CompactDatabase _
    "Provider=Microsoft.Jet.OLEDB.4.0; Data Source=C:\temp\pubs.mdb", _
    "Provider=Microsoft.Jet.OLEDB.4.0; Data Source=C:\temp\newpubs.mdb"
```

The connection string only allows a limited set of provider specific properties – all other properties are ignored. The allowed properties are:

Property	Source	Destination
Provider	✓	✓
Data Source	✓	✓
User Id	✓	
Password	✓	
Locale Identifier		✓
Jet OLEDB:Database Password	✓	✓
Jet OLEDB:Engine Type	✓	✓
Jet OLEDB:Registry Path	✓	
Jet OLEDB:System Database	✓	
Jet OLEDB:Encrypt Database		✓
Jet OLEDB:Don't Copy Locale on Compact		✓
Jet OLEDB:Compact Without Relationships		✓
Jet OLEDB:Compact Without Replica Repair		✓

These properties are added to the connection string in the usual way. For example:

```
objJE.CompactDatabase _
    "Provider=Microsoft.Jet.OLEDB.4.0; Data Source=C:\temp\pubs.mdb; " & _
                        "User Id=davids; Password=abc123", _
    "Provider=Microsoft.Jet.OLEDB.4.0; Data Source=C:\temp\newpubs.mdb;" & _
                        "Jet OLEDB:Encrypt Database=True"
```

For more details on these properties consult the ADO Properties collection in Appendix C.

The RefreshCache Method

RefreshCache allows you to force any pending writes to the database, and refresh memory with the latest data from the database.

JetEngine.**RefreshCache(***Connection***)**

Parameter	Type	Description
Connection	Connection	An open ADO Connection object for which the cache should be refreshed.

In high multi-user applications you can use this method to free memory locks.

11

Data Shaping and Internet Publishing

In this chapter, we'll take a look at two of the providers that are shipped with ADO 2.1. The Data Shape provider originally shipped with ADO 2.0. It provides a way to arrange sets of related data hierarchically; it also provides an efficient way to transfer related sets of data from the server to a client. ADO 2.1 has added some new features to the Data Shaping Provider:

❑ **Hierarchy Reshaping**, which will allow the creation of new hierarchies based upon existing data.

❑ **Grandchild Aggregates**, to allow aggregation of the values of specific grandchildren in a hierarchy into a higher aggregation level.

❑ **Parameterized Computed Children**, to allow an aggregate level to be inserted between a parent and parameterized child.

Examples of these are shown later in the chapter.

This chapter also features a look at the Provider for Internet Publishing – a new OLEDB Provider that is supplied with ADO 2.1. This provider allows ADO to connect to web servers that support the Microsoft FrontPage Server Extensions, or the Distributed Authoring and Versioning (DAV) protocol. It's covered in more detail towards the end of the chapter.

Data Shaping

Data shaping was one of the new features in ADO 2.0, so if you've only just converted to version 2 you might not know anything about it. The easiest way to understand data shaping is to use another term that is often employed – **hierarchical recordsets**. Think about all of those times that you've had master and detail recordsets – publishers and books are a good example. The easiest way to imagine this is to think of the windows where you have folders and sub-folders. In data shaping terms you have recordsets and sub-recordsets. Take a look at the following diagram, which shows a shape involving publishers, titles and sales from the pubs database:

This could be created with the following SHAPE command:

```
SHAPE {SELECT * FROM publishers}
APPEND ((SHAPE {SELECT * FROM titles}
    APPEND ({SELECT * FROM sales}
    RELATE title_id TO title_id))
RELATE pub_id TO pub_id)
```

What this produces is a recordset for the publishers, with an extra column containing another recordset for titles. The titles recordset also has an extra column for sales. These child recordsets are often called **chapters** – and the data type of the column would be adChapter. In the above example only three recordsets are created - for each of sales, titles and publishers.

The child column actually contains the details that relate the parent to the child, and when you access the child column, the child recordset is filtered so only the correct rows are shown. So, creating the above hierarchy against SQL Server, you can see (using SQL Trace in SQL 6.5 or SQL Profiler in SQL 7) three statements sent to the server:

```
select * from publishers
select * from titles
select * from sales
```

These are all sent in one command, and returned as multiple recordsets. All of the data is sent back at once. The client only has three recordsets, so resource usage is kept to a minimum.

The shape provider performs no optimization on the SQL statements sent to the server. For example, consider the following SHAPE command:

```
SHAPE {select * from publishers where state = 'ca'}
APPEND ({select * from titles}
RELATE pub_id TO pub_id)
```

This returns two recordsets – the first containing details of all `publishers` where the `state` is `ca`, and the second containing all `titles`. This isn't a joined query, so the titles query returns all `titles`, not just those for publishers in `ca`. The data shaping actually takes place on the client, and the Data Provider is just the supplier of data.

Child Data Freshness

You can force the Shape Provider to query the data source for the child data each time a parent row is accessed. To do this, set the `Cache Child Rows` dynamic property to `False`:

```
objRec.Properties("Cache Child Rows") = False
```

Normally this property is `True` – this tells the local cursor service to cache the child data. By setting it to `False`, you ensure that the cursor service requeries the data provider for new information each time a parent row is accessed. This ensures that the data for the child is up-to-date, but it does impose a performance penalty.

Child Recordsets

When you access a row in the parent recordset, the child recordset automatically reflects the values related to the parent – in fact the child recordset is closed and then reopened with the new values.

You can change this behavior so that when you move to a new record the child recordset does not change. This behavior is controlled by the `StayInSync` property of the `Recordset`. Setting this to `True` (the default) keeps the child recordset synchronized with its parent. Setting it to `False` ensures that no synchronization takes place. For example:

```
objRec.StayInSync = False
```

Using Data Shaping

There are two important things to know if you want to use data shaping:

❑   You have to use the `MSDataShape` provider. Your provider that supplies the data becomes the `Data Provider`.

❑   You have to use a special data shape language, which is a superset of SQL

If you've got Visual Basic 6 then there's a really quick way to produce your shape commands using the Data Environment Designer. You'll see an example of this later in the chapter. It is also worth looking at the syntax, because it's not always convenient to load Visual Basic just to create a shaped recordset (unless you're developing a Visual Basic application, of course!).

The Shape Language

The shape command has its own formal grammar, which we won't list here (it's included in the ADO 2.1 documentation), but we will go through the way you use this command. In general, your shape command will look something like this:

```
SHAPE {parent_command} [[AS] table_alias]
APPEND ({child_command} [[AS] child_table_alias]
     RELATE parent_column TO child_column) [[AS] column_name]
```

This defines the parent and the child, and how they relate. You can happily omit the `table_alias`, but the `column_name` is extremely useful as it defines the name of the column containing the child recordset. The command is a SQL command. If we take the `pubs` database – the sample database supplied with SQL Server – and show an example using publishers and titles:

```
SHAPE {SELECT * FROM publishers}
APPEND ({SELECT * FROM titles}
        RELATE pub_id TO pub_id) AS recTitles
```

So, the first line is the parent – this will be a list of publishers:

```
SHAPE {SELECT * FROM publishers}
```

For each publisher we want a list of titles, so we APPEND a query that lists the titles:

```
APPEND ({SELECT * FROM titles}
```

Now we identify how the two commands are linked together. This is the primary key in the parent table and the foreign key in the child table:

```
        RELATE pub_id TO pub_id) AS recTitles
```

The alias used here is what the new column will be called. The shape provider creates this new column on the parent, and for each entry, this column contains a recordset of its own.

Here's a simple piece of VB code that creates a shape and navigates through the records in both the parent and the child – you'll need to change the connect string to point to your server for this:

```
Dim objConn      As New ADODB.Connection
Dim objRec       As New ADODB.Recordset
Dim objRecTitle  As ADODB.Recordset
Dim strShape     As String

' use the data shape provider,
' with SQL Server as the source of the data
objConn.Provider = "MSDataShape"
objConn.Open "Data Provider=SQLOLEDB; Data Source=Tigger; " & _
             "Initial Catalog=pubs; User Id=sa; Password="

' define our shape string and open the recordset
strShape = "SHAPE {SELECT * FROM publishers}" & _
           " APPEND ({SELECT * FROM titles}" & _
           " RELATE pub_id TO pub_id) AS recTitles"
objRec.Open strShape, objConn

' loop through the parent records
While Not objRec.EOF
    Debug.Print objRec("pub_name")

    ' set the recordset for the child
    ' records and loop through them
    Set objRecTitle = objRec("recTitles").Value
    While Not objRecTitle.EOF
        Debug.Print vbTab; objRecTitle("title")
        objRecTitle.MoveNext
    Wend
    objRec.MoveNext
Wend
```

```
objRec.Close
objConn.Close
Set objRec = Nothing
Set objConn = Nothing
Set objRecTitle = Nothing
```

The first thing to notice about this is that we set the `Data Provider` to point to the OLEDB provider that actually supplies the data, and we set the `Provider` property to `MSDataShape`. So the actual OLEDB Provider is `MSDataShape` – its job is to get the data from somewhere else and shape it. This means we have to tell the data shape provider where we want the actual data to come from – we've done that here through the `Data Provider` part of the connection string. This means that the data shape provider can take data from any existing OLEDB provider.

The shape command becomes the source of our recordset, and we can loop through this as normal. Notice that we use a second recordset to point to the child recordset, which is stored as a column in the first recordset. The `Value` of this column is the child recordset. This produces the following output:

New Moon Books
    You Can Combat Computer Stress!
    Is Anger the Enemy?
    Life Without Fear
    Prolonged Data Deprivation: Four Case Studies
    Emotional Security: A New Algorithm
Binnet & Hardley
    Silicon Valley Gastronomic Treats
    The Gourmet Microwave
    The Psychology of Computer Cooking
    Computer Phobic AND Non-Phobic Individuals: Behavior Variations
    Onions, Leeks, and Garlic: Cooking Secrets of the Mediterranean
    Fifty Years in Buckingham Palace Kitchens
    Sushi, Anyone?
Algodata Infosystems
    The Busy Executive's Database Guide
    Cooking with Computers: Surreptitious Balance Sheets
    Straight Talk About Computers
    But Is It User Friendly?
    Secrets of Silicon Valley
    Net Etiquette
Five Lakes Publishing
Ramona Publishers
GGG&G
Scootney Books
Lucerne Publishing

Notice that some records don't have child records. In this case an empty recordset is created.

You don't have to assign the child recordset to a `Recordset` object if you don't want to; instead, you can access the child recordset directly:

```
objRec("recTitles").Value.Fields("title")
```

Multiple Children

In the above example we saw publishers and titles, but a parent recordset is not restricted to only one child recordset. For example, the publishers also have employees, and we may wish to include this information in our data schema:

```
SHAPE {SELECT * FROM  publishers}
APPEND ({SELECT * FROM  titles}
        RELATE pub_id TO pub_id) AS recTitles,
       ({SELECT * FROM employee}
        RELATE pub_id TO pub_id) AS recEmployees
```

This follows the same rules as the above example, but we are appending two commands. The parent is publishers, to which we APPEND two select queries (separated by a comma), giving them names of titles and employees. The syntax for these is the same, indicating the relationship of the parent to the child:

```
SHAPE {parent_command} [[AS] table_alias]
APPEND ({child_command_1} [[AS] child_table_1_alias]
        RELATE parent_column TO child_column_1) [[AS] column_name_1],
       {child_command_2} [[AS] child_table_2_alias]
        RELATE parent_column TO child_column_2) [[AS] column_name_2]
```

Your recordset would now have two extra columns, which you could use in the same way as above:

```
Set objRecTitles = objRec("recTitles").Value
Set objRecEmps = objRec("recEmployees").Value
```

Grandchildren

Data shaping doesn't have to be limited to sets of data one level deep. Each of the child records can have its own child. For example, suppose we wanted to add the sales for each title, showing the date purchased and the number sold. The SHAPE command now becomes:

```
SHAPE {SELECT * FROM publishers}
APPEND (( SHAPE {SELECT * FROM titles}
    APPEND ({SELECT * FROM sales}
    RELATE title_id TO title_id) AS recSales)
RELATE pub_id TO pub_id) AS RecTitles
```

This just adds another APPEND and RELATE command to relate the new child table to its parent. So now you could change your code accordingly. Add a new variable declaration:

```
Dim objRecSales As ADODB.Recordset
```

And then add the loop to print the sales:

```
Set objRecTitle = objRec("recTitles").Value
While Not objRecTitle.EOF
    Debug.Print vbTab; objRecTitle("title")
    Set objRecSales = objRecTitle("recSales").Value
    While Not objRecSales.EOF
        Debug.Print vbTab; vbTab; objRecSales("ord_date");
                         vbTab; objRecSales("qty")
        objRecSales.MoveNext
    Wend
    objRecTitle.MoveNext
Wend
```

What you now see is this:

```
Binnet & Hardley
    Silicon Valley Gastronomic Treats
        12/12/93   10
    The Gourmet Microwave
        14/09/94   25
        14/09/94   15
    The Psychology of Computer Cooking
    Computer Phobic AND Non-Phobic Individuals: Behavior Variations
        29/05/93   20
    Onions, Leeks, and Garlic: Cooking Secrets of the Mediterranean
        15/06/92   40
```

The SQL statement is not limited to just SELECT *, and you can use almost any SQL statement you like. The only restriction is that you must have matching columns in the parent and child SELECTs, but this is not different from a normal SQL join or sub-query.

Summarizing with Shapes

The data shape language also has a way to produce summary information, allowing your parent to hold summary details, whilst the children hold the individual details. This is really useful for those management information systems drill-down situations – where you show a total, and then you can drill-down into the details. For example, imagine that you wanted to find out the total sales of books for each type of book, as well as being able to see the total sales for the books.

For this type of data shape, you need to use a different form of the shaping language:

```
SHAPE {child_command} [[AS] table_alias]
COMPUTE aggregate_field_list
BY group_field_list
```

For example, you could construct a shape command like this:

```
SHAPE {SELECT * FROM titles}  AS recTitlesSales
COMPUTE TitlesSales, SUM(TitlesSales.ytd_sales) AS NumberSold
BY type
```

The first line is familiar – you are creating a shape, and it's to be called TitlesSales. You want to sum the ytd_sales column of this shape, grouping on the type column. Your parent recordset will contain three columns:

❑   type, which is the column we grouped on

❑   NumberSold, which is the column we summed

❑   recTitlesSales, which is the child recordset

The child recordset contains the SQL statement from the first line, and, as a result of this, everything in the titles table.

You could access the result with code like this:

```
While Not objRec.EOF
    Debug.Print objRec("type"); vbTab; objRec("NumberSold")

    Set objRecSales = objRec("TitlesSales").Value
    While Not objRecAuth.EOF
        Debug.Print vbTab; objRecSales("title"); _
                    vbTab; objRecSales("ytd_sales")
        objRecSales.MoveNext
    Wend
    objRec.MoveNext
Wend
```

And the results it produces would be like this:

business   30788
   The Busy Executive's Database Guide   4095
   Cooking with Computers: Surreptitious Balance Sheets   3876
   You Can Combat Computer Stress!   18722
   Straight Talk About Computers   4095
mod_cook   24278
   Silicon Valley Gastronomic Treats   2032
   The Gourmet Microwave   22246

Stored Procedures

In addition to using SELECT queries in your shape commands, you can also use stored procedures. For example, imagine two stored procedures:

```
CREATE PROCEDURE usp_AllPublishers
AS
    SELECT *
    FROM    publishers
```

and

```
CREATE PROCEDURE usp_TitlesByPubID
    @PubID char(4)
AS
    SELECT *
    FROM    titles
    WHERE   pub_id = @PubID
```

The first just returns all publishers, and the second returns all titles for a given publisher. You could create a shape command to use these two as follows:

```
SHAPE {{CALL dbo.usp_AllPublishers }}
APPEND ({{CALL dbo.usp_TitlesByPubID( ? )  }}
RELATE pub_id TO  PARAMETER 0) AS recTitlesByPubID
```

Notice that instead of the SELECT commands we previously had, there is now a call to the stored procedure. The stored procedure for the child takes a parameter – since the parameter is to be filled in by the parent, we RELATE the pub_id field to the parameter. The shape command processor automatically takes care of filling in this parameter for each child recordset. Whilst this might look cool, you should be aware that this can have a detrimental effect on performance, as the child stored procedure is executed each time it is referenced. If you have stored procedures that are children, then all parameters must participate in the relationship.

If you wanted the parent stored procedure to accept an argument, such as the country, then it could be written like this:

```
CREATE PROCEDURE usp_PublishersByCountry
    @Country varchar(30)
AS
    SELECT *
    FROM    publishers
    WHERE   country = @Country
```

The shape command would now become:

```
SHAPE {{CALL dbo.usp_PublishersByCountry( ?) }}
APPEND ({{CALL dbo.usp_TitlesByPubID( ?) }}
RELATE pub_id TO  PARAMETER 0) AS recTitlesByPubID
```

You can pass parameters into this command in three ways. The first is to add it in manually:

```
SHAPE {{CALL dbo.usp_PublishersByCountry('USA') }}
APPEND ({{CALL dbo.usp_TitlesByPubID( ?) }}
RELATE pub_id TO  PARAMETER 0) AS recTitlesByPubID
```

The second is to create a `Command` object and use the `Parameters` collection:

```
strShape = "SHAPE {{CALL dbo.usp_PublishersByCountry(?) }}" & _
    "APPEND ({{CALL dbo.usp_TitlesByPubID(?) }}" & _
    "RELATE pub_id TO PARAMETER 0) AS recTitlesByPubID "
objCmd.CommandText = strShape
objCmd.Parameters.Append objCmd.CreateParameter("@Country", _
                                adVarChar, adParamInput, 30, "USA")
Set objCmd.ActiveConnection = objConn
Set objRec = objCmd.Execute
```

The third is again to use a `Command` object, but this time pass the parameter into the `Execute` method:

```
objCmd.CommandText = strShape
Set objRec = objCmd.Execute  (, Array("USA"))
```

You can pass in multiple parameters using any of these methods.

Parameter Based Shapes

When using a parameter-based hierarchy, the data is not fetched all at once as the command is executed. When parent row is accessed, the parameter query is executed with the parameter details from the parent. This data is then cached locally. This means that there will be a trip back to the server to fetch data the first time a new row is accessed. However, this approach can be a lot more efficient if the user is only interested in a subset of parent rows.

You can change this behavior by setting the `Cache Child Rows` dynamic property, as discussed earlier.

Updating Shaped Recordsets

Using data shaping doesn't mean that your recordsets behave any differently from normal recordsets. Assuming that your recordset allows updating, then you can treat shaped recordsets as you would normally: adding, updating and deleting records. For example:

```
Set objRecTitles = objRec("titles").Value
objRecTitles("qty") = objRecTitles("qty") + 1
objRecTitles.Update
```

This sets a variable, objRecTitles, to point to the child recordset, and then updates a value. Changing the relating field in the parent recordset means that the child recordset may become orphaned. Likewise, changing the relating field in the child recordset will stop it being related to the parent.

Data Shaping in Visual Basic 6

Having shown you the hard way to create shape commands, you won't be surprised to find that Visual Basic 6 has a quick (and rather cool) way to do this, as part of its Data Environment. To create a data shape command you first add a command to the Data Environment. I created a connection to the pubs database, and then added a command, pointing to the publishers table. You can do this by selecting the connection, right-mouse clicking, and selecting **Add Command**, and then adding the command details. You'll have to enter SQL query details, via the **General** tab of the Properties...of the command.

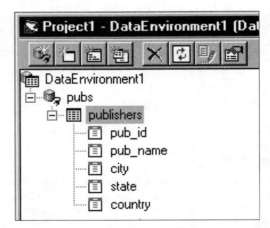

Then you add a child command (right-click on the existing publishers command) – in this case we'll write a command to query the titles table. With child commands you have to specify the relationship (after adding the SQL query details into the General tab's SQL Statement box):

Once the child command has been added, you'll see it appear under its parent:

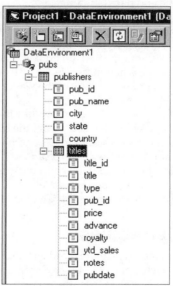

If you then right-mouse click on the parent, you can pick Hierarchy Info... from the menu to see the shape command:

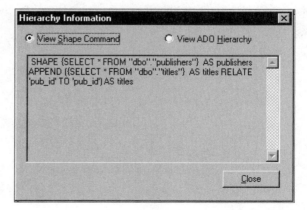

Another great thing about VB6 is that it has a grid, the Hierarchical FlexGrid, which binds directly to hierarchical recordsets, allowing you to drill down to the child data.

Of course, if you haven't got Visual Basic 6 you'll have to do it manually.

Why Data Shaping?

All of this might seem very smart, but what's the real use, especially when you can achieve the same result by joining the tables together? Well, imagine a parent recordset that has a hundred rows and ten columns. It has a child recordset containing ten rows per parent row. Now look at a normal join:

```
SELECT * FROM parent INNER JOIN child
ON parent.id = child.id
```

For each child row, there will also be a parent row containing ten columns. Those ten parent columns will be the same for each of the childrens' ten rows. That's an awful lot of wasted network traffic and data handling.

If you use data shaping, then the parent row is only included once, so instead of 1000 rows containing the parent data we only have 100. You still have 1000 rows of child data, but the parent data is not repeated. Overall, it's smaller, easier to manage, and produces less network traffic when marshaled over the Internet as a disconnected recordset. However, you should be aware of the way that data shaping actually works.

When you create a simple relation (for example, like the relation between publishers and titles), then both tables will be fetched before the hierarchy is created. A new field (a pointer to the child recordset) is added to the parent recordset — and when the child is referenced, a filter is applied to the child recordset. This means that all child recordsets are fetched in advance, so if the child recordsets are large you might find that this slower than a normally joined recordset, and may lead to more network congestion. This concept is also examined in Chapter 9.

Reshaping Hierarchies

Reshaping allows you to reuse existing recordsets held by the shape provider, allowing them to become children of new shape commands. If the new shape command doesn't require new data from the original data provider, then the shaping is performed entirely within the shape provider on the client.

The easiest way to understand this is via a few examples. Consider the following shape command:

```
SHAPE {SELECT * FROM titles} AS rsTitles
    APPEND ({SELECT * FROM sales} AS rsSales
         RELATE title_id TO title_id)
```

This will give the following:

Here we have a recordset containing the details from the `titles` table. The last column, `rsSales`, is a Chapter column containing the recordset of the `sales` table.

A new recordset can be created using a new shape command:

```
SHAPE rsSales
      COMPUTE rsSales, SUM(rsSales.qty) AS Sum_qty1 BY stor_id
```

This creates the following structure:

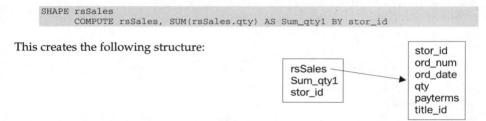

The existing `rsSales` recordset is reshaped, with a new parent being added, which contains summary details of the sales quantity. The original recordset is unchanged by this new shape.

```
SHAPE {SELECT * FROM publishers}
      APPEND (rsTitles RELATE pub_id TO pub_id)
```

Another parent addition could be:

This creates a new shape using the publishers as the top level, and appending the already existing shape `rsTitles` to it:

Notice that the APPENDed chapter has been given the default name of Chapter1 – this is because in the code fragment above, we didn't use the AS clause to assign a specific name to rsTitles.

You can also use reshaping to gain access to all of the records in a child recordset. For example, consider this shape command:

```
SHAPE {SELECT * FROM titles} as rsTitles
      APPEND ({SELECT * FROM sales} AS rsSales
            RELATE title_id TO title_id)
```

When you access the child recordset you only ever see the records related to the parent. However, we know that there are actually two recordsets in existence – one for the parent and one for the child – and that it's just filtering that takes place to show the correct records. Since reshaping allows access to recordsets without querying the data provider, you can use the following shape command to access the complete set of records for the child:

```
SHAPE rsSales
```

This would give you a recordset of all sales items.

Limitations

Reshaping allows quite a lot of flexibility but there are some limitations to its use:

❑ You cannot APPEND new columns to an existing shaped recordset.

❑ You cannot reshape parameterized recordsets.

Usage

The actual commands to reshape are no different from those used to create an initial shape. For example, consider the following Visual Basic code:

```
objConn.Open strConn

strShape = "SHAPE {SELECT * FROM titles} as rsTitles" & _
           " APPEND ({SELECT * FROM sales} AS rsSales" & _
           " RELATE title_id TO title_id)"

objRec.Open strShape, objConn

objRec1.Open "SHAPE rsSales " & _
             "COMPUTE rsSales, SUM(rsSales.qty) BY stor_id", objConn

objRec2.Open "SHAPE {select * from publishers} " & _
             " APPEND (rsTitles RELATE pub_id TO pub_id)", objConn
```

Once the original recordset has been opened, the data shape provider caches the shape details, and they then become available for use in reshaping.

Grandchild Aggregates

When using aggregation to produce summary values, you are not limited to just one level, and you can aggregate multiple levels down by including the full object hierarchy. For example, imagine you wanted to list the quantity of books sold, broken down by publisher, store and book. Something like this:

New Moon Books	208
You Can Combat Computer Stress!	35
Fricative Bookshop	35
Is Anger the Enemy?	108
Eric the Read Books	3
Barnum's	75
News & Brews	10
Doc-U-Mat: Quality Laundry and Books	20
Life Without Fear	25
Doc-U-Mat: Quality Laundry and Books	25
Prolonged Data Deprivation: Four Case Studies	15
Doc-U-Mat: Quality Laundry and Books	15
Emotional Security: A New Algorithm	25
Doc-U-Mat: Quality Laundry and Books	25
Binnet & Hardley	150
Silicon Valley Gastronomic Treats	10
Fricative Bookshop	10
The Gourmet Microwave	40
Doc-U-Mat: Quality Laundry and Books	25
Bookbeat	15
The Psychology of Computer Cooking	
Computer Phobic AND Non-Phobic Individuals...	20
Doc-U-Mat: Quality Laundry and Books	20
Onions, Leeks, and Garlic: Cooking Secrets of ...	40
News & Brews	40
Fifty Years in Buckingham Palace Kitchens	20
News & Brews	20
Sushi, Anyone?	20
News & Brews	20

etc.

So, what you need is a structure like this:

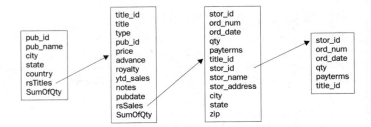

If the quantity sold is only held at the bottom level, then you need to be able to sum this value from the parent, and the grandparent. Here's the SHAPE command:

```
SHAPE {SELECT * FROM publishers}
APPEND ((SHAPE {SELECT * FROM titles}
  APPEND ({SELECT * FROM sales INNER JOIN
          stores on sales.stor_id = stores.stor_id}
    RELATE title_id TO title_id) AS recSales
  , SUM(recSales.qty) AS SumOfQty)
    RELATE pub_id TO pub_id) AS recTitles
  , SUM(recTitles.recSales.qty) As SumOfQty
```

The SUM statement at the bottom applies to the parent, so it includes the names for both the child and the grandchild. You can produce the table of data with the following Visual Basic code:

```
objRecPubs.Open strShape, objConn

While Not objRecPubs.EOF
    Debug.Print objRecPubs("pub_name")~ "~~~"~ objRecPubs("SumOfQty")
    Set objRecTitles = objRecPubs("recTitles").Value
    While Not objRecTitles.EOF
        Debug.Print "~"~ objRecTitles("title")~ _
                    "~~"~ objRecTitles("SumOfQty")
        Set objRecStoreSales = objRecTitles("recSales").Value
        While Not objRecStoreSales.EOF
            Debug.Print "~~"~ objRecStoreSales("stor_name")~ _
                        "~"~ objRecStoreSales("qty")
            objRecStoreSales.MoveNext
        Wend
        objRecTitles.MoveNext
    Wend
    objRecPubs.MoveNext
Wend
```

I've used the tilde symbol (~) to separate the columns being produced – this makes it easy to convert into a Word table.

Parameterized Computed Children

If a shape command has a child based on a parameterized stored procedure, there's no reason why you can't have an intermediate table to perform grouping on certain values in the procedure. For example, imagine you want to show the book titles grouped by book type and by publisher. Something like this:

```
New Moon Books
        business
                You Can Combat Computer Stress!
        psychology
                Is Anger the Enemy?
                Life Without Fear
                Prolonged Data Deprivation: Four Case Studies
                Emotional Security: A New Algorithm
Binnet & Hardley
        mod_cook
                Silicon Valley Gastronomic Treats
                The Gourmet Microwave
        psychology
                Computer Phobic AND Non-Phobic Individuals: Behavior Variations
        UNDECIDED
                The Psychology of Computer Cooking
Algodata Infosystems
        business
                The Busy Executive's Database Guide
                Cooking with Computers: Surreptitious Balance Sheets
```

The code used to produce this is similar to the parent/child/grandchild example shown earlier.

Here's the structure that will give us this analysis:

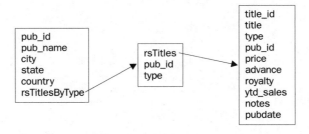

This is easy to do with three SQL commands, but suppose you want to use a parameterized query for the book titles so that you always see the latest data. Here's the SHAPE command:

```
SHAPE {{CALL dbo.usp_PublishersByCountry('?')}}
APPEND ((SHAPE {{CALL dbo.usp_TitlesByPubID('?')}} AS recTitles
COMPUTE recTitles By pub_id, type)
RELATE pub_id TO PARAMETER 0) AS recTitlesByType
```

The advantage of using a COMPUTE statement for the book types is that the COMPUTE is based upon the child. Since the child is a parameterized query it always shows the latest data, therefore so does the COMPUTE. If a new book is added with a new book type this is automatically reflected by the COMPUTE.

Creating New Shapes

The shape language allows you to create shaped recordsets that are not bound to a data provider. This is useful if you want to create a local storage of complex data, perhaps to replace collections.

To create a new shape you need to set the Data Provider option in the connection string to none:

```
Provider=MSDataShape; Data Provider=none
```

You can then construct your recordset in the shape command:

```
SHAPE APPEND
 NEW adChar(4) AS pub_id,
 NEW adVarChar(40) AS pub_name,
 NEW adVarChar(20) AS city,
 NEW adChar(2)      AS state,
 NEW adVarChar(30) AS country,
 ((SHAPE APPEND
   NEW adVarChar(6)  AS title_id,
   NEW adVarChar(80) AS title,
   NEW adCurrency    AS price,
   NEW adChar(4)      AS pub_id)
 RELATE pub_id TO pub_id) AS rsTitles
```

You can then open the recordset and add records. Here's an example in Visual Basic:

```
' open the new shape
objRec.Open strShape, objConn, adOpenStatic, adLockOptimistic

' add some records
With objRec
    .AddNew
    .Fields("pub_id") = "1234"
    .Fields("pub_name") = "Wrox Press"
    .Fields("city") = "Birmingham"
    .Fields("state") = "WM"
    .Fields("country") = "England"
    .Update
End With

' now some children
Set objRecT = objRec("rsTitles").Value
With objRecT
    .AddNew
    .Fields("title_id") = "2688"
    .Fields("title") = "ADO 2.1 Prog Ref"
    .Fields("price") = 29.99
    .Update

    .AddNew
    .Fields("title_id") = "1266"
    .Fields("title") = "Professional ASP 2.0"
    .Fields("price") = 59.95
    .Update
End With
```

Once created the shaped recordset behaves exactly like a shaped recordset created from a data provider.

Dynamic Properties

The shape provider now has some new dynamic properties to help with the shape service. These apply to the Recordset and are set using the dynamic Properties collection:

```
objRec.Properties("property_name") = value
```

The Name Property

The Name property is a read-only property that identifies the name of the Recordset in a shape. The recordset name is generally defined by the AS keyword in the shape language – if this is omitted the shape provider will generate a name for you. For example, in the following code fragment there is a parent recordset named rsTitles, and a child recordset named rsSales:

```
SHAPE {SELECT * FROM titles} AS rsTitles
    APPEND ({SELECT * FROM sales} AS rsSales
        RELATE title_id TO title_id)
```

The Unique Reshape Names Property

The Unique Reshape Names property specifies whether or not unique values for the name are generated. For example, a shape command that assigned the same name (using the AS keyword) to two different recordsets can be forced to be unique by setting the Unique Reshape Names property to True.

Internet Publishing

Internet Publishing is a big new feature of ADO 2.1 (although it hasn't had a great deal of publicity), and it revolves around the OLEDB Provider for Internet Publishing. Internet Publishing is the ability to read and write data from Web resources, such as Web servers. For some time, Microsoft Internet Information Server has supported the FrontPage Server Extensions, which allowed FrontPage to edit files directly on the Web Server, and from beta 3 of Windows 2000, IIS will support WebDAV. Using ADO 2.1 we can access IIS Web Servers that support Front Page extenstions, or any Web server that supports WebDAV.

A new initiative called Distributed Authoring and Versioning (DAV) is currently underway by the World Wide Web Consortium to formalize a standard for the DAV protocol. There are several web servers (including IIS with Windows 2000) that support the current version of the standard. Check out the WebDAV Working Group home page at http://www.ics.uci.edu/pub/ietf/webdav/ for more details.

What DAV will give us is the ability to edit resources remotely, using the HTTP protocol. You'll be able to add, delete and update most resources stored by a DAV client server, as well as being able to version your changes to a resource. This will bring true collaboration to the Web authoring world.

Support for Internet Publishing

The following Servers support Internet Publishing:

❑   Microsoft IIS 3.0 and FrontPage 97

❑   Microsoft IIS 4.0 and FrontPage 98

❑   Microsoft IIS 4.0, SP4, and FrontPage 2000

❑   Microsoft IIS 4.0, SP4, and Office 2000 Server Extensions

❑   Microsoft PWS 2.0 and FrontPage 2000

❑   Apache Web Server 1.2 and FrontPage 2000

❑   Netscape Enterprise Server 3.0 and FrontPage 2000

❑   Netscape FastTrack Server 2.0 and FrontPage 2000

❑   O'Reilly WebSite 1.2 and FrontPage 2000

❑   Stronghold Apache-SSL Web Server 2.0 and FrontPage 2000

❑   Any Web server supporting WebDAV, such as Zope (www.zope.org), or Microsoft IIS 5.0.

If you wish to connect to a WebDAV-compliant server then you should consult the software list at http://www.webdav.org. This is also an excellent site for further details on WebDAV.

ADO Support

Internet Publishing and the OLEDB Provider are still developing technologies, and because of their intended purpose, they don't support all aspects of ADO.

In ADO 2.1 you are limited to just getting back a recordset from the Web server. The Connection string is:

```
Provider=MSDAIPP.DSO;Data Source=URL
```

Future versions of ADO will allow full control of resources.

The following sections list which features of ADO are supported by the Internet Publishing Provider.

Methods

ADO object	Supported	Not Supported
Errors, Fields, Parameters, Properties	Clear Delete Item Refresh	Append
Command	Execute (*Options* must be adCmdText)	CreateParameter Cancel
Connection	Close Execute (*Options* must be adCmdText) Open OpenSchema	BeginTrans Cancel CommitTrans RollbackTrans
Field	AppendChunk GetChunk	
Parameter		AppendChunk
Recordset	AddNew CancelBatch CancelUpdate Clone Close CompareBookmarks Delete Find GetRows GetString Move MoveFirst MoveLast MoveNext MovePrevious Open Requery Save Seek Supports Update UpdateBatch	Cancel NextRecordset Resync

Properties

ADO object	Supported	Not Supported
Command	ActiveConnection CommandText CommandType State	CommandTimeout Prepared Name
Connection	Attributes ConnectionString CursorLocation Mode Provider State Version	CommandTimeout ConnectionTimeout DefaultDatabase IsolationLevel
Error	Description NativeError Number Source	HelpContext HelpFile SQLState
Field	ActualSize Attributes DefinedSize Name NumericScale OriginalValue Precision Type UnderlyingValue Value	DataFormat
Parameter		Attributes Direction Name NumericScale Precision Size Type Value
Property	Attributes Name Type Value	

ADO object	Supported	Not Supported
Recordset	ActiveCommand ActiveConnection BOF Bookmark CacheSize CursorLocation CursorType EditMode EOF Filter Locktype Sort Source State Status	AbsolutePage AbsolutePosition DataMember DataSource MarshalOptions MaxRecords PageCount PageSize RecordCount StayInSync

Collections

ADO object	Supported	Not Supported
Command	Properties	Parameters
Connection	Errors Properties	
Field	Properties	
Parameter		Properties
Recordset	Fields Properties	

Security Limitations

Since the Provider for Internet Publisher allows you to manipulate resources, there are certain operations that are deemed unsafe, and are therefore not allowed:

❑ Copy or Move between servers.

❑ Copy, Move or Delete for file-based URLs.

❑ Delete on a URL hosted by a server other than the server that supplied the page.

12

Performance

This chapter will look at one of the most critical issues for all data store programmers – that of **performance**. Microsoft has stated that one of its goals for ADO was to achieve the best performance possible; however, during testing and through its various versions, the newsgroups have contained several messages regarding poor performance. What we plan to do here is show you whether or not those criticisms were justified.

Most of the performance statistics were generated using a Test Tool, built especially for this purpose in Visual Basic 5. The source code for this tool is available from the Wrox Press web site, at http://webdev.wrox.co.uk/books/2688, along with a test Access database, some SQL Scripts for creating the test database in SQL Server, and an Access database for logging the results.

This tool is provided as is, with no warranty of its fitness for purpose. You can use it as you find it, or extend it in your own environment. For obvious reasons we can't guarantee the same results on your systems. At the end of this chapter you'll see how this tool works, but we won't cover it in depth. Its sole purpose is to run various queries under different conditions, and to time them. Not all of the tests were carried out using this tool, and we created several tools just for test purposes. Some of these are also available on the Web site.

The tests were run on a Dell Dimension Pentium II 450MHz, with 128Mb memory and 8Gb EIDE disk, running NT Workstation 4. We tested both Access 97 and Access 2000 databases, and these generally gave similar results. Any major differences have been highlighted. SQL Server versions 6.5 and 7.0 were both tested. The machine with version 6.5 was a Pentium 166, with 128Mb and 9Gb UW SCSI running NT Server 4. I've avoided explicit performance tests between versions 6.5 and 7.0 because these are beyond the scope of this chapter – the intention was not to compare performance of the two versions of SQL Server, but to test ADO. There are some major differences between 6.5 and 7.0, and these have been highlighted where appropriate.

All tests were run on this machine, so those involving client cursors don't have the added network lag to contend with. Although this is less realistic, it ensures that only the difference between cursor types (and not the network) is tested. This is important because network traffic can vary widely from situation to situation, and it's unlikely that my three machines – all within 10 feet of each other – would ever give any kind of useful indication. It would therefore be wrong for me to say 'these timings take into account network usage', when this is quite clearly not the case. So, when running the tests yourself, make sure you allow for this.

One further thing to note is that ADO and the data stores were not under any stress here. The tests were performed in a single-user environment, and you may experience difference results if your server and data store are being used heavily. The tests were also run 10 times and the results averaged, to take account of cached data. The standard deviations were generally very small.

For the majority of tests, the following table was used:

Column	Type	Length
KeyCol	int (IDENTITY)	
Description	varchar	(50)
ForeignKey	int	
TextField	varchar	(10)
CurrencyField	money	
BitField	bit	

There were several copies of this table, all with varying amounts of dummy data. When testing ADO yourself you should use your own tables and data to get a more accurate picture.

I've tried to explain why some of the tests give the results that they do – although in some cases this is not possible, simply because I don't know what OLEDB and the providers are actually doing underneath. It would be nice to have these details explained, but as an ADO programmer it's not really necessary. As long as we know which mechanisms to use to give us best performance, and we have a way of testing that, we should be relatively happy.

Cursor Type, Location and Locking

Here are three questions that are often asked, by beginning and experienced users alike:

- ❑ What's the best cursor type to use?
- ❑ Should I use server-side or client-side cursors?
- ❑ What locking scheme should I use?

Like many design questions, the answer is always the same: it depends. The cursor type and location that you choose will not only affect performance, but also the functionality. So, whilst in some cases it's easy to establish a particular cursor type as the fastest, it may not be the type that best suits your particular business needs.

The OLEDB Driver for Jet

The charts below show the results from opening and closing a table, using the OLEDB Driver for Access. The code used for this test is simple:

```
objRec.Open "table_name", objConn
objRec.Close
```

We timed only this fragment of the code, adding the various locking modes and cursor types to the Open command. This was run 10 times (that is, we performed the Open/Close combination ten times), and the average taken. We took an average in this way in all of the tests performed, to ensure that the first run didn't distort the results because of data not being cached. Times are given in milliseconds.

Server-Side Cursors

The following figures were produced using server-side cursors, with a table holding 100 rows.

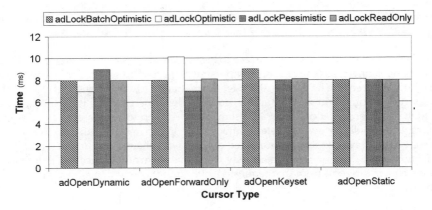

You might wonder why there is so little difference between the cursor types – but recall that, when using server-side cursors, Access only supports keyset cursors (unless you specify a read-only recordset). So if you are locking your recordset, Access will always return a keyset cursor – no matter what cursor type you request.

You might also expect that larger tables would have an impact, but the times are almost exactly the same – even for a table of the same type with 100,000 records! The lack of difference in speed when using larger tables is because, if you are using server-side cursors, only the first batch of data is read into the recordset. Consequently, it doesn't matter how many records there are when you open the table. And that's an important point. This test is essentially just opening and closing the table, without reading any data in.

Client-Side Cursors

The following chart shows the speed using client-side cursors, with the test table holding 100 rows.

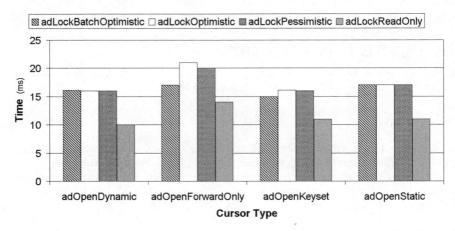

You can see that client-side cursors are much slower than server-side cursors, being generally twice as slow. Relatively, however, cursors with no locking are faster than the other cursor types. Client-side cursors are inherently slower because they actually copy the data into a cache on the local machine, using the memory and disk space if necessary. This is why they are named client-side cursors – the cursor facility is located in the central OLEDB handler, rather than being provided by the data store.

Comparing locking cursors, you can see that the read-only cursor is faster than the other two locking types (optimistic and pessimistic) – and between those two there is very little difference. The graphs also suggest that there's little difference between the cursor types. You might wonder at this, but note that when locking is required, the OLEDB Provider for Jet only supports static cursors: therefore, whatever cursor type you request, you'll always get a static cursor back. In fact, a static cursor is the only cursor type that really makes sense when dealing with client-side cursors. The `Errors` collection of the `Connection` object may well have a warning indicating that the cursor type is different from that requested, although this will depend upon the provider.

The reasons for the time differences between read-only and updateable locking should be fairly clear. With read-only cursors, Jet can stream out the data without having to keep track of the records, as it knows that no changes will ever take place. This is obviously going to be faster than trying to keep track of the changes. For updateable cursors, the cursor type has to be changed – but this fact can be ignored, because you can see that for a static cursor the timings are approximately the same.

Have a look at the same test over a table with 1000 rows:

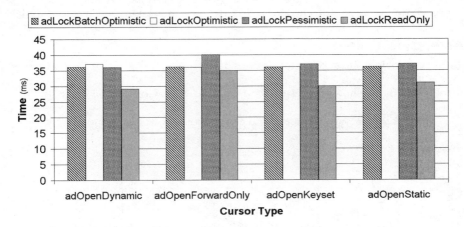

Again, not much difference between the locking types, but the difference in speed between read-only access and read/write access is not as marked as before. The overall times have increased, reflecting that much more data is being pushed to the client, as compared to the server-side cursors, where there was little difference.

With 50,000 records, the result looks like this:

Now we see some more interesting results, with a much greater variation between the various cursor types and locking mechanisms. Again, the average times have increased to reflect the amount of data.

The OLEDB Driver for SQL Server

The same tests for SQL Server show remarkably different results. Again, these are comprised of opening and closing a recordset 10 times, then taking the average figure.

Server-Side Cursors

SQL Server provides full support for server-side cursors.

The following figure shows the results for a table of 100 rows on SQL 6.5 and SQL 7.0.

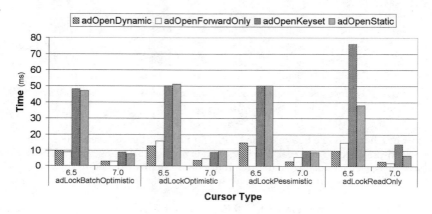

This shows a dramatic improvement in performance when using dynamic and forward-only cursors over keyset and static cursors on SQL 6.5. The reason for this is simple: in SQL 6.5, both keyset and static cursors require a copy of the data to be put into the temporary database (*tempdb*) in the SQL Server before the cursor is created. In fact, a keyset cursor only puts the keys and the first buffer full of data into temporary storage. SQL 7.0 doesn't appear to suffer from this problem, although I've yet to confirm whether this is due to a general improvement in performance in SQL 7.0, or if it handles keyset and static cursors in a different way.

You can see how this has a marked effect as the number of rows increases. For a table with 1000 rows, the change is significant:

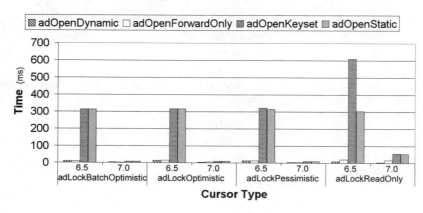

On SQL Server 6.5, the figures for the dynamic and forward-only cursors don't change much; however, the times for the keyset and static cursors increase significantly. This is because of the use of *tempdb*. SQL 7.0 on the other hand shows that the difference between cursor types is extremely small. The differences shown above become even more exaggerated as the table size increases, so if you've got a table with large data and you are working on SQL 6.5 it's probably worth upgrading to SQL 7.0.

Client-Side Cursors

So how does this compare with client-side cursors, given that all the client-side cursor types were slower in Jet? For the initial test of 100 rows we get the following figure:

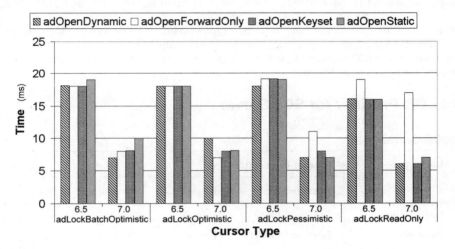

These seem to bear out what we know about client cursors - they are slower because all of the data is read into the client. Overall, the performance is close for all cursor types and lock types, and this remains so as we scale the table up to 50,000 rows. On the other hand, the overall speed is slower than server-based dynamic and forward-only cursors (as expected) because all of the data is returned to the client.

> *If you want to learn more about SQL Server cursor types and how they are used, then by far the best description can be found in* Inside Microsoft SQL Server 6.5 *(Microsoft Press, ISBN 1-57231-331-5). In fact, this book is full of extremely useful information for the SQL Server developer. A new version for SQL 7.0 (ISBN 0-73560-517-3) was released in April 1999.*

The OLEDB Driver for ODBC

For ODBC, the tests show similar results for the cursor types, locations, and locking mechanisms. We'll be contrasting the OLEDB Driver for ODBC against the native driver later in this chapter.

Cursor Summary

Despite the figures you've seen so far, it's not always possible to use the faster method because it may not meet your needs. For example, although server-side cursors are quicker to open, they don't always provide the same functionality that client-side cursors do, and cannot be used if you need to disconnect your recordsets. In the n-tier world of client–server development you may well be using disconnected recordsets to pass data between the various tiers in your application, so you'll have to use client cursors. If this is the case, then you want to minimize the amount of data being passed around.

With locking, you can see that in most cases read-only mode is faster, as you would expect. Use this to your advantage if you are just providing data browsing capabilities.

You've seen that in comes cases, the cursor type you get is not necessarily the one you requested – this depends upon the provider, the cursor location, and the locking mechanism used. The following tables describe the cursor type that you receive according to these conditions.

OLEDB Provider for SQL Server

adUseServer

Lock type	Cursor type requested			
	Forward-Only	Keyset	Dynamic	Static
Read-Only	Forward-Only	Keyset	Dynamic	Static
Pessimistic	Forward-Only	Keyset	Dynamic	Keyset
Optimistic	Forward-Only	Keyset	Dynamic	Keyset
BatchOptimistic	Forward-Only	Keyset	Dynamic	Keyset

adUseClient

Lock type	Cursor type requested			
	Forward-Only	Keyset	Dynamic	Static
Read-Only	Static	Static	Static	Static
Pessimistic	Static	Static	Static	Static
Optimistic	Static	Static	Static	Static
BatchOptimistic	Static	Static	Static	Static

OLEDB Provider for Jet

adUseServer

Lock type	Cursor type requested			
	Forward-Only	Keyset	Dynamic	Static
Read-Only	Forward-Only	Keyset	Static	Static
Pessimistic	Keyset	Keyset	Keyset	Keyset
Optimistic	Keyset	Keyset	Keyset	Keyset
BatchOptimistic	Keyset	Keyset	Keyset	Keyset

adUseClient

Lock type	Cursor type requested			
	Forward-Only	Keyset	Dynamic	Static
Read-Only	Static	Static	Static	Static
Pessimistic	Static	Static	Static	Static
Optimistic	Static	Static	Static	Static
BatchOptimistic	Static	Static	Static	Static

OLEDB Provider for ODBC with SQL Server

adUseServer

Lock type	Cursor type requested			
	Forward-Only	Keyset	Dynamic	Static
Read-Only	Forward-Only	Keyset	Dynamic	Static
Pessimistic	Forward-Only	Keyset	Dynamic	Keyset
Optimistic	Forward-Only	Keyset	Dynamic	Keyset
BatchOptimistic	Forward-Only	Keyset	Dynamic	Keyset

adUseClient

Lock type	Cursor type requested			
	Forward-Only	Keyset	Dynamic	Static
Read-Only	Static	Static	Static	Static
Pessimistic	Static	Static	Static	Static
Optimistic	Static	Static	Static	Static
BatchOptimistic	Static	Static	Static	Static

OLEDB Provider for ODBC with Access

adUseServer

Lock type	Cursor type requested			
	Forward-Only	Keyset	Dynamic	Static
Read-Only	Forward-Only	Keyset	Keyset	Static
Pessimistic	Forward-Only	Keyset	Keyset	Keyset
Optimistic	Forward-Only	Keyset	Keyset	Keyset
BatchOptimistic	Forward-Only	Keyset	Keyset	Keyset

adUseClient

Lock type	Cursor type requested			
	Forward-Only	Keyset	Dynamic	Static
Read-Only	Static	Static	Static	Static
Pessimistic	Static	Static	Static	Static
Optimistic	Static	Static	Static	Static
BatchOptimistic	Static	Static	Static	Static

Moving Through Records

Since you very rarely just open and close a recordset, we need to look at moving through records, where the cursor type and mode can also have an impact on performance. The opening and closing of the recordset were not included as part of the timing, so this just includes the movement.

There are two main ways of getting at the data in a recordset. The first is to use
MoveNext to move from one end of the recordset to the other, and the second is to
GetRows to read the data into an array. For client-based cursors, of any type and
locking mode, the figures were extremely close between using MoveNext and
GetRows. This is because the data is already on the client, and in both cases, the client
cursor service is fetching the data from its local cache. For server-based cursors,
however, there are differences.

GetRows can also be used to fetch a smaller number of rows, and then repeating this
operation until the whole recordset is read, although this method, called
GetRows(chunked) in the graph, is less common. Consider a table of 1,000 rows, on
SQL Server 7.0 (the figures were very similar for Optimistic, Batch Optimistic and
Pessimistic locking modes):

Here you can see that MoveNext is clearly the fastest method, but that using GetRows
with small chunks is faster than trying to retrieve all of the records into an array at
once. The interesting figures come when you use a read-only cursor:

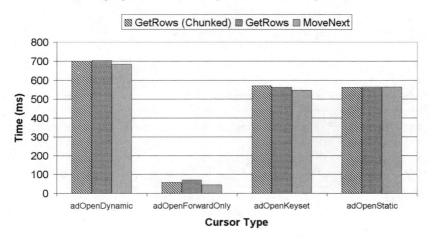

With a forward-only cursor that is a vast improvement in the speed, because using server-based forward-only cursors makes use of the SQL Server native cursor, which is much faster than other cursor types.

If you switch to the Jet provider, the results are again different:

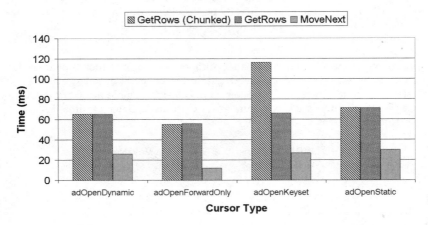

Because Jet doesn't have its own server-based cursors, the results for cursor types are very similar. However, using MoveNext is far quicker than using GetRows.

Cache Size

The Recordset object's CacheSize property identifies how many records are fetched in one go and stored in a local cache on the client. The default value for this property is 1, so with a large table you are able to fetch each record individually (if you desire). This could be quite time consuming if moving through the records. For example, imagine a table with 1000 rows. If the CacheSize property is equal to 1, then it would require 1000 fetches to create a recordset on this table and move through all 1000 rows. If the CacheSize property is equal to 100, the same task would take only 10 fetches (each visit fetching 100 records).

The graph below shows the results of changing the cache size for a client-side cursor on a table of 1000 rows in SQL 7.0.

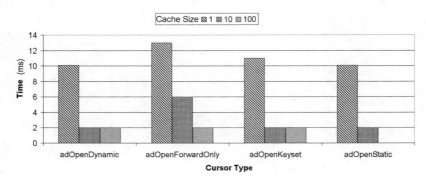

Notice that using a larger cache size is much faster. In some cases there's no difference between a cache size of 10 and 100, so you'll need to experiment. For server-side cursors the results are even more significant:

Here you can see that moving from a cache size of 1 to 10 has a dramatic effect, and for some cursor types this can be improved even more by increasing the cache size to 100.

Although you might never fetch 1000 rows directly for processing, the cache size can have a big impact even on small tables. For processing large tables, you are nearly always better building SQL statements and executing them on the server.

Command and Recordset Options

ADO 2.0 introduced a new constant value, adCmdTableDirect, for the CommandTypeEnum constant type. adCmdTableDirect gives us a new option when specifying the command type, by indicating that the provider is to return all rows from the table named in the CommandText property. The documentation states that using this will cause some internal code to work differently, but does it make any performance difference? Under ADO 2.0 it did make a small difference, with the use of adCmdTableDirect being marginally quicker. Under ADO 2.1 the difference between adCmdTable and adCmdTableDirect was negligible under our tests. So yes, use this option, but don't expect a sudden speed increase.

ADO 2.0 also introduced a new option into the ExecuteOptionEnum constant set: adExecuteNoRecords tells ADO that an action query will not return any records. To test this, the following code was used without the option set:

```
strSQL = "UPDATE tblOneThousand SET TextField = 'abc 123'" & _
    "WHERE KeyField = 587"
Set objRec = objConn.Execute(strSQL, , adCmdText)
```

and compared against code with the extra option added in:

```
Set objRec = objConn.Execute(strSQL, , adCmdText + adExecuteNoRecords)
```

Whilst this test might not be a command that you perform frequently, it does show that this option can speed up action queries.

Stored Procedure Or Direct SQL?

Many people often put SQL statements directly into their programs, and there are a couple of reasons why:

- ❑ They feel it keeps everything required to run the program together.
- ❑ They are unsure about stored procedures and the benefits they can bring.

Using stored procedures not only allows you alter them without affecting your program, but brings the performance advantage of compiled SQL. When you run SQL statements they are parsed by SQL Server, and then executed. The SQL engine has to carry this every time the statement is used. When you create a stored procedure, the SQL is converted into a compiled form – thus eliminating this step when the procedure is run. In addition, stored procedures are placed into a procedure cache, which is an in-memory store of the compiled SQL – improving performance even more. Of course, if your table statistics change frequently, then the stored execution plan for stored procedures could become out of date.

You can bring the stored procedure benefit to straight SQL text strings, by setting the `Prepared` property of the `Command` object before execution – but this is only useful if you intend to run the command several times on the same connection. With `Prepared` set to `True`, a prepared statement is created the first time the command is run; and subsequent runs of the command on the same connection will use the prepared statement. So the first run will be slower, but subsequent runs after the first will be quicker. In ASP you will not see any benefit to prepared statements, because you should always work in a disconnected mode, creating database connections as you require them, which means subsequent runs of the SQL will use a new connection, and will therefore prepare a new statement.

On SQL Server 6.5 prepared statements are compiled into temporary stored procedures. On SQL Server 7 prepared statements are fully supported.

Consider the following SQL statement, using the `pubs` database, to analyze sales by publisher, state, and author:

```
SELECT publishers.pub_name, publishers.state,
       (au_lname + ', ' + au_fname) AS author,
       Sum(sales.qty) AS SumOfqty
FROM ((publishers INNER JOIN titles ON publishers.pub_id = titles.pub_id)
   INNER JOIN (authors INNER JOIN titleauthor
                    ON authors.au_id = titleauthor.au_id)
   ON titles.title_id = titleauthor.title_id)
INNER JOIN sales ON titles.title_id = sales.title_id
GROUP BY publishers.pub_name, publishers.state,
       (au_lname + ', ' + au_fname)
```

Executing this statement 10 times on the same connection resulted in the following:

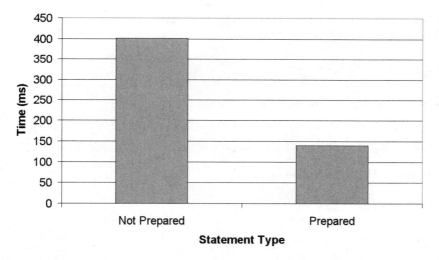

You can clearly see that prepared statements are faster for concurrent executions. Simple SQL statements may yield less impressive performance improvements, as the SQL optimizer will have less to do.

Parameters

When I started using ADO I had a lot of trouble using parameters, partly because of the data types. I then discovered the `Refresh` method, and I started to use this during development to print out details of what the parameters should be. If you use **SQL Trace** when connecting to SQL Server, you can clearly see that using `Refresh` can have a big overhead as it makes a trip back to the server to get the parameters. However, I did wonder what the speed difference was between the following three methods:

- ❑ Using direct SQL.
- ❑ Using the *Parameters* argument of the `Command`'s `Execute` method.
- ❑ Using the `Parameters` collection.

The following test used the **pubs** database supplied with SQL Server. The stored procedure contains the following commands:

```
CREATE PROCEDURE usp_SalesTest
      @iQty          int,
      @sPayTerms     varchar(12)
AS
      SELECT     *
      FROM       sales
      WHERE      qty = @iQty
      OR         payterms = @sPayTerms
```

The parameters to be searched for will be `20` for the quantity and `Net 60` for the payment terms.

A `Command` object was created for each of the three tests, giving us three sections of code. For the direct SQL statement I used:

```
objCmd.CommandText = "SELECT * FROM sales WHERE qty=60 OR payterms='Net 60'"
objCmd.CommandType = adCmdText
Set objRec = objCmd.Execute
```

Passing the parameters into the `Execute` method, I used:

```
objCmd.CommandText = "usp_SalesTest"
objCmd.CommandType = adCmdStoredProc
Set objRec = objCmd.Execute(, Array(20, "Net 60"))
```

To create a `Parameters` collection I used:

```
objCmd.CommandText = "usp_SalesTest"
objCmd.CommandType = adCmdStoredProc
objCmd.Parameters.Append objCmd.CreateParameter("@iQty", adInteger, _
                                   adParamInput, 8, 20)
objCmd.Parameters.Append objCmd.CreateParameter("@sPayTerms", adVarChar, _
                                   adParamInput, 12, "Net 60")
Set objRec = objCmd.Execute
```

Again, these were run 10 times and the average taken, and each set of runs executed three times, closing the connection between runs. The diagram below shows three runs for SQL 6.5 and 7.0.

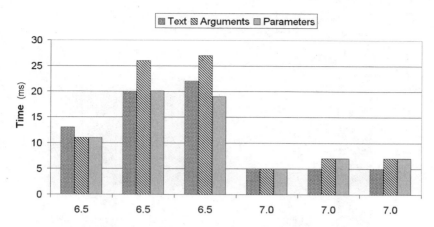

The SQL Server 6.5 tests show a small difference between the various methods, while the SQL Server 7.0 tests show even less of a difference. The `Parameter` method has the advantage of making the parameters explicit, and of course you have to use this method if you require output parameters. Many databases don't support the extraction of parameters, so you might have to use explicit parameters.

Connection Pooling

The subject of connection pooling is a constant source of confusion. The documentation states that to free a connection you should set the connection variable to `Nothing`. However, the question has arisen as to whether this cleared the connection from the pool of connections, and therefore had a detrimental effect on performance. So, using the `Open/Close` method again, using SQL Server, we'll try it with and without clearing the memory, and see if that has an impact. For the first test, the code was as follows:

```
For intLoop = 1 To 10
    objConn.Open strConn
    objConn.Close
Next
```

And for the second:

```
For intLoop = 1 To 10
    objConn.Open strConn
    objConn.Close
    Set objConn = Nothing
Next
```

The figures for ADO 2.0 were as follows:

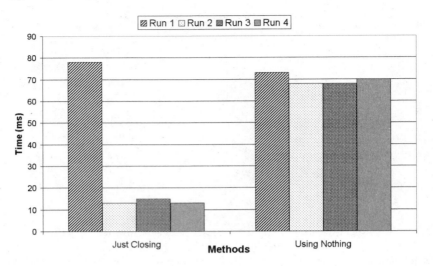

The results show four consecutive runs of the code shown above. The figures on the left clearly show that, after the first time, just closing the recordset is considerably faster, because the connection has been pooled. The figures on the right however, show that setting the connection object variable to Nothing produces very similar figures for all four batches.

But does this really answer the question about connection pooling? Setting the object variable to Nothing deallocates the COM object, so it could be just the creation of the COM object that is time-consuming. If you run SQL Trace whilst testing this, you'll see that for the first test only one connection is made. However for the second test, there are ten connection/disconnections in a row.

In fact, if you put the two pieces of code on two separate command buttons and watch SQL Trace as you press them you'll see that for the first code, where we just open and close the recordset, SQL Trace just shows a connection without a disconnection. Pressing the button again doesn't show another connection because the first is still active and held in the pool. If you don't press a button for 60 seconds you'll see the disconnection. With the second command button, where we set the object variable to Nothing, each time you press the button you get both a connection and a disconnection.

In ADO 2.1, you can set the Connection object variable to Nothing and this will *not* remove the connection from the connection pool. Thus, the test demonstrated on ADO 2.0 above gives a very different conclusion when run against ADO 2.1 – in both parts of the test, the outcome looks very similar to the left-hand section of the graph shown above.

Performance Summary

The first thing to remember is that these figures only show certain traits, under certain circumstances, so don't rely on them. Perform your own analysis, using your own data and see what results you achieve. You should also make sure that you test your application under circumstances that are similar to those in which it will run – that is, on a well used network, on a server that is heavily used, on a database with multiple users, etc. You can use this chapter as a guideline for some of the criteria to test.

Having said that, there are some key points we've established from these tests:

❑ When opening recordsets, server-side cursors are generally quicker than client-side cursors, because less data is initially being transferred. However, the fetching of data is then slower.

❑ If you need to use disconnected recordsets, then you'll have to use client-side cursors. In this case, keep the amount of data transferred to a minimum.

❑ If using SQL Server 6.5 and server-side cursors, then dynamic or forward-only cursors are more efficient when selecting data. This is because the data is not copied into *tempdb* first. For SQL Server 7.0, this effect is greatly reduced.

❑ Use the native OLEDB providers, because they are quicker and offer more functionality than the ODBC ones. However, if you are using Oracle you may want to use the OLEDB Provider for ODBC and the ODBC Drivers for Oracle, since they have greater functionality than the OLEDB Provider for Oracle.

❑ Use the correct cursor types. If you're not going to change any data, then use read-only cursors. Don't waste the resources of the data store.

There is also the performance aspect of performing large batch jobs on the server, and only transferring data to the client when required. These are general ways to improve application performance, and should be used in conjunction with any ADO performance enhancements.

The Performance Test Tool

As mentioned at the beginning of this chapter, this tool is intended to help you do your own performance tests. It began its life in the form of few small routines, used to help decide a few issues, and has grown into the program that is now available from http://webdev.wrox.co.uk/books/2688. I considered expanding this into a large test suite, and supplying it as a fully finished program, but then decided that – as a programmer – this is probably not what you really want. Therefore we've decided to give it away as it stands. Bear in mind that it's a far-from-complete product, has little or no error handling, and has some options that won't work under all conditions. Having said that, it does perform basic tests fairly well.

The opening screen allows you to connect to a data store:

Here you can pick a provider (and, if using ODBC, pick a DSN or a driver). The Connect String box will supply some default values, and you should overwrite these with your specific values before connecting. The Log To box allows you to pick the database to log timings to. Currently this is an Access database, but there's no reason why you couldn't convert the code to use another database.

Once you've connected you get to the main timing screen:

The tab control allows you to select from tables, queries, or your own SQL text. To the right you pick which test you want to run, but remember that some of these may not be suitable for SQL queries that don't return recordsets. Below this you can select whether records are to be returned. The asynchronous option isn't implemented, and was added to give you the opportunity to supply this. You can specify the number of times that the test is run, and add some marker text (to be written to the logging database) so that you can identify individual tests. At the bottom of the screen you can pick the cursor type, lock type and cursor location. In order to run a test, you must select at least one of each – and you can pick more options to allow several tests to be compared.

The logging database just consists of one simple table into which the results are written. The graphs in this chapter were produced by pulling the figures from this table into Excel; it's often easier to appreciate the performance differences in visual form, so you may wish to consider doing the same.

Summary

In this chapter, we've shown you the results of our experimentation with the various options available in ADO 2.1. In particular, we've looked at the performance implications of using different data providers, as well as the (often significant) differences given by the various cursor types and locking options. To finish, we discussed the VB tool that we used to run the tests with, and encouraged you to download it use it, or customize it for your own purposes. You can download it from our website: you'll find the samples page that supports this book at http://webdev.wrox.co.uk/books/2688.

With this consideration of the performance implications of ADO 2.1, our discussion of ADO is complete. The appendices that follow this chapter are intended to provide a reference for using ADO 2.1; the documentation Microsoft supply is not quite complete, and wherever possible we have tried to include undocumented features.

ADO Object Summary

Microsoft ActiveX Data Objects 2.1 Library Reference

Properties and methods that are new to version 2.1 are indicated in the first column.

> **All properties are read/write unless otherwise stated.**

The Objects

The Main Objects	Description
Command	A Command object is a definition of a specific command that you intend to execute against a data source.
Connection	A Connection object represents an open connection to a data store.
Recordset	A Recordset object represents the entire set of records from a base table or the results of an executed command. At any given time, the 'current record' of a Recordset object refers to a single record within the recordset.

The Other Objects	Description
Error	An Error object contains the details of data access errors pertaining to a single operation involving the provider.
Field	A Field object represents a column of data within a common data type.

Table Continued on Following Page

The Other Objects	Description
Parameter	A `Parameter` object represents a parameter or argument associated with a `Command` object based on a parameterized query or stored procedure.
Property	A `Property` object represents a dynamic characteristic of an ADO object that is defined by the provider.

The Collections	Description
Errors	The `Errors` collection contains all of the `Error` objects created in response to a single failure involving the provider.
Fields	A `Fields` collection contains all of the `Field` objects of a `Recordset` object.
Parameters	A `Parameters` collection contains all the `Parameter` objects of a `Command` object.
Properties	A `Properties` collection contains all the `Property` objects for a specific instance of an object.

The Command Object

Methods of the Command Object	Return Type	Description
Cancel		Cancels execution of a pending `Execute` or `Open` call.
CreateParameter	Parameter	Creates a new `Parameter` object.
Execute	Recordset	Executes the query, SQL statement, or stored procedure specified in the `CommandText` property.

Properties of the Command Object	Return Type	Description
ActiveConnection	Variant	Indicates to which `Connection` object the command currently belongs.
CommandText	String	Contains the text of a command to be issued against a data provider.
CommandTimeout	Long	Indicates how long to wait, in seconds, while executing a command before terminating the command and generating an error. Default is 30.

Properties of the Command Object	Return Type	Description
CommandType	CommandType Enum	Indicates the type of command specified by the `Command` object.
Name	String	Indicates the name of the `Command` object.
Prepared	Boolean	Indicates whether or not to save a compiled version of a command before execution.
State	Long	Describes whether the `Command` object is open or closed. Read only.

Collections of the Command Object	Return Type	Description
Parameters	Parameters	Contains all of the `Parameter` objects for a `Command` object.
Properties	Properties	Contains all of the `Property` objects for a `Command` object.

The Connection Object

Methods of the Connection Object	Return Type	Description
BeginTrans	Integer	Begins a new transaction.
Cancel		Cancels the execution of a pending, asynchronous `Execute` or `Open` operation.
Close		Closes an open connection and any dependent objects.
CommitTrans		Saves any changes and ends the current transaction.
Execute	Recordset	Executes the query, SQL statement, stored procedure, or provider-specific text.
Open		Opens a connection to a data source, so that commands can be executed against it.
OpenSchema	Recordset	Obtains database schema information from the provider.
RollbackTrans		Cancels any changes made during the current transaction and ends the transaction.

Table Continued on Following Page

Properties of the Connection Object	Return Type	Description
Attributes	Long	Indicates one or more characteristics of a Connection object. Default is 0.
CommandTimeout	Long	Indicates how long, in seconds, to wait while executing a command before terminating the command and generating an error. The default is 30.
ConnectionString	String	Contains the information used to establish a connection to a data source.
ConnectionTimeout	Long	Indicates how long, in seconds, to wait while establishing a connection before terminating the attempt and generating an error. Default is 15.
CursorLocation	CursorLocation Enum	Sets or returns the location of the cursor engine.
DefaultDatabase	String	Indicates the default database for a Connection object.
IsolationLevel	IsolationLevel Enum	Indicates the level of transaction isolation for a Connection object. Write only.
Mode	ConnectMode Enum	Indicates the available permissions for modifying data in a Connection.
Provider	String	Indicates the name of the provider for a Connection object.
State	Long	Describes whether the Connection object is open or closed. Read only.
Version	String	Indicates the ADO version number. Read only.

Collections of the Connection Object	Return Type	Description
Errors	Errors	Contains all of the Error objects created in response to a single failure involving the provider.
Properties	Properties	Contains all of the Property objects for a Connection object.

Events of the Connection Object	Description
BeginTransComplete	Fired after a `BeginTrans` operation finishes executing.
CommitTransComplete	Fired after a `CommitTrans` operation finishes executing.
ConnectComplete	Fired after a connection starts.
Disconnect	Fired after a connection ends.
ExecuteComplete	Fired after a command has finished executing.
InfoMessage	Fired whenever a `ConnectionEvent` operation completes successfully and additional information is returned by the provider.
RollbackTransComplete	Fired after a `RollbackTrans` operation finished executing.
WillConnect	Fired before a connection starts.
WillExecute	Fired before a pending command executes on the connection.

The Error Object

Properties of the Error Object	Return Type	Description
Description	String	A description string associated with the error. Read only.
HelpContext	Integer	Indicates the `ContextID` in the help file for the associated error. Read only.
HelpFile	String	Indicates the name of the help file. Read only.
NativeError	Long	Indicates the provider-specific error code for the associated error. Read only.
Number	Long	Indicates the number that uniquely identifies an `Error` object. Read only.
Source	String	Indicates the name of the object or application that originally generated the error. Read only.
SQLState	String	Indicates the SQL state for a given `Error` object. It is a five-character string that follows the ANSI SQL standard. Read only.

The Errors Collection

Methods of the Errors Collection	Return Type	Description
Clear		Removes all of the Error objects from the Errors collection.
Refresh		Updates the Error objects with information from the provider.

Properties of the Errors Collection	Return Type	Description
Count	Long	Indicates the number of Error objects in the Errors collection. Read only.
Item	Error	Allows indexing into the Errors collection to reference a specific Error object. Read only.

The Field Object

Methods of the Field Object	Return Type	Description
AppendChunk		Appends data to a large or binary Field object.
GetChunk	Variant	Returns all or a portion of the contents of a large or binary Field object.

Properties of the Field Object	Return Type	Description
ActualSize	Long	Indicates the actual length of a field's value. Read only.
Attributes	Long	Indicates one or more characteristics of a Field object.
DataFormat	Variant	Identifies the format in which data should be displayed.
DefinedSize	Long	Indicates the defined size of the Field object. Write only.
Name	String	Indicates the name of the Field object.
NumericScale	Byte	Indicates the scale of numeric values for the Field object. Write only.

Properties of the Field Object	Return Type	Description
OriginalValue	Variant	Indicates the value of a `Field` object that existed in the record before any changes were made. Read only.
Precision	Byte	Indicates the degree of precision for numeric values in the `Field` object. Read only.
Type	DataTypeEnum	Indicates the data type of the `Field` object.
UnderlyingValue	Variant	Indicates a `Field` object's current value in the database. Read only.
Value	Variant	Indicates the value assigned to the `Field` object.

Collections of the Field Object	Return Type	Description
Properties	Properties	Contains all of the `Property` objects for a `Field` object.

The Fields Collection

Methods of the Fields Collection	Return Type	Description
Append		Appends a `Field` object to the `Fields` collection.
Delete		Deletes a `Field` object from the `Fields` collection.
Refresh		Updates the `Field` objects in the `Fields` collection.

Properties of the Fields Collection	Return Type	Description
Count	Long	Indicates the number of `Field` objects in the `Fields` collection. Read only.
Item	Field	Allows indexing into the `Fields` collection to reference a specific `Field` object. Read only.

The Parameter Object

Methods of the Parameter Object	Return Type	Description
AppendChunk		Appends data to a large or binary `Parameter` object.

Properties of the Parameter Object	Return Type	Description
Attributes	Long	Indicates one or more characteristics of a `Parameter` object.
Direction	ParameterDirection Enum	Indicates whether the `Parameter` object represents an input parameter, an output parameter, or and input/output parameter, or if the parameter is a return value from a stored procedure.
Name	String	Indicates the name of the `Parameter` object.
NumericScale	Byte	Indicates the scale of numeric values for the `Parameter` object.
Precision	Byte	Indicates the degree of precision for numeric values in the `Parameter` object.
Size	Long	Indicates the maximum size (in bytes or characters) of a `Parameter` object.
Type	DataTypeEnum	Indicates the data type of the `Parameter` object.
Value	Variant	Indicates the value assigned to the `Parameter` object.

Collections of the Parameter Object	Return Type	Description
Properties	Properties	Contains all of the `Property` objects for a `Parameter` object.

The Parameters Collection

Methods of the Parameters Collection	Return Type	Description
Append		Appends a `Parameter` object to the `Parameters` collection.
Delete		Deletes a `Parameter` object from the `Parameters` collection.
Refresh		Updates the `Parameter` objects in the `Parameters` collection.

Properties of the Parameters Collection	Return Type	Description
Count	Long	Indicates the number of `Parameter` objects in the `Parameters` collection. Read only.
Item	Parameter	Allows indexing into the `Parameters` collection to reference a specific `Parameter` object. Read only.

The Properties Collection

Methods of the Properties Collection	Return Type	Description
Refresh		Updates the `Property` objects in the `Properties` collection with the details from the provider.

Properties of the Properties Collection	Return Type	Description
Count	Long	Indicates the number of `Property` objects in the `Properties` collection. Read only.
Item	Property	Allows indexing into the `Properties` collection to reference a specific `Property` object. Read only.

The Property Object

Properties of the Property Object	Return Type	Description
Attributes	Long	Indicates one or more characteristics of a `Property` object.
Name	String	Indicates the name of the `Property` object. Read only.
Type	DataTypeEnum	Indicates the data type of the `Property` object.
Value	Variant	Indicates the value assigned to the `Property` object.

The Recordset Object

Methods of the Recordset Object	Return Type	Description
AddNew		Creates a new record for an updateable `Recordset` object.
Cancel		Cancels execution of a pending asynchronous `Open` operation.
CancelBatch		Cancels a pending batch update.
CancelUpdate		Cancels any changes made to the current record, or to a new record prior to calling the `Update` method.
Clone	Recordset	Creates a duplicate `Recordset` object from an existing `Recordset` object.
Close		Closes the `Recordset` object and any dependent objects.
CompareBookmarks	CompareEnum	Compares two bookmarks and returns an indication of the relative values.
Delete		Deletes the current record or group of records.
Find		Searches the `Recordset` for a record that matches the specified criteria.
GetRows	Variant	Retrieves multiple records of a `Recordset` object into an array.
GetString	String	Returns a `Recordset` as a string.

Methods of the Recordset Object	Return Type	Description
Move		Moves the position of the current record in a `Recordset`.
MoveFirst		Moves the position of the current record to the first record in the `Recordset`.
MoveLast		Moves the position of the current record to the last record in the `Recordset`.
MoveNext		Moves the position of the current record to the next record in the `Recordset`.
MovePrevious		Moves the position of the current record to the previous record in the `Recordset`.
NextRecordset	Recordset	Clears the current `Recordset` object and returns the next `Recordset` by advancing to the next in a series of commands.
Open		Opens a `Recordset`.
Requery		Updates the data in a `Recordset` object by re-executing the query on which the object is based.
Resync		Refreshes the data in the current `Recordset` object from the underlying database.
Save		Saves the `Recordset` to a file.
Seek (new in ADO 2.1)		Searches the recordset index to locate a value
Supports	Boolean	Determines whether a specified `Recordset` object supports particular functionality.
Update		Saves any changes made to the current `Recordset` object.
UpdateBatch		Writes all pending batch updates to disk.

Properties of the Recordset Object	Return Type	Description
AbsolutePage	PositionEnum	Specifies in which page the current record resides.
AbsolutePosition	PositionEnum	Specifies the ordinal position of the `Recordset` object's current record.

Table Continued on Following Page

Appendix A

Properties of the Recordset Object	Return Type	Description
ActiveCommand	Object	Indicates the Command object that created the associated Recordset object. Read only.
ActiveConnection	Variant	Indicates to which Connection object the Recordset object currently belongs.
BOF	Boolean	Indicates whether the record pointer is pointing before the first record in the Recordset object. Read only.
Bookmark	Variant	Returns a bookmark that uniquely identifies the current record in the Recordset object, or sets the record pointer to point to the record identified by a valid bookmark.
CacheSize	Long	Indicates the number of records from the Recordset object that are cached locally in memory.
CursorLocation	CursorLocationEnum	Sets or returns the location of the cursor engine.
CursorType	CursorTypeEnum	Indicates the type of cursor used in the Recordset object.
DataMember	String	Specifies the name of the data member to be retrieved from the object referenced by the DataSource property. Write only.
DataSource	Object	Specifies an object containing data, to be represented by the Recordset object. Write only.
EditMode	EditModeEnum	Indicates the editing status of the current record. Read only.
EOF	Boolean	Indicates whether the record pointer is pointing beyond the last record in the Recordset object. Read only.
Filter	Variant	Indicates a filter for data in the Recordset.
Index (new in ADO 2.1)	String	Identifies the name of the index currently being used.
LockType	LockTypeEnum	Indicates the type of locks placed on records during editing.

Properties of the Recordset Object	Return Type	Description
MarshalOptions	MarshalOptionsEnum	Indicates which records are to be marshaled back to the server.
MaxRecords	Long	Indicates the maximum number of records that can be returned to the Recordset object from a query. Default is zero (no limit).
PageCount	Long	Indicates how many pages of data are contained in the Recordset object (and is thus dependent on the values of PageSize and RecordCount). Read only.
PageSize	Long	Indicates how many records constitute one page in the Recordset.
RecordCount	Long	Indicates the current number of records in the Recordset object. Read only.
Sort	String	Specifies one or more field names the Recordset is sorted on, and the direction of the sort.
Source	String	Indicates the source for the data in the Recordset object.
State	Long	Indicates whether the recordset is open, closed, or whether it is executing an asynchronous operation. Read only.
Status	Integer	Indicates the status of the current record with respect to match updates or other bulk operations. Read only.
StayInSync	Boolean	Indicates, in a hierarchical Recordset object, whether the parent row should change when the set of underlying child records changes. Read only.

Collections of the Recordset Object	Return Type	Description
Fields	Fields	Contains all of the Field objects for the Recordset object.
Properties	Properties	Contains all of the Property objects for the current Recordset object.

Events of the Recordset Object	Description
EndOfRecordset	Fired when there is an attempt to move to a row past the end of the `Recordset`.
FetchComplete	Fired after all the records in an asynchronous operation have been retrieved into the `Recordset`.
FetchProgress	Fired periodically during a lengthy asynchronous operation, to report how many rows have currently been retrieved.
FieldChangeComplete	Fired after the value of one or more `Field` object has been changed.
MoveComplete	Fired after the current position in the `Recordset` changes.
RecordChangeComplete	Fired after one or more records change.
RecordsetChangeComplete	Fired after the `Recordset` has changed.
WillChangeField	Fired before a pending operation changes the value of one or more `Field` objects.
WillChangeRecord	Fired before one or more rows in the `Recordset` change.
WillChangeRecordset	Fired before a pending operation changes the `Recordset`.
WillMove	Fired before a pending operation changes the current position in the `Recordset`.

ADO Method Calls – Quick Reference

Command Object Methods

Command.Cancel
Parameter = Command.CreateParameter(*Name As String, Type As DataTypeEnum,_
    Direction As ParameterDirectionEnum, Size As Integer, [Value As Variant]*)
Recordset = Command.Execute(*RecordsAffected As Variant, Parameters As Variant, _
    Options As Integer*)

Connection Object Methods

Integer = Connection.BeginTrans
Connection.Cancel
Connection.Close
Connection.CommitTrans
Recordset = Connection.Execute(*CommandText As String, RecordsAffected As Variant, _
    Options As Integer*)
Connection.Open(*ConnectionString As String, UserID As String, Password As String, _
    Options As Integer*)
Recordset = Connection.OpenSchema(*Schema As SchemaEnum, [Restrictions As Variant], _
    [SchemaID As Variant]*)
Connection.RollbackTrans

Errors Collection Methods

Errors.Clear
Errors.Refresh

Field Object Methods

Field.AppendChunk(*Data As Variant*)
Variant = Field.GetChunk(*Length As Integer*)

Fields Collection Methods

Fields.Append(*Name As String, Type As DataTypeEnum, DefinedSize As Integer, _*
    Attrib As FieldAttributeEnum)
Fields.Delete(*Index As Variant*)
Fields.Refresh

Parameter Object Methods

Parameter.AppendChunk(*Val As Variant*)

Parameters Collection Methods

Parameters.Append(*Object As Object*)
Parameters.Delete(*Index As Variant*)
Parameters.Refresh

Properties Collection Methods

Properties.Refresh

RecordsetObject Methods

Recordset.AddNew([*FieldList As Variant*], [*Values As Variant*])
Recordset.Cancel
Recordset.CancelBatch(*AffectRecords As AffectEnum*)
Recordset.CancelUpdate
Recordset = Recordset.Clone(*LockType As LockTypeEnum*)
Recordset.Close
CompareEnum = Recordset.CompareBookmarks(*Bookmark1 As Variant, Bookmark2 As*
Variant)
Recordset.Delete(*AffectRecords As AffectEnum*)
Recordset.Find(*Criteria As String, SkipRecords As Integer, _*
    SearchDirection As SearchDirectionEnum, [Start As Variant])
Variant = Recordset.GetRows(*Rows As Integer, [Start As Variant], [Fields As Variant]*)
String = Recordset.GetString(*StringFormat As StringFormatEnum, _*
    NumRows As Integer, ColumnDelimeter As String, RowDelimeter As String, _
    NullExpr As String)
Recordset.Move(*NumRecords As Integer, [Start As Variant]*)
Recordset.MoveFirst
Recordset.MoveLast
Recordset.MoveNext
Recordset.MovePrevious

Recordset = Recordset.NextRecordset(*[RecordsAffected As Variant]*)
Recordset.Open(*Source As Variant, ActiveConnection As Variant, _*
    CursorType As CursorTypeEnum, LockType As LockTypeEnum, _
    Options As Integer)
Recordset.Requery(*Options As Integer*)
Recordset.Resync(*AffectRecords As AffectEnum, ResyncValues As ResyncEnum*)
Recordset.Save(*FileName As String, PersistFormat As PersistFormatEnum*)
Recordset.Seek(*KeyValues As Variant, SeekOption As SeekEnum*)
Boolean = Recordset.Supports(*CursorOptions As CursorOptionEnum*)
Recordset.Update(*[Fields As Variant], [Values As Variant]*)
Recordset.UpdateBatch(*AffectRecords As AffectEnum*)

ADO Constants

Standard Constants

The following constants are predefined by ADO. For scripting languages these are included in `adovbs.inc` or `adojava.inc`, which can be found in the `Program Files\Common Files\System\ado` directory. In Visual Basic, these constants are included automatically when you reference the ADO library.

AffectEnum

Name	Value	Description
adAffectAll	3	Operation affects all records in the recordset.
adAffectAllChapters	4	Operation affects all child (chapter) records.
adAffectCurrent	1	Operation affects only the current record.
adAffectGroup	2	Operation affects records that satisfy the current `Filter` property.

BookmarkEnum

Name	Value	Description
adBookmarkCurrent	0	Default. Start at the current record.
adBookmarkFirst	1	Start at the first record.
adBookmarkLast	2	Start at the last record.

Appendix B

CEResyncEnum

Name	Value	Description
adResyncAll	15	Resynchronizes the data for each pending row.
adResyncAutoIncrement	1	Resynchronizes the auto-increment values for all successfully inserted rows. This is the default.
adResyncConflicts	2	Resynchronizes all rows for which an update or delete operation failed due to concurrency conflicts.
adResyncInserts	8	Resynchronizes all successfully inserted rows, including the values of their identity columns.
adResyncNone	0	No resynchronization is performed.
adResyncUpdates	4	Resynchronizes all successfully updated rows.

CommandTypeEnum

Name	Value	Description
adCmdFile	256	Indicates that the provider should evaluate CommandText as a previously persisted file.
adCmdStoredProc	4	Indicates that the provider should evaluate CommandText as a stored procedure.
adCmdTable	2	Indicates that the provider should generate a SQL query to return all rows from the table named in CommandText.
adCmdTableDirect	512	Indicates that the provider should return all rows from the table named in CommandText.
adCmdText	1	Indicates that the provider should evaluate CommandText as textual definition of a command, such as a SQL statement.
adCmdUnknown	8	Indicates that the type of command in CommandText unknown.
adCmdUnspecified	-1	The command type is unspecified.

CompareEnum

Name	Value	Description
adCompareEqual	1	The bookmarks are equal.
adCompareGreaterThan	2	The first bookmark is after the second.
adCompareLessThan	0	The first bookmark is before the second.
adCompareNotComparable	4	The bookmarks cannot be compared.
adCompareNotEqual	3	The bookmarks are not equal and not ordered.

ConnectModeEnum

Name	Value	Description
adModeRead	1	Indicates read-only permissions.
adModeReadWrite	3	Indicates read/write permissions.
adModeShareDenyNone	16	Prevents others from opening connection with any permissions.
adModeShareDenyRead	4	Prevents others from opening connection with read permissions.
adModeShareDenyWrite	8	Prevents others from opening connection with write permissions.
adModeShareExclusive	12	Prevents others from opening connection.
adModeUnknown	0	Default. Indicates that the permissions have not yet been set or cannot be determined.
adModeWrite	2	Indicates write-only permissions.

ConnectOptionEnum

Name	Value	Description
adAsyncConnect	16	Open the connection asynchronously
adConnectUnspecified	-1	The connection mode is unspecified.

ConnectPromptEnum

Name	Value	Description
adPromptAlways	1	Always prompt for connection information.
adPromptComplete	2	Only prompt if not enough information was supplied.
adPromptCompleteRequired	3	Only prompt if not enough information was supplied, but disable any options not directly applicable to the connection.
adPromptNever	4	Default. Never prompt for connection information.

CursorLocationEnum

Name	Value	Description
adUseClient	3	Use client-side cursors supplied by the local cursor library.
adUseClientBatch	3	Use client-side cursors supplied by the local cursor library.
adUseNone	1	No cursor services are used.
adUseServer	2	Default. Uses data provider driver supplied cursors.

CursorOptionEnum

Name	Value	Description
adAddNew	16778240	You can use the AddNew method to add new records.
adApproxPosition	16384	You can read and set the AbsolutePosition and AbsolutePage properties.
adBookmark	8192	You can use the Bookmark property to access specific records.
adDelete	16779264	You can use the Delete method to delete records.
adFind	524288	You can use the Find method to find records.
adHoldRecords	256	You can retrieve more records or change the next retrieve position without committing all pending changes.

Name	Value	Description
adIndex	8388608	You can use the Index property to set the current index.
adMovePrevious	512	You can use the MoveFirst, MovePrevious, Move and GetRows methods.
adNotify	262144	The recordset supports Notifications.
adResync	131072	You can update the cursor with the data visible in the underlying database with the Resync method.
adSeek	4194304	You can use the Seek method to find records by an index.
adUpdate	16809984	You can use the Update method to modify existing records.
adUpdateBatch	65536	You can use the UpdateBatch or CancelBatch methods to transfer changes to the provider in groups.

CursorTypeEnum

Name	Value	Description
adOpenDynamic	2	Opens a dynamic type cursor.
adOpenForwardOnly	0	Default. Opens a forward-only type cursor.
adOpenKeyset	1	Opens a keyset type cursor.
adOpenStatic	3	Opens a static type cursor.
adOpenUnspecified	-1	Indicates as unspecified value for cursor type.

DataTypeEnum

Name	Value	Description
adBigInt	20	An 8-byte signed integer.
adBinary	128	A binary value.
adBoolean	11	A Boolean value.
adBSTR	8	A null-terminated character string.
adChapter	136	A chapter type, indicating a child recordset.
adChar	129	A String value.

Table Continued on Following Page

Name	Value	Description
adCurrency	6	A currency value. An 8-byte signed integer scaled by 10,000, with 4 digits to the right of the decimal point.
adDate	7	A Date value. A Double where the whole part is the number of days since December 30 1899, and the fractional part is a fraction of the day.
adDBDate	133	A date value (yyyymmdd).
adDBFileTime	137	A database file time.
adDBTime	134	A time value (hhmmss).
adDBTimeStamp	135	A date-time stamp (yyyymmddhhmmss plus a fraction in billionths).
adDecimal	14	An exact numeric value with fixed precision and scale.
adDouble	5	A double-precision floating point value.
adEmpty	0	No value was specified.
adError	10	A 32-bit error code.
adFileTime	64	A DOS/Win32 file time. The number of 100-nanosecond intervals since Jan 1 1601.
adGUID	72	A globally unique identifier.
adIDispatch	9	A pointer to an `IDispatch` interface on an OLE object.
adInteger	3	A 4-byte signed integer.
adIUnknown	13	A pointer to an `IUnknown` interface on an OLE object.
adLongVarBinary	205	A long binary value.
adLongVarChar	201	A long String value.
adLongVarWChar	203	A long null-terminated string value.
adNumeric	131	An exact numeric value with a fixed precision and scale.
adPropVariant	138	A variant that is not equivalent to an Automation variant.
adSingle	4	A single-precision floating point value.
adSmallInt	2	A 2-byte signed integer.

Name	Value	Description
adTinyInt	16	A 1-byte signed integer.
adUnsignedBigInt	21	An 8-byte unsigned integer.
adUnsignedInt	19	An 4-byte unsigned integer.
adUnsignedSmallInt	18	An 2-byte unsigned integer.
adUnsignedTinyInt	17	An 1-byte unsigned integer.
adUserDefined	132	A user-defined variable.
adVarBinary	204	A binary value.
adVarChar	200	A String value.
adVariant	12	An Automation Variant.
adVarNumeric	139	A variable width exact numeric, with a signed scale value.
adVarWChar	202	A null-terminated Unicode character string.
adWChar	130	A null-terminated Unicode character string.

EditModeEnum

Name	Value	Description
adEditAdd	2	Indicates that the AddNew method has been invoked and the current record in the buffer is a new record that hasn't been saved to the database.
adEditDelete	4	Indicates that the Delete method has been invoked.
adEditInProgress	1	Indicates that data in the current record has been modified but not saved.
adEditNone	0	Indicates that no editing is in progress.

ErrorValueEnum

Name	Value	Description
adErrBoundToCommand	3707	The application cannot change the ActiveConnection property of a Recordset object with a Command object as its source.
adErrDataConversion	3421	The application is using a value of the wrong type for the current application.

Table Continued on Following Page

Appendix B

Name	Value	Description
adErrFeatureNotAvailable	3251	The operation requested by the application is not supported by the provider.
adErrIllegalOperation	3219	The operation requested by the application is not allowed in this context.
adErrInTransaction	3246	The application cannot explicitly close a `Connection` object while in the middle of a transaction.
adErrInvalidArgument	3001	The application is using arguments that are the wrong type, are out of the acceptable range, or are in conflict with one another.
adErrInvalidConnection	3709	The application requested an operation on an object with a reference to a closed or invalid `Connection` object.
adErrInvalidParamInfo	3708	The application has improperly defined a `Parameter` object.
adErrItemNotFound	3265	ADO could not find the object in the collection.
adErrNoCurrentRecord	3021	Either `BOF` or `EOF` is `True`, or the current record has been deleted. The operation requested by the application requires a current record.
adErrNotExecuting	3715	The operation is not executing.
adErrNotReentrant	3710	The operation is not reentrant.
adErrObjectClosed	3704	The operation requested by the application is not allowed if the object is closed.
adErrObjectInCollection	3367	Can't append. Object already in collection.
adErrObjectNotSet	3420	The object referenced by the application no longer points to a valid object.
adErrObjectOpen	3705	The operation requested by the application is not allowed if the object is open.
adErrOperationCancelled	3712	The operation was cancelled.

Name	Value	Description
adErrProviderNotFound	3706	ADO could not find the specified provider.
adErrStillConnecting	3713	The operation is still connecting.
adErrStillExecuting	3711	The operation is still executing.
adErrUnsafeOperation	3716	The operation is unsafe under these circumstances.

EventReasonEnum

Name	Value	Description
adRsnAddNew	1	A new record is to be added.
adRsnClose	9	The object is being closed.
adRsnDelete	2	The record is being deleted.
adRsnFirstChange	11	The record has been changed for the first time.
adRsnMove	10	A Move has been invoked and the current record pointer is being moved.
adRsnMoveFirst	12	A MoveFirst has been invoked and the current record pointer is being moved.
adRsnMoveLast	15	A MoveLast has been invoked and the current record pointer is being moved.
adRsnMoveNext	13	A MoveNext has been invoked and the current record pointer is being moved.
adRsnMovePrevious	14	A MovePrevious has been invoked and the current record pointer is being moved.
adRsnRequery	7	The recordset was requeried.
adRsnResynch	8	The recordset was resynchronized.
adRsnUndoAddNew	5	The addition of a new record has been cancelled.
adRsnUndoDelete	6	The deletion of a record has been cancelled.
adRsnUndoUpdate	4	The update of a record has been cancelled.
adRsnUpdate	3	The record is being updated.

EventStatusEnum

Name	Value	Description
adStatusCancel	4	Request cancellation of the operation that is about to occur.
adStatusCantDeny	3	A `Will` event cannot request cancellation of the operation about to occur.
adStatusErrorsOccurred	2	The operation completed unsuccessfully, or a `Will...` event cancelled the operation.
adStatusOK	1	The operation completed successfully.
adStatusUnwantedEvent	5	Events for this operation are no longer required.

ExecuteOptionEnum

Name	Value	Description
adAsyncExecute	16	The operation is executed asynchronously.
adAsyncFetch	32	The records are fetched asynchronously.
adAsyncFetchNonBlocking	64	The records are fetched asynchronously without blocking subsequent operations.
adExecuteNoRecords	128	Indicates `CommandText` is a command or stored procedure that does not return rows. Always combined with `adCmdText` or `adCmdStoreProc`.

FieldAttributeEnum

Name	Value	Description
adFldCacheDeferred	4096	Indicates that the provider caches field values and that subsequent reads are done from the cache.
adFldFixed	16	Indicates that the field contains fixed-length data.
adFldIsNullable	32	Indicates that the field accepts Null values.
adFldKeyColumn	32768	The field is part of a key column.
adFldLong	128	Indicates that the field is a long binary field, and that the `AppendChunk` and `GetChunk` methods can be used.

Name	Value	Description
adFldMayBeNull	64	Indicates that you can read Null values from the field.
adFldMayDefer	2	Indicates that the field is deferred, that is, the field values are not retrieved from the data source with the whole record, but only when you access them.
adFldNegativeScale	16384	The field has a negative scale.
adFldRowID	256	Indicates that the field some kind of record ID.
adFldRowVersion	512	Indicates that the field time or date stamp used to track updates.
adFldUnknownUpdatable	8	Indicates that the provider cannot determine if you can write to the field.
adFldUnspecified	-1	Attributes of the field are unspecified.
adFldUpdatable	4	Indicates that you can write to the field.

FilterGroupEnum

Name	Value	Description
adFilterAffectedRecords	2	Allows you to view only records affected by the last Delete, Resync, UpdateBatch or CancelBatch method.
adFilterConflictingRecords	5	Allows you to view the records that failed the last batch update attempt.
adFilterFetchedRecords	3	Allows you to view records in the current cache.
adFilterNone	0	Removes the current filter and restores all records to view.
adFilterPendingRecords	1	Allows you to view only the records that have changed but have not been sent to the server. Only applicable for batch update mode.
adFilterPredicate	4	Allows you to view records that failed the last batch update attempt.

Appendix B

GetRowsOptionEnum

Name	Value	Description
adGetRowsRest	-1	Retrieves the remainder of the rows in the recordset.

IsolationLevelEnum

Name	Value	Description
adXactBrowse	256	Indicates that from one transaction you can view uncommitted changes in other transactions.
adXactChaos	16	Default. Indicates that you cannot overwrite pending changes from more highly isolated transactions.
adXactCursorStability	4096	Default. Indicates that from one transaction you can view changes in other transactions only after they have been committed.
adXactIsolated	1048576	Indicates that transactions are conducted in isolation of other transactions.
adXactReadCommitted	4096	Same as adXactCursorStability.
adXactReadUncommitted	256	Same as adXactBrowse.
adXactRepeatableRead	65536	Indicates that from one transaction you cannot see changes made in other transactions, but that requerying can bring new recordsets.
adXactSerializable	1048576	Same as adXactIsolated.
adXactUnspecified	-1	Indicates that the provider is using a different IsolationLevel than specified, but that the level cannot be identified.

LockTypeEnum

Name	Value	Description
adLockBatchOptimistic	4	Optimistic batch updates.
adLockOptimistic	3	Optimistic locking, record by record. The provider locks records when Update is called.

Name	Value	Description
adLockPessimistic	2	Pessimistic locking, record by record. The provider locks the record immediately upon editing.
adLockReadOnly	1	Default. Read only, data cannot be modified.
adLockUnspecified	-1	The clone is created with the same lock type as the original.

MarshalOptionsEnum

Name	Value	Description
adMarshalAll	0	Default. Indicates that all rows are returned to the server.
adMarshalModifiedOnly	1	Indicates that only modified rows are returned to the server.

ObjectStateEnum

Name	Value	Description
adStateClosed	0	Default. Indicates that the object is closed.
adStateConnecting	2	Indicates that the object is connecting.
adStateExecuting	4	Indicates that the object is executing a command.
adStateFetching	8	Indicates that the rows of the recordset are being fetched.
adStateOpen	1	Indicates that the object is open.

ParameterAttributesEnum

Name	Value	Description
adParamLong	128	Indicates that the parameter accepts long binary data.
adParamNullable	64	Indicates that the parameter accepts Null values.
adParamSigned	16	Default. Indicates that the parameter accepts signed values.

ParameterDirectionEnum

Name	Value	Description
adParamInput	1	Default. Indicates an input parameter.
adParamInputOutput	3	Indicates both an input and output parameter.
adParamOutput	2	Indicates an output parameter.
adParamReturnValue	4	Indicates a return value.
adParamUnknown	0	Indicates parameter direction is unknown.

PersistFormatEnum

Name	Value	Description
adPersistADTG	0	Default. Persist data in Advanced Data TableGram format.
adPersistXML	1	Persist data in XML format.

PositionEnum

Name	Value	Description
adPosBOF	-2	The current record pointer is at BOF.
adPosEOF	-3	The current record pointer is at EOF.
adPosUnknown	-1	The Recordset is empty, or the current position is unknown, or the provider does not support the AbsolutePage property.

PropertyAttributesEnum

Name	Value	Description
adPropNotSupported	0	Indicates that the property is not supported by the provider.
adPropOptional	2	Indicates that the user does not need to specify a value for this property before the data source is initialized.
adPropRead	512	Indicates that the user can read the property.
adPropRequired	1	Indicates that the user must specify a value for this property before the data source is initialized.
adPropWrite	1024	Indicates that the user can set the property.

RecordStatusEnum

Name	Value	Description
adRecCanceled	256	The record was not saved because the operation was cancelled.
adRecCantRelease	1024	The new record was not saved because of existing record locks.
adRecConcurrencyViolation	2048	The record was not saved because optimistic concurrency was in use.
adRecDBDeleted	262144	The record has already been deleted from the data source.
adRecDeleted	4	The record was deleted.
adRecIntegrityViolation	4096	The record was not saved because the user violated integrity constraints.
adRecInvalid	16	The record was not saved because its bookmark is invalid.
adRecMaxChangesExceeded	8192	The record was not saved because there were too many pending changes.
adRecModified	2	The record was modified.
adRecMultipleChanges	64	The record was not saved because it would have affected multiple records.
adRecNew	1	The record is new.
adRecObjectOpen	16384	The record was not saved because of a conflict with an open storage object.
adRecOK	0	The record was successfully updated.
adRecOutOfMemory	32768	The record was not saved because the computer has run out of memory.
adRecPendingChanges	128	The record was not saved because it refers to a pending insert.
adRecPermissionDenied	65536	The record was not saved because the user has insufficient permissions.
adRecSchemaViolation	131072	The record was not saved because it violates the structure of the underlying database.
adRecUnmodified	8	The record was not modified.

Appendix B

ResyncEnum

Name	Value	Description
adResyncAllValues	2	Default. Data is overwritten and pending updates are cancelled.
adResyncUnderlyingValues	1	Data is not overwritten and pending updates are not cancelled.

SchemaEnum

Name	Value	Description
adSchemaAsserts	0	Request assert information.
adSchemaCatalogs	1	Request catalog information.
adSchemaCharacterSets	2	Request character set information.
adSchemaCheckConstraints	5	Request check constraint information.
adSchemaCollations	3	Request collation information.
adSchemaColumnPrivileges	13	Request column privilege information.
adSchemaColumns	4	Request column information.
adSchemaColumnsDomainUsage	11	Request column domain usage information.
adSchemaConstraintColumnUsage	6	Request column constraint usage information.
adSchemaConstraintTableUsage	7	Request table constraint usage information.
adSchemaCubes	32	For multi-dimensional data, view the Cubes schema.
adSchemaDBInfoKeywords	30	Request the keywords from the provider.
adSchemaDBInfoLiterals	31	Request the literals from the provider.
adSchemaDimensions	33	For multi-dimensional data, view the Dimensions schema.
adSchemaForeignKeys	27	Request foreign key information.
adSchemaHierarchies	34	For multi-dimensional data, view the Hierarchies schema.
adSchemaIndexes	12	Request index information.

Name	Value	Description
adSchemaKeyColumnUsage	8	Request key column usage information.
adSchemaLevels	35	For multi-dimensional data, view the Levels schema.
adSchemaMeasures	36	For multi-dimensional data, view the Measures schema.
adSchemaMembers	38	For multi-dimensional data, view the Members schema.
adSchemaPrimaryKeys	28	Request primary key information.
adSchemaProcedureColumns	29	Request stored procedure column information.
adSchemaProcedureParameters	26	Request stored procedure parameter information.
adSchemaProcedures	16	Request stored procedure information.
adSchemaProperties	37	For multi-dimensional data, view the Properties schema.
adSchemaProviderSpecific	-1	Request provider specific information.
adSchemaProviderTypes	22	Request provider type information.
adSchemaReferentialContraints	9	Request referential constraint information.
adSchemaReferentialConstraints	9	Request referential constraint information.
adSchemaSchemata	17	Request schema information.
adSchemaSQLLanguages	18	Request SQL language support information.
adSchemaStatistics	19	Request statistics information.
adSchemaTableConstraints	10	Request table constraint information.
adSchemaTablePrivileges	14	Request table privilege information.
adSchemaTables	20	Request information about the tables.

Table Continued on Following Page

Name	Value	Description
adSchemaTranslations	21	Request character set translation information.
adSchemaTrustees	39	Request trustee information.
adSchemaUsagePrivileges	15	Request user privilege information.
adSchemaViewColumnUsage	24	Request column usage in views information.
adSchemaViews	23	Request view information.
adSchemaViewTableUsage	25	Request table usage in views information.

Due to a misspelling in the type library, adSchemaReferentialConstraints is included twice – once for the original spelling and once for the corrected spelling.

SearchDirectionEnum

Name	Value	Description
adSearchBackward	-1	Search backward from the current record.
adSearchForward	1	Search forward from the current record.

SeekEnum

Name	Value	Description
adSeekAfter	8	Seek the key just after the match.
adSeekAfterEQ	4	Seek the key equal to or just after the match.
adSeekBefore	32	See the key just before the match.
adSeekBeforeEQ	16	Seek the key equal to or just before the match.
adSeekFirstEQ	1	Seek the first key equal to the match.
adSeekLastEQ	2	Seek the last key equal to the match.

StringFormatEnum

Name	Value	Description
adClipString	2	Rows are delimited by user defined values.

XactAttributeEnum

Name	Value	Description
adXactAbortRetaining	262144	The provider will automatically start a new transaction after a `RollbackTrans` method call.
adXactAsyncPhaseOne	524288	Perform an asynchronous commit.
adXactCommitRetaining	131072	The provider will automatically start a new transaction after a `CommitTrans` method call.
adXactSyncPhaseOne	1048576	Performs an synchronous commit.

Miscellaneous Constants

These values are not included in the standard `adovbs.inc` include file (and are not automatically supplied when using Visual Basic), but can be found in `adocon.inc` (for ASP) and `adocon.bas` (for Visual Basic) from the supporting web site, http://webdev.wrox.co.uk/books/2688.

Many of these may not be necessary to you as an ADO programmer, but they are included here for completeness, and are only really useful as bitmask values for entries in the `Properties` collection.

DBBINDURLFLAG

Name	Value	Description
DBBINDURLFLAG_ DELAYFETCHCOLUMNS	32768	This value is not supported by this version of ADO.
DBBINDURLFLAG_ DELAYFETCHSTREAM	16384	This value is not supported by this version of ADO.
DBBINDURLFLAG_ OUTPUT	8388608	Bind to the executed output, rather than the resource source.
DBBINDURLFLAG_ RECURSIVE	4191304	This value is not supported by this version of ADO.

DB_COLLATION

Name	Value	Description
DB_COLLATION_ASC	1	The sort sequence for the column is ascending.
DB_COLLATION_DESC	2	The sort sequence for the column is descending.

DB_IMP_LEVEL

Name	Value	Description
DB_IMP_LEVEL_ ANONYMOUS	0	The client is anonymous to the server, and the server process cannot obtain identification information about the client and cannot impersonate the client.
DB_IMP_LEVEL_ DELEGATE	3	The process can impersonate the client's security context while acting on behalf of the client. The server process can also make outgoing calls to other servers while acting on behalf of the client.
DB_IMP_LEVEL_ IDENTIFY	1	The server can obtain the client's identity, and can impersonate the client for ACL checking, but cannot access system objects as the client.
DB_IMP_LEVEL_ IMPERSONATE	2	The server process can impersonate the client's security context whilst acting on behalf of the client. This information is obtained upon connection and not on every call.

DB_MODE

Name	Value	Description
DB_MODE_READ	1	Read only.
DB_MODE_READWRITE	3	Read/Write (equal to DB_MODE_READ + DB_MODE_WRITE).
DB_MODE_SHARE_DENY_ NONE	16	Neither read nor write access can be denied to others.
DB_MODE_SHARE_DENY_ READ	4	Prevents others from opening in read mode.
DB_MODE_SHARE_DENY_ WRITE	8	Prevents others from opening in write mode.
DB_MODE_SHARE_ EXCLUSIVE	12	Prevents others from opening in read/write mode (equal to DB_MODE_SHARE_DENY_WRITE + DB_MODE_SHARE_DENY_WRITE).
DB_MODE_WRITE	2	Write only.

DB_PROT_LEVEL

Name	Value	Description
DB_PROT_LEVEL_ CALL	2	Authenticates the source of the data at the beginning of each request from the client to the server.
DB_PROT_LEVEL_ CONNECT	1	Authenticates only when the client establishes the connection with the server.
DB_PROT_LEVEL_ NONE	0	Performs no authentication of data sent to the server.
DB_PROT_LEVEL_ PKT	3	Authenticates that all data received is from the client.
DB_PROT_LEVEL_ PKT_INTEGRITY	4	Authenticates that all data received is from the client and that it has not been changed in transit.
DB_PROT_LEVEL_ PKT_PRIVACY	5	Authenticates that all data received is from the client, that it has not been changed in transit, and protects the privacy of the data by encrypting it.

DB_PT

Name	Value	Description
DB_PT_FUNCTION	3	Function; there is a returned value.
DB_PT_PROCEDURE	2	Procedure; there is no returned value.
DB_PT_UNKNOWN	1	It is not known whether there is a returned value.

DB_SEARCHABLE

Name	Value	Description
DB_ALL_EXCEPT_LIKE	3	The data type can be used in a WHERE clause with all comparison operators except LIKE.
DB_LIKE_ONLY	2	The data type can be used in a WHERE clause only with the LIKE predicate.
DB_SEARCHABLE	4	The data type can be used in a WHERE clause with any comparison operator.
DB_UNSEARCHABLE	1	The data type cannot be used in a WHERE clause.

DBCOLUMNDESCFLAG

Name	Value	Description
DBCOLUMNDESCFLAG _CLSID	8	The CLSID portion of the column description can be changed when altering the column.
DBCOLUMNDESCFLAG _COLSIZE	16	The column size portion of the column description can be changed when altering the column.

Table Continued on Following Page

Name	Value	Description
DBCOLUMNDESCFLAG _DBCID	32	The DBCID portion of the column description can be changed when altering the column.
DBCOLUMNDESCFLAG _ITYPEINFO	2	The type information portion of the column description can be changed when altering the column.
DBCOLUMNDESCFLAG _PRECISION	128	The precision portion of the column description can be changed when altering the column.
DBCOLUMNDESCFLAG _PROPERTIES	4	The property sets portion of the column description can be changed when altering the column.
DBCOLUMNDESCFLAG _SCALE	256	The numeric scale portion of the column description can be changed when altering the column.
DBCOLUMNDESCFLAG _TYPENAME	1	The type name portion of the column description can be changed when altering the column.
DBCOLUMNDESCFLAG _WTYPE	64	The data type portion of the column description can be changed when altering the column.

DBCOLUMNFLAGS

Name	Value	Description
DBCOLUMNFLAGS_ CACHEDEFERRED	4096	Indicates that the value of a deferred column is cached when it is first read.
DBCOLUMNFLAGS_ISCHAPTER	8192	The column contains a Chapter value.
DBCOLUMNFLAGS_ ISFIXEDLENGTH	16	All of the data in the column is of a fixed length.
DBCOLUMNFLAGS_ISLONG	128	The column contains a BLOB value that contains long data.
DBCOLUMNFLAGS_ISNULLABLE	32	The column can be set to NULL, or the provider cannot determine whether the column can be set to NULL.
DBCOLUMNFLAGS_ISROWID	256	The column contains a persistent row identifier.
DBCOLUMNFLAGS_ISROWVER	512	The column contains a timestamp or other row versioning data type.
DBCOLUMNFLAGS_MAYBENULL	64	NULLs can be got from the column.
DBCOLUMNFLAGS_MAYDEFER	2	The column is deferred.
DBCOLUMNFLAGS_WRITE	4	The column may be updated.
DBCOLUMNFLAGS_ WRITEUNKNOWN	8	It is not known if the column can be updated.

DBLITERAL

Name	Value	Description
DBLITERAL_INVALID		An invalid value.
DBLITERAL_BINARY_LITERAL		A binary literal in a text command.
DBLITERAL_CATALOG_NAME		A catalog name in a text command.
DBLITERAL_CATALOG_SEPARATOR		The character that separates the catalog name from the rest of the identifier in a text command.
DBLITERAL_CHAR_LITERAL		A character literal in a text command.
DBLITERAL_COLUMN_ALIAS		A column alias in a text command.
DBLITERAL_COLUMN_NAME		A column name used in a text command or in a data-definition interface.
DBLITERAL_CORRELATION_NAME		A correlation name (table alias) in a text command.
DBLITERAL_CURSOR_NAME		A cursor name in a text command.
DBLITERAL_ESCAPE_PERCENT_PREFIX		The character used in a LIKE clause to escape the character returned for the DBLITERAL_LIKE_PERCENT literal.
DBLITERAL_ESCAPE_PERCENT_SUFFIX		The escape character, if any, used to suffix the character returned for the DBLITERAL_LIKE_PERCENT literal.
DBLITERAL_ESCAPE_UNDERSCORE_PREFIX		The character used in a LIKE clause to escape the character returned for the DBLITERAL_LIKE_UNDERSCORE literal.
DBLITERAL_ESCAPE_UNDERSCORE_SUFFIX		The escape character, if any, used to suffix the character returned for the DBLITERAL_LIKE_UNDERSCORE literal.
DBLITERAL_INDEX_NAME		An index name used in a text command or in a data-definition interface.
DBLITERAL_LIKE_PERCENT		The character used in a LIKE clause to match zero or more characters.
DBLITERAL_LIKE_UNDERSCORE		The character used in a LIKE clause to match exactly one character.
DBLITERAL_PROCEDURE_NAME		A procedure name in a text command.
DBLITERAL_SCHEMA_NAME		A schema name in a text command.

Table Continued on Following Page

Name	Value	Description
DBLITERAL_SCHEMA_SEPARATOR		The character that separates the schema name from the rest of the identifier in a text command.
DBLITERAL_TABLE_NAME		A table name used in a text command or in a data-definition interface.
DBLITERAL_TEXT_COMMAND		A text command, such as an SQL statement.
DBLITERAL_USER_NAME		A user name in a text command.
DBLITERAL_VIEW_NAME		A view name in a text command.
DBLITERAL_QUOTE_PREFIX		The character used in a text command as the opening quote for quoting identifiers that contain special characters.
DBLITERAL_QUOTE_SUFFIX		The character used in a text command as the closing quote for quoting identifiers that contain special characters.

DBPARAMTYPE

Name	Value	Description
DBPARAMTYPE_INPUT	1	The parameter is an input parameter.
DBPARAMTYPE_INPUTOUTPUT	2	The parameter is both an input and an output parameter.
DBPARAMTYPE_OUTPUT	3	The parameter is an output parameter.
DBPARAMTYPE_RETURNVALUE	4	The parameter is a return value.

DBPROMPT

Name	Value	Description
DBPROMPT_COMPLETE	2	Prompt the user only if more information is needed.
DBPROMPT_COMPLETEREQUIRED	3	Prompt the user only if more information is required. Do not allow the user to enter optional information.
DBPROMPT_NOPROMPT	4	Do not prompt the user.
DBPROMPT_PROMPT	1	Always prompt the user for initialization information.

DBPROPVAL_AO

Name	Value	Description
DBPROPVAL_AO_RANDOM	2	Columns can be accessed in any order.
DBPROPVAL_AO_SEQUENTIAL	0	All columns must be accessed in sequential order determined by the column ordinal.
DBPROPVAL_AO_SEQUENTIAL STORAGEOBJECTS	1	Columns bound as storage objects can only be accessed in sequential order as determined by the column ordinal.

DBPROPVAL_ASYNCH

Name	Value	Description
DBPROPVAL_ASYNCH_ BACKGROUNDPOPULATION	8	The rowset is populated asynchronously in the background.
DBPROPVAL_ASYNCH_ INITIALIZE	1	Initialization is performed asynchronously.
DBPROPVAL_ASYNCH_ POPULATEONDEMAND	32	The consumer prefers to optimize for getting each individual request for data returned as quickly as possible.
DBPROPVAL_ASYNCH_ PREPOPULATE	16	The consumer prefers to optimize for retrieving all data when the row set is materialized.
DBPROPVAL_ASYNCH_ RANDOMPOPULATION	4	Rowset population is performed asynchronously in a random manner.
DBPROPVAL_ASYNCH_ SEQUENTIALPOPULATION	2	Rowset population is performed asynchronously in a sequential manner.

DBPROPVAL_BG

Name	Value	Description
DBPROPVAL_GB_ COLLATE	16	A COLLATE clause can be specified at the end of each grouping column.
DBPROPVAL_GB_ CONTAINS_SELECT	4	The GROUP BY clause must contain all non-aggregated columns in the select list. It can contain columns that are not in the select list.
DBPROPVAL_GB_ EQUALS_SELECT	2	The GROUP BY clause must contain all non-aggregated columns in the select list. It cannot contain any other columns.
DBPROPVAL_GB_ NO_RELATION	8	The columns in the GROUP BY clause and the select list are not related. The meaning on non-grouped, non-aggregated columns in the select list is data source dependent.
DBPROPVAL_GB_ NOT_SUPPORTED	1	GROUP BY clauses are not supported.

DBPROPVAL_BI

Name	Value	Description
DBPROPVAL_BI_CROSSROWSET	1	Bookmark values are valid across all rowsets generated on this table.

DBPROPVAL_BMK

Name	Value	Description
DBPROPVAL_BMK_KEY	2	The bookmark type is key.
DBPROPVAL_BMK_NUMERIC	1	The bookmark type is numeric.

DBPROPVAL_BO

Name	Value	Description
DBPROPVAL_BO_NOINDEXUPDATE	1	The provider is not required to update indexes based on inserts or changes to the rowset. Any indexes need to be re-created following changes made through the rowset.
DBPROPVAL_BO_NOLOG	0	The provider is not required to log inserts or changes to the rowset.
DBPROPVAL_BO_REFINTEGRITY	2	Referential integrity constraints do not need to be checked or enforced for changes made through the rowset.

DBPROPVAL_BP

Name	Value	Description
DBPROPVAL_BP_NOPARTIAL	2	Fail the bulk operation if there is a single error.
DBPROPVAL_BP_PARTIAL	1	Allow the bulk operation to partially complete, possibly resulting in inconsistent data.

DBPROPVAL_BT

Name	Value	Description
DBPROPVAL_BT_DEFAULT	0	Use the value defined in the dynamic property Jet OLEDB:Global Bulk Transactions
DBPROPVAL_BT_NOBULKTRANSACTIONS	1	Bulk operations are not transacted.
DBPROPVAL_BT_BULKTRANSACTION	2	Bulk operations are transacted.

DBPROPVAL_CB

Name	Value	Description
DBPROPVAL_CB_NON_NULL	2	The result is the concatenation of the non-NULL valued column or columns.
DBPROPVAL_CB_NULL	1	The result is NULL valued.

DBPROPVAL_CB

Name	Value	Description
DBPROPVAL_CB_DELETE	1	Aborting a transaction deletes prepared commands.
DBPROPVAL_CB_PRESERVE	2	Aborting a transaction preserves prepared commands.

DBPROPVAL_CD

Name	Value	Description
DBPROPVAL_CD_NOTNULL	1	Columns can be created non-nullable.

DBPROPVAL_CL

Name	Value	Description
DBPROPVAL_CL_END	2	The catalog name appears at the end of the fully qualified name.
DBPROPVAL_CL_START	1	The catalog name appears at the start of the fully qualified name.

DBPROPVAL_CO

Name	Value	Description
DBPROPVAL_CO_BEGINSWITH	32	Provider supports the BEGINSWITH and NOTBEGINSWITH operators.
DBPROPVAL_CO_CASEINSENSITIVE	8	Provider supports the CASEINSENSITIVE operator.
DBPROPVAL_CO_CASESENSITIVE	4	Provider supports the CASESENSITIVE operator.
DBPROPVAL_CO_CONTAINS	16	Provider supports the CONTAINS and NOTCONTAINS operators.
DBPROPVAL_CO_EQUALITY	1	Provider supports the following operators: LT, LE, EQ, GE, GT, NE.
DBPROPVAL_CO_STRING	2	Provider supports the BEGINSWITH operator.

DBPROPVAL_CS

Name	Value	Description
DBPROPVAL_CS_COMMUNICATIONFAILURE	2	The DSO is unable to communicate with the data store.
DBPROPVAL_CS_INITIALIZED	1	The DSO is in an initialized state and able to communicate with the data store.
DBPROPVAL_CS_UNINITIALIZED	0	The DSO is in an uninitialized state.

DBPROPVAL_CU

Name	Value	Description
DBPROPVAL_CU_DML_STATEMENTS	1	Catalog names are supported in all Data Manipulation Language statements.
DBPROPVAL_CU_INDEX_DEFINITION	4	Catalog names are supported in all index definition statements.
DBPROPVAL_CU_PRIVILEGE_DEFINITION	8	Catalog names are supported in all privilege definition statements.
DBPROPVAL_CU_TABLE_DEFINITION	2	Catalog names are supported in all table definition statements.

DBPROPVAL_DF

Name	Value	Description
DBPROPVAL_DF_INITIALLY_DEFERRED	1	The foreign key is initially deferred.
DBPROPVAL_DF_INITIALLY_IMMEDIATE	2	The foreign key is initially immediate.
DBPROPVAL_DF_NOT_DEFERRABLE	3	The foreign key is not deferrable.

DBPROPVAL_DL

Name	Value	Description
DBPROPVAL_DL_OLDMODE	0	Mode used in previous versions of the Jet database.
DBPROPVAL_DL_ALCATRAZ	1	Use new method, allowing row level locking.

DBPROPVAL_DST

Name	Value	Description
DBPROPVAL_DST_MDP	2	The provider is a multidimensional provider (MD).
DBPROPVAL_DST_TDP	1	The provider is a tabular data provider (TDP).
DBPROPVAL_DST_TDPANDMDP	3	The provider is both a TDP and a MD provider.
DBPROPVAL_DST_DOCSOURCE	4	The provider is a document source (Internet Publishing Provider)

DBPROPVAL_GU

Name	Value	Description
DBPROPVAL_GU_NOTSUPPORTED	1	URL suffixes are not supported. This is the only option supported by the Internet Publishing Provider in this version of ADO.
DBPROPVAL_GU_SUFFIX	2	URL suffixes are generated by the Internet Publishing Provider.

DBPROPVAL_HT

Name	Value	Description
DBPROPVAL_HT_DIFFERENT_CATALOGS	1	The provider supports heterogeneous joins between catalogs.
DBPROPVAL_HT_DIFFERENT_PROVIDERS	2	The provider supports heterogeneous joins between providers.

DBPROPVAL_IC

Name	Value	Description
DBPROPVAL_IC_LOWER	2	Identifiers in SQL are case insensitive and are stored in lower case in system catalog.
DBPROPVAL_IC_MIXED	8	Identifiers in SQL are case insensitive and are stored in mixed case in system catalog.
DBPROPVAL_IC_SENSITIVE	4	Identifiers in SQL are case sensitive and are stored in mixed case in system catalog.
DBPROPVAL_IC_UPPER	1	Identifiers in SQL are case insensitive and are stored in upper case in system catalog.

DBPROPVAL_IN

Name	Value	Description
DBPROPVAL_IN_ALLOWNULL	0	The index allows NULL values to be inserted.
DBPROPVAL_IN_DISALLOWNULL	1	The index does not allow entries where the key columns are NULL. An error will be generated if the consumer attempts to insert a NULL value into a key column.
DBPROPVAL_IN_IGNOREANYNULL	4	The index does not insert entries containing NULL keys.
DBPROPVAL_IN_IGNORENULL	2	The index does not insert entries where some column key has a NULL value.

DBPROPVAL_IT

Name	Value	Description
DBPROPVAL_IT_BTREE	1	The index is a B+ tree.
DBPROPVAL_IT_CONTENT	3	The index is a content index.
DBPROPVAL_IT_HASH	2	The index is a hash file using linear or extensible hashing.
DBPROPVAL_IT_OTHER	4	The index is some other type of index.

DBPROPVAL_JCC

Name	Value	Description
DBPROPVAL_JCC_PASSIVESHUTDOWN	1	New connections to the database are disallowed.
DBPROPVAL_JCC_NORMAL	2	Users are allowed to connect to the database.

DBPROPVAL_LG

Name	Value	Description
DBPROPVAL_LG_PAGE	1	Use page locking.
DBPROPVAL_LG_ALCATRAZ	2	Use row-level locking.

DBPROPVAL_LM

Name	Value	Description
DBPROPVAL_LM_INTENT	4	The provider uses the maximum level of locking to ensure that changes will not fail due to a concurrency violation.
DBPROPVAL_LM_NONE	1	The provider is not required to lock rows at any time to ensure successful updates.
DBPROPVAL_LM_READ	2	The provider uses the minimum level of locking to ensure that changes will not fail due to a concurrency violation.
DBPROPVAL_LM_RITE	8	
DBPROPVAL_LM_SINGLEROW	2	The provider uses the minimum level of locking to ensure that changes will not fail due to a concurrency violation.

DBPROPVAL_MR

Name	Value	Description
DBPROPVAL_MR_CONCURRENT	2	More than one rowset create by the same multiple results object can exist concurrently.
DBPROPVAL_MR_NOTSUPPORTED	0	Multiple results objects are not supported.
DBPROPVAL_MR_SUPPORTED	1	The provider supports multiple results objects.

DBPROPVAL_NC

Name	Value	Description
DBPROPVAL_NC_END	1	NULLs are sorted at the end of the list, regardless of the sort order.
DBPROPVAL_NC_HIGH	2	NULLs are sorted at the high end of the list.
DBPROPVAL_NC_LOW	4	NULLs are sorted at the low end of the list.
DBPROPVAL_NC_START	8	NULLs are sorted at the start of the list, regardless of the sort order.

DBPROPVAL_NP

Name	Value	Description
DBPROPVAL_NP_ABOUTTODO	2	The consumer will be notified before an action (ie the Will event).
DBPROPVAL_NP_DIDEVENT	16	The consumer will be notified after an action (ie the Complete event).

Table Continued on Following Page

Name	Value	Description
DBPROPVAL_NP_FAILEDTODO	8	The consumer will be notified if an action failed (ie a Will or Complete event).
DBPROPVAL_NP_OKTODO	1	The consumer will be notified of events.
DBPROPVAL_NP_SYNCHAFTER	4	The consumer will be notified when the rowset is resynchronized.

DBPROPVAL_NT

Name	Value	Description
DBPROPVAL_NT_MULTIPLEROWS	2	For methods that operate on multiple rows, and generate multiphased notifications (events), then the provider calls OnRowChange once for all rows that succeed and once for all rows that fail.
DBPROPVAL_NT_SINGLEROW	1	For methods that operate on multiple rows, and generate multiphased notifications (events), then the provider calls OnRowChange separately for each phase for each row.

DBPROPVAL_OA

Name	Value	Description
DBPROPVAL_OA_ATEXECUTE	2	Output parameter data is available immediately after the Command.Execute returns.
DBPROPVAL_OA_ATROWRELEASE	4	Output parameter data is available when the rowset is released. For a single rowset operation this is when the rowset is completely released (closed) and for a multiple rowset operation this is when the next rowset if fetched. The consumer's bound memory is in an indeterminate state before the parameter data becomes available.
DBPROPVAL_OA_NOTSUPPORTED	1	Output parameters are not supported.

DBPROPVAL_OO

Name	Value	Description
DBPROPVAL_OO_BLOB	1	The provider supports access to BLOBs as structured storage objects.
DBPROPVAL_OO_DIRECTBIND	16	The provider supports direct binding to BLOBs.
DBPROPVAL_OO_IPERSIST	2	The provider supports access to OLE objects through OLE.
DBPROPVAL_OO_SCOPED	8	

DBPROPVAL_ORS

Name	Value	Description
DBPROPVAL_ORS_TABLE		The provider supports opening tables.
DBPROPVAL_ORS_INDEX		The provider supports opening indexes.
DBPROPVAL_ORS_INTEGRATEDINDEX		The provider supports both the table and index in the same open method.
DBPROPVAL_ORS_STOREDPROPC		The provider supports opening rowsets over stored procedures.

DBPROPVAL_OS

Name	Value	Description
DBPROPVAL_OS_ENABLEALL	-1	All services should be invoked. This is the default.
DBPROPVAL_OS_RESOURCEPOOLING	1	Resources should be pooled.
DBPROPVAL_OS_TXNENLISTMENT	2	Sessions in an MTS environment should automatically be enlisted in a global transaction where required.
DBPROPVAL_OS_CLIENT_CURSOR	4	Disable client cursor.
DBPROPVAL_OS_DISABLEALL	0	All services should be disabled.

DBPROPVAL_PT

Name	Value	Description
DBPROPVAL_PT_GUID	8	The GUID is used as the persistent ID type.
DBPROPVAL_PT_GUID_NAME	1	The GUID Name is used as the persistent ID type.
DBPROPVAL_PT_GUID_PROPID	2	The GUID Property ID is used as the persistent ID type.
DBPROPVAL_PT_NAME	4	The Name is used as the persistent ID type.
DBPROPVAL_PT_PGUID_NAME	32	The Property GUID name is used as the persistent ID type.
DBPROPVAL_PT_PGUID_PROPID	64	The Property GUID Property ID is used as the persistent ID type.
DBPROPVAL_PT_PROPID	16	The Property ID is used as the persistent ID type.

DBPROPVAL_RD

Name	Value	Description
DBPROPVAL_RD_RESETALL	-1	The provider should reset all state associated with the data source, with the exception that any open object is not released.

Appendix B

DBPROPVAL_RT

Name	Value	Description
DBPROPVAL_RT_APTMTTHREAD	2	The DSO is apartment threaded.
DBPROPVAL_RT_FREETHREAD	1	The DSO is free threaded.
DBPROPVAL_RT_SINGLETHREAD	4	The DSO is single threaded.

DBPROPVAL_SQ

Name	Value	Description
DBPROPVAL_SQ_COMPARISON	2	All predicates that support subqueries support comparison subqueries.
DBPROPVAL_SQ_CORRELATEDSUBQUERIES	1	All predicates that support subqueries support correlated subqueries.
DBPROPVAL_SQ_EXISTS	4	All predicates that support subqueries support EXISTS subqueries.
DBPROPVAL_SQ_IN	8	All predicates that support subqueries support IN subqueries.
DBPROPVAL_SQ_QUANTIFIED	16	All predicates that support subqueries support quantified subqueries.

DBPROPVAL_SQL

Name	Value	Description
DBPROPVAL_SQL_ANDI89_IEF	8	The provider supports the ANSI SQL89 IEF level.
DBPROPVAL_SQL_ANSI92_ENTRY	16	The provider supports the ANSI SQL92 Entry level.
DBPROPVAL_SQL_ANSI92_FULL	128	The provider supports the ANSI SQL92 Full level.
DBPROPVAL_SQL_ANSI92_INTERMEDIATE	64	The provider supports the ANSI SQL92 Intermediate level.
DBPROPVAL_SQL_CORE	2	The provider supports the ODBC 2.5 Core SQL level.
DBPROPVAL_SQL_ESCAPECLAUSES	256	The provider supports the ODBC escape clauses syntax.
DBPROPVAL_SQL_EXTENDED	4	The provider supports the ODBC 2.5 EXTENDED SQL level.
DBPROPVAL_SQL_FIPS_TRANSITIONAL	32	The provider supports the ANSI SQL92 Transitional level.

Name	Value	Description
DBPROPVAL_SQL_MINIMUM	1	The provider supports the ODBC 2.5 EXTENDED SQL level.
DBPROPVAL_SQL_NONE	0	SQL is not supported.
DBPROPVAL_SQL_ODBC_CORE	2	The provider supports the ODBC 2.5 Core SQL level.
DBPROPVAL_SQL_ODBC_EXTENDED	4	The provider supports the ODBC 2.5 EXTENDED SQL level.
DBPROPVAL_SQL_ODBC_MINIMUM	1	The provider supports the ODBC 2.5 EXTENDED SQL level.
DBPROPVAL_SQL_SUBMINIMUM	512	The provider supports the DBGUID_SQL dialect and parses the command text according to SQL rules, but does not support wither the minimum ODBC level nor the ANSI SQL92 Entry level.

DBPROPVAL_SS

Name	Value	Description
DBPROPVAL_SS_ILOCKBYTES	8	The provider supports IlockBytes.
DBPROPVAL_SS_ISEQUENTIALSTREAM	1	The provider supports IsequentialStream.
DBPROPVAL_SS_ISTORAGE	4	The provider supports Istorage.
DBPROPVAL_SS_ISTREAM	2	The provider supports IStream.

DBPROPVAL_SU

Name	Value	Description
DBPROPVAL_SU_DML_STATEMENTS	1	Schema names are supported in all Data Manipulation Language statements.
DBPROPVAL_SU_INDEX_DEFINITION	4	Schema names are supported in all index definition statements.
DBPROPVAL_SU_PRIIVILEGE_DEFINITION	8	Schema names are supported in all privilege definition statements.
DBPROPVAL_SU_TABLE_DEFINITION	2	Schema names are supported in all table definition statements.

DBPROPVAL_TC

Name	Value	Description
DBPROPVAL_TC_ALL	8	Transactions can contain DDL and DML statements in any order.
DBPROPVAL_TC_DDL_COMMIT	2	Transactions can contain DML statements. DDL statements within a transaction cause the transaction to be committed.
DBPROPVAL_TC_DDL_IGNORE	4	Transactions can only contain DML statements. DDL statements within a transaction are ignored.

Name	Value	Description
DBPROPVAL_TC_DDL_LOCK	16	
DBPROPVAL_TC_DML	1	Transactions can only contain Data Manipulation (DML) statements. DDL statements within a transaction cause an error.
DBPROPVAL_TC_NONE	0	Transactions are not supported.

DBPROPVAL_TI

Name	Value	Description
DBPROPVAL_TI_BROWSE	256	Changes made by other transactions are visible before they are committed.
DBPROPVAL_TI_CHAOS	16	Transactions cannot overwrite pending changes from more highly isolated transactions. This is the default.
DBPROPVAL_TI_CURSORSTABILITY	4096	Changes made by other transactions are not visible until those transactions are committed.
DBPROPVAL_TI_ISOLATED	1048576	All concurrent transactions will interact only in ways that produce the same effect as if each transaction were entirely executed one after the other.
DBPROPVAL_TI_READCOMMITTED	4096	Changes made by other transactions are not visible until those transactions are committed.
DBPROPVAL_TI_READUNCOMMITTED	256	Changes made by other transactions are visible before they are committed.

Name	Value	Description
DBPROPVAL_TI_REPEATABLEREAD	65536	Changes made by other transactions are not visible.
DBPROPVAL_TI_SERIALIZABLE	1048576	All concurrent transactions will interact only in ways that produce the same effect as if each transaction were entirely executed one after the other.

DBPROPVAL_TR

Name	Value	Description
DBPROPVAL_TR_ABORT	16	The transaction preserves its isolation context (ie, it preserves its locks if that is how isolation is implemented) across the retaining abort.
DBPROPVAL_TR_ABORT_DC	8	The transaction may either preserve or dispose of isolation context across a retaining abort.
DBPROPVAL_TR_ABORT_NO	32	The transaction is explicitly not to preserve its isolation across a retaining abort.
DBPROPVAL_TR_BOTH	128	Isolation is preserved across both a retaining commit and a retaining abort.
DBPROPVAL_TR_COMMIT	2	The transaction preserves its isolation context (ie, it preserves its locks if that is how isolation is implemented) across the retaining commit.
DBPROPVAL_TR_COMMIT_DC	1	The transaction may either preserve or dispose of isolation context across a retaining commit.
DBPROPVAL_TR_COMMIT_NO	4	The transaction is explicitly not to preserve its isolation across a retaining commit.
DBPROPVAL_TR_DONTCARE	64	The transaction may either preserve or dispose of isolation context across a retaining commit or abort. This is the default.
DBPROPVAL_TR_NONE	256	Isolation is explicitly not to be retained across either a retaining commit or abort.
DBPROPVAL_TR_OPTIMISTIC	512	Optimistic concurrency control is to be used.

DBPROPVAL_UP

Name	Value	Description
DBPROPVAL_UP_CHANGE	1	Indicates that SetData is supported.
DBPROPVAL_UP_DELETE	2	Indicates that DeleteRows is supported.
DBPROPVAL_UP_INSERT	4	Indicates that InsertRow is supported.

JET_ENGINETYPE

Name	Value	Description
JET_ENGINETYPE_UNKNOWN	0	The database type is unknown.
JET_ENGINETYPE_JET10	1	Jet 1.0
JET_ENGINETYPE_JET11	2	Jet 1.1
JET_ENGINETYPE_JET2X	3	Jet 2.x
JET_ENGINETYPE_JET3X	4	Jet 3.x
JET_ENGINETYPE_JET4X	5	Jet 4.x
JET_ENGINETYPE_DBASE3	10	DBase III
JET_ENGINETYPE_DBASE4	11	DBase IV
JET_ENGINETYPE_DBASE5	12	DBase V
JET_ENGINETYPE_EXCEL30	20	Excel 3
JET_ENGINETYPE_EXCEL40	21	Excel 4
JET_ENGINETYPE_EXCEL50	22	Excel 5 (Excel 95)
JET_ENGINETYPE_EXCEL80	23	Excel 8 (Excel 97)
JET_ENGINETYPE_EXCEL90	24	Excel 9 (Excel 2000)
JET_ENGINETYPE_EXCHANGE4	30	Exchange Server
JET_ENGINETYPE_LOTUSWK1	40	Lotus 1
JET_ENGINETYPE_LOTUSWK3	41	Lotus 3
JET_ENGINETYPE_LOTUSWK4	42	Lotus 4
JET_ENGINETYPE_PARADOX3X	50	Paradox 3.x
JET_ENGINETYPE_PARADOX4X	51	Paradox 4.5
JET_ENGINETYPE_PARADOX5X	52	Paradox 5.x
JET_ENGINETYPE_PARADOX7X	53	Paradox 7.x
JET_ENGINETYPE_TEXT1X	60	Text
JET_ENGINETYPE_HTML1X	70	HTML

MD_DIMTYPE

Name	Value	Description
MD_DIMTYPE_MEASURE	2	A measure dimension.
MD_DIMTYPE_OTHER	3	The dimension is neither a time nor a measure dimension.
MD_DIMTYPE_TIME	1	A time dimension.
MD_DIMTYPE_UNKNOWN	0	The provider is unable to classify the dimension.

SQL_FN_NUM

Name	Value	Description
SQL_FN_NUM_ABS	1	The ABS function is supported by the data source.
SQL_FN_NUM_ACOS	2	The ACOS function is supported by the data source.
SQL_FN_NUM_ASIN	4	The ASIN function is supported by the data source.
SQL_FN_NUM_ATAN	8	The ATAN function is supported by the data source.
SQL_FN_NUM_ATAN2	16	The ATAN2 function is supported by the data source.
SQL_FN_NUM_CEILING	32	The CEILING function is supported by the data source.
SQL_FN_NUM_COS	64	The COS function is supported by the data source.
SQL_FN_NUM_COT	128	The COT function is supported by the data source.
SQL_FN_NUM_DEGREES	262144	The DEGREES function is supported by the data source.
SQL_FN_NUM_EXP	256	The EXP function is supported by the data source.
SQL_FN_NUM_FLOOR	512	The FLOOR function is supported by the data source.
SQL_FN_NUM_LOG	1024	The LOG function is supported by the data source.
SQL_FN_NUM_LOG10	524288	The LOG10 function is supported by the data source.
SQL_FN_NUM_MOD	2048	The MOD function is supported by the data source.
SQL_FN_NUM_PI	65536	The PI function is supported by the data source.

Table Continued on Following Page

Appendix B

Name	Value	Description
SQL_FN_NUM_POWER	1048576	The POWER function is supported by the data source.
SQL_FN_NUM_RADIANS	2097152	The RADIANS function is supported by the data source.
SQL_FN_NUM_RAND	131072	The RAND function is supported by the data source.
SQL_FN_NUM_ROUND	4194304	The ROUND function is supported by the data source.
SQL_FN_NUM_SIGN	4096	The SIGN function is supported by the data source.
SQL_FN_NUM_SIN	8192	The SIN function is supported by the data source.
SQL_FN_NUM_SQRT	10384	The SQRT function is supported by the data source.
SQL_FN_NUM_TAN	32768	The TAN function is supported by the data source.
SQL_FN_NUM_TRUNCATE	8388608	The TRUNCATE function is supported by the data source.

SQL_FN_STR

Name	Value	Description
SQL_FN_STR_ASCII	8192	The ASCII function is supported by the data source.
SQL_FN_STR_BIT_LENGTH	524288	The BIT_LENGTH function is supported by the data source.
SQL_FN_STR_CHAR	16384	The CHAR function is supported by the data source.
SQL_FN_STR_CHAR_LENGTH	1048576	The CHAR_LENGTH function is supported by the data source.
SQL_FN_STR_CHARACTER_LENGTH	2097152	The CHARACTER_LENGTH function is supported by the data source.
SQL_FN_STR_CONCAT	1	The CONCAT function is supported by the data source.
SQL_FN_STR_DIFFERENCE	32768	The DIFFERENCE function is supported by the data source.
SQL_FN_STR_INSERT	2	The INSERT function is supported by the data source.
SQL_FN_STR_LCASE	64	The LCASE function is supported by the data source.
SQL_FN_STR_LEFT	4	The LEFT function is supported by the data source.

Name	Value	Description
SQL_FN_STR_LENGTH	16	The LENGTH function is supported by the data source.
SQL_FN_STR_LOCATE	32	The LOCATE function is supported by the data source.
SQL_FN_STR_LOCATE_2	65536	The LOCATE_2 function is supported by the data source.
SQL_FN_STR_LTRIM	8	The LTRIM function is supported by the data source.
SQL_FN_STR_OCTET_LENGTH	4194304	The OCTET_LENGTH function is supported by the data source.
SQL_FN_STR_POSITION	8388608	The POSITION function is supported by the data source.
SQL_FN_STR_REPEAT	128	The REPEAT function is supported by the data source.
SQL_FN_STR_REPLACE	256	The REPLACE function is supported by the data source.
SQL_FN_STR_RIGHT	512	The RIGHT function is supported by the data source.
SQL_FN_STR_RTRIM	1024	The RTRIM function is supported by the data source.
SQL_FN_STR_SOUNDEX	131072	The SOUNDEX function is supported by the data source.
SQL_FN_STR_SPACE	262144	The SPACE function is supported by the data source.
SQL_FN_STR_SUBSTRING	2048	The SUBSTRING function is supported by the data source.
SQL_FN_STR_UCASE	4096	The UCASE function is supported by the data source.

SQL_FN_SYS

Name	Value	Description
SQL_FN_SYS_DBNAME	2	The DBNAME system function is supported.
SQL_FN_SYS_IFNULL	4	The IFNULL system function is supported.
SQL_FN_SYS_USERNAME	1	The USERNAME system function is supported.

Appendix B

SQL_OJ

Name	Value	Description
SQL_OJ_ALL_COMPARISON_OPS	64	The comparison operator in the ON clause can be any of the ODBC comparison operators. If this is not set, only the equals (=) comparison operator can be used in an outer join.
SQL_OJ_FULL	4	Full outer joins are supported.
SQL_OJ_INNER	32	The inner table (the right table in a left outer join or the left table in a right outer join) can also be used in an inner join. This does not apply to full out joins, which do not have an inner table.
SQL_OJ_LEFT	1	Left outer joins are supported.
SQL_OJ_NESTED	8	Nested outer joins are supported.
SQL_OJ_NOT_ORDERED	16	The column names in the ON clause of the outer join do not have to be in the same order as their respective table names in the OUTER JOIN clause.
SQL_OJ_RIGHT	2	Right outer joins are supported.

SQL_SDF_CURRENT

Name	Value	Description
SQL_SDF_CURRENT_DATE	1	The CURRENT_DATE system function is supported.
SQL_SDF_CURRENT_TIME	2	The CURRENT_TIME system function is supported.
SQL_SDF_CURRENT_TIMESTAMP	4	The CURRENT_TIMESTAMP system function is supported.

SSPROP_CONCUR

Name	Value	Description
SSPROP_CONCUR_LOCK	4	Use row locking to prevent concurrent access.
SSPROP_CONCUR_READ_ONLY	8	The rowset is read-only. Full concurrency is supported.
SSPROP_CONCUR_ROWVER	1	Use row versioning to determining concurrent access violations. The SQL Table or tables must contain a timestamp column.
SSPROP_CONCUR_VALUES	2	Use the values in of columns in the rowset row.

SSPROPVAL_USEPROCFORPREP

Name	Value	Description
SSPROPVAL_USEPROCFORPREP_OFF	0	A temporary stored procedure is not created when a command is prepared.
SSPROPVAL_USEPROCFORPREP_ON	1	A temporary stored procedure is created when a command is prepared. Temporary stored procedures are dropped when the session is released.
SSPROPVAL_USEPROCFORPREP_ON_DROP	2	A temporary stored procedure is created when a command is prepared. The procedure is dropped when the command is unprepared, or a new command text is set, or when all application references to the command are released.

ADO Properties Collection

We've seen that each ADO object has its own fixed set of properties (things like `Name` and `Value`). Since ADO is designed for use with different providers, we *also* need a way to allow providers to specify their *own* properties. Therefore, ADO gives us the `Properties` collection, which deals with dynamic properties that are specific to the provider. This appendix deals with which providers support which properties, and what these properties actually do.

Some of the properties refer to **rowsets**. This is just the OLE DB term for recordsets.

Property Usage

As you can see from the tables in this appendix, there are very many properties – however, using them is actually quite simple. You simply index into the `Properties` collection by using the property name itself. For example, to find out the name the provider gives to procedures you could do this:

```
Print objConn.Properties("Procedure Term")
```

For SQL Server, this returns `stored procedure` and for Access this returns `STORED QUERY`.

You can iterate through the entire set of properties very simply:

```
For Each objProp In objConn.Properties
    Print objProp.Name
    Print objProp.Value
Next
```

This will print out the property name and value.

For those properties that return custom types, you need to identify whether these return a bitmask or a simple value – the property description identifies this, as it says 'one of' or 'one or more of'. In its simplest forms, these properties will just return a single value. For example, to find out whether your provider supports output parameters on stored procedures you can query the `Output Parameter Availability` property. This is defined as returning values of type DBPROPVAL_OA, which are as follows:

Constant	Value
DBPROPVAL_OA_ATEXECUTE	2
DBPROPVAL_OA_ATROWRELEASE	4
DBPROPVAL_OA_NOTSUPPORTED	1

Examining this property when connected to SQL Server gives you a value of 4, indicating that output parameters are available when the recordset is closed. Access, on the other hand, returns a value of 1, indicating that output parameters are not supported.

For those properties that return bitmask, you'll need to use Boolean logic to identify which values are set. For example, to query the provider and examine what features of SQL are supported, you can use the SQL Support property. For Access this returns 512, which corresponds to DBPROPVAL_SQL_SUBMINIMUM, indicating that not even the ANSI SQL92 Entry level SQL facilities are provided. On the other hand, SQL Server returns 283, but there isn't a single value for this, so it must be a combination of values. In fact, it corresponds to the sum of the following:

Constant	Value
DBPROPVAL_SQL_ESCAPECLAUSES	256
DBPROPVAL_SQL_ANSI92_ENTRY	16
DBPROPVAL_SQL_ANDI89_IEF	8
DBPROPVAL_SQL_CORE	2
DBPROPVAL_SQL_MINIMUM	1

In order to see whether a specific value is set, use the Boolean AND operator. For example:

```
lngSQLSupport = oConn.Properties("SQL Support")
If (lngSQLSupport AND DBPROPVAL_SQL_CORE) = DBPROPVAL_SQL_CORE Then
    'core facilities are supported
End If
```

A full description of the constants is given in Appendix B.

Property Support

The following table shows a list of all OLEDB properties, and indicates which of them are supported by three widely-used drivers: the Microsoft OLEDB driver for Jet, the Microsoft OLEDB driver for ODBC, and the Microsoft OLEDB driver for SQL Server. Since this list contains dynamic properties, not every property may show up under all circumstances. Other providers may also implement properties not listed in this table.

A tick (✓) indicates that the property is supported, and a blank space indicates it is not supported. Note that support for recordset properties may depend upon the locking type, cursor type and cursor location.

> Note. This list doesn't include the **I**property (such as IRowset, etc) properties. Although these are part of the collection they are not particularly useful for the ADO programmer.

For the *Object Type* column, the following applies:

    R = Recordset

    C = Connection

    F = Field

Property Name	Object Type (R/F/C)	ODBC	Jet	SQL	Internet Publishing	MSDataShape	Persist	Remote	Index Server
Access Order	R	✓	✓	✓	✓	✓	✓	✓	
Access Permission	C				✓				
Accessible Procedures	C	✓							
Accessible Tables	C	✓							
Active Sessions	C	✓	✓	✓	✓				✓
Active Statements	C	✓							
Alter Column Support	C		✓						
Always use content index	R								✓
Append-Only Rowset	R	✓	✓	✓	✓	✓	✓	✓	
Application Name	C			✓					
Asynchable Abort	C	✓	✓	✓					
Asynchable Commit	C	✓	✓	✓					

Appendix C

Property Name	Object Type (R/F/C)	ODBC	Jet	SQL	Internet Publishing	MSDataShape	Persist	Remote	Index Server
Asynchronous Processing	C					✓			
Asynchronous Rowset Processing	R	✓	✓	✓	✓	✓	✓	✓	
Auto Recalc	R	✓	✓	✓	✓	✓	✓	✓	
Auto Translate	C			✓					
Autocommit Isolation Levels	C	✓	✓	✓		✓	✓	✓	✓
Background Fetch Size	R	✓	✓	✓	✓	✓	✓	✓	
Background thread Priority	R	✓	✓	✓	✓	✓	✓	✓	
BASECATALOG NAME	F	✓	✓	✓	✓	✓	✓	✓	
BASECOLUMN NAME	F	✓	✓	✓	✓	✓	✓	✓	
BASESCHEMA NAME	F	✓	✓	✓	✓	✓	✓	✓	
BASETABLE NAME	F	✓	✓	✓	✓	✓	✓	✓	
Batch Size	R	✓	✓	✓	✓	✓	✓	✓	
Bind Flags	C				✓				
BLOB accessibility on Forward-Only cursor	R	✓							
Blocking Storage Objects	R	✓	✓	✓	✓	✓	✓	✓	✓
Bookmark Information	R	✓		✓					
Bookmark Type	R	✓	✓	✓	✓	✓	✓	✓	✓

Property Name	Object Type (R/F/C)	ODBC	Jet	SQL	Internet Publishing	MSDataShape	Persist	Remote	Index Server
Bookmarkable	R	✓	✓	✓	✓	✓	✓	✓	✓
Bookmarks Ordered	R	✓	✓	✓	✓	✓	✓	✓	✓
Cache Aggressively	C				✓				
Cache Authentication	C		✓			✓		✓	
Cache Child Rows	R	✓	✓	✓	✓	✓	✓	✓	
Cache Deferred Columns	R	✓	✓	✓	✓	✓	✓	✓	
CALCULATION INFO	F	✓	✓	✓	✓	✓	✓	✓	
Catalog Location	C	✓	✓	✓					
Catalog Term	C	✓	✓	✓					
Catalog Usage	C	✓		✓					
Change Inserted Rows	R	✓	✓	✓	✓	✓	✓	✓	
Chapter	C						✓		
CLSID	F	✓							
COLLATING SEQUENCE	F	✓	✓						
Column Definition	C	✓	✓	✓					✓
Column Privileges	R	✓	✓	✓	✓	✓	✓	✓	✓
Column Set Notification	R	✓	✓	✓	✓	✓	✓	✓	
Column Writable	R	✓	✓	✓	✓	✓	✓	✓	
Command Properties	C							✓	

Property Name	Object Type (R/F/C)	ODBC	Jet	SQL	Internet Publishing	MSDataShape	Persist	Remote	Index Server
Command Time Out	R	✓	✓	✓	✓	✓	✓	✓	✓
COMPUTEMODE	F	✓							
Connect Timeout	C	✓		✓	✓	✓	✓	✓	
Connection Status	C	✓		✓					
Current Catalog	C	✓	✓	✓					✓
Current DFMode	C							✓	
Current Language	C			✓					
Cursor Engine Version	R	✓	✓	✓	✓	✓	✓	✓	
Data Provider	C					✓			
Data Source	C	✓	✓	✓	✓	✓		✓	✓
Data Source Name	C	✓	✓	✓					
Data Source Object Threading Model	C	✓	✓	✓		✓		✓	✓
Datasource Type	C				✓				
DATETIME PRECISION	F	✓		✓					
DBMS Name	C	✓	✓	✓					✓
DBMS Version	C	✓	✓	✓					✓
DEFAULTVALUE	F	✓							
Defer Column	R	✓	✓	✓	✓	✓	✓	✓	
Defer scope and security testing	R								✓
Delay Storage Object Updates	R	✓	✓	✓	✓	✓	✓	✓	

Property Name	Object Type (R/F/C)	ODBC	Jet	SQL	Internet Publishing	MSDataShape	Persist	Remote	Index Server
DFMode	C							✓	
DOMAIN CATALOG	F	✓							
DOMAINNAME	F	✓							
DOMAINSCHE MA	F	✓							
Driver Name	C	✓							
Driver ODBC Version	C	✓							
Driver Version	C	✓							
Enable Fastload	C			✓					
Encrypt Password	C		✓			✓		✓	
Extended Properties	C	✓	✓	✓		✓		✓	
Fastload Options	R			✓					
Fetch Backwards	R	✓	✓	✓	✓	✓	✓	✓	✓
File Usage	C	✓							
Filter Operations	R	✓	✓	✓	✓	✓	✓	✓	
Find Operations	R	✓	✓	✓	✓	✓	✓	✓	
Force no command preparation when executing a parameterized command	R	✓							
Force no command reexecution when failure to satisfy all required properties	R	✓							

Appendix C

Property Name	Object Type (R/F/C)	ODBC	Jet	SQL	Internet Publishing	MSDataShape	Persist	Remote	Index Server
Force no parameter rebinding when executing a command	R	✓							
Force SQL Server Firehose Mode cursor	R	✓							
Generate a Rowset that can be marshalled	R	✓							
Generate URL	C				✓				
GROUP BY Support	C	✓	✓	✓					✓
Handler	C							✓	
HASDEFAULT	F	✓							
Heterogeneous Table Support	C	✓	✓	✓					✓
Hidden Columns	R	✓	✓	✓	✓	✓	✓	✓	
Hold Rows	R	✓	✓	✓	✓	✓	✓	✓	✓
Identifier Case Sensitivity	C	✓	✓	✓					
Ignore Cached Data	C				✓				
Immobile Rows	R	✓	✓	✓	✓	✓	✓	✓	
Impersonation Level	C					✓		✓	
Include SQL_FLOAT, SQL_DOUBLE, and SQL_REAL in QBU where clauses	R	✓							

Property Name	Object Type (R/F/C)	ODBC	Jet	SQL	Internet Publishing	MSDataShape	Persist	Remote	Index Server
Initial Catalog	C	✓		✓		✓		✓	
Initial Fetch Size	R	✓	✓	✓	✓	✓	✓	✓	
Initial File Name	C			✓					
Integrated Security	C			✓		✓		✓	
Integrity Enhancement Facility	C	✓							
Internet Timeout	C							✓	
ISAUTO INCREMENT	F	✓	✓	✓	✓	✓	✓	✓	
ISCASESENSITIVE	F	✓	✓	✓					
Isolation Levels	C	✓	✓	✓					✓
Isolation Retention	C	✓	✓	✓					✓
ISSEARCHABLE	F	✓		✓					
ISUNIQUE	F	✓							
Jet OLEDB:Bulk Transactions	R		✓						
Jet OLEDB:Compact Reclaimed Space Amount	C		✓						
Jet OLEDB:Compact Without Replica Repair	C		✓						
Jet OLEDB: Connection Control	C		✓						
Jet OLEDB:Create System Database	C		✓						
Jet OLEDB:Database Locking Mode	C		✓						

Appendix C

Property Name	Object Type (R/F/C)	ODBC	Jet	SQL	Internet Publishing	MSDataShape	Persist	Remote	Index Server
Jet OLEDB:Database Password	C		✓						
Jet OLEDB:Don't Copy Locale on Compact	C		✓						
Jet OLEDB:Enable Fat Cursors	R		✓						
Jet OLEDB:Encrypt Database	C		✓						
Jet OLEDB:Engine Type	C		✓						
Jet OLEDB:Exclusive Async Delay	C		✓						
Jet OLEDB:Fat Cursor Cache Size	R		✓						
Jet OLEDB:Flush Transaction Timeout	C		✓						
Jet OLEDB:Global Bulk Transactions	C		✓						
Jet OLEDB:Global Partial Bulk Ops	C		✓						
Jet OLEDB:Grbit Value	R		✓						
Jet OLEDB:Implicit Commit Sync	C		✓						
Jet OLEDB:Inconsist ent	R		✓						

Property Name	Object Type (R/F/C)	ODBC	Jet	SQL	Internet Publishing	MSDataShape	Persist	Remote	Index Server
Jet OLEDB:Lock Delay	C		✓						
Jet OLEDB:Lock Retry	C		✓						
Jet OLEDB:Locking Granularity	R		✓						
Jet OLEDB:Max Buffer Size	C		✓						
Jet OLEDB:Max Locks Per File	C		✓						
Jet OLEDB:New Database Password	C		✓						
Jet OLEDB:ODBC Command Time Out	C		✓						
Jet OLEDB:ODBC Parsing	C		✓						
Jet OLEDB:ODBC Pass-Through Statement	R		✓						
Jet OLEDB:Page Locks to Table Lock	C		✓						
Jet OLEDB:Page Timeout	C		✓						
Jet OLEDB:Partial Bulk Ops	R		✓						
Jet OLEDB:Pass Through Query Bulk-Op	R		✓						
Jet OLEDB:Pass Through Query Connect String	R		✓						

Property Name	Object Type (R/F/C)	ODBC	Jet	SQL	Internet Publishing	MSDataShape	Persist	Remote	Index Server
Jet OLEDB:Recycle Long-Valued Pages	C		✓						
Jet OLEDB:Registry Path	C		✓						
Jet OLEDB:Reset ISAM Stats	C		✓						
Jet OLEDB:Sandbox Mode	C		✓						
Jet OLEDB:SFP	C		✓						
Jet OLEDB:Shared Async Delay	C		✓						
Jet OLEDB:Stored Query	R		✓						
Jet OLEDB:System database	C		✓						
Jet OLEDB:Transaction Commit Mode	C		✓						
Jet OLEDB:Use Grbit	R		✓						
Jet OLEDB:User Commit Sync	C		✓						
Jet OLEDB:Validate Rules On Set	R		✓						
Keep Identity	R			✓					
Keep Nulls	R			✓					

Property Name	Object Type (R/F/C)	ODBC	Jet	SQL	Internet Publishing	MSDataShape	Persist	Remote	Index Server
KEYCOLUMN	F	✓	✓	✓	✓	✓	✓	✓	
Like Escape Clause	C	✓							
Literal Bookmarks	R	✓	✓	✓	✓	✓	✓	✓	✓
Literal Row Identity	R	✓	✓	✓	✓	✓	✓	✓	✓
Locale Identifier	C	✓	✓	✓	✓	✓		✓	✓
Location	C	✓				✓		✓	✓
Lock Mode	R		✓	✓					
Lock Owner	C				✓				
Maintain Change Status	R	✓	✓	✓	✓	✓	✓	✓	
Maintain Property Values	C						✓		
Mark For Offline	C				✓				
Mask Password	C		✓			✓		✓	
Max Columns in Group By	C	✓							
Max Columns in Index	C	✓							
Max Columns in Order By	C	✓							
Max Columns in Select	C	✓							
Max Columns in Table	C	✓							
Maximum BLOB Length	R			✓					
Maximum Index Size	C	✓	✓	✓					

Appendix C

Property Name	Object Type (R/F/C)	ODBC	Jet	SQL	Internet Publishing	MSDataShape	Persist	Remote	Index Server
Maximum Open Chapters	C			✓					✓
Maximum Open Rows	R	✓	✓	✓	✓	✓	✓	✓	✓
Maximum Pending Rows	R	✓	✓	✓	✓	✓	✓	✓	
Maximum Row Size	C	✓	✓	✓					✓
Maximum Row Size Includes BLOB	C	✓	✓	✓					
Maximum Rows	R	✓	✓	✓	✓	✓	✓	✓	✓
Maximum Tables in SELECT	C	✓	✓	✓					✓
Memory Usage	R	✓	✓	✓	✓	✓	✓	✓	✓
Mode	C	✓	✓		✓	✓		✓	
Multi-Table Update	C	✓	✓	✓					
Multiple Connections	C			✓					
Multiple Parameter Sets	C	✓	✓	✓				✓	✓
Multiple Results	C	✓	✓	✓		✓		✓	✓
Multiple Storage Objects	C	✓	✓	✓					✓
Network Address	C			✓					
Network Library	C			✓					
Notification Granularity	R	✓	✓	✓	✓	✓	✓	✓	
Notification Phases	R	✓	✓	✓	✓	✓	✓	✓	

Property Name	Object Type (R/F/C)	ODBC	Jet	SQL	Internet Publishing	MSDataShape	Persist	Remote	Index Server
NULL Collation Order	C	✓	✓	✓					✓
NULL Concatenation Behavior	C	✓	✓	✓					
Numeric Functions	C	✓							
Objects Transacted	R	✓	✓	✓	✓	✓	✓	✓	
OCTETLENGTH	F	✓		✓					
ODBC Concurrency Type	R	✓							
ODBC Cursor Type	R	✓							
OLE DB Services	C	✓							
OLE DB Version	C	✓	✓	✓	✓			✓	✓
OLE Object Support	C	✓	✓	✓					✓
OLE Objects	C				✓				
Open Rowset Support	C	✓	✓	✓					
OPTIMIZE	F	✓	✓	✓	✓	✓	✓	✓	
ORDER BY Columns in Select List	C	✓	✓	✓					✓
Others' Changes Visible	R	✓	✓	✓	✓	✓	✓	✓	✓
Others' Inserts Visible	R	✓	✓	✓	✓	✓	✓	✓	✓
Outer Join Capabilities	C	✓							

Property Name	Object Type (R/F/C)	ODBC	Jet	SQL	Internet Publishing	MSDataShape	Persist	Remote	Index Server
Outer Joins	C	✓							
Output Parameter Availability	C	✓	✓	✓				✓	✓
Own Changes Visible	R	✓	✓	✓	✓	✓	✓	✓	
Own Inserts Visible	R	✓	✓	✓	✓	✓	✓	✓	
Packet Size	C			✓					
Pass By Ref Accessors	C	✓	✓	✓					✓
Password	C	✓	✓	✓	✓	✓		✓	
Persist Encrypted	C					✓			
Persist Format	C						✓		
Persist Schema	C						✓		
Persist Security Info	C	✓		✓		✓		✓	
Persistent ID Type	C	✓	✓	✓					✓
Position on the last row after insert	R	✓							
Prepare Abort Behavior	C	✓	✓	✓					
Prepare Commit Behavior	C	✓	✓	✓					
Preserve on Abort	R	✓	✓	✓	✓	✓	✓	✓	
Preserve on Commit	R	✓	✓	✓	✓	✓	✓	✓	
Procedure Term	C	✓	✓	✓					

Property Name	Object Type (R/F/C)	ODBC	Jet	SQL	Internet Publishing	MSDataShape	Persist	Remote	Index Server
Prompt	C	✓	✓	✓	✓	✓		✓	✓
Protection Level	C					✓		✓	
Protocol Provider	C				✓				
Provider Friendly Name	C	✓	✓	✓				✓	
Provider Name	C	✓	✓	✓	✓			✓	✓
Provider Version	C	✓	✓	✓	✓			✓	✓
Query Based Updates/Deletes/Inserts	R	✓							
Query Restriction	R								✓
Quick Restart	R	✓	✓	✓	✓	✓	✓	✓	✓
Quoted Catalog Names	C			✓					
Quoted Identifier Sensitivity	C	✓		✓					
Read-Only Data Source	C	✓	✓	✓					✓
Reentrant Events	R	✓	✓	✓	✓	✓	✓	✓	✓
RELATIONCONDITIONS	F	✓	✓	✓	✓	✓	✓	✓	
Remote Provider	C							✓	
Remote Server	C							✓	
Remove Deleted Rows	R	✓	✓	✓	✓	✓	✓	✓	✓
Report Multiple Changes	R	✓	✓	✓	✓	✓	✓	✓	
Reshape Name	R	✓	✓	✓	✓	✓	✓	✓	
Resync Command	R	✓	✓	✓	✓	✓	✓	✓	

Appendix C

Property Name	Object Type (R/F/C)	ODBC	Jet	SQL	Internet Publishing	MSDataShape	Persist	Remote	Index Server
Return PROPVARIANTs in variant binding	R								✓
Return Pending Inserts	R	✓	✓	✓	✓	✓	✓	✓	
Row Delete Notification	R	✓	✓	✓	✓	✓	✓	✓	
Row First Change Notification	R	✓	✓	✓	✓	✓	✓	✓	
Row Insert Notification	R	✓	✓	✓	✓	✓	✓	✓	
Row Privileges	R	✓	✓	✓	✓	✓	✓	✓	✓
Row Resynchronization Notification	R	✓	✓	✓	✓	✓	✓	✓	
Row Threading Model	R	✓	✓	✓	✓	✓	✓	✓	✓
Row Undo Change Notification	R	✓	✓	✓	✓	✓	✓	✓	
Row Undo Delete Notification	R	✓	✓	✓	✓	✓	✓	✓	
Row Undo Insert Notification	R	✓	✓	✓	✓	✓	✓	✓	
Row Update Notification	R	✓	✓	✓	✓	✓	✓	✓	
Rowset Conversions on Command	C	✓	✓	✓					✓
Rowset Fetch Position Change Notification	R	✓	✓	✓	✓	✓	✓	✓	
Rowset Query Status	R								✓

Property Name	Object Type (R/F/C)	ODBC	Jet	SQL	Internet Publishing	MSDataShape	Persist	Remote	Index Server
Rowset Release Notification	R	✓	✓	✓	✓	✓	✓	✓	
Schema Term	C	✓	✓	✓					
Schema Usage	C	✓	✓	✓					
Scroll Backwards	R	✓	✓	✓	✓	✓	✓	✓	✓
Server Cursor	R	✓	✓	✓	✓	✓	✓	✓	✓
Server Data on Insert	R		✓	✓					
Server Name	C	✓		✓					
Skip Deleted Bookmarks	R	✓	✓	✓	✓	✓	✓	✓	✓
Special Characters	C	✓							
SQL Content Query Locale String	R								✓
SQL Grammar Support	C	✓							
SQL Support	C	✓	✓	✓					✓
Stored Procedures	C	✓							
String Functions	C	✓							
Strong Row Identity	R	✓	✓	✓	✓	✓	✓	✓	✓
Structured Storage	C	✓	✓	✓					✓
Subquery Support	C	✓	✓	✓					✓
System Functions	C	✓							
Table Term	C	✓	✓	✓					

Property Name	Object Type (R/F/C)	ODBC	Jet	SQL	Internet Publishing	MSDataShape	Persist	Remote	Index Server
Time/Date Functions	C	✓							
Transact Updates	C							✓	
Transaction DDL	C	✓	✓	✓					✓
Treat As Offline	C				✓				
Unicode Comparison Style	C			✓					
Unicode Locale Id	C			✓					
Unique Catalog	R	✓	✓	✓	✓	✓	✓	✓	
Unique Reshape Names	C					✓			
Unique Rows	R	✓	✓	✓	✓	✓	✓	✓	
Unique Schema	R	✓	✓	✓	✓	✓	✓	✓	
Unique Table	R	✓	✓	✓	✓	✓	✓	✓	
Updatability	R	✓	✓	✓	✓	✓	✓	✓	✓
Update Criteria	R	✓	✓	✓	✓	✓	✓	✓	
Update Resync	R	✓	✓	✓	✓	✓	✓	✓	
Use Bookmarks	R	✓	✓	✓	✓	✓	✓	✓	✓
Use Procedure for Prepare	C			✓					
User ID	C	✓	✓	✓	✓	✓		✓	
User Name	C	✓	✓	✓					
Window Handle	C	✓	✓	✓	✓	✓		✓	✓
Workstation ID	C			✓					

Object Properties

This section details the properties by object type, including the enumerated values that they support. These values are not included in the standard adovbs.inc include file (and are not automatically supplied when using Visual Basic), but can be found in adoconvb.inc and adoconjs.inc (for ASP, in VBScript and JScript format) and adocon.bas (for Visual Basic) from the supporting web site, http://webdev.wrox.co.uk/books/2688.

> *Some properties in this list are undocumented, and I've had to make an educated guess as to their purpose. I've marked these properties with a ** *symbol in their description field.*

The Connection Object's Properties

Property Name	Description	DataType
Access Permissions	Identifies the permissions used to access the data source. Read/Write.	ConnectModeEnum
Accessible Procedures	Identifies accessible procedures. Read-only.	Boolean
Accessible Tables	Identifies accessible tables. Read-only.	Boolean
Active Sessions	The maximum number of sessions that can exist at the same time. A value of 0 indicates no limit. Read-only.	Long
Active Statements	The maximum number of statements that can exist at the same time. Read-only.	Long
Alter Column Support	Identifies which portions of the column can be altered.	DBCOLUMNDESC FLAG
Application Name	Identifies the client application name. Read/Write.	String
Asynchable Abort	Whether transactions can be aborted asynchronously. Read-only.	Boolean
Asynchable Commit	Whether transactions can be committed asynchronously. Read-only.	Boolean

Table Continued on Following Page

Property Name	Description	DataType
Asynchronous Processing	Specifies the asynchronous processing performed on the rowset. Read/Write.	DBPROPVAL_ ASYNCH
Auto Translate	Indicates whether OEM/ANSI character conversion is used. Read/Write.	Boolean
Autocommit Isolation Level	Identifies the transaction isolation level while in auto-commit mode. Read/Write.	DBPROPVAL_OS
Bind Flags	Identifies the binding behaviour for resources. Allows binding to the results of a resource, rather than the resource itself.	DBBINDURLFLAG
Cache Aggressively	Identifies whether or not the provider will download and cache all properties of the resource, and its stream.	Boolean
Cache Authentication	Whether or not the data source object can cache sensitive authentication information, such as passwords, in an internal cache. Read/Write.	Boolean
Catalog Location	The position of the catalog name in a table name in a text command. Returns 1 (DBPROPVAL_CL_START) if the catalog is at the start of the name (such as Access with \Temp\Database.mdb), and 2 (DBPROPVAL_CL_END) if the catalog is at the end of name (such as Oracle with ADMIN.EMP@EMPDATA). Read/Write.	DBPROPVAL_CL
Catalog Term	The name the data source uses for a catalog, e.g. 'catalog' or 'database'. Read/Write.	String

Property Name	Description	DataType
Catalog Usage	Specifies how catalog names can be used in text commands. A combination of zero or more of DBPROPVAL_CU constants. Read/Write.	DBPROPVAL_CU
Column Definition	Defines the valid clauses for the definition of a column. Read/Write.	DBPROPVAL_CD
Command Properties	The dynamic properties of the Command.[#]	String
Connect Timeout	The amount of time, in seconds, to wait for the initialization to complete. Read/Write.	Long
Connection Status	The status of the current connection. Read-only.	DBPROPVAL_CS
Current Catalog	The name of the current catalog. Read/Write.	String
Current DFMode	Identifies the actual version of the Data Factory on the server. Can be: "21" (the default) for version 2.1 "20" for version 2.0 "15" for version 1.5	String
Current Language	Identifies the language used for system messages selection and formatting. The language must be installed on the SQL Server or initialization of the data source fails. Read/Write.	Boolean
Data Provider	For a shaped (hierarchical) recordset, this identifies the provider who supplies the data.	String
Data Source	The name of the data source to connect to. Read/Write.	String

Table Continued on Following Page

Property Name	Description	DataType
Data Source Name	The name of the data source. Read-only.	String
Data Source Object Threading Model	Specifies the threading models supported by the data source object. Read-only.	DBPROPVAL_RT
Datasource Type	The type of data source.	DBPROPVAL_DST
DBMS Name	The name of the product accessed by the provider. Read-only.	String
DBMS Version	The version of the product accessed by the provider. Read-only.	String
DFMode	Identifies the Data Factory mode. Can be: "21" (the default) for version 2.1 "20" for version 2.0 "15" for version 1.5	String
Driver Name	Identifies the ODBC Driver name. Read-only.	String
Driver ODBC Version	Identifies the ODBC Driver version. Read-only.	String
Driver Version	Identifies the Driver ODBC version. Read-only.	String
Enable Fastload	Indicates whether bulk-copy operations can be used between the SQL Server and the consumer.	Boolean
Encrypt Password	Whether the consumer required that the password be sent to the data source in an encrypted form. Read/Write.	Boolean
Extended Properties	Contains provider specific, extended connection information. Read/Write.	String
File Usage	Identifies the usage count of the ODBC driver. Read-only.	Long

Property Name	Description	DataType
Generate URL	Identifies the level of support of the Internet Server for generating URL suffixes.	DBPROPVAL_GU
GROUP BY Support	The relationship between the columns in a GROUP BY clause and the non-aggregated columns in the select list. Read-only.	DBPROPVAL_BG
Handler	The name of the server-side customization program, and any parameters the program uses.	String
Heterogeneous Table Support	Specifies whether the provider can join tables from different catalogs or providers. Read-only.	DBPROPVAL_HT
Identifier Case Sensitivity	How identifiers treats case. Read-only.	DBPROPVAL_IC
Ignore Cached Data	Identifies whether the provider should ignore any cached data for this resource.	Boolean
Impersonation Level	Identifies the level of client impersonation the server can take whilst performing actions on behalf of the client.	DB_IMP_LEVEL
Initial Catalog	The name of the initial, or default, catalog to use when connecting to the data source. If the provider supports changing the catalog for an initialized data source, a different catalog name can be specified in the Current Catalog property. Read/Write.	String
Initial File Name	The primary file name of an attachable database. [*]	String

Table Continued on Following Page

Property Name	Description	DataType
Integrated Security	Contains the name of the authentication service used by the server to identify the user. Read/Write.	String
Integrity Enhancement Facility	Indicates whether the data source supports the optional Integrity Enhancement Facility. Read-only.	Boolean
Internet Timeout	The maximum number of milliseconds to wait before generating an error.	Long
Isolation Levels	Identifies the supported transaction isolation levels. Read-only.	DBPROPVAL_TI
Isolation Retention	Identifies the supported transaction isolation retention levels. Read-only.	DBPROPVAL_TR
Jet OLEDB:Compact Reclaimed Space Amount	The amount of space reclaimed during a compaction.[#]	Long
Jet OLEDB:Compact Without Replica Repair	Indicates whether or not to find and repair damaged replicas.	Boolean
Jet OLEDB:Compact Without Relationships	Indicates whether or not to copy relationships to the new database.	Boolean
Jet OLEDB:Connection Control	Identifies the state of the connection, indicating whether other users are allowed to connect to the database or not.	DBPROPVAL_JCC
Jet OLEDB:Create System Database	Indicates whether or not a system database is generated when creating a new data source.	Boolean
Jet OLEDB:Database Locking Mode	Identifies the mode to use when locking the database. The first person to open a database identifies the mode.	DBPROPVAL_DL
Jet OLEDB:Database Password	The database password. Read/Write.	String

Property Name	Description	DataType
Jet OLEDB:Don't Copy Locale on Compact	Indicates that the database sort order should be used when compacting, rather than the locale.	Boolean
Jet OLEDB:Encrypt Database	Indicates whether or not to encrypt the new database.	Boolean
Jet OLEDB:Engine Type	Identifies the version of the database to open, or the version of the database to create.	JET_ENGINETYPE
Jet OLEDB:Exclusive Async Delay	The maximum time (in milliseconds) that Jet will delay asynchronous writes to disk, when the database is open in exclusive mode.	Long
Jet OLEDB:Flush Transaction Timeout	Amount of time of inactivity before the asynchronous write cache is written to the disk.	Long
Jet OLEDB:Global Bulk Transactions	Identifies whether bulk operations are transacted.	DBPROPVAL_BT
Jet OLEDB:Global Partial Bulk Ops	Identifies whether Bulk operations are allowed with partial values. Read/Write.	DBPROPVAL_BP
Jet OLEDB:Implicit Commit Sync	Indicates whether or not implicit transactions are written synchronously.	Boolean
Jet OLEDB:Lock Delay	The number of times to repeat attempts to access a locked page.	Long
Jet OLEDB:Lock Retry	The number of attempts made to access a locked page.	Long
Jet OLEDB:Max Buffer Size	The largest amount of memory (in Kb) that can be used before it starts flushing changes to disk.	Long

Table Continued on Following Page

Property Name	Description	DataType
Jet OLEDB:Max Locks Per File	The maximum number of locks that can be placed on a database. This defaults to 9500.	Long
Jet OLEDB:New Database Password	Sets the database password.	String
Jet OLEDB:ODBC Command Time Out	The number of seconds before remote ODBC queries timeout.	Long
Jet OLEDB:ODBC Parsing	Indicates whether or not Jet performs parsing of SQL statements on ODBC connections. #	Boolean
Jet OLEDB:Page Locks to Table Lock	The percentage of page locks to apply to a table before escalating the lock to a table lock. #	Long
Jet OLEDB:Page Timeout	The amount of time (in milliseconds) to delay before Jet checks to see if the cache is out of date with the database.	Long
Jet OLEDB:Recycle Long-Valued Pages	Indicates whether or not Jet aggressively tries to reclaim BLOB pages when they are freed.	Boolean
Jet OLEDB:Registry Path	The registry key that contains values for the Jet database engine. Read/Write.	String
Jet OLEDB:Reset ISAM Stats	Determines whether or not the ISAM statistics should be reset after the information has been returned.	Boolean
Jet OLEDB:Sandbox Mode	Indicates whether the database is in Sandbox mode. #	Boolean
Jet OLEDB:Shared Async Delay	The maximum time (in milliseconds) to delay asynchronous writes when in multi-user mode.	Long

Property Name	Description	DataType
Jet OLEDB:System database	The path and file name for the workgroup file. Read/Write.	String
Jet OLEDB:Transaction Commit Mode	A value if 1 indicates that the database commits updates immediately, rather than caching them.	Long
Jet OLEDB:User Commit Sync	Indicates whether or not explicit user transactions are written synchronously.	Boolean
Like Escape Clause	Identifies the LIKE escape clause. Read-only.	String
Locale Identifier	The locale ID of preference for the consumer. Read/Write.	Long
Location	The location of the data source to connect to. Typically this will be the server name. Read/Write.	String
Lock Owner	The string to show when you lock a resource and other users attempt to access that resource. Ignored for the WEC protocol, used with FrontPage Server Extensions. Read/Write.	String
Log text and image writes	Identifies whether writes to text and images fields are logged in the transaction log. Read/Write.	Boolean
Maintain Property Values	Indicates whether or not the property values are persisted along with the data when saving a recordset. Defaults to `True`. #	Boolean
Mark For Offline	Indicates that the URL can be marked for offline use. #	Integer

Table Continued on Following Page

Property Name	Description	DataType
Mask Password	The consumer requires that the password be sent to the data source in masked form. Read/Write.	Boolean
Max Columns in Group By	Identifies the maximum number of columns in a GROUP BY clause. Read-only.	Long
Max Columns in Index	Identifies the maximum number of columns in an index. Read-only.	Long
Max Columns in Order By	Identifies the maximum number of columns in an ORDER BY clause. Read-only.	Long
Max Columns in Select	Identifies the maximum number of columns in a SELECT statement. Read-only.	Long
Max Columns in Table	Identifies the maximum number of columns in a table. Read-only.	Long
Maximum Index Size	The maximum number of bytes allowed in the combined columns of an index. This is 0 if there is no specified limit or the limit is unknown. Read-only.	Long
Maximum Open Chapters	The maximum number of chapters that can be open at any one time. If a chapter must be released before a new chapter can be opened, the value is 1. If the provider does not support chapters, the value is 0. Read-only.	Long

Property Name	Description	DataType
Maximum OR Conditions	The maximum number of disjunct conditions that can be supported in a view filter. Multiple conditions of a view filter are joined in a logical OR. Providers that do not support joining multiple conditions return a value of 1, and providers that do not support view filters return a value of 0. Read-only.	Long
Maximum Row Size	The maximum length of a single row in a table. This is 0 if there is no specified limit or the limit is unknown. Read-only.	Long
Maximum Row Size Includes BLOB	Identifies whether Maximum Row Size includes the length for BLOB data. Read-only.	Boolean
Maximum Sort Columns	The maximum number of columns that can be supported in a View Sort. This is 0 if there is no specified limit or the limit is unknown. Read-only.	Long
Maximum Tables in SELECT	The maximum number of tables allowed in the FROM clause of a SELECT statement. This is 0 if there is no specified limit or the limit is unknown. Read-only.	Long
Mode	Specifies the access permissions. Read/Write.	DB_MODE
Multi-Table Update	Identifies whether the provider can update rowsets derived from multiple tables. Read-only.	Boolean

Table Continued on Following Page

Property Name	Description	DataType
Multiple Connections	Identifies whether the provider silently creates additional connections to support concurrent `Command`, `Connection` or `Recordset` objects. This only applies to providers that have to spawn multiple connections, and not to providers that support multiple connections natively. Read/Write.	Boolean
Multiple Parameter Sets	Identifies whether the provider supports multiple parameter sets. Read-only.	Boolean
Multiple Results	Identifies whether the provider supports multiple results objects and what restrictions it places on those objects. Read-only.	DBPROPVAL_MR
Multiple Storage Objects	Identifies whether the provider supports multiple, open storage objects at the same time. Read-only.	Boolean
Network Address	Identifies the network address of the SQL Server. Read/Write.	String
Network Library	Identifies the name of the Net-Library (DLL) used to communicate with SQL Server. Read/Write.	String
NULL Collation Order	Identifies where NULLs are sorted in a list. Read-only.	DBPROPVAL_NC
NULL Concatenation Behavior	How the data source handles concatenation of NULL-valued character data type columns with non-NULL valued character data type columns. Read-only.	DBPROPVAL_CB
Numeric Functions	Identifies the numeric functions supported by the ODBC driver and data source. Read-only.	SQL_FN_NUM

Property Name	Description	DataType
OLE DB Services	Specifies the OLEDB services to enable. Read/Write.	DBPROPVAL_OS
OLE DB Version	Specifies the version of OLEDB supported by the provider. Read-only.	String
OLE Object Support	Specifies the way on which the provider supports access to BLOBs and OLE objects stored in columns. Read-only.	DBPROPVAL_OO
OLE Objects	Indicates the level of binding support for OLE Objects.	DBPROPVAL_OO
Open Rowset Support	Indicates the level of support for opening rowsets.	DBPROPVAL_ORS
ORDER BY Columns in Select List	Identifies whether columns in an ORDER BY clause must be in the SELECT list. Read-only.	Boolean
Outer Join Capabilities	Identifies the outer join capabilities of the ODBC data source. Read-only.	SQL_OJ
Outer Joins	Identifies whether outer joins are supported or not. Read-only.	Boolean
Outer Join Capabilities	Identifies the outer join capabilities of the ODBC data source. Read-only.	SQL_OJ
Output Parameter Availability	Identifies the time at which output parameter values become available. Read-only.	DBPROPVAL_OA
Packet Size	Specifies the network packet size in bytes. It must be between 512 and 32767. The default is 4096. Read/Write.	Long

Table Continued on Following Page

Property Name	Description	DataType
Pass By Ref Accessors	Whether the provider supports the DBACCESSOR_PASSBYREF flag. Read-only.	Boolean
Password	The password to be used to connect to the data source. Read/Write.	String
Persist Encrypted	Whether or not the consumer requires that the data source object persist sensitive authentication information, such as a password, in encrypted form. Read/Write.	Boolean
Persist Format	Indicates the format for persisting data.	PersistFormatEnum
Persist Schema	Indicates whether or not the schema is persisted along with the data.	Boolean
Persist Security Info	Whether or not the data source object is allowed to persist sensitive authentication information, such as a password, along with other authentication information. Read/Write.	Boolean
Persistent ID Type	Specifies the type of DBID that the provider uses when persisting DBIDs for tables, indexes and columns. Read-only.	DBPROPVAL_PT
Prepare Abort Behavior	Identifies how aborting a transaction affects prepared commands. Read-only.	DBPROPVAL_CB
Prepare Commit Behavior	Identifies how committing a transaction affects prepared commands. Read-only.	DBPROPVAL_CB
Procedure Term	Specifies the data source providers name for a procedure, e.g. 'database procedure' or 'stored procedure'. Read-only.	String

Property Name	Description	DataType
Prompt	Specifies whether to prompt the user during initialization. Read/Write.	DBPROMPT
Protection Level	The level of protection of data sent between client and server. This property applies only to network connections other than RPC. Read/Write.	DB_PROT_LEVEL
Protocol Provider	The protocol to use when using the IPP to connect to a resource. This should be WEC to use the FrontPage Web Extender Client protocol, and DAV to use the Web Distributed Authoring and Versioning (WebDAV) protocol.	String
Provider Friendly Name	The friendly name of the provider. Read-only.	String
Provider Name	The filename of the provider. Read-only.	String
Provider Version	The version of the provider. Read-only.	String
Quoted Catalog Names	Indicates whether or not quoted identifiers are allowed for catalog names.	Boolean
Quoted Identifier Sensitivity	Identifies how quoted identifiers treat case. Read-only.	DBPROPVAL_IC
Read-Only Data Source	Whether or not the data source is read-only. Read-only.	Boolean
Remote Provider	The data provide used to supply the data from a remote connection.	String
Remote Server	The name of the server supplying data from a remote connection.	String

Table Continued on Following Page

Property Name	Description	DataType
Reset Datasource	Specifies the data source state to reset. Write only.	DBPROPVAL_RD
Rowset Conversions on Command	Identifies whether callers can enquire on a command and about conversions supported by the command. Read-only.	Boolean
Schema Term	The name the data source uses for a schema, e.g. 'schema' or 'owner'. Read-only.	String
Schema Usage	Identifies how schema names can be used in commands. Read-only.	DBPROPVAL_SU
Server Name	The name of the server. Read-only.	String
Sort on Index	Specifies whether the provider supports setting a sort order only for columns contained in an index. Read-only.	Boolean
Special Characters	Identifies the data store's special characters. Read-only.	String
SQL Grammar Support	Identifies the SQL grammar level supported by the ODBC driver. 0 represents no conformance, 1 indicates Level 1 conformance, and 2 represents Level 2 conformance. Read-only.	Long
SQL Support	Identifies the level of support for SQL. Read-only.	DBPROPVAL_SQL
SQLOLE execute a SET TEXTLENGTH	Identifies whether SQLOLE executes a SET TEXTLENGTH before accessing BLOB fields [#]. Read-only.	Boolean
Stored Procedures	Indicates whether stored procedures are available. Read-only.	Boolean

Property Name	Description	DataType
String Functions	Identifies the string functions supported by the ODBC driver and data source. Read-only.	SQL_FN_STR
Structured Storage	Identifies what interfaces the rowset supports on storage objects. Read-only.	DBPROPVAL_SS
Subquery Support	Identifies the predicates in text commands that support sub-queries. Read-only.	DBPROPVAL_SQ
System Functions	Identifies the system functions supported by the ODBC Driver and data source. Read-only.	SQL_FN_SYS
Table Term	The name the data source uses for a table, e.g. 'table' or 'file'. Read-only.	String
Time/Date Functions	Identifies the time/date functions supported by the ODBC Driver and data source. Read-only.	SQL_SDF_CURRENT
Transact Updates	Indicates whether or not updates on the remote server are transacted. #	Boolean
Transaction DDL	Indicates whether Data Definition Language (DDL) statements are supported in transactions. Read-only.	DBPROPVAL_TC
Treat As Offline	Indicates whether or not the resource should be treated as an offline resource.	Boolean
Unicode Comparison Style	Determines the sorting options used for Unicode data.	Long
Unicode Locale Id	The locale ID to use for Unicode sorting.	Long
Unique Reshape Names	Indicates whether or not the value of the Name property of a recordset would conflict with an existing name, resulting in a unique name being generated.	Boolean

Table Continued on Following Page

Property Name	Description	DataType
Use Procedure for Prepare	Indicates whether SQL Server is to use temporary stored procedures for prepared statements. Read/Write.	SSPROPVAL_USEPR OCFORPREP
User Authentication mode	Indicates whether Windows NT Authentication is used to access SQL Server. Read/Write.	Boolean
User ID	The User ID to be used when connecting to the data source. Read/Write.	String
User Name	The User Name used in a particular database. Read-only.	String
Window Handle	The window handle to be used if the data source object needs to prompt for additional information. Read/Write.	Long
Workstation ID	Identifies the workstation. Read/Write.	String

The Recordset Object's Properties

Property Name	Description	DataType
Access Order	Indicates the order in which columns must be accessed on the rowset. Read/Write.	DBPROPVAL_ AO
Always use content index	Indicates whether or not to use the content index to resolve queries, even if the index is out of date.	Boolean
Append-Only Rowset	A rowset opened with this property will initially contain no rows. Read/Write.	Boolean
Asynchronous Rowset Processing	Identifies the asynchronous processing performed on the rowset. Read/Write.	DBPROPVAL_ ASYNCH

Property Name	Description	DataType
Auto Recalc	For chaptered recordsets using `COMPUTE`, automatically recalculate the summary if the detail lines change [#]. Read/Write.	Integer
Background Fetch Size	The number of rows to fetch in each batch, during asynchronous reads.	Long
Background thread Priority	The priority of the background thread for asynchronous actions. Read/Write.	Integer
Batch Size	The number of rows in a batch. Read/Write.	Integer
BLOB accessibility on Forward-Only cursor	Indicates whether or not BLOB columns can be accessed irrespective of their position in the column list. If True then the BLOB column can be accessed even if it is not the last column. If False then the BLOB column can only be accessed if it the last BLOB column, and any non-BLOB columns after this column will not be accessible. Read/Write.	Boolean
Blocking Storage Objects	Indicates whether storage objects might prevent use of other methods on the rowset. Read/Write.	Boolean
Bookmark Information	Identifies additional information about bookmarks over the rowset. Read-only.	DBPROPVAL_BI
Bookmark Type	Identifies the bookmark type supported by the rowset. Read/Write.	DBPROPVAL_BMK
Bookmarkable	Indicates whether bookmarks are supported. Read-only.	Boolean
Bookmarks Ordered	Indicates whether boomarks can be compared to determine the relative position of their rows in the rowset. Read/Write.	Boolean

Table Continued on Following Page

Property Name	Description	DataType
Bulk Operations	Identifies optimizations that a provider may take for updates to the rowset. Read-only.	DBPROPVAL_ BO
Cache Child Rows	Indicates whether child rows in a chaptered recordset are cached [*]. Read/Write.	Boolean
Cache Deferred Columns	Indicates whether the provider caches the value of a deferred column when the consumer first gets a value from that column. Read/Write.	Boolean
Change Inserted Rows	Indicates whether the consumer can delete or update newly inserted rows. An inserted row is assumed to be one that has been transmitted to the data source, as opposed to a pending insert row. Read/Write.	Boolean
Column Privileges	Indicates whether access rights are restricted on a column-by-column basis. Read-only.	Boolean
Column Set Notification	Indicates whether changing a column set is cancelable. Read-only.	DBPROPVAL_ NP
Column Writable	Indicates whether a particular column is writable. Read/Write.	Boolean
Command Time Out	The number of seconds to wait before a command times out. A value of 0 indicates an infinite timeout. Read/Write.	Long
Concurrency control method	Identifies the method used for concurrency control when using server based cursors. Read/Write.	SSPROPVAL_ CONCUR
Cursor Engine Version	Identifies the version of the cursor engine. Read-only.	String
Defer Column	Indicates whether the data in a column is not fetched until specifically requested. Read/Write.	Boolean

Property Name	Description	DataType
Defer scope and security testing	Indicates whether or not the search will defer scope and security testing.	Boolean
Delay Storage Object Updates	Indicates whether, when in delayed update mode, if storage objects are also used in delayed update mode. Read/Write.	Boolean
Fastload Options	Indicates the options to use when in Fastload mode.	String
Fetch Backward	Indicates whether a rowset can fetch backwards. Read/Write.	Boolean
Filter Operations	Identifies which comparison operations are supported when using Filter on a particular column. Read-only.	DBPROPVAL_CO
Find Operations	Identifies which comparison operations are supported when using Find on a particular column. Read-only.	DBPROPVAL_CO
FOR BROWSE versioning columns	Indicates the rowset contains the primary key or a timestamp column. Only applicable with rowsets created with the SQL FOR BROWSE statement. Read/Write.	Boolean
Force no command preparation when executing a parameterized command	Identifies whether or not a temporary statement is created for parameterized commands.[#] Read/Write.	Boolean
Force no command reexecution when failure to satisfy all required properties	Identifies whether or not the command is re-executed if the command properties are invalid.[#] Read/Write.	Boolean
Force no parameter rebinding when executing a command	Identifies whether or not the command parameters are rebound every time the command is executed.[#] Read/Write.	Boolean
Force SQL Server Firehose Mode cursor	Identifies whether or not a forward-only, read-only cursor is always created.[#] Read/Write.	Boolean

Table Continued on Following Page

Property Name	Description	DataType
Generate a Rowset that can be marshalled	Identifies whether or not the rowset that is to be created can be marshalled across process boundaries. * Read/Write.	Boolean
Hidden Columns	Indicates the number of hidden columns in the rowset added by the provider to uniquely identify rows.	Long
Hold Rows	Indicates whether the rowset allows the consumer to retrieve more rows or change the next fetch position whilst holding previously fetched rows with pending changes. Read/Write.	Boolean
Immobile Rows	Indicates whether the rowset will reorder insert or updated rows. Read/Write.	Boolean
Include SQL_FLOAT, SQL_DOUBLE, and SQL_REAL in QBU where clauses	When using a query-based update, setting this to True will include REAL, FLOAT and DOUBLE numeric types in the WHERE clause, otherwise they will be omitted. Read/Write.	Boolean
Initial Fetch Size	Identifies the initial size of the cache into which records are fetched. * Read/Write.	Long
Jet OLEDB:Bulk Transaction	Determines whether bulk operations are transacted.	DBPROPVAL_BT
Jet OLEDB:Enable Fat Cursors	Indicates whether or not Jet caches multiple rows for remote row sources.	Boolean
Jet OLEDB:Fat Cursor Cache Size	The number of rows that should be cached if the dynamic property Jet OLEDB:Enable Fat Cursors is set to True.	Long
Jet OLEDB:Inconsistent	Indicates whether or not inconsistent updates are allowed on queries.	Boolean
Jet OLEDB:Locking Granularity	Identifies the lock mode used to open a table. This only applies if Jet OLEDB:Database Locking Mode is set to DBPROPVAL_DL_ALCATRAZ.	DBPROPVAL_LG

Property Name	Description	DataType
Jet OLEDB:ODBC Pass-Through Statement	Identifies the statement used for a SQL Pass through statement. Read/Write.	String
Jet OLEDB:Partial Bulk Ops	Indicates whether on not bulk operations will complete if some of the values fail.	
Jet OLEDB:Pass Through Query Bulk-Op	Indicates whether or not pass-through queries allow bulk operations. [#]	Boolean
Jet OLEDB:Pass Through Query Connect String	Identifies the Connect string for an ODBC pass through query. Read/Write.	String
Jet OLEDB:Stored Query	Indicates whether or not the command should be interpreted as a stored query.	Boolean
Jet OLEDB:Validate Rules On Set	Indicates whether Jet validation rules are applied when the value in a column is set (`True`) or when the changes are committed (`False`).	Boolean
Keep Identity	Indicates whether or not IDENTITY columns should keep the values if supplied by the client during an INSERT. [#]	Boolean
Keep Nulls	Indicates whether or not NULL values supplied by the client should be kept if DEFAULT values exist on the columns. [#]	Boolean
Literal Bookmarks	Indicates whether bookmarks can be compared literally, i.e. as a series of bytes. Read/Write.	Boolean
Literal Row Identity	Indicates whether the consumer can perform a binary comparison of two row handles to determine whether they point to the same row. Read-only.	Boolean
Lock Mode	Identifies the level of locking performed by the rowset. Read/Write.	DBPROPVAL_LM

Table Continued on Following Page

Property Name	Description	DataType
Maintain Change Status	Indicates whether or not to maintain the status of a row if a conflict happens during row updates. [#]	Boolean
Maximum BLOB Length	Identifies the maximum length of a BLOB field. Read-only.	Long
Maximum Open Rows	Specifies the maximum number of rows that can be active at the same time. Read/Write.	Long
Maximum Pending Rows	Specifies the maximum number of rows that can have pending changes at the same time. Read/Write.	Long
Maximum Rows	Specifies the maximum number of rows that can be returned in the rowset. This is 0 if there is no limit. Read/Write.	Long
Memory Usage	Estimates the amount of memory that can be used by the rowset. If set to 0 the amount is unlimited. If between 1 and 99 it specifies a percentage of the available virtual memory. If 100 or greater it specifies the number of kilobytes. Read/Write.	Long
Notification Granularity	Identifies when the consumer is notified for methods that operate on multiple rows. Read/Write.	DBPROPVAL_NT
Notification Phases	Identifies the notification phases supported by the provider. Read-only.	DBPROPVAL_NP
Objects Transacted	Indicates whether any object created on the specified column is transacted. Read/Write.	Boolean
ODBC Concurrency Type	Identifies the ODBC concurrency type. Read-only.	Integer
ODBC Cursor Type	Identifies the ODBC cursor type. Read-only.	Integer
Others' Changes Visible	Indicates whether the rowset can see updates and deletes made by someone other that the consumer of the rowset. Read/Write.	Boolean

Property Name	Description	DataType
Others' Inserts Visible	Indicates whether the rowset can see rows inserted by someone other than the consumer of the rowset. Read/Write.	Boolean
Own Changes Visible	Indicates whether the rowset can see its own updates and deletes. Read/Write.	Boolean
Own Inserts Visible	Indicates whether the rowset can see its own inserts. Read/Write.	Boolean
Position on the last row after insert	Identifies whether or not the cursor is placed on the last row after an insert. # Read-only.	Boolean
Preserve on Abort	Indicates whether, after aborting a transaction, the rowset remains active. Read/Write.	Boolean
Preserve on Commit	Indicates whether after committing a transaction the rowset remains active. Read/Write.	Boolean
Query Based Updates/Deletes/ Inserts	Identifies whether or not queries can be used for updates, deletes, and inserts. # Read/Write.	Boolean
Quick Restart	Indicates whether RestartPosition is relatively quick to execute. Read/Write.	Boolean
Query Restriction	Indicates the restriction to use for a query.	String
Reentrant Events	Indicates whether the provider supports re-entrancy during callbacks. Read-only.	Boolean
Remove Deleted Rows	Indicates whether the provider removes rows it detects as having been deleted from the rowset. Read/Write.	Boolean
Report Multiple Changes	Indicates whether an update or delete can affect multiple rows and the provider can detect that multiple rows have been updated or deleted. Read-only.	Boolean

Table Continued on Following Page

Property Name	Description	DataType
Reshape Name	Indicates the name of the recordset that can be used in reshaping commands.	String
Resync Command	The command string that the `Resync` method will use to refresh data in the `Unique Table`.	String
Return PROPVARIANTs in variant binding	Indicates whether or not to return PROPVARIANTS when binding to variant columns.	Boolean
Return Pending Inserts	Indicates whether methods that fetch rows can return pending insert rows. Read-only.	Boolean
Row Delete Notification	Indicates whether deleting a row is cancellable. Read-only.	DBPROPVAL_NP
Row First Change Notification	Indicates whether changing the first row is cancellable. Read-only.	DBPROPVAL_NP
Row Insert Notification	Indicates whether inserting a new row is cancellable. Read-only.	DBPROPVAL_NP
Row Privileges	Indicates whether access rights are restricted on a row-by-row basis. Read-only.	Boolean
Row Resynchronization Notification	Indicates whether resynchronizing a row is cancellable. Read-only.	DBPROPVAL_NP
Row Threading Model	Identifies the threading models supported by the rowset. Read/Write.	DBPROPVAL_RT
Row Undo Change Notification	Indicates whether undoing a change is cancellable. Read-only.	DBPROPVAL_NP
Row Undo Delete Notification	Indicates whether undoing a delete is cancellable. Read-only.	DBPROPVAL_NP
Row Undo Insert Notification	Indicates whether undoing an insert is cancellable. Read-only.	DBPROPVAL_NP
Row Update Notification	Indicates whether updating a row is cancellable. Read-only.	DBPROPVAL_NP

Property Name	Description	DataType
Rowset Fetch Position Change Notification	Indicates whether changing the fetch position is cancellable Indicates whether changing the fetch position is cancellable. Read-only.	DBPROPVAL_ NP
Rowset Release Notification	Indicates whether releasing a rowset is cancellable. Read-only.	DBPROPVAL_ NP
Scroll Backward	Indicates whether the rowset can scroll backward. Read/Write.	Boolean
Server Cursor	Indicates whether the cursor underlying the rowset (if any) must be materialized on the server. Read/Write.	Boolean
Server Data on Insert	Indicates whether, at the time an insert is transmitted to the server, the provider retrieves data from the server to update to update the local row cache. Read/Write.	Boolean
Skip Deleted Bookmarks	Indicates whether the rowset allows positioning to continue if a bookmark row was deleted. Read/Write.	Boolean
SQL Content Query Locale String	The locale string to use for queries.	String
Strong Row Identity	Indicates whether the handles of newly inserted rows can be compared. Read-only.	Boolean
Unique Catalog	Specifies the catalog, or database name containing the table named in the Unique Table property.	String
Unique Rows	Indicates whether each row is uniquely identified by its column values. Read/Write.	Boolean
Unique Schema	Specifies the schema, or owner of the table named in the Unique Table property.	String
Unique Table	Specifies the name of the base table upon which edits are allowed. This is required when updateable recordsets are created from one-to-many JOIN statements.	String

Table Continued on Following Page

Property Name	Description	DataType
Updatability	Identifies the supported methods for updating a rowset. Read/Write.	DBPROPVAL_UP
Update Criteria	For chaptered recordsets, identifies the criteria used when performing a requery. # Read/Write.	String
Update Operation	For chaptered recordsets, identifies the operation to be performed with a requery. Read/Write.	String
Update Resync	Specifies whether an implicit `Resync` method is called directly after an `UpdateBatch` method	CEResyncEnum
Use Bookmarks	Indicates whether the rowset supports bookmarks. Read/Write.	Boolean

The Field Object's Properties

The field properties names are different from the other properties because they are less readable and appear more like the schema column names.

Property Name	Description	DataType
BASECATALOGNAME	The name of the catalog. Read-only.	String
BASECOLUMNNAME	The name of the column. Read-only.	String
BASESCHEMANAME	The name of the schema. Read-only.	String
BASETABLENAME	The table name. Read-only.	String
CALCULATIONINFO	This is only available of client cursors.	Binary
CLSID	The class id of the field.	GUID
COLLATINGSEQUENCE	The locale ID of the sort sequence.	Long
COMPUTEMODE	Indicates the mode of recalculation for computed fields.	DBCOMPUTEMODE

Property Name	Description	DataType
DATETIMEPRECISION	The number of digits in the fraction seconds portion if a datetime column. Read-only.	Long
DEFAULTVALUE	The default value of the field.	Variant
DOMAINCATALOG	The name of the catalog containing this column's domain.	String
DOMAINNAME	The name of the domain of which this column is a member.	String
DOMAINSCHEMA	The name of the schema containing this column's domain.	String
HASDEFAULT	Indicates whether or not the field has a default value.	Boolean
ISAUTOINCREMENT	Identifies whether the column is an auto increment column, such as an Access AutoNumber or a SQL Server IDENTITY column. Read-only.	Boolean
ISCASESENSITIVE	Identifies whether the contents of the column are case sensitive. Useful when searching. Read-only.	Boolean
ISSEARCHABLE	Identifies the searchability of the column. Read-only.	DB_SEARCHABLE
ISUNIQUE	Indicates whether or not the field uniquely identifies the row.	Boolean
KEYCOLUMN	Identifies whether or not the column is a key column, used to uniquely identify the row. Read-only.	Boolean
OCTETLENGTH	The maximum column length in bytes, for character or binary data columns. Read-only.	Long
OPTIMIZE	Identifies whether the column is indexed locally. This is only available of client cursors. Read/Write.	Boolean
RELATIONCONDITIONS	Identifies the relationship between fields. This is only available on client cursors. [#]	Binary

Schemas

There are two terms that are important when dealing with schemas:

❑ A **Catalog** is like a normal paper catalog, but contains a list of schemas. It always contains a schema named INFORMATION_SCHEMA, which is the information schema. When dealing with Microsoft SQL Server and Access, a catalog is a database.

❑ A **Schema** is a collection of database objects that are owned (or have been created by) a particular user. Microsoft Access does not have an equivalent to a schema, and so all database objects appear in a single schema.

This appendix details the schema objects that can be accessed using the OpenSchema method of the Connection object.

The table below shows the main providers and the list of schemas supported by them:

Schema	ODBC Access 97	ODBC Access 2000	ODBC SQL 6.5	ODBC SQL 7	OLEDB Access 97	OLEDB Access 2000	OLEDB SQL 6.5	OLEDB SQL 7	OLAP
adSchemaAsserts									
adSchemaCatalogs	✓	✓	✓	✓				✓	✓
adSchemaCharacterSets									
adSchemaCheckConstraints					✓	✓			
adSchemaCollations									
adSchemaColumnPrivileges			✓	✓				✓	
adSchemaColumns	✓	✓	✓	✓	✓	✓		✓	✓

Table Continued on Following Page

Schema	ODBC Access 97	ODBC Access 2000	ODBC SQL 6.5	ODBC SQL 7	OLEDB Access 97	OLEDB Access 2000	OLEDB SQL 6.5	OLEDB SQL 7	OLAP
adSchemaColumnsDomainUsage									
adSchemaConstraintColumnUsage					✓	✓			
adSchemaConstraintTableUsage									
adSchemaCubes									✓
adSchemaDBInfoKeywords	✓	✓	✓	✓	✓	✓	✓	✓	✓
adSchemaDBInfoLiterals	✓	✓	✓	✓	✓	✓	✓	✓	✓
adSchemaDimensions									✓
adSchemaForeignKeys			✓	✓	✓	✓		✓	
adSchemaHierarchies									✓
adSchemaIndexes	✓	✓	✓	✓	✓	✓		✓	
adSchemaKeyColumnUsage					✓	✓			
adSchemaLevels									✓
adSchemaMeasures									✓
adSchemaMembers									✓
adSchemaPrimaryKeys			✓	✓	✓	✓		✓	
adSchemaProcedureColumns	✓	✓							
adSchemaProcedureParameters	✓	✓	✓	✓				✓	
adSchemaProcedures	✓	✓	✓	✓	✓	✓		✓	
adSchemaProperties									✓
adSchemaProviderTypes	✓	✓	✓	✓	✓	✓		✓	✓
adSchemaReferentialContraints					✓	✓			
adSchemaSchemata			✓	✓				✓	
adSchemaSQLLanguages									
adSchemaStatistics					✓	✓		✓	
adSchemaTableConstraints					✓	✓		✓	
adSchemaTablePrivileges								✓	
adSchemaTables	✓	✓	✓	✓	✓	✓		✓	✓
adSchemaTranslations									
adSchemaTrustees									
adSchemaUsagePrivileges									
adSchemaViewColumnUsage									
adSchemaViews					✓	✓			
adSchemaViewTableUsage									

Schema Usage

Using schemas is quite easy, since all you need to do is use the OpenSchema method of the connection object. For example, to list all of the tables on a particular connection:

```
Set objRec = objConn.OpenSchema (adSchemaTables)
While Not objRec.EOF
  Print objRec("TABLE_NAME")
  objRec.MoveNext
Wend
```

This simply opens a recordset on the tables schema and loops through it, printing each table name. You can use the TABLE_TYPE column to check for system tables:

```
Set objRec = objConn.OpenSchema (adSchemaTables)
While Not objRec.EOF
  If objRec("TABLE_TYPE") <> "SYSTEM TABLE" Then
     Print objRec("TABLE_NAME")
  End If
  objRec.MoveNext
Wend
```

You can use the Restrictions argument of OpenSchema to return only certain rows. This argument accepts an array that matches the column names. For example, to find only the system tables:

```
Set objRec = objConn.OpenSchema (adSchemaTables, _
                       Array (Empty, Empty, Empty, "SYSTEM_TABLE"))
```

Since the type is the fourth column in the recordset, you need to specify empty values for the columns you wish to skip.

For multi-dimensional providers using adSchemaMembers, the restrictions can either be the columns in the members schema, or one of the MDTREEOP constants, as defined in Appendix L.

When connecting to Microsoft Access, there are some interesting things you should be aware of. If you wish to see the queries, then you might have to use both adSchemaProcedures and adSchemaViews depending upon the query type. Normal select queries appear as Views, whereas action queries (Update, Delete, etc) and CrossTab queries appear as procedures. This is only for the native Jet provider. For the ODBC provider, select and crosstab queries appear as tables with a table type set to VIEW.

adSchemaAsserts

This identifies the assertions defined in the catalog.

Column name	Type	Description
CONSTRAINT_CATALOG	String	Catalog name, or Null if the provider does not support catalogs.
CONSTRAINT_SCHEMA	String	Schema name, or Null if the provider does not support schemas.

Table Continued on Following Page

Column name	Type	Description
CONSTRAINT_NAME	String	Constraint name.
IS_DEFERRABLE	Boolean	True if the assertion is deferrable, False otherwise
INITIALLY_DEFERRED	Boolean	True if the assertion is initially deferred, False otherwise.
DESCRIPTION	String	Description of the assertion.

adSchemaCatalogs

This defines the physical attributes of the catalogs of a database. When using SQL Server the catalogs are the databases within the Server, and for Access the catalogs contain the current database.

Column name	Type	Description
CATALOG_NAME	String	Catalog name.
DESCRIPTION	String	Catalog description.

adSchemaCharacterSets

This identifies the character sets supported by the catalog.

Column name	Type	Description
CHARACTER_SET_CATALOG	String	Catalog name, or Null if the provider does not support catalogs.
CHARACTER_SET_SCHEMA	String	Schema name, or Null if the provider does not support schemas.
CHARACTER_SET_NAME	String	Character set name.
FORM_OF_USE	String	Name of form-of-use of the character set.
NUMBER_OF_CHARACTERS	Big Integer	Number of characters in the character repertoire.
DEFAULT_COLLATE_CATALOG	String	Catalog name containing the default collation, or Null if the provider does not support catalogs or different collations.

Column name	Type	Description
DEFAULT_COLLATE_SCHEMA	String	Schema name containing the default collation, or Null if the provider does not support schemas or different collations.
DEFAULT_COLLATE_NAME	String	Default collation name, or Null if the provider does not support different collations.

adSchemaCheckConstraints

This identifies the check constraints available in the catalog. Check constraints identify the valid values allowed for columns.

Column name	Type	Description
CONSTRAINT_CATALOG	String	Catalog name, or Null if the provider does not support catalogs.
CONSTRAINT_SCHEMA	String	Schema name, or Null if the provider does not support schemas.
CONSTRAINT_NAME	String	Constraint name.
CHECK_CLAUSE	String	The WHERE clause specified in the CHECK constraint.
DESCRIPTION	String	Check constraint description.

adSchemaCollations

Collations identify how the catalog sorts data.

Column name	Type	Description
COLLATION_CATALOG	String	Catalog name, or Null if the provider does not support catalogs.
COLLATION_SCHEMA	String	Schema name, or Null if the provider does not support schemas.
COLLATION_NAME	String	Collation name.
CHARACTER_SET_CATALOG	String	Catalog name containing the character set on which the collation is defined, or Null if the provider does not support catalogs or different character sets.

Table Continued on Following Page

Column name	Type	Description
CHARACTER_SET_SCHEMA	String	Schema name containing the character set on which the collation is defined, or Null if the provider does not support schema or different character sets.
CHARACTER_SET_NAME	String	Character set name on which the collation is defined, or Null if the provider does not support different character sets.
PAD_ATTRIBUTE	String	'NO PAD' if the collation being described has the NO PAD attribute, 'PAD SPACE' if the collation being described has the PAD SPACE attribute. This identifies whether variable length character columns are padded with spaces.

adSchemaColumnDomainUsage

This identifies the columns that use domains for integrity checking.

Column name	Type	Description
DOMAIN_CATALOG	String	Catalog name, or Null if the provider does not support catalogs.
DOMAIN_SCHEMA	String	Schema name, or Null if the provider does not support schemas.
DOMAIN_NAME	String	View name.
TABLE_CATALOG	String	Catalog name in which the table is defined, or Null if the provider does not support catalogs.
TABLE_SCHEMA	String	Unqualified schema name in which the table is defined, or Null if the provider does not support schemas.
TABLE_NAME	String	Table name.
COLUMN_NAME	String	Column name. This column, together with the COLUMN_GUID and COLUMN_PROPID columns, forms the column ID. One or more of these columns will be Null depending on which elements of the DBID structure the provider uses.
COLUMN_GUID	GUID	Column GUID.
COLUMN_PROPID	Long	Column property ID.

adSchemaColumnPrivileges

This identifies the privileges on table columns for a given user.

Column name	Type	Description
GRANTOR	String	User who granted the privileges on the table in TABLE_NAME.
GRANTEE	String	User name (or "PUBLIC") to whom the privilege has been granted.
TABLE_CATALOG	String	Catalog name in which the table is defined, or Null if the provider does not support catalogs.
TABLE_SCHEMA	String	Schema name in which the table is defined, or Null if the provider does not support schemas.
TABLE_NAME	String	Table name.
COLUMN_NAME	String	Column name.
COLUMN_GUID	GUID	Column GUID.
COLUMN_PROPID	Long	Column property ID.
PRIVILEGE_TYPE	String	Privilege type. One of the following: SELECT, DELETE, INSERT, UPDATE, REFERENCES
IS_GRANTABLE	Boolean	True if the privilege being described was granted with the WITH GRANT OPTION clause; False if the privilege being described was not granted with the WITH GRANT OPTION clause.

adSchemaColumns

This identifies the columns of tables.

Column name	Type	Description
TABLE_CATALOG	String	Catalog name, or Null if the provider does not support catalogs.
TABLE_SCHEMA	Long	Schema name, or Null if the provider does not support schemas.
TABLE_NAME	String	Table name. This column cannot contain a Null.
COLUMN_NAME	String	The name of the column, or Null if this cannot be determined.

Table Continued on Following Page

Column name	Type	Description
COLUMN_GUID	GUID	Column GUID, or Null for providers that do not use GUIDs to identify columns.
COLUMN_PROPID	Long	Column property ID, or Null for providers that do not associate PROPIDs with columns.
ORDINAL_POSITION	Long	The ordinal of the column, or Null if there is no stable ordinal value for the column. Columns are numbered starting from one.
COLUMN_HASDEFAULT	Boolean	True if column has a default value, False if the column does not have a default value or it is unknown whether the column has a default value.
COLUMN_DEFAULT	String	Default value of the column.
COLUMN_FLAGS	Long	A bitmask that describes column characteristics. The DBCOLUMNFLAGS enumerated type specifies the bits in the bitmask. The values for DBCOLUMNFLAGS can be found in Appendix B. This column cannot contain a Null value.
IS_NULLABLE	Boolean	True if the column might be nullable, False if the column is known not to be nullable.
DATA_TYPE	Integer	The column's data type. If the data type of the column varies from row to row, this must be a Variant. This column cannot contain Null. For a list of valid Types, see DataTypeEnum in Appendix B.
TYPE_GUID	GUID	The GUID of the column's data type. Providers that do not use GUIDs to identify data types should return Null in this column.
CHARACTER_MAXIMUM_LENGTH	Long	The maximum possible length of a value in the column. See below

Column name	Type	Description
CHARACTER_OCTET_LENGTH	Long	Maximum length in octets (bytes) of the column, if the type of the column is character or binary. A value of zero means the column has no maximum length. Null for all other types of columns.
NUMERIC_PRECISION	Integer	If the column's data type is numeric, this is the maximum precision of the column. The precision of columns with a data type of Decimal or Numeric depends on the definition of the column
		If the column's data type is not numeric, this is Null.
NUMERIC_SCALE	Integer	If the column's Type is Decimal or Numeric, this is the number of digits to the right of the decimal point. Otherwise, this is Null.
DATETIME_PRECISION	Long	Datetime precision (number of digits in the fractional seconds portion) of the column if the column is a datetime or interval type. If the column's data type is not datetime, this is Null.
CHARACTER_SET_CATALOG	String	Catalog name in which the character set is defined, or Null if the provider does not support catalogs or different character sets.
CHARACTER_SET_SCHEMA	String	Schema name in which the character set is defined, or Null if the provider does not support schemas or different character sets.
CHARACTER_SET_NAME	String	Character set name, or Null if the provider does not support different character sets.
COLLATION_CATALOG	String	Catalog name in which the collation is defined, or Null if the provider does not support catalogs or different collations.

Table Continued on Following Page

Column name	Type	Description
COLLATION_SCHEMA	String	Schema name in which the collation is defined, or Null if the provider does not support schemas or different collations.
COLLATION_NAME	String	Collation name, or Null if the provider does not support different collations.
DOMAIN_CATALOG	String	Catalog name in which the domain is defined, or Null if the provider does not support catalogs or domains.
DOMAIN_SCHEMA	String	Unqualified schema name in which the domain is defined, or Null if the provider does not support schemas or domains.
DOMAIN_NAME	String	Domain name, or Null if the provider does not support domains.
DESCRIPTION	String	Description of the column, or Null if there is no description associated with the column.
SS_DATA_TYPE	Integer	SQL Server data type.

CHARACTER_MAXIMUM_LENGTH will vary depending upon the data type of the column. For character, binary, or bit columns, this is one of the following:

❑ The maximum length of the column in characters, bytes, or bits, respectively, if one is defined. For example, a CHAR(5) column in an SQL table has a maximum length of five (5).

❑ The maximum length of the data type in characters, bytes, or bits, respectively, if the column does not have a defined length.

❑ Zero (0) if neither the column nor the data type has a defined maximum length.

It will be Null for all other types of columns.

adSchemaConstraintColumnUsage

This identifies the columns used for referential integrity constraints, unique constraints, check constraints, and assertions.

Column name	Type	Description
TABLE_CATALOG	String	Catalog name in which the table is defined, or Null if the provider does not support catalogs.
TABLE_SCHEMA	String	Schema name in which the table is defined, or Null if the provider does not support schemas.

Column name	Type	Description
TABLE_NAME	String	Table name.
COLUMN_NAME	String	Column name.
COLUMN_GUID	GUID	Column GUID.
COLUMN_PROPID	Long	Column property ID.
CONSTRAINT_CATALOG	String	Catalog name, or Null if the provider does not support catalogs.
CONSTRAINT_SCHEMA	String	Schema name, or Null if the provider does not support schemas.
CONSTRAINT_NAME	String	Constraint name.

adSchemaConstraintTableUsage

This identifies the tables used for referential integrity constraints, unique constraints, check constraints, and assertions.

Column name	Type	Description
TABLE_CATALOG	String	Catalog name in which the table is defined, or Null if the provider does not support catalogs.
TABLE_SCHEMA	String	Schema name in which the table is defined, or Null if the provider does not support schemas.
TABLE_NAME	String	Table name.
CONSTRAINT_CATALOG	String	Catalog name, or Null if the provider does not support catalogs.
CONSTRAINT_SCHEMA	String	Schema name, or Null if the provider does not support schemas.
CONSTRAINT_NAME	String	Constraint name.

adSchemaCubes

Identifies the Cubes in an OLAP Catalog.

Column name	Type	Description
CATALOG_NAME	String	Catalog name in which the table is defined, or Null if the provider does not support catalogs.
SCHEMA_NAME	String	Schema name in which the table is defined, or Null if the provider does not support schemas.

Table Continued on Following Page

Column name	Type	Description
CUBE_NAME	String	The name of the cube
CUBE_TYPE	String	Either CUBE to indicate a regular cube, or VIRTUAL CUBE to indicate a virtual cube.
CUBE_GUID	String	The GUID of the cube, or Null if no GUID exists.
CREATED_ON	Date	Date and time cube was created.
LAST_SCHEMA_UPDATE	Date	Date and time schema was last updated.
SCHEMA_UPDATED_BY	String	User ID of person who last updated the schema.
LAST_DATA_UPDATE	Date	Date and time data was last updated
DATA_UPDATED_BY	String	User ID of person who last updated the data.
Description	String	The cube description.

adSchemaDimensions

Identifies the Dimensions in an OLAP Catalog.

Column name	Type	Description
CATALOG_NAME	String	Catalog name in which the table is defined, or Null if the provider does not support catalogs.
SCHEMA_NAME	String	Schema name in which the table is defined, or Null if the provider does not support schemas.
CUBE_NAME	String	The name of the Cube to which this dimension belongs
DIMENSION_NAME	String	The name of the dimension
DIMENSION_UNIQUE_NAME	String	The fully qualified name of the dimension.
DIMENSION_GUID	GUID	The GUID of the dimension, or Null if no GUID exists.
DIMENSION_CAPTION	String	The name of the dimension.
DIMENSION_ORDINAL	Long	The number of the ordinal. This is 0 based.

Column name	Type	Description
DIMENSION_TYPE	Integer	The type of the dimension. Can be one of: `MD_DIMTYPE_MEASURE`, to indicate a measure dimension `MD_DIMTYPE_TIME`, to indicate a time dimension `MD_DIMTYPE_OTHER`, to indicate neither a measure nor a time dimension. `MD_DIM_TYPE_UNKNOWN`, to indicate the type is unknown.
DIMENSION_CARDINALITY	Long	The number of members in the dimension. This figure is not guaranteed to be accurate.
DEFAULT_HIERARCHY	String	The default hierarchy for this dimension, or Null if no default exists.
DESCRIPTION	String	The description of the hierarchy.
IS_VIRTUAL	Boolean	True if the dimension is a virtual one, False otherwise.

adSchemaForeignKeys

This identifies the foreign key columns, as used in referential integrity checks.

Column name	Type	Description
PK_TABLE_CATALOG	String	Catalog name in which the primary key table is defined, or Null if the provider does not support catalogs.
PK_TABLE_SCHEMA	String	Schema name in which the primary key table is defined, or Null if the provider does not support schemas.
PK_TABLE_NAME	String	Primary key table name.
PK_COLUMN_NAME	String	Primary key column name.
PK_COLUMN_GUID	GUID	Primary key column GUID.
PK_COLUMN_PROPID	Long	Primary key column property ID.
FK_TABLE_CATALOG	String	Catalog name in which the foreign key table is defined, or Null if the provider does not support catalogs.

Table Continued on Following Page

Column name	Type	Description
FK_TABLE_SCHEMA	String	Schema name in which the foreign key table is defined, or Null if the provider does not support schemas.
FK_TABLE_NAME	String	Foreign key table name.
FK_COLUMN_NAME	String	Foreign key column name.
FK_COLUMN_GUID	GUID	Foreign key column GUID.
FK_COLUMN_PROPID	Long	Foreign key column property ID.
ORDINAL	Long	The order of the column in the key. For example, a table might contain several foreign key references to another table. The ordinal starts over for each reference; for example, two references to a three-column key would return 1, 2, 3, 1, 2, 3.
UPDATE_RULE	String	The action if an UPDATE rule was specified. This will be Null only if the provider cannot determine the UPDATE_RULE. In most cases, this implies a default of NO ACTION.
DELETE_RULE	String	The action if a DELETE rule was specified. This will be Null if the provider cannot determine the DELETE_RULE. In most cases, this implies a default of NO ACTION.
FK_NAME	String	Foreign key name, or Null if the provider does not support named foreign key constraints.
PK_NAME	String	Primary key name, or Null if the provider does not support named primary key constraints.
DEFERRABILITY	Integer	Deferability of the foreign key. Value is one of the following DBPROPVAL_DF types, as shown in Appendix B.

For UPDATE_RULE and DELETE_RULE, the value will be one of the following:

CASCADE	A referential action of CASCADE was specified.
SET NULL	A referential action of SET NULL was specified.
SET DEFAULT	A referential action of SET DEFAULT was specified.
NO ACTION	A referential action of NO ACTION was specified.

adSchemaHierarchies

Identifies the Hierarchies in an OLAP Catalog.

Column name	Type	Description
CATALOG_NAME	String	Catalog name in which the table is defined or Null if the provider does not support catalogs.
SCHEMA_NAME	String	Schema name in which the table is defined or Null if the provider does not support schemas.
CUBE_NAME	String	The name of the Cube to which this Hierarchy belongs
DIMENSION_UNIQUE_NAME	String	The fully qualified name of the Dimension to which this Hierarchy belongs.
HIERARCHY_NAME	String	The name of the Hierarchy.
HIERARCHY_UNIQUE_NAME	String	The fully qualified name of the Hierarchy
HIERARCHY_GUID	GUID	The GUID of the Hierarchy, or Null if no GUID exists.
HIERARCHY_CAPTION	String	The name of the Hierarchy.
DIMENSION_TYPE	Integer	The type of the dimension. Can be one of: MD_DIMTYPE_MEASURE, to indicate a measure dimension MD_DIMTYPE_TIME, to indicate a time dimension MD_DIMTYPE_OTHER, to indicate neither a measure nor a time dimension MD_DIMTYPE_UNKNOWN, to indicate the type is unknown.
HIERARCHY_CARDINALITY	Long	The number of members in the Hierarchy. This figure is not guaranteed to be accurate.
DEFAULT_MEMBER	String	The default Level for this Hierarchy, or Null if no default exists.
ALL_MEMBER	String	The name of the default member if the first level is All, or Null if the first level is not All.
DESCRIPTION	String	The description of the hierarchy.

adSchemaIndexes

Identifies the list of indexes in the catalog.

Column name	Type	Description
TABLE_CATALOG	String	Catalog name, or Null if the provider does not support catalogs.
TABLE_SCHEMA	String	Unqualified schema name, or Null if the provider does not support schemas.
TABLE_NAME	String	Table name.
INDEX_CATALOG	String	Catalog name, or Null if the provider does not support catalogs.
INDEX_SCHEMA	String	Schema name, or Null if the provider does not support schemas.
INDEX_NAME	String	Index name.
PRIMARY_KEY	Boolean	Whether the index represents the primary key on the table, or Null if this is not known.
UNIQUE	Boolean	Whether index keys must be unique. This will be True if the index keys must be unique, and False if duplicate keys are allowed.
CLUSTERED	Boolean	Whether an index is clustered.
TYPE	Integer	The type of the index. One of the DBPROPVAL_IT constants as shown in Appendix B
FILL_FACTOR	Long	For a B+-tree index, this property represents the storage utilization factor of page nodes during the creation of the index.
INITIAL_SIZE	Long	The total amount of bytes allocated to this structure at creation time.
NULLS	Long	Whether null keys are allowed. This will be one of the DBPROVAL_IN constants as shown in Appendix B.
SORT_BOOKMARKS	Boolean	How the index treats repeated keys. This will be True if the index sorts repeated keys by bookmark, and False if it doesn't.

Column name	Type	Description
AUTO_UPDATE	Boolean	Whether the index is maintained automatically when changes are made to the corresponding base table. This will be True if the index is automatically maintained, and False if it isn't.
NULL_COLLATION	Long	How Nulls are collated in the index. This will be one of the DBPROPVAL_NC constants as shown in Appendix B.
ORDINAL_POSITION	Long	Ordinal position of the column in the index, starting with one.
COLUMN_NAME	String	Column name.
COLUMN_GUID	GUID	Column GUID.
COLUMN_PROPID	Long	Column property ID.
COLLATION	Integer	Identifies the sort order, and will be one of the DB_COLLATION constants as shown in Appendix B.
CARDINALITY	Unsigned Big Integer	Number of unique values in the index.
PAGES	Long	Number of pages used to store the index.
FILTER_CONDITION	String	The WHERE clause identifying the filtering restriction.
INTEGRATED	Boolean	Whether the index is integrated, that is, all base table columns are available from the index. This will be True if the index is integrated, and False if it isn't. Clustered indexes always set this value to True.

adSchemaInfoKeywords

This identifies a list of provider-specific keywords.

Column name	Type	Description
Keyword	String	The Keyword supported by the provider

adSchemaInfoLiterals

This identifies a list of provider-specific literals used in text commands.

Column name	Type	Description
LiteralName	String	The literal name.
LiteralValue	String	The literal value.
InvalidChars	String	Characters which are invalid as part of a literal.
InvalidStartingChars	String	Characters which the literal cannot start with.
Literal	Integer	The literal type. This can be one of the DBLITERAL constants described in Appendix B.
Supported	Boolean	True if the provider supports the literal.
Maxlen	Integer	Maximum length of the literal name.

adSchemaKeyColumnUsage

This identifies the key columns, and table names, in the catalog.

Column name	Type	Description
CONSTRAINT_CATALOG	String	Catalog name, or Null if the provider does not support catalogs.
CONSTRAINT_SCHEMA	String	Schema name, or Null if the provider does not support schemas.
CONSTRAINT_NAME	String	Constraint name.
TABLE_CATALOG	String	Catalog name in which the table containing the key column is defined, or Null if the provider does not support catalogs.
TABLE_SCHEMA	String	Schema name in which the table containing the key column is defined, or Null if the provider does not support schemas.
TABLE_NAME	String	Table name containing the key column.
COLUMN_NAME	String	Name of the column participating in the unique, primary, or foreign key.

Column name	Type	Description
COLUMN_GUID	GUID	Column GUID.
COLUMN_PROPID	Long	Column property ID.
ORDINAL_POSITION	Long	Ordinal position of the column in the constraint being described.

adSchemaLevels

Identifies the Levels in an OLAP Catalog.

Column name	Type	Description
CATALOG_NAME	String	Catalog name, or Null if the provider does not support catalogs.
SCHEMA_NAME	String	Schema name, or Null if the provider does not support schemas.
CUBE_NAME	String	The Cube name to which the level belongs.
DIMENSION_UNIQUE_NAME	String	The unique name of the Dimension to which the level belongs.
HIERARCHY_UNIQUE_NAME	String	The unique name of the hierarchy to which the level belongs.
LEVEL_NAME	String	The level name.
LEVEL_UNIQUE_NAME	String	The unique level name.
LEVEL_GUID	String	The GUID of the level, or Null if no GUID exists.
LEVEL_CAPTION	String	The Caption of the level.
LEVEL_NUMBER	String	The index number of the level.
LEVEL_CARDINALITY	Long	The number of members in the level. This figure is not guaranteed to be accurate.
LEVEL_TYPE	Integer	The Type of the level. This can be one of the MDLEVEL constants, as described in Appendix L.
DESCRIPTION	String	The description of the level.

adSchemaMeasures

Identifies the Measures in an OLAP Catalog.

Column name	Type	Description
CATALOG_NAME	String	Catalog name, or Null if the provider does not support catalogs.
SCHEMA_NAME	String	Schema name, or Null if the provider does not support schemas.
CUBE_NAME	String	The Cube name to which the measure belongs.
MEASURE_NAME	String	The name of the measure.
MEASURE_UNIQUE_NAME	String	The unique name of the measure.
MEASURE_CAPTION	String	The caption of the measure.
MEASURE_GUID	GUID	The GUID of the measure, or Null if no GUID exists.
MEASURE_AGGEGATOR	Long	The type of aggregation for the measure. This can be one of the MDMEASURE_AGGR constants, as described in Appendix L.
DATA_TYPE	Integer	The data type the most closely matches the OLAP Provider type.
NUMERIC_PRECISION	Integer	The numeric precision of the data type.
NUMERIC_SCALE	Integer	The numeric scale of the data type.
MEASURE_UNITS	String	The unit of measurement for the measure.
DESCRIPTION	String	Description of the measure.
EXPRESSION	String	The expression that the measure is based upon.

adSchemaMembers

Identifies the Members in an OLAP Catalog.

Column name	Type	Description
CATALOG_NAME	String	Catalog name, or Null if the provider does not support catalogs.
SCHEMA_NAME	String	Schema name, or Null if the provider does not support schemas.
CUBE_NAME	String	The Cube name to which the member belongs.
DIMENSION_UNIQUE_NAME	String	The unique name of the dimension to which the member belongs.
HIERARCHY_UNIQUE_NAME	String	The unique name of the hierarchy to which the member belongs.
LEVEL_UNIQUE_NAME	String	The unique name of the level to which the member belongs.
LEVEL_NUMBER	Long	The position of the member.
MEMBER_ORDINAL	Long	The ordinal of the member, indicating the sorting rank.
MEMBER_NAME	String	The name of the member.
MEMBER_UNIQUE_NAME	String	The unique name of the member.
MEMBER_TYPE	Integer	The type of the member. Can be one of the MemberTypeEnum constants, as detailed in Appendix L.
MEMBER_GUID	GUID	The GUID of the member, or Null if no GUID exists.
MEMBER_CAPTION	String	The caption of the member.
CHILDREN_CARDINALITY	Long	The number of children that the member contains. This number is not guaranteed to be accurate.
PARENT_LEVEL	Long	The position, or level number, of the member's parent.
PARENT_UNIQUE_NAME	String	The unique name of the member's parent.
PARENT_COUNT	Long	The number of parents that this member has.
DESCRIPTION	String	The description of the member.

adSchemaPrimaryKeys

This identifies the primary keys, and table name, in the catalog.

Column name	Type	Description
TABLE_CATALOG	String	Catalog name in which the table is defined, or Null if the provider does not support catalogs.
TABLE_SCHEMA	String	Schema name in which the table is defined, or Null if the provider does not support schemas.
TABLE_NAME	String	Table name.
COLUMN_NAME	String	Primary key column name.
COLUMN_GUID	GUID	Primary key column GUID.
COLUMN_PROPID	Long	Primary key column property ID.
ORDINAL	Long	The order of the column names (and GUIDs and property IDs) in the key.
PK_NAME	String	Primary key name, or Null if the provider does not support primary key constraints.

adSchemaProcedureColumns

This identifies the columns used in procedures.

Column name	Type	Description
PROCEDURE_CATALOG	String	Catalog name, or Null if the provider does not support catalogs.
PROCEDURE_SCHEMA	String	Schema name, or Null if the provider does not support schemas.
PROCEDURE_NAME	String	Table name.
COLUMN_NAME	String	The name of the column, or Null if this cannot be determined. This might not be unique.
COLUMN_GUID	GUID	Column GUID.
COLUMN_PROPID	Long	Column property ID.
ROWSET_NUMBER	Long	Number of the rowset containing the column. This is greater than one only if the procedure returns multiple rowsets.

Column name	Type	Description
ORDINAL_POSITION	Long	The ordinal of the column. Columns are numbered starting from one, or Null if there is no stable ordinal value for the column.
IS_NULLABLE	Boolean	Will be True if the column might be nullable, or False if the column is known not to be nullable.
DATA_TYPE	Integer	The indicator of the column's data type. For a list of valid Types, see DataTypeEnum in Appendix B.
TYPE_GUID	GUID	The GUID of the column's data type.
CHARACTER_MAXIMUM_ LENGTH	Long	The maximum possible length of a value in the column. See below
CHARACTER_OCTET_ LENGTH	Long	Maximum length in octets (bytes) of the column, if the type of the column is character or binary. A value of zero means the column has no maximum length. Null for all other types of columns.
NUMERIC_PRECISION	Integer	If the column's data type is numeric, this is the maximum precision of the column. If the column's data type is not numeric, this is Null.
NUMERIC_SCALE	Integer	If the column's Type is DBTYPE_DECIMAL or DBTYPE_NUMERIC, this is the number of digits to the right of the decimal point. Otherwise, this is Null.
DESCRIPTION	String	Column description

CHARACTER_MAXIMUM_LENGTH will vary depending upon the data type of the column. For character, binary, or bit columns, this is one of the following:

❑ The maximum length of the column in characters, bytes, or bits, respectively, if one is defined. For example, a CHAR(5) column in an SQL table has a maximum length of five (5).

❑ The maximum length of the data type in characters, bytes, or bits, respectively, if the column does not have a defined length.

❑ Zero (0) if neither the column nor the data type has a defined maximum length.

It will be Null for all other types of columns.

adSchemaProcedureParameters

This identifies the parameters of stored procedures.

Column name	Type	Description
PROCEDURE_CATALOG	String	Catalog name, or Null if the provider does not support catalogs.
PROCEDURE_SCHEMA	String	Schema name, or Null if the provider does not support catalogs.
PROCEDURE_NAME	String	Procedure name.
PARAMETER_NAME	String	Parameter name, or Null if the parameter is not named.
ORDINAL_POSITION	Integer	If the parameter is an input, input/output, or output parameter, this is the one-based ordinal position of the parameter in the procedure call.
		If the parameter is the return value, this is zero.
PARAMETER_TYPE	Integer	The type (direction) of the parameter, which will be one of the DBPARAMTYPE constants, as shown in Appendix B. If the provider cannot determine the parameter type, this is Null.
PARAMETER_HASDEFAULT	Boolean	True if the parameter has a default value, or False if it doesn't or the provider doesn't know whether it has a default value.
PARAMETER_DEFAULT	String	Default value of parameter. A default value of Null is a valid default.
IS_NULLABLE	Boolean	True if the parameter might be nullable, or False if the parameter is not nullable.
DATA_TYPE	Integer	The indicator of the parameter's data type. For a list of valid Types, see DataTypeEnum in Appendix B.

Column name	Type	Description
CHARACTER_MAXIMUM_LENGTH	Long	The maximum possible length of a value in the parameter.
CHARACTER_OCTET_LENGTH	Long	Maximum length in octets (bytes) of the parameter, if the type of the parameter is character or binary. A value of zero means the parameter has no maximum length. Null for all other types of parameters.
NUMERIC_PRECISION	Integer	If the column's data type is numeric, this is the maximum precision of the column. If the column's data type is not numeric, this is Null.
NUMERIC_SCALE	Integer	If the column's Type is DBTYPE_DECIMAL or DBTYPE_NUMERIC, this is the number of digits to the right of the decimal point. Otherwise, this is Null.
DESCRIPTION	String	Parameter description
TYPE_NAME	String	Provider-specific data type name.
LOCAL_TYPE_NAME	String	Localized version of TYPE_NAME, or Null if the data provider does not support a localized name.
SS_DATA_TYPE	Integer	The SQL Server data type.

CHARACTER_MAXIMUM_LENGTH will vary depending upon the data type of the column. For character, binary, or bit columns, this is one of the following:

❏ The maximum length of the column in characters, bytes, or bits, respectively, if one is defined. For example, a CHAR(5) column in an SQL table has a maximum length of five (5).

❏ The maximum length of the data type in characters, bytes, or bits, respectively, if the column does not have a defined length.

❏ Zero (0) if neither the column nor the data type has a defined maximum length.

It will be Null for all other types of columns.

adSchemaProcedures

This identifies the stored procedures or queries.

Column name	Type	Description
PROCEDURE_CATALOG	String	Catalog name, or Null if the provider does not support catalogs.
PROCEDURE_SCHEMA	String	Schema name, or Null if the provider does not support schemas.
PROCEDURE_NAME	String	Procedure name.
PROCEDURE_TYPE	Integer	Identifies whether there will be a return value or not, and will be one of the DB_PT constants as defined in Appendix B.
PROCEDURE_DEFINITION	String	Procedure definition.
DESCRIPTION	String	Procedures description.
DATE_CREATED	Date/Time	Date when the procedure was created or Null if the provider does not have this information.
DATE_MODIFIED	Date/Time	Date when the procedure definition was last modified or Null if the provider does not have this information.

adSchemaProperties

This identifies the properties for each level of a dimension.

Column name	Type	Description
CATALOG_NAME	String	The name of the catalog to which the property belongs.
SCHEMA_NAME	String	The name of the schema to which the property belongs.
CUBE_NAME	String	The name of the cube to which the property belongs.
DIMENSION_UNIQUE_NAME	String	The unique name of the dimension.
HIERARCHY_UNIQUE_NAME	String	The unique name of the hierarchy.
LEVEL_UNIQUE_NAME	String	The unique name of the level.

Column name	Type	Description
MEMBER_UNIQUE_NAME	String	The unique name of the member.
PROPERTY_TYPE	Integer	The type of the property. Can be one of:
		MDPROP_MEMBER to indicate the property relates to a member MDPROP_CELL, to indicate the property relates to a cell.
PROPERTY_NAME	String	The name of the property.
PROPERTY_CAPTION	String	The caption of the property.
DATA_TYPE	Long	The data type of the property. For a list of valid Types, see DataTypeEnum in Appendix B.
CHARACTER_MAXIMUM_LENGTH	Long	The maximum possible length of data in the property, or 0 to indicate no defined maximum.
CHARACTER_OCTET_LENGTH	Long	The maximum length in bytes of the property, for character and binary data types, or 0 to indicate no defined maximum.
NUMERIC_PRECISION	Integer	The numeric precision of the data type.
NUMERIC_SCALE	Integer	The numeric scale of the data type.
DESCRIPTION	String	The description of the property.

adSchemaProviderSpecific

The contents returned by this setting are dependent upon the provider, and you should consult the provider-specific information for details regarding them.

adSchemaProviderTypes

This identifies the data types supported by the provider.

Column name	Type	Description
TYPE_NAME	String	Provider-specific data type name.
DATA_TYPE	Integer	The indicator of the data type.

Table Continued on Following Page

Column name	Type	Description
COLUMN_SIZE	Long	The length of a non-numeric column or parameter refers to either the maximum or the defined length for this type by the provider. For character data, this is the maximum or defined length in characters. For datetime data types, this is the length of the String representation (assuming the maximum allowed precision of the fractional seconds component). If the data type is numeric, this is the upper bound on the maximum precision of the data type.
LITERAL_PREFIX	String	Character or characters used to prefix a literal of this type in a text command.
LITERAL_SUFFIX	String	Character or characters used to suffix a literal of this type in a text command.
CREATE_PARAMS	String	The creation parameters are specified by the consumer when creating a column of this data type. For example, the SQL data type DECIMAL needs a precision and a scale. In this case, the creation parameters might be the String "precision,scale". In a text command to create a DECIMAL column with a precision of 10 and a scale of 2, the value of the TYPE_NAME column might be DECIMAL() and the complete type specification would be DECIMAL(10,2).
IS_NULLABLE	Boolean	True if the data type is nullable, False if the data type is not nullable, and Null if it is not known whether the data type is nullable.
CASE_SENSITIVE	Boolean	True if the data type is a character type and is case sensitive, or False if the data type is not a character type or is not case sensitive.
SEARCHABLE	Long	Identifies whether the column can be used in WHERE clauses, and will be one of the DB_SEARCHABLE constants as shown in Appendix B.

Column name	Type	Description
UNSIGNED_ATTRIBUTE	Boolean	True if the data type is unsigned, False if the data type is signed, or Null if not applicable to data type.
FIXED_PREC_SCALE	Boolean	True if the data type has a fixed precision and scale, or False if the data type does not have a fixed precision and scale.
AUTO_UNIQUE_VALUE	Boolean	True if values of this type can be autoincrementing, or False if values of this type cannot be autoincrementing.
LOCAL_TYPE_NAME	String	Localized version of TYPE_NAME, or Null if a localized name is not supported by the data provider.
MINIMUM_SCALE	Integer	The minimum number of digits allowed to the right of the decimal point, for decimal and numeric data types. Otherwise, this is Null.
MAXIMUM_SCALE	Integer	The maximum number of digits allowed to the right of the decimal point, for a decimal and numeric data types. Otherwise, this is Null.
GUID	GUID	The GUID of the type. All types supported by a provider are described in a type library, so each type has a corresponding GUID.
TYPELIB	String	The type library containing the description of this type.
VERSION	String	The version of the type definition. Providers may wish to version type definitions. Different providers may use different version schemes, such as a timestamp or number (integer or float), or Null if not supported.
IS_LONG	Boolean	True if the data type is a BLOB that contains very long data; the definition of very long data is provider-specific, or False if the data type is a BLOB that does not contain very long data or is not a BLOB.

Table Continued on Following Page

Column name	Type	Description
BEST_MATCH	Boolean	True if the data type is the best match between all data types in the data source and the OLEDB data type indicated by the value in the DATA_TYPE column, or False if the data type is not the best match.
IS_FIXEDLENGTH	Boolean	True if columns of this type created by the DDL will be of fixed length. False if columns of this type created by the DDL will be of variable length.
		If the field is Null, it is not known whether the provider will map this field with a fixed or variable length.

adSchemaReferentialConstraints

This identifies the referential integrity constraints for the catalog.

Column name	Type	Description
CONSTRAINT_CATALOG	String	Catalog name, or Null if the provider does not support catalogs.
CONSTRAINT_SCHEMA	String	Schema name, or Null if the provider does not support schemas.
CONSTRAINT_NAME	String	Constraint name.
UNIQUE_CONSTRAINT_CATALOG	String	Catalog name in which the unique or primary key constraint is defined, or Null if the provider does not support catalogs.
UNIQUE_CONSTRAINT_SCHEMA	String	Unqualified schema name in which the unique or primary key constraint is defined, or Null if the provider does not support schemas.
UNIQUE_CONSTRAINT_NAME	String	Unique or primary key constraint name.
MATCH_OPTION	String	The type of match that was specified.
UPDATE_RULE	String	The action if an UPDATE rule was specified. This will be Null only if the provider cannot determine the UPDATE_RULE. In most cases, this implies a default of NO ACTION.

Column name	Type	Description
DELETE_RULE	String	The action if a DELETE rule was specified. This will be Null if the provider cannot determine the DELETE_RULE. In most cases, this implies a default of NO ACTION.
DESCRIPTION	String	Human-readable description of the constraint.

For MATCH_OPTION, the values will be one of:

NONE   No match type was specified.
PARTIAL   A match type of PARTIAL was specified.
FULL   A match type of FULL was specified.

For UPDATE_RULE and DELETE_RULE, the value will be one of the following:

CASCADE   A referential action of CASCADE was specified.
SET NULL   A referential action of SET NULL was specified.
SET DEFAULT   A referential action of SET DEFAULT was specified.
NO ACTION   A referential action of NO ACTION was specified.

adSchemaSchemata

This identifies the schemas that are owned by a particular user.

Column name	Type	Description
CATALOG_NAME	String	Catalog name, or Null if the provider does not support catalogs.
SCHEMA_NAME	String	Unqualified schema name.
SCHEMA_OWNER	String	User that owns the schemas.
DEFAULT_CHARACTER_SET_CATALOG	String	Catalog name of the default character set for columns and domains in the schemas, or Null if the provider does not support catalogs or different character sets.
DEFAULT_CHARACTER_SET_SCHEMA	String	Unqualified schema name of the default character set for columns and domains in the schemas, or Null if the provider does not support different character sets.
DEFAULT_CHARACTER_SET_NAME	String	Default character set name, or Null if the provider does not support different character sets.

adSchemaSQLLanguages

This identifies the conformance levels and other options supported by the catalog.

Column name	Type	Description
SQL_LANGUAGE_SOURCE	String	Should be "ISO 9075" for standard SQL.
SQL_LANGUAGE_YEAR	String	Should be "1992" for ANSI SQL92-compliant SQL.
SQL_LANGUAGE_CONFORMANCE	String	The language conformance level.
SQL_LANGUAGE_INTEGRITY	String	This will be Yes if optional integrity feature is supported, or No if optional integrity feature is not supported.
SQL_LANGUAGE_IMPLEMENTATION	String	Null for "ISO 9075" implementation.
SQL_LANGUAGE_BINDING_STYLE	String	"DIRECT" for C/C++ callable direct execution of SQL.
SQL_LANGUAGE_PROGRAMMING_LANGUAGE	String	Null.

SQL_LANGUAGE_CONFORMANCE will be one of the following values:

ENTRY	For entry level conformance
INTERMEDIATE	for intermediate conformance
FULL	for full conformance

adSchemaStatistics

This identifies the catalog statistics.

Column name	Type	Description
TABLE_CATALOG	String	Catalog name, or Null if the provider does not support catalogs.
TABLE_SCHEMA	String	Schema name, or Null if the provider does not support schemas.
TABLE_NAME	String	Table name.
CARDINALITY	Unsigned Big Integer	Cardinality (number of rows) of the table.

adSchemaTableConstraints

This identifies the referential table constraints.

Column name	Type	Description
CONSTRAINT_CATALOG	String	Catalog name, or Null if the provider does not support catalogs.
CONSTRAINT_SCHEMA	String	Schema name, or Null if the provider does not support schemas.
CONSTRAINT_NAME	String	Constraint name.
TABLE_CATALOG	String	Catalog name in which the table is defined, or Null if the provider does not support catalogs.
TABLE_SCHEMA	String	Unqualified schema name in which the table is defined, or Null if the provider does not support schemas.
TABLE_NAME	String	Table name.
CONSTRAINT_TYPE	String	The constraint type.
IS_DEFERRABLE	Boolean	True if the table constraint is deferrable, or False if the table constraint is not deferrable.
INITIALLY_DEFERRED	Boolean	True if the table constraint is initially deferred, or False if the table constraint is initially immediate.
DESCRIPTION	String	Column description

CONSTRAINT_TYPE will be one of the following values:

UNIQUE	for a unique constraint
PRIMARY KEY	for a primary key constraint
FOREIGN KEY	for a foreign key constraint
CHECK	for a check constraint

adSchemaTablePrivileges

This identifies the user privileges of tables.

Column name	Type	Description
GRANTOR	String	User who granted the privileges on the table in TABLE_NAME.
GRANTEE	String	User name (or "PUBLIC") to whom the privilege has been granted.
TABLE_CATALOG	String	Catalog name in which the table is defined, or Null if the provider does not support catalogs.
TABLE_SCHEMA	String	Unqualified schema name in which the table is defined, or Null if the provider does not support schemas.
TABLE_NAME	String	Table name.
PRIVILEGE_TYPE	String	Privilege type.
IS_GRANTABLE	Boolean	False if the privilege being described was granted with the WITH GRANT OPTION clause, or True if the privilege being described was not granted with the WITH GRANT OPTION clause.

PRIVILEGE_TYPE will be one of the following values:

SELECT	for SELECT privileges
DELETE	for DELETE privileges
INSERT	for INSERT privileges
UPDATE	for UPDATE privileges
REFERENCES	for REFERENCE privileges

adSchemaTables

This identifies the tables in a catalog.

Column name	Type	Description
TABLE_CATALOG	String	Catalog name, or Null if the provider does not support catalogs.
TABLE_SCHEMA	String	Schema name, or Null if the provider does not support schemas.
TABLE_NAME	String	Table name. This column cannot contain a Null.

Column name	Type	Description
TABLE_TYPE	String	Table type. This column cannot contain a Null.
TABLE_GUID	GUID	GUID that uniquely identifies the table. Providers that do not use GUIDs to identify tables should return Null in this column.
DESCRIPTION	String	Human-readable description of the table, or Null if there is no description associated with the column.
TABLE_PROPID	Long	Property ID of the table. Providers which do not use PROPIDs to identify columns should return Null in this column.
DATE_CREATED	Date/ Time	Date when the table was created or Null if the provider does not have this information.
DATE_MODIFIED	Date/ Time	Date when the table definition was last modified or Null if the provider does not have this information.

TABLE_TYPE will be on of the following, or a provider-specific value.

ALIAS	The table is an alias
TABLE	The table is a normal table
SYNONYM	The table is a synonym
SYSTEM TABLE	The table is a system table
VIEW	The table is a view
GLOBAL TEMPORARY	The table is a global, temporary table
LOCAL TEMPORARY	The table is a local, temporary table

Provider specific values should be defined in the provider documentation. For example, Access returns **PASS-THROUGH** for linked tables.

adSchemaTranslations

This identifies character translations that the catalog supports.

Column name	Type	Description
TRANSLATION_CATALOG	String	Catalog name, or Null if the provider does not support catalogs.
TRANSLATION_SCHEMA	String	Schema name, or Null if the provider does not support schemas.
TRANSLATION_NAME	String	Translation name.

Table Continued on Following Page

Column name	Type	Description
SOURCE_CHARACTER _SET_CATALOG	String	Catalog name containing the source character set on which the translation is defined, or Null if the provider does not support catalogs.
SOURCE_CHARACTER _SET_SCHEMA	String	Unqualified schema name containing the source character set on which the translation is defined, or Null if the provider does not support schemas.
SOURCE_CHARACTER _SET_NAME	String	Source character set name on which the translation is defined.
TARGET_CHARACTER _SET_CATALOG	String	Catalog name containing the target character set on which the translation is defined, or Null if the provider does not support catalogs.
TARGET_CHARACTER _SET_SCHEMA	String	Unqualified schema name containing the target character set on which the translation is defined, or Null if the provider does not support schemas.
TARGET_CHARACTER _SET_NAME	String	Target character set name on which the translation is defined.

adSchemaUsagePrivileges

This identifies the usage privileges that are available to a user.

Column name	Type	Description
GRANTOR	String	User who granted the privileges on the object in OBJECT_NAME.
GRANTEE	String	User name (or "PUBLIC") to whom the privilege has been granted.
OBJECT_CATALOG	String	Catalog name in which the object is defined, or Null if the provider does not support catalogs.
OBJECT_SCHEMA	String	Unqualified schema name in which the object is defined, or Null if the provider does not support schemas.
OBJECT_NAME	String	Object name.
OBJECT_TYPE	String	Object type.

Column name	Type	Description
PRIVILEGE_TYPE	String	Privilege type.
IS_GRANTABLE	Boolean	True if the privilege being described was granted with the WITH GRANT OPTION clause, or False if the privilege being described was not granted with the WITH GRANT OPTION clause.

OBJECT_TYPE will be one of the following values:

DOMAIN	The object is a domain
CHARACTER SET	The object is a character set
COLLATION	The object is a collation
TRANSLATION	The object is a translation

adSchemaViewColumnUsage

This identifies the columns used in views.

Column name	Type	Description
VIEW_CATALOG	String	Catalog name, or Null if the provider does not support catalogs.
VIEW_SCHEMA	String	Schema name, or Null if the provider does not support schemas.
VIEW_NAME	String	View name.
TABLE_CATALOG	String	Catalog name in which the table is defined, or Null if the provider does not support catalogs.
TABLE_SCHEMA	String	Schema name in which the table is defined, or Null if the provider does not support schemas.
TABLE_NAME	String	Table name.
COLUMN_NAME	String	Column name.
COLUMN_GUID	GUID	Column GUID.
COLUMN_PROPID	Long	Column property ID.

adSchemaViewTableUsage

This identifies the tables used in views.

Column name	Type	Description
VIEW_CATALOG	String	Catalog name, or Null if the provider does not support catalogs.
VIEW_SCHEMA	String	Schema name, or Null if the provider does not support schemas.
VIEW_NAME	String	View name.
TABLE_CATALOG	String	Catalog name in which the table is defined, or Null if the provider does not support catalogs.
TABLE_SCHEMA	String	Schema name in which the table is defined, or Null if the provider does not support schemas.
TABLE_NAME	String	Table name.

adSchemaViews

This identifies the views in the catalog.

Column name	Type	Description
TABLE_CATALOG	String	Catalog name, or Null if the provider does not support catalogs.
TABLE_SCHEMA	String	Schema name, or Null if the provider does not support schemas.
TABLE_NAME	String	View name.
VIEW_DEFINITION	String	View definition. This is a query expression.
CHECK_OPTION	Boolean	True if local update checking only, or False for cascaded update checking (same as no CHECK OPTION specified on view definition).
IS_UPDATABLE	Boolean	True if the view is updateable, or False if the view is not updateable.
DESCRIPTION	String	View description
DATE_CREATED	Date/Time	Date when the view was created or Null if the provider does not have this information.
DATE_MODIFIED	Date/Time	Date when the view definition was last modified or Null if the provider does not have this information.

ADO Data Types

You might find the large array of data types supported by ADO confusing, especially since your language or database might not support them all. This appendix details the `DataTypeEnum` constants and how they map to SQL and Access data types.

ODBC to Access 97

Database Type	ADO Type
Text	adVarChar
Memo	adLongVarChar
Number (Byte)	adUnsignedTinyInt
Number (Integer)	adSmallInt
Number (Long Integer)	adInteger
Number (Single)	adSingle
Number (Double)	adDouble
Number (Replication ID)	adGUID
Date/Time	adDBTimeStamp
Currency	adCurrency
Long Integer	adInteger
Yes/No	adBoolean
OLE Object	adLongVarBinary
Hyperlink	adLongVarChar

ODBC to Access 2000

Database Type	ADO Type
Text	adVarWChar
Memo	adLongVarWChar
Number (Byte)	adUnsignedTinyInt
Number (Integer)	adSmallInt
Number (Long Integer)	adInteger
Number (Single)	adSingle
Number (Double)	adDouble
Number (Replication ID)	adGUID
Number (Decimal)	adNumeric
Date/Time	adDBTimeStamp
Currency	adCurrency
AutoNumber	adInteger
Yes/No	adBoolean
OLE Object	adLongVarBinary
Hyperlink	adLongVarWChar

ODBC to SQL 6.5

Database Type	ADO Type
binary	adBinary
bit	adBoolean
char	adChar
datetime	adDBTimeStamp
decimal	adNumeric
float	adDouble
image	adLongVarBinary
int	adInteger
money	adCurrency
numeric	adNumeric

Database Type	ADO Type
real	adSingle
smalldatetime	adDBTimeStamp
smallint	adSmallInt
smallmoney	adCurrency
sysname	adVarChar
text	adLongVarChar
timestamp	adBinary
tinyint	adUnsignedTinyInt
varbinary	adVarBinary
varchar	adVarChar

ODBC to SQL 7.0

Database Type	ADO Type
binary	adBinary
bit	adBoolean
char	adChar
datetime	adDBTimeStamp
decimal	adNumeric
float	adDouble
image	adLongVarBinary
int	adInteger
money	adCurrency
nchar	adWChar
ntext	adLongVarWChar
numeric	adNumeric
nvarchar	adVarWChar
real	adSingle
smalldatetime	adDBTimeStamp
smallint	adSmallInt

Table Continued on Following Page

Database Type	ADO Type
smallmoney	adCurrency
text	adLongVarChar
timestamp	adBinary
tinyint	adUnsignedTinyInt
uniqueidentifier	adGUID
varbinary	adVarBinary
varchar	adVarChar

Native Jet Provider to Access 97

Database Type	ADO Type
Text	adVarWChar
Memo	adLongVarWChar
Number (Byte)	adUnsignedTinyInt
Number (Integer)	adSmallInt
Number (Long Integer)	adInteger
Number (Single)	adSingle
Number (Double)	adDouble
Number (Replication ID)	adGUID
Date/Time	adDate
Currency	adCurrency
Long Integer	adInteger
Yes/No	adBoolean
OLE Object	adLongVarBinary
Hyperlink	adLongVarWChar

Native Jet Provider to Access 2000

Database Type	ADO Type
Text	adVarWChar
Memo	adLongVarWChar
Number (Byte)	adUnsignedTinyInt
Number (Integer)	adSmallInt
Number (Long Integer)	adInteger
Number (Single)	adSingle
Number (Double)	adDouble
Number (Replication ID)	adGUID
Number (Decimal)	adNumeric
Date/Time	adDate
Currency	adCurrency
AutoNumber	adInteger
Yes/No	adBoolean
OLE Object	adLongVarBinary
Hyperlink	adLongVarWChar

Native SQL Provider to SQL Server 6.5

Database Type	ADO Type
binary	adBinary
bit	adBoolean
char	adChar
datetime	adDBTimeStamp
decimal	adNumeric
float	adDouble
image	adLongVarBinary
int	adInteger
money	adCurrency
numeric	adNumeric

Table Continued on Following Page

Database Type	ADO Type
real	adSingle
smalldatetime	adDBTimeStamp
smallint	adSmallInt
smallmoney	adCurrency
sysname	adVarChar
text	adLongVarChar
timestamp	adBinary
tinyint	adUnsignedTinyInt
varbinary	adVarBinary
varchar	adVarChar

Native SQL Provider to SQL Server 7.0

Database Type	ADO Type
binary	adBinary
bit	adBoolean
char	adChar
datetime	adDBTimeStamp
decimal	adNumeric
float	adDouble
image	adLongVarBinary
int	adInteger
money	adCurrency
nchar	adWChar
ntext	adLongVarWChar
numeric	adNumeric
nvarchar	adVarWChar
real	adSingle
smalldatetime	adDBTimeStamp
smallint	adSmallInt
smallmoney	adCurrency

Database Type	ADO Type
text	adLongVarChar
timestamp	adBinary
tinyint	adUnsignedTinyInt
uniqueidentifier	adGUID
varbinary	adVarBinary
varchar	adVarChar

Language Types

The following table lists the data types you should use in your programming language.

A blank value indicates that the language does not natively support the data type, although there may be support in other libraries, or other data types might be used instead. For example, the com.ms.wfc.data import library for J++ has support for dates and timestamp types, amongst others, but these are not supported by J++ natively.

Constant	Visual Basic	Visual C++	Visual J++
adBinary	Variant		
adBoolean	Boolean	bool	boolean
adChar	String	char[]	String
adCurrency	Currency		
adDate	Date		
adDBTimeStamp	Variant		
adDouble	Double	double	double
adGUID		char[]	String, char[]
adInteger	Long	int	int
adLongVarBinary	Variant		
adLongVarChar	String		
adNumeric			
adSingle	Single	float	float
adSmallInt	Integer	short	short
adUnsignedTinyInt	Byte	char	byte
adVarBinary		char[]	byte[]
adVarChar	String	char[]	String, byte[]
adVarWChar	String	char[]	String, byte[]

RDS Object Summary

The Remote Data Service (RDS) provides a set of objects that can be used to allow a client machine to access data remotely over HTTP protocol. This section lists the properties, methods and events for two RDS controls – the **RDS/ADC Data Source Object** (DSO) and the **Tabular Data Control** (TDC). It also lists the properties, methods, events and constants for the DataSpace and DataFactory objects that are used by the RDS/ADC control.

> All properties are read/write unless otherwise stated.

The RDS Advanced Data Control (RDS/ADC)

The RDS/ADC Data Control is used on the client to provide read/write access to a data store or custom business object on the server. To instantiate the control in a Web page, an <OBJECT> tag is used:

```
<OBJECT CLASSID="clsid:BD96C556-65A3-11D0-983A-00C04FC29E33"
        ID="dsoBookList" HEIGHT=0 WIDTH=0>
  <PARAM NAME="Server" VALUE="http://www.yourserver.com">
  <PARAM NAME="Connect" VALUE="DSN=yourdsn;UID=anon;PWD=">
  <PARAM NAME="SQL" VALUE="SELECT * FROM BookList">
</OBJECT>
```

The <PARAM> elements are used to set the properties of the control at design time. They can be changed at run-time using script code. The following tables list the properties, methods and events for the control.

Properties of the RDS ADC	Return Type	Description
Connect	String	The data store connection string or DSN.
ExecuteOptions	Integer	Specifies if the control will execute asynchronously. Can be one of the ADCExecuteOptionEnum constants, as detailed in Appendix G.
FetchOptions	Integer	Specifies if the data will be fetched asynchronously. Can be one of the ADCFetchOptionEnum constants, as detailed in Appendix G.
FilterColumn	String	Name of the column to filter on.
FilterCriterion	String	The criteria for the filter, can be <, <=, >, >=, =, or <>.
FilterValue	String	The value to match values in FilterColumn with when filtering.
Handler	String	Specifies the server-side security handler to use with the control if not the default.
InternetTimeout	Long	Indicates the timeout (in milliseconds) for the HTTP connection.
ReadyState	Integer	Indicates the state of the control as data is received. Can be one of the ADCReadyStateEnum constants, as detailed in Appendix G. Read only.
Recordset	Object	Provides a reference to the ADO recordset object in use by the control. Read only.
Server	String	Specifies the communication protocol and the address of the server to execute the query on.
SortColumn	String	Name of the column to sort on.
SortDirection	Boolean	The sort direction for the column. The default is ascending order (True). Use False for descending order.
SourceRecordset	Object	Can be used to bind the control to a different recordset object at run time. Write only.
SQL	String	The SQL statement used to extract the data from the data store.
URL	String	URL to the path of the file.

Methods of the RDS ADC	Description
Cancel	Cancels an asynchronous action such as fetching data.
CancelUpdate	Cancels all changes made to the source recordset.
CreateRecordSet	Creates and returns an empty, disconnected recordset on the client.
MoveFirst	Moves to the first record in a displayed recordset.
MoveLast	Moves to the last record in a displayed recordset.
MoveNext	Moves to the next record in a displayed recordset.
MovePrevious	Moves to the previous record in a displayed recordset.
Refresh	Refreshes the client-side recordset from the data source.
Reset	Updates the local recordset to reflect current filter and sort criteria.
SubmitChanges	Sends changes to the client-side recordset back to the data store.

Methods Syntax

datacontrol.Cancel
datacontrol.CancelUpdate
(Set) *object* = *datacontrol*.CreateRecordSet (*varColumnInfos As Variant*)
datacontrol.Recordset.MoveFirst
datacontrol.Recordset.MoveLast
datacontrol.Recordset.MoveNext
datacontrol.Recordset.MovePrevious
datacontrol.Refresh
datacontrol.Reset (*re-filter As Integer*)
datacontrol.SubmitChanges

Events of the RDS ADC	Description
onerror	Occurs if an error prevents the data being fetched from the server, or a user action being carried out.
onreadystatechange	Occurs when the value of the ReadyState property changes.

Events Syntax

onError (*StatusCode*, *Description*, *Source*, *CancelDisplay*)
onReadyStateChange ()

The Tabular Data Control

The Tabular Data Control (TDC) uses a formatted text file that is downloaded to the client and exposed there as an ADO recordset. The control cannot be used to update the server data store. To instantiate the control in a Web page, an <OBJECT> tag is used:

```
<OBJECT CLASSID="clsid:333C7BC4-460F-11D0-BC04-0080C7055A83"
       ID="dsoBookList" WIDTH=0 HEIGHT=0>
 <PARAM NAME="DataURL" VALUE="/data/booklist.txt">
 <PARAM NAME="FieldDelim" VALUE=";">
 <PARAM NAME="UseHeader" VALUE="true">
 <PARAM NAME="Sort" VALUE="tCategory; -dReleasedate">
 <PARAM NAME="Filter" VALUE="tCode=16-1*" >
 <PARAM NAME="EscapeChar" VALUE="\">
</OBJECT>
```

The <PARAM> elements are used to set the properties of the control at design time. They can be changed at run-time using script code. The following tables list the properties, methods and events for the control.

Properties of the TDC	Return Type	Description
AppendData	Boolean	If True, specifies that the Reset method will attempt to append returned data to the existing recordset rather than replacing the recordset. Default value is False.
CaseSensitive	Boolean	Specifies whether string comparisons will be case sensitive. Default is True.
CharSet	String	Specifies the character set for the data. Default is windows-1252 (Western).
DataURL	String	The URL or location of the source text data file.
EscapeChar	String	Single character string that is used to avoid the meaning of the other special characters specified by the FieldDelim, RowDelim, and TextQualifier properties.
FieldDelim	String	Specifies the character in the file that delimits each column (field). Default –if none specified– is a comma. Only a single character may be used.
Filter	String	Specifies the complete filter that will be applied to the data, such as "Name=Jonson". An asterisk acts as a wildcard for any set of characters.
FilterColumn	String	Name of the column to filter on. Not supported in all versions of the TDC.

Properties of the TDC	Return Type	Description
FilterCriterion	String	The criteria for the filter, can be <, <=, >, >=, =, or <>. Not supported in all versions of the TDC.
FilterValue	String	The value to match values in FilterColumn with when filtering. Not supported in all versions of the TDC.
Language	String	Specifies the language of the data file. Default is en-us (US English).
ReadyState	Integer	Indicates the state of the control as data is received. Can be one of the ADCReadyStateEnum constants, as detailed in Appendix G. Read only.
RowDelim	String	Specifies the character in the file that delimits each row (record). Default if not specified is a carriage return. Only a single character may be used.
Sort	String	Specifies the sort order for the data, as a comma-delimited list of column names. Prefix column name with a minus sign (-) for descending order.
SortAscending	Boolean	The sort direction for the column. The default is ascending order (True). Use False for descending order. Not supported in all versions of the TDC.
SortColumn	String	Name of the column to sort on. Not supported in all versions of the TDC.
TextQualifier	String	The character in the data file used to enclose field values. Default is the double-quote (") character.
UseHeader	Boolean	If True, specifies that the first line of the data file is a set of column (field) names and (optionally) the field data type definitions.

Methods of the TDC	Description
Reset	Updates the local recordset to reflect current filter and sort criteria.

Events of the TDC	Description
onreadystatechange	Occurs when the value of the ReadyState property changes.

The RDS DataSpace Object

The DataSpace object is responsible for caching the recordset on the client, and connecting it to a data source control. To instantiate the object in a Web page, an <OBJECT> tag is used:

```
<OBJECT ID="dspDataSpace"
        CLASSID="CLSID:BD96C556-65A3-11D0-983A-00C04FC29E36">
</OBJECT>
```

A DataSpace object is also created automatically when a data source object (such as the RDS/ADC) is instantiated. The DataSpace object exposes one property and one method:

Properties of the RDS DataSpace Object	Return Type	Description
InternetTimeout	Long	Indicates the timeout (in milliseconds) for the HTTP connection.

Methods of the RDS Dataspace Object	Description
CreateObject	Creates a data factory or custom object of type specified by a class string, at a location specified by the connection (address) parameter.

Methods Syntax

variant = *dataspace*.CreateObject(*bstrProgId* As String, *bstrConnection* As String)

For a connection over HTTP, the connection parameter is the URL of the server, while over DCOM the UNC machine name is used. When the CreateObject method is used to create in-process objects, the connection should be a null string.

The RDS DataFactory Object

The DataFactory object handles transport of the data from server to client and vice versa. It creates a stub and proxy that can communicate over HTTP. To instantiate the object, the CreateObject method of an existing DataSpace control is used. The class string for the DataFactory object is RDSServer.DataFactory, and the address of the server on which the object is to be created must also be provided:

```
<OBJECT ID="dspDataSpace"
        CLASSID="CLSID:BD96C556-65A3-11D0-983A-00C04FC29E36">
</OBJECT>
...
<SCRIPT LANGUAGE="JavaScript">
  <myDataFactory = dspDataSpace.CreateObject("RDSServer.DataFactory",
                                    "http://servername.com");
</SCRIPT>
```

A `DataFactory` object is also created automatically when a data source object (such as the RDS/ADC) is instantiated. The `DataFactory` object provides four methods:

Methods of the RDS Datafactory Object	Return Type	Description
ConvertToString	String	Converts a recordset into a MIME64-encoded string.
CreateRecordSet	Object	Creates and returns an empty recordset.
Query	Object	Executes a valid SQL string query over a specified connection and returns an ADO recordset object.
SubmitChanges		Marshals the records and submits them to the server for updating the source data store.

Methods Syntax

string = *datafactory*.`ConvertToString`(*recordset* As Object)
(Set) *recordset* = *datafactory*.`CreateRecordSet`(*varColumnInfos* As Variant)
(Set) *recordset* = *datafactory*.`Query`(*bstrConnection* As String, *bstrQuery* As String)
datafactory.`SubmitChanges`(*bstrConnection* As String, *pRecordset* As Object)

RDS Constants

ADCPROP_UPDATECRITERIA_ENUM

Name	Value	Description
adCriteriaAllCols	1	Collisions should be detected if there is a change to any column.
adCriteriaKey	0	Collisions should be detected if there is a change to the key column.
adCriteriaTimeStamp	3	Collisions should be detected if a row has been accessed.
adCriteriaUpdCols	2	Collisions should be detected if there is a change to columns being updated.

RDS Constants

ADCExecuteOptionEnum

Name	Value	Description
adcExecAsync	2	The next Refresh of the recordset is executed asynchronously.
adcExecSync	1	The next Refresh of the recordset is executed synchronously.

ADCFetchOptionEnum

Name	Value	Description
adcFetchAsync	3	Records are fetched in the background and control is returned to the application immediately. Attempts to access a record not yet read will cause control to return immediately, and the nearest record to the sought record returned. This indicates that the end of the recordset has been reached, even though there may be more records.
adcFetchBackground	2	The first batch of records is read and control returns to the application. Access to records not in the first batch will cause a wait until the requested record is fetched.
adcFetchUpFront	1	The complete Recordset is fetched before control is returned to the application.

ADCReadyStateEnum

Name	Value	Description
adcReadyStateComplete	4	All rows have been fetched.
adcReadyStateInteractive	3	Rows are still being fetched, although some rows are available.
adcReadyStateLoaded	2	The recordset is not available for use as the rows are still being loaded.

ADOX Object Summary

Microsoft ActiveX Data Objects 2.1 Extensions for DDL and Security Library Reference

The ADOX Objects

Name	Description
Catalog	Acts as a parent for the `Tables`, `Groups`, `Users`, `Procedures` and `Views` collections.
Column	An individual `Column` in a `Table`, `Index` or `Key`.
Columns	Contains one or more `Column` objects.
Group	An individual `Group` account describing data store permissions, and containing a `Users` collection describing the members of the group.
Groups	Contains one or more `Group` objects.
Index	An individual index on a `Table`, containing a `Columns` collection describing the columns that comprise the index.
Indexes	Contains one or more `Index` objects.
Key	An individual `Key` representing a primary or foreign key for a table, and containing a `Columns` collection to describe the columns that the `Key` comprises.
Keys	Contains one or more `Key` objects.
Procedure	Describes a stored procedure, and contains an ADO `Command` object to obtain the details of the procedure.
Procedures	Contains one or more `Procedure` objects.

Table Continued on Following Page

Name	Description
Properties	Contains one or more Property objects.
Property	Describes an individual property of a particular object.
Table	Describes an individual data store table, and contains Columns, Indexes, Keys and Properties collections.
Tables	Contains one or more Table objects.
User	An individual User account describing an authorized user of the data store, and containing a Groups collection to indicate the groups to which the user belongs.
Users	Contains one or more User objects.
View	Describes a virtual table, or a filtered set of records from the data store, and contains and ADO Command object to obtain the exact details of the view.
Views	Contains one or more View objects.

The Catalog Object

Methods of the Catalog Object	Return Type	Description
Create	Variant	Creates a new catalog, using its argument as a connection string for the catalog.
GetObjectOwner	String	Obtains the name of the user or group that owns a particular catalog object.
SetObjectOwner		Sets the owner for a particular catalog object.

Properties of the Catalog Object	Return Type	Description
ActiveConnection	Object	Sets or returns the ADO Connection object or string to which the catalog belongs.

Collections of the Catalog Object	Return Type	Description
Groups	Groups	Contains one or more Group objects. Read only
Procedures	Procedures	Contains one or more Procedure objects. Read only
Tables	Tables	Contains one or more Table objects. Read only

Collections of the Catalog Object	Return Type	Description
Users	Users	Contains one or more User objects. Read only
Views	Views	Contains one or more View objects. Read only

The Column Object

Properties of the Column Object	Return Type	Description
Attributes	ColumnAttributes Enum	Describes the characteristics of the column.
DefinedSize	Long	Indicates the maximum size for a column.
Name	String	The name of the column.
NumericScale	Byte	The numeric scale of the column. Read only for existing columns.
ParentCatalog	Catalog	Indicates the Catalog to which the columns parent object belongs.
Precision	Integer	The maximum precision of data in the column. Read only for existing columns.
RelatedColumn	String	For key columns this indicates the name of the related column in the related table. Read only for existing columns.
SortOrder	SortOrderEnum	Indicates the order in which the column is sorted. Only applies to columns in an Index.
Type	DataTypeEnum	Identifies the data type of the column. Read only once the column is appended to a collection.

Collections of the Column Object	Return Type	Description
Properties	Properties	Contains one or more provider specific column properties. Read only

The Columns Collection

Methods of the Columns Collection	Return Type	Description
Append		Appends a `Column` object to the `Columns` collection.
Delete		Deletes a `Column` object from the `Columns` collection.
Refresh		Updates the `Column` objects in the `Columns` collection.

Properties of the Columns Collection	Return Type	Description
Count	Integer	Indicates the number of `Column` objects in the `Columns` collection. Read only
Item	Column	Allows indexing into the `Columns` collection to reference a specific `Column` object. Read only

The Group Object

Methods of the Group Object	Return Type	Description
GetPermissions	RightsEnum	Obtains the permissions on a catalog object for the `Group`.
SetPermissions		Sets the permissions on a catalog object for the `Group`.

Properties of the Group Object	Return Type	Description
Name	String	The name of the group.

Collections of the Group Object	Return Type	Description
Users	Users	Contains the `User` objects that belong to this group. Read only

The Groups Collection

Methods of the Groups Collection	Return Type	Description
Append		Appends a Group object to the Groups collection.
Delete		Deletes a Group object from the Groups collection.
Refresh		Updates the Group objects in the Groups collection.

Properties of the Groups Collection	Return Type	Description
Count	Integer	Indicates the number of Group objects in the Groups collection. Read only
Item	Column	Allows indexing into the Groups collection to reference a specific Group object. Read only

The Index Object

Properties of the Index Object	Return Type	Description
Clustered	Boolean	Indicates whether or not the Index is clustered. Read only on Index objects already appended to a collection.
IndexNulls	AllowNullsEnum	Indicates whether or not index entries are created for records that have null values. Read only on Index objects already appended to a collection.
Name	String	The name of the Index.
PrimaryKey	Boolean	Indicates whether or not the index is the primary key. Read only on Index objects already appended to a collection.
Unique	Boolean	Indicates whether or not the keys in the Index must be unique. Read only on Index objects already appended to a collection.

Collections of the Index Object	Return Type	Description
Columns	Columns	Contains one or more `Column` objects, which make up the `Index` object. Read only
Properties	Properties	Contains provider specific properties for the `Index` object. Read only

The Indexes Collection

Methods of the Indexes Collection	Return Type	Description
Append		Appends a `Index` object to the `Indexes` collection.
Delete		Deletes a `Index` object from the `Indexes` collection.
Refresh		Updates the `Index` objects in the `Indexes` collection.

Properties of the Indexes Collection	Return Type	Description
Count	Integer	Indicates the number of `Index` objects in the `Indexes` collection. Read only
Item	Column	Allows indexing into the `Indexes` collection to reference a specific `Index` object. Read only

The Key Object

Properties of the Key Object	Return Type	Description
DeleteRule	RuleEnum	Indicates what happens to the key values when a primary key is deleted. Read only on `Key` objects already appended to a collection.
Name	String	The name of the Key.
RelatedTable	String	For foreign keys indicates the name of the foreign table.
Type	KeyTypeEnum	Specifies the type of the Key. Read only on `Key` objects already appended to a collection.

Properties of the Key Object	Return Type	Description
UpdateRule	RuleEnum	Indicates what happens to the key values when a primary key is updated. Read only on Key objects already appended to a collection.

Collections of the Key Object	Return Type	Description
Columns	Columns	Contains one or more Column objects that make up the Key. Read only

The Keys Collection

Methods of the Keys Collection	Return Type	Description
Append		Appends a Key object to the Keys collection.
Delete		Deletes a Key object from the Keys collection.
Refresh		Updates the Key objects in the Keys collection.

Properties of the Keys Collection	Return Type	Description
Count	Integer	Indicates the number of Key objects in the Keys collection. Read only
Item	Column	Allows indexing into the Keys collection to reference a specific Key object. Read only

The Procedure Object

Properties of the Procedure Object	Return Type	Description
Command	Object	Specifies an ADO Command object containing the details of the procedure.
DateCreated	Variant	The date the Procedure was created. Read only
DateModified	Variant	The date the Procedure was last modified. Read only
Name	String	The name of the Procedure. Read only

The Procedures Collection

Methods of the Procedures Collection	Return Type	Description
Append		Appends a `Procedure` object to the `Procedures` collection.
Delete		Deletes a `Procedure` object from the `Procedures` collection.
Refresh		Updates the `Procedure` objects in the `Procedures` collection.

Properties of the Procedures Collection	Return Type	Description
Count	Integer	Indicates the number of `Procedure` objects in the `Procedures` collection. Read only
Item	Column	Allows indexing into the `Procedures` collection to reference a specific `Procedure` object. Read only

The Properties Collection

Methods of the Properties Collection	Return Type	Description
Refresh		Updates the `Property` objects in the `Properties` collection.

Properties of the Properties Collection	Return Type	Description
Count	Integer	Indicates the number of `Property` objects in the `Properties` collection. Read only
Item	Column	Allows indexing into the `Properties` collection to reference a specific `Property` object. Read only

The Property Object

Properties of the Property Object	Return Type	Description
Attributes	Integer	Indicates one or more characteristics of the Property.
Name	String	The Property Name. Read only
Type	DataTypeEnum	The data type of the Property. Read only
Value	Variant	The value assigned to the Property.

The Table Object

Properties of the Table Object	Return Type	Description
DateCreated	Variant	The date the Table was created. Read only
DateModified	Variant	The date the Table was last modified. Read only
Name	String	The name of the Table.
ParentCatalog	Catalog	The Catalog to which the Table belongs.
Type	String	Indicates whether the Table is a permanent, temporary, or system table. Read only

Collections of the Table Object	Return Type	Description
Columns	Columns	One or more Column objects that make up the Table. Read only
Indexes	Indexes	Zero or more Index objects that belong to the Table. Read only
Keys	Keys	Zero or more Key objects that the Table contains. Read only
Properties	Properties	One or more Property objects describing provider specific properties. Read only

The Tables Collection

Methods of the Tables Collection	Return Type	Description
Append		Appends a Table object to the Tables collection.
Delete		Deletes a Table object from the Tables collection.
Refresh		Updates the Table objects in the Tables collection.

Properties of the Tables Collection	Return Type	Description
Count	Integer	Indicates the number of Table objects in the Tables collection. Read only
Item	Column	Allows indexing into the Tables collection to reference a specific Table object. Read only

The User Object

Methods of the User Object	Return Type	Description
ChangePassword		Changes the password for a User.
GetPermissions	RightsEnum	Gets the permissions on a Catalog object for a User.
SetPermissions		Sets the permissions on a Catalog object for a User.

Properties of the User Object	Return Type	Description
Name	String	The user name.

Collections of the User Object	Return Type	Description
Groups	Groups	One or more Group objects, to which the user belongs. Read only

The Users Collection

Methods of the Users Collection	Return Type	Description
Append		Appends a User object to the Users collection.
Delete		Deletes a User object from the Users collection.
Refresh		Updates the User objects in the Users collection.

Properties of the Users Collection	Return Type	Description
Count	Integer	Indicates the number of User objects in the Users collection. Read only
Item	Column	Allows indexing into the Users collection to reference a specific User object. Read only

The View Object

Properties of the View Object	Return Type	Description
Command	Object	Specifies an ADO Command object containing the details of the View.
DateCreated	Variant	The date the View was created. Read only
DateModified	Variant	The date the View was last modified. Read only
Name	String	The name of the View. Read only

The Views Collection

Methods of the Views Collection	Return Type	Description
Append		Appends a View object to the Views collection.
Delete		Deletes a View object from the Views collection.
Refresh		Updates the View objects in the Views collection.

Properties of the Views Collection	Return Type	Description
Count	Integer	Indicates the number of View objects in the Views collection. Read only
Item	Column	Allows indexing into the Views collection to reference a specific View object. Read only

Method Calls

The Catalog Object

Variant = Catalog.Create(*ConnectString As String*)
String = Catalog.GetObjectOwner(*ObjectName As String, _*
ObjectType As ObjectTypeEnum, [ObjectTypeId As Variant])
Catalog.SetObjectOwner(*ObjectName As String, ObjectType As ObjectTypeEnum, _*
UserName As String, [ObjectTypeId As Variant])

The Columns Collection

Columns.Append(*Item As Variant, Type As DataTypeEnum, DefinedSize As Integer*)
Columns.Delete(*Item As Variant*)
Columns.Refresh

The Group Object

RightsEnum = Group.GetPermissions(*Name As Variant, _*
ObjectType As ObjectTypeEnum, [ObjectTypeId As Variant])
Group.SetPermissions(*Name As Variant, ObjectType As ObjectTypeEnum, _*
Action As ActionEnum, Rights As RightsEnum, Inherit As InheritTypeEnum, _
[ObjectTypeId As Variant])

The Groups Collection

Groups.Append(*Item As Variant*)
Groups.Delete(*Item As Variant*)
Groups.Refresh

The Indexes Collection

Indexes.Append(*Item As Variant, [Columns As Variant]*)
Indexes.Delete(*Item As Variant*)
Indexes.Refresh

The Keys Collection

Keys.Append(*Item As Variant, Type As KeyTypeEnum, Column As Variant, _*
RelatedTable As String, RelatedColumn As String)
Keys.Delete(*Item As Variant*)
Keys.Refresh

The Procedures Collection

Procedures.Append(*Name As String, Command As Object*)
Procedures.Delete(*Item As Variant*)
Procedures.Refresh

The Properties Collection

Properties.Refresh

The Tables Collection

Tables.Append(*Item As Variant*)
Tables.Delete(*Item As Variant*)
Tables.Refresh

The User Object

User.ChangePassword(*OldPassword As String, NewPassord As String*)
RightsEnum = User.GetPermissions(*Name As Variant, _*
    ObjectType As ObjectTypeEnum, [ObjectTypeId As Variant])
User.SetPermissions(*Name As Variant, ObjectType As ObjectTypeEnum, _*
    Action As ActionEnum, Rights As RightsEnum, Inherit As InheritTypeEnum, _
    [ObjectTypeId As Variant])

The Users Collection

Users.Append(*Item As Variant, [Password As String]*)
Users.Delete(*Item As Variant*)
Users.Refresh

The Views Collection

Views.Append(*Name As String, Command As Object*)
Views.Delete(*Item As Variant*)
Views.Refresh

ADOX Constants

ActionEnum

Constant Name	Value	Description
adAccessDeny	3	Deny the specific permissions to the Group or User.
adAccessGrant	1	Grant the specific permissions to the Group or User. Other permissions may remain in effect.
adAccessRevoke	4	Revoke any specific access rights to the Group or User.
adAccessSet	2	Set the exact permissions for the Group or User. Other permissions will not remain in effect.

Note: The documentation indicates that adAccessAuditSuccess and adAccessAuditFailure are allowable values for the Action. This is incorrect – these constants are not supported.

AllowNullsEnum

Constant Name	Value	Description
adIndexNullsAllow	0	Key columns with null values have index values.
adIndexNullsDisallow	1	Do not allow index entries if the key columns are null.
adIndexNullsIgnore	2	Null values in key columns are ignored and an index entry is not created.
adIndexNullsIgnoreAny	4	Null values in any part of the key (for multiple columns) are ignored, and an index entry is not created.

Appendix I

ColumnAttributesEnum

Constant Name	Value	Description
adColFixed	1	The column is of a fixed length.
adColNullable	2	The column may contain null values.

DataTypeEnum

The ADOX data type constants are the same as the ADO data type constants. See the listing for DataTypeEnum in Appendix B.

InheritTypeEnum

Constant Name	Value	Description
adInheritBoth	3	Permissions for the object are inherited by both objects and other containers.
adInheritContainers	2	Permissions for the object are inherited by other containers.
adInheritNone	0	No permissions are inherited.
adInheritNoPropogate	4	The `adInheritObjects` and `adInheritContainers` permissions are not propagated to child objects.
adInheritObjects	1	Permissions are only inherited by objects that are not containers.

Note: *The documentation states that* `adInheritOnly` *is an allowable option for the InheritType. This is incorrect – this constant is not supported.*

KeyTypeEnum

Constant Name	Value	Description
adKeyForeign	2	The key is a foreign key.
adKeyPrimary	1	The key is a primary key.
adKeyUnique	3	The key is unique.

ObjectTypeEnum

Constant Name	Value	Description
adPermObjColumn	2	The object is a column.
adPermObjDatabase	3	The object is a database.
adPermObjProcedure	4	The object is a procedure.

Constant Name	Value	Description
adPermObjProviderSpecific	-1	The object is of a provider specific type.
adPermObjTable	1	The object is a table.
adPermObjView	5	The object is a view.

Note: The documentation mentions adPermObjSchema, adPermObjDomain, adPermObjCollation, adPermObjSchemaRowset, adPermObjCharacterSet, adPermObjTranslation *as allowable options for the object type. This is incorrect – these constants are not supported.*

RightsEnum

Constant Name	Value	Description
adRightCreate	16384	The User or Group has permission to create the object.
adRightDelete	65536	The User or Group has permission to delete the object.
adRightDrop	256	The User or Group has permission to drop the object.
adRightExclusive	512	The User or Group has permission to obtain exclusive access to the object.
adRightExecute	536870912	The User or Group has permission to execute the object.
adRightFull	268435456	The User or Group has full permissions on the object.
adRightInsert	32768	The User or Group has permission to insert the object.
adRightMaximumAllowed	33554432	The User or Group has the maximum number of permissions allowed by the provider.
adRightNone	0	The User or Group has no permissions on the object.
adRightRead	-2147483648	The User or Group has permission to read the object.

Table Continued on Following Page

Constant Name	Value	Description
adRightReadDesign	1024	The User or Group has permission to read the design of the object.
adRightReadPermissions	131072	The User or Group has permission to read the permissions of the object.
adRightReference	8192	The User or Group has permission to reference the object.
adRightUpdate	1073741824	The User or Group has permission to update the object.
adRightWithGrant	4096	The User or Group has permission to grant permissions to other Users or Groups.
adRightWriteDesign	2048	The User or Group has permission to change the design of the object.
adRightWriteOwner	524288	The User or Group has permission to change the owner of the object.
adRightWritePermissions	262144	The User or Group has permission to change the permissions of the object.

RuleEnum

Constant Name	Value	Description
adRICascade	1	Updates and deletes are cascaded.
adRINone	0	Updates and deletes are not cascaded.
adRISetDefault	3	Set the foreign key to its default value for updates and deletes.
adRISetNull	2	Set the foreign key to null for updates and deletes.

SortOrderEnum

Constant Name	Value	Description
adSortAscending	1	The key column is in ascending order.
adSortDescending	2	The key column is in descending order.

DBPROPVAL_NC

Constant Name	Value	Description
DBPROPVAL_NC_END	1	Null values are collated at the end of the list, irrespective of the collation order.
DBPROPVAL_NC_HIGH	2	Null values are collated at the high end of the list.
DBPROPVAL_NC_LOW	4	Null values are collated at the low end of the list.
DBPROPVAL_NC_START	8	Null values are collated at the start of the list, irrespective of the collation order.

DBPROPVAL_IN

Constant Name	Value	Description
DBPROPVAL_IN_ DISALLOWNULL	1	Keys containing NULL values are not allowed. Generate an error if an attempt is made to insert a key that contains NULL.
DBPROPVAL_IN_ IGNORENULL	2	Keys containing NULL values are allowed, but are ignored and not added to the index. No error is generated.
DBPROPVAL_IN_ IGNOREANYNULL	4	Keys consisting of multi-columns will allow a NULL in any column, but the key is ignored and not added to the index. No error is generated.

DBPROPVAL_IT

Constant Name	Value	Description
DBPROPVAL_IT_BTREE	1	The index is a B+ tree.
DBPROPVAL_IT_CONTENT	3	The index is a content index.
DBPROPVAL_IT_HASH	2	The index is a hash file using linear or extensible hashing.
DBPROPVAL_IT_OTHER	4	The index is some other type of index.

ADOX Properties Collection

Property Support

The following table shows a list of all OLE DB properties, and indicates which of them are supported by Microsoft Access and Microsoft SQL Server. The property support is the same whether using the OLE DB Provider for ODBC or the native OLE DB Providers. Since this list contains dynamic properties, not every property may show up under all circumstances. Other providers may also implement properties not listed in this table.

A tick indicates the property is supported, and a blank space indicates it is not supported.

Property Name	Object	Jet	SQL
Auto-Update	Index	✓	
Autoincrement	Column	✓	✓
Clustered	Index	✓	✓
Default	Column	✓	✓
Description	Column	✓	
Fill Factor	Index	✓	✓
Fixed Length	Column	✓	✓
Increment	Column	✓	
Index Type	Index	✓	
Initial Size	Index	✓	
Jet OLEDB:Allow Zero Length	Column	✓	

Table Continued on Following Page

Property Name	Object	Jet	SQL
Jet OLEDB:AutoGenerate	Column	✓	
Jet OLEDB:Cache Link Name/Password	Table	✓	
Jet OLEDB:Column Validation Rule	Column	✓	
Jet OLEDB:Column Validation Text	Column	✓	
Jet OLEDB:Compressed UNICODE Strings	Column	✓	
Jet OLEDB:Create Link	Table	✓	
Jet OLEDB:Exclusive Link	Table	✓	
Jet OLEDB:Hyperlink	Column	✓	
Jet OLEDB:IISAM Not Last Column	Column	✓	
Jet OLEDB:Link Datasource	Table	✓	
Jet OLEDB:Link Provider String	Table	✓	
Jet OLEDB:One BLOB per Page	Column	✓	
Jet OLEDB:Remote Table Name	Table	✓	
Jet OLEDB:Table Hidden In Access	Table	✓	
Jet OLEDB:Table Validation Rule	Table	✓	
Jet OLEDB:Table Validation Text	Table	✓	
NULL Collation	Index	✓	
NULL Keys	Index	✓	
Nullable	Column	✓	✓
Primary Key	Column		✓
Primary Key	Index	✓	✓
Seed	Column	✓	
Sort Bookmarks	Index	✓	
Temporary Index	Index	✓	
Temporary Table	Table	✓	✓
Unique	Column		✓
Unique	Index	✓	✓

The Column Object's Properties

Name	Description	Data Type
Autoincrement	Indicates whether or not the column is autoincrementing.	Boolean
Default	Specifies the default value for the column, to be used if no explicit value is supplied.	Variant
Description	The column description.	String
Fixed Length	Indicates whether or not the column holds fixed length data.	Boolean
Increment	The value by which auto-increment columns are increased.	Long
Jet OLEDB:Allow Zero Length	Indicates whether or not zero length strings can be inserted into the field.	Boolean
Jet OLEDB:Autogenerate	Indicates whether or not, for a GUID data type, a GUID should be automatically created.	Boolean
Jet OLEDB:Column Validation Rule	The validation rule to apply to column values before allowing the column to be set.	String
Jet OLEDB:Column Validation Text	Errors string to display if changes to a row do not meet the column validation rule.	String
Jet OLEDB:Compressed UNICODE Strings	Indicates whether or not Jet should compress UNICODE strings. Only applicable to Jet 4.0 databases.	Boolean
Jet OLEDB:Hyperlink	Indicates whether or not the column is a hyperlink.	Boolean
Jet OLEDB:IISAM Not Last Column	When creating columns (or a table) for installable IISAMS, this indicates whether or nor this is the last column.	Boolean
Jet OLEDB:One BLOB Per Page	Indicates whether or not BLOB columns can share data pages.	Boolean
Nullable	Indicates whether or not the column can contain NULL values.	Boolean
Primary Key	Indicates whether or not the column is part of the primary key.	Boolean
Seed	The initial seed value of an auto-increment column.	Long
Unique	Indicates whether or not the column allows unique values.	Boolean

The Index Object's Properties

Property Name	Description	DataType
Auto-Update	Indicates whether or not the index is maintained automatically when changes are made to rows.	Boolean
Clustered	Indicates whether or not the index is clustered.	Boolean
Fill Factor	Identifies the fill-factor of the index. This is the storage use of page-nodes during index creation. It is always 100 for the Jet provider.	Long
Index Type	The type of the index.	DBPROPVAL_IT
Initial Size	The total number of bytes allocated to the index when it is first created.	Long
NULL Collation	Specifies how NULL values are collated in the index.	DBPROPVAL_NC
NULL Keys	Specifies whether key values containing NULLs are allowed.	DBPROPVAL_IN
Primary Key	Indicates whether or not the index represents the primary key on the table.	Boolean
Sort Bookmarks	Indicates whether or not repeated keys are sorted by bookmarks.	Boolean
Temporary Index	Indicates whether or not the index is temporary.	Boolean
Unique	Indicates whether or not index keys must be unique.	Boolean

The Table Object's Properties

Property Name	Description	Data Type
Jet OLEDB:Cache Link Name/Password	Indicates whether or not the authentication information for a linked table should be cached locally in the Jet database.	Boolean
Jet OLEDB:Create Link	Indicates whether or not a link is created to a remote data source when creating a new table.	Boolean

Property Name	Description	Data Type
Jet OLEDB:Exclusive Link	Indicates whether or not the remote data source is opened exclusively when creating a link.	Boolean
Jet OLEDB:Link Datasource	The name of the remote data source to link to.	String
Jet OLEDB:Link Provider String	The connection string to the remote provider.	String
Jet OLEDB:Remote Table Name	The name of the remote table in a link.	String
Jet OLEDB:Table Hidden In Access	Indicates whether or not the table is shown in the Access user interface.	Boolean
Jet OLEDB:Table Validation Rule	The validation rule to apply to row values before committing changes to the row.	String
Jet OLEDB:Table Validation Text	Errors string to display if changes to a row do not meet the table validation rule.	String
Temporary Table	Indicates whether or not the table is a temporary table.	Boolean

ADOMD Object Summary

Microsoft ActiveX Data Objects (Multi-dimensional) 1.0 Library Reference

The ADOMD Objects

Name	Description
Axes	Contains an `Axis` object for each axis in the `Cellset`.
Axis	An `Axis` of a `Cellset`, containing members of one or more dimensions.
Catalog	Contains the multi-dimensional schema information.
Cell	The data at an intersection of `Axis` coordinates.
Cellset	The results of a multi-dimensional query.
CubeDef	A `Cube` from a multi-dimensional schema, containing related `Dimension` objects.
CubeDefs	One or more `CubeDef` objects contained within a `Catalog`.
Dimension	A dimension of a multi-dimensional cube, containing one or more `Hierarchy` objects.
Dimensions	One or more `Dimension` objects, making up the dimensions of a `CubeDef`.
Hierarchies	One or more `Hierarchy` objects, representing the ways a `Dimension` can be aggregated.

Table Continued on Following Page

Name	Description
Hierarchy	Indicates one way in which aggregation of a `Dimension` can take place.
Level	Contains the members which make up the `Hierarchy`.
Levels	Contains one or more `Level` objects contained within the `Hierarchy`.
Member	An individual member of a the `Members` collection
Members	A collection of `Member` objects for the level.
Position	A position in the cellset.
Positions	A collection of `Position` objects in the cellset.

The Axes Collection

Methods of the Axes Collection	Return Type	Description
Refresh		Refreshes the collection with details from the provider

Properties of the Axes Collection	Return Type	Description
Count	Long	The number of `Axis` objects in the collection. Read only
Item	Axis	The default property, allowing indexing into the collection. Read only

The Axis Object

Properties of the Axis Object	Return Type	Description
DimensionCount	Long	The number of Dimensions on this `Axis`. Read only
Name	String	The name of the `Axis`. Read only

Collections of the Axis Object	Return Type	Description
Positions	Positions	A collection of `Position` objects in the `Axis`. Read only
Properties	Properties	A collection of provider specific properties for the `Axis`. Read only

The Catalog Object

Properties of the Catalog Object	Return Type	Description
ActiveConnection	Object	The ADO `Connection` object or string, indicating the data provider to which the catalog is attached.
Name	String	The name of the `Catalog`. Read only

Collections of the Catalog Object	Return Type	Description
CubeDefs	CubeDefs	A collection of `CubeDef` objects available in the catalog. Read only

The Cell Object

Properties

Properties of the Cell Object	Return Type	Description
FormattedValue	String	The formatted value of the cell.
Ordinal	Long	The unique number identifying a cell. Read only
Value	Variant	The value of the cell.

Collections of the Cell Object	Return Type	Description
Positions	Positions	A collection of `Position` objects available for the cell. Read only
Properties	Properties	A collection of provider-specific properties for the cell. Read only

The Cellset Object

Methods of the Cellset Object	Return Type	Description
Close		Closes the cellset.
Open		Opens the cellset.

Properties of the Cellset Object	Return Type	Description
ActiveConnection	Object	The ADO Connection object or string, indicating the data provider to which the catalog is attached.
FilterAxis	Axis	Indicates the filtering information for the cellset. Read only
Item	Cell	The default property, which allows indexing into the cellset. Read only
Source	Variant	The multi-dimensional query used to generate the cellset.
State	Long	Indicates whether the cellset is open or closed. Read only

Collections of the Cellset Object	Return Type	Description
Axes	Axes	A collection of Axis objects in the cellset. Read only
Properties	Properties	A collection of provider-specific properties for the cellset. Read only

The CubeDef Object

Properties of the CubeDef Object	Return Type	Description
Description	String	Text describing the cube. Read only
Name	String	The name of the cube. Read only

Collections of the CubeDef Object	Return Type	Description
Dimensions	Dimensions	A collection of Dimensions available in the cube. Read only
Properties	Properties	A collection of provider-specific properties for the CubeDef. Read only

The CubeDefs Collection

Methods of the CubeDefs Collection	Return Type	Description
Refresh		Refreshes the CubeDef objects from the provider.

Properties of the CubeDefs Collection	Return Type	Description
Count	Long	Indicates the number of `CubeDef` objects in the collection. Read only
Item	CubeDef	The default property, which allows indexing into the collection. Read only

The Dimension Object

Properties of the Dimension Object	Return Type	Description
Description	String	A description of the dimension. Read only
Name	String	The name of the dimension. Read only
UniqueName	String	The unique name of the dimension. Read only

Collections of the Dimension Object	Return Type	Description
Hierarchies	Hierarchies	A collection of hierarchies available in the dimension. Read only
Properties	Properties	A collection of provider-specific properties for the dimension. Read only

The Dimensions Collection

Methods of the Dimensions Collection	Return Type	Description
Refresh		Refreshes the `Dimensions` collection from the provider.

Properties of the Dimensions Collection	Return Type	Description
Count	Long	The number of `Dimension` objects in the collection. Read only
Item	Dimension	The default property, which allows indexing into the collection. Read only

The Hierarchies Collection

Methods of the Hierarchies Collection	Return Type	Description
Refresh		Refreshes the `Hierarchies` collection from the provider.

Properties of the Hierarchies Collection	Return Type	Description
Count	Long	The number of Hierarchy objects in the collection. Read only
Item	Hierarchy	The default property, which allows indexing into the collection. Read only

The Hierarchy Object

Properties of the Hierarchy Object	Return Type	Description
Description	String	The description of the hierarchy. Read only
Name	String	The name of the hierarchy. Read only
UniqueName	String	The unique name of the hierarchy. Read only

Collections of the Hierarchy Object	Return Type	Description
Levels	Levels	A collection of levels in the hierachy. Read only
Properties	Properties	A collection of provider specific properties for thehierarchy. Read only

The Level Object

Properties of the Level Object	Return Type	Description
Caption	String	The caption of the level. Read only
Depth	Integer	How deep in the hierarchy this level is. Read only
Description	String	The description of the level. Read only
Name	String	The name of the level. Read only
UniqueName	String	The unique name of the level. Read only

Collections of the Level Object	Return Type	Description
Members	Members	A collection of Member objects available in this level. Read only
Properties	Properties	A collection of provider-specific properties for the level. Read only

The Levels Collection

Methods of the Levels Collection	Return Type	Description
Refresh		Refreshes the Levels collection from the provider.

Properties of the Levels Collection	Return Type	Description
Count	Long	The number of Level objects in the collection. Read only
Item	Level	The default property, which allows indexing into the collection. Read only

The Member Object

Properties of the Member Object	Return Type	Description
Caption	String	The caption of the member. Read only
ChildCount	Long	The number of children belonging to this member. Read only
Description	String	A description of the member. Read only
DrilledDown	Boolean	Indicates whether or not this is a leaf node (contains children). Read only
LevelDepth	Long	How deep in the collection this member is. Read only
LevelName	String	The name of the Level to which this member belongs. Read only
Name	String	The name of the member. Read only
Parent	Member	The Member object which is the parent of this member. Read only

Table Continued on Following Page

Properties of the Member Object	Return Type	Description
ParentSameAsPrev	Boolean	Indicates whether the `Parent` member is the same as the `Parent` member of the previous member in the collection. Read only
Type	MemberTypeEnum	The type of the member. Read only
UniqueName	String	The unique name of the member. Read only

Collections of the Member Object	Return Type	Description
Children	Members	A collection of `Member` objects which are children of this member. Read only
Properties	Properties	A collection of provider specific properties for the member. Read only

The Members Collection

Methods of the Members Collection	Return Type	Description
Refresh		Refreshes the `Members` collection from the provider.

Properties of the Members Collection	Return Type	Description
Count	Long	The number of `Member` objects in the collection. Read only
Item	Member	The default property, which allows indexing into the collection. Read only

The Position Object

Properties of the Position Object	Return Type	Description
Ordinal	Long	A unique identifier, indicating the location of the position in the collection. Read only

Collections of the Position Object	Return Type	Description
Members	Members	A collection of Member objects in this position. Read only

The Positions Collection

Methods of the Positions Collection	Return Type	Description
Refresh		Refreshes the Positions collection from the provider.

Properties of the Positions Collection	Return Type	Description
Count	Long	The number of Position objects in the collection. Read only
Item	Position	The default property, which allows indexing into the collection. Read only

ADOMD Method Calls

The Axes Collection
Axes.Refresh

The CubeDefs Collection
CubeDefs.Refresh

The Dimensions Collection
Dimensions.Refresh

The Hierarchies Collection
Hierarchies.Refresh

The Cellset Object
Cellset.Close
Cellset.Open(*[DataSource As Variant], [ActiveConnection As Variant]*)

The Levels Collection
Levels.Refresh

The Members Collection
Members.Refresh

The Positions Collection
Positions.Refresh

ADOMD Constants

MemberTypeEnum

Constant Name	Value	Description
adMemberAll	2	The member is the All member, at the top of the members hierachy.
adMemberFormula	4	The member identifies a formula.
adMemberMeasure	3	The member identifies a Measure.
adMemberRegular	1	The member identifies a regular member.
adMemberUnknown	0	The type of member is unknown.

MD_DIMTYPE

Constant Name	Value	Description
MD_DIMTYPE_UNKNOWN	0	The dimension type is unknown.
MD_DIMTYPE_TIME	1	The dimension is a time dimension.
MD_DIMTYPE_MEASURE	2	The dimension is a measure dimension.
MD_DIMTYPE_OTHER	3	The dimension is neither a time nor a measure dimenstion.

MDLEVEL_TYPE

Constant Name	Value	Description
MDLEVEL_TYPE_REGULAR	0	The level is a regular level
MDLEVEL_TYPE_ALL	1	The level identifies the top of the hierarchy, or All levels.
MDLEVEL_TYPE_CALCULATED	2	The level is a calculated level.
MDLEVEL_TYPE_TIME	4	The level is a time level.
MDLEVEL_TYPE_TIME_YEARS	20	The level is a time level, based on years.
MDLEVEL_TYPE_TIME_HALF_YEAR	36	The level is a time level, based on half-years.
MDLEVEL_TYPE_TIME_QUARTERS	68	The level is a time level, based on quarters.
MDLEVEL_TYPE_TIME_MONTHS	132	The level is a time level, based on months.
MDLEVEL_TYPE_TIME_WEEKS	260	The level is a time level, based on weeks.
MDLEVEL_TYPE_TIME_DAYS	516	The level is a time level, based on days.
MDLEVEL_TYPE_TIME_HOURS	772	The level is a time level, based on hours.
MDLEVEL_TYPE_TIME_MINUTES	1028	The level is a time level, based on minutes.
MDLEVEL_TYPE_TIME_SECONDS	2052	The level is a time level, based on seconds.
MDLEVEL_TYPE_TIME_UNDEFINED	4100	The level type is not defined.
MDLEVEL_TYPE_UNKNOWN	0	The level type is unknown.

MDMEASURE_AGGR

Constant Name	Value	Description
MDMEASURE_AGGR_SUM	1	The aggregate function is SUM.
MDMEASURE_AGGR_COUNT	2	The aggregate function is COUNT.
MDMEASURE_AGGR_MIN	3	The aggregate function is MIN.
MDMEASURE_AGGR_MAX	4	The aggregate function is MAX.

Constant Name	Value	Description
MDMEASURE_AGGR_AVG	5	The aggregate function is AVG.
MDMEASURE_AGGR_VAR	6	The aggregate function is VAR.
MDMEASURE_AGGR_STD	7	The aggregate function is one of SUM, COUNT, MIN, MAX, AVG, VAR, STDEV.
MDMEASURE_AGGR_CALCULATED	127	The aggregate function is derived from formula that is not a standard one.
MDMEASURE_AGGR_UNKNOWN	0	The aggregate function is not known.

MDPROPVAL_AU

Constant Name	Value	Description
MDPROPVAL_AU_UNSUPPORTED	0	Updating of aggregated cells is not supported.
MDPROPVAL_AU_UNCHANGED	1	Aggregated cells can be changed, but the cells that make up the aggregation remain unchanged.
MDPROPVAL_AU_UNKNOWN	2	Aggregated cells can be changed, but the cells that make up the aggregation remain undefined.

MDPROPVAL_FS

Constant Name	Value	Description
MDPROPVAL_FS_FULL_SUPPORT	1	The provider supports flattening.
MDPROPVAL_FS_GENERATED_COLUMN	2	The provider supports flattening by using dummy names.
MDPROPVAL_FS_GENERATED_DIMENSION	3	The provider supports flattening by generating one column per dimension.
MDPROPVAL_FS_NO_SUPPORT	4	The provider does not support flattening.

MDPROPVAL_MC

Constant Name	Value	Description
MDPROPVAL_MC_SINGLECASE	1	The provider supports simple case statements.
MDPROPVAL_MC_SEARCHEDCASE	2	The provider supports searched case statements.

MDPROPVAL_MD

Constant Name	Value	Description
MDPROPVAL_MD_BEFORE	2	The BEFORE flag is supported.
MDPROPVAL_MD_AFTER	4	The AFTER flag is supported.
MDPROPVAL_MD_SELF	1	The SELF flag is supported.

MDPROPVAL_MF

Constant Name	Value	Description
MDPROPVAL_MF_WITH_CALCMEMBERS	1	Calculated members are supported by use of the WITH clause.
MDPROPVAL_MF_WITH_NAMEDSETS	2	Named sets are supported by use of the WITH clause.
MDPROPVAL_MF_CREATE_CALCMEMBERS	4	Named calculated members are supported by use of the CREATE clause.
MDPROPVAL_MF_CREATE_NAMEDSETS	8	Named sets are supported by use of the CREATE clause.
MDPROPVAL_MF_SCOPE_SESSION	16	The scope value of SESSION is supported during the creation of named sets and calculated members.
MDPROPVAL_MF_SCOPE_GLOBAL	32	The scope value of GLOBAL is supported during the creation of named sets and calculated members

MDPROPVAL_MJC

Constant Name	Value	Description
MDPROPVAL_MJC_IMPLICITCUBE	4	An empty FROM clause is supported, and the cube is implictly resolved.
MDPROPVAL_MJC_SINGLECUBE	1	Only one cube is supported in the FROM clause.
MDPROPVAL_MJC_MULTICUBES	2	More than one cube is supported in the FROM clause.

MDPROPVAL_MMF

Constant Name	Value	Description
MDPROPVAL_MMF_COUSIN	1	The COUSIN function is supported.
MDPROPVAL_MMF_PARALLELPERIOD	2	The PARALLELPERIOD function is supported.
MDPROPVAL_MMF_OPENINGPERIOD	4	The OPENINGPERIOD function is supported.
MDPROPVAL_MMF_CLOSINGPERIOD	8	The CLOSINGPERIOD function is supported.

MDPROPVAL_MNF

Constant Name	Value	Description
MDPROPVAL_MNF_MEDIAN	1	The MEDIAN function is supoprted.
MDPROPVAL_MNF_VAR	2	The VAR function is supported.
MDPROPVAL_MNF_STDDEV	4	The STDDEV function is supported.
MDPROPVAL_MNF_RANK	8	The RANK function is supported.
MDPROPVAL_MNF_AGGREGATE	16	The AGGREGATE function is supported.
MDPROPVAL_MNF_COVARIANCE	32	The COVARIANCE function is supported.
MDPROPVAL_MNF_CORRELATION	64	The CORRELATION function is supported.
MDPROPVAL_MNF_LINREGSLOPE	128	The LINREGSLOPE function is supported.
MDPROPVAL_MNF_LINREGVARIANCE	256	The LINREGVARIANCE function is supported.
MDPROPVAL_MNF_LINREGR2	512	The LINREGR2function is supported.
MDPROPVAL_MNF_LINREGPOINT	1024	The LINREGPOINT function is supported.
MDPROPVAL_MNF_LINREGINTERCEPT	2048	The LINREGINTERCEPT function is supported.

MDPROPVAL_MO

Constant Name	Value	Description
MDPROPVAL_MO_TUPLE		The tuple.[VALUE] clause can be qualified by a cube name as an argument.

MDPROPVAL_MOQ

Constant Name	Value	Description
MDPROPVAL_MOQ_DATASOURCE_ CUBE	1	Cubes can be qualified by the data source name.
MDPROPVAL_MOQ_CATALOG_ CUBE	2	Cubes can be qualified by the catalog name.
MDPROPVAL_MOQ_SCHEMA_CUBE	4	Cubes can be qualified by the schema name.
MDPROPVAL_MOQ_CUBE_DIM	8	Dimensions can be qualified by the cube name.
MDPROPVAL_MOQ_DIM_HIER	16	Hierarchies can be qualified by the dimension name.
MDPROPVAL_MOQ_DIMHIER_ LEVEL	32	Levels can be qualified by the schema name, and/or the hierarchy name.
MDPROPVAL_MOQ_LEVEL_ MEMBER	64	Members can be qualified by a level name.
MDPROPVAL_MOQ_MEMBER_ MEMBER	128	Members can be qualified by their ancestor names.

MDPROPVAL_MS

Constant Name	Value	Description
MDPROPVAL_MS_SINGLETUPLE	2	Only one tuple is supported in the WHERE clause.
MDPROPVAL_MS_MULTIPLETUPLES	1	Multiple tuples are supported in the WHERE clause.

MDPROPVAL_MSC

Constant Name	Value	Description
MDPROPVAL_MSC_LESSTHAN	1	The provider supports the less than operator.
MDPROPVAL_MSC_GREATERTHAN	2	The provider supports the greater than operator.
MDPROPVAL_MSC_LESSTHANEQUAL	4	The provider supports the less than or equal to operator.
MDPROPVAL_MSC_ GREATERTHANEQUAL	8	The provider supports the greater than or equal to operator.

MDPROPVAL_MSF

Constant Name	Value	Description
MDPROPVAL_MSF_ TOPPERCENT	1	The TOPPERCENT function is supported.
MDPROPVAL_MSF_ BOTTOMPERCENT	2	The BOTTOMPERCENT function is supported.
MDPROPVAL_MSF_ TOPSUM	4	The TOPSUM function is supported.
MDPROPVAL_MSF_ BOTTOMSUM	8	The BOTTOMSUM function is supported.
MDPROPVAL_MSF_ DRILLDOWNLEVEL	2048	The DRILLDOWNLEVEL function is supported.
MDPROPVAL_MSF_ DRILLDOWNMEMBER	1024	The DRILLDOWNMEMBER function is supported.
MDPROPVAL_MSF_ DRILLDOWNMEMBERTOP	4096	The DRILLDOWNMEMBERTOP function is supported.
MDPROPVAL_MSF_ DRILLDOWNMEMBERBOTTOM	8192	The DRILLDOWNMEMBERBOTTOM function is supported.
MDPROPVAL_MSF_ DRILLDOWNLEVELTOP	16384	The DRILLDOWNLEVELTOP function is supported.

Table Continued on Following Page

Constant Name	Value	Description
MDPROPVAL_MSF_ DRILLDOWNLEVELBOTTOM	32768	The DRILLDOWNLEVELBOTTOM function is supported.
MDPROPVAL_MSF_ DRILLUPMEMBER	65536	The DRILLUPMEMBER function is supported.
MDPROPVAL_MSF_ DRILLUPLEVEL	131072	The DRILLUPLEVEL function is supported.
MDPROPVAL_MSF_ PERIODSTODATE	16	The PERIODSTODATE function is supported.
MDPROPVAL_MSF_ LASTPERIODS	32	The LASTPERIODS function is supported.
MDPROPVAL_MSF_YTD	64	The YTD function is supported.
MDPROPVAL_MSF_QTD	128	The QTD function is supported.
MDPROPVAL_MSF_MTD	256	The MTD function is supported.
MDPROPVAL_MSF_WTD	512	The WTD function is supported.

MDPROPVAL_NL

Constant Name	Value	Description
MDPROPVAL_NL_NAMEDLEVELS	1	The provider supports named levels
MDPROPVAL_NL_NUMBEREDLEVELS	2	The provider supports numbered levels.
MDPROPVAL_NL_SCHEMAONLY	4	The provider supports 'dummy' levels, for display only.

MDPROPVAL_RR

Constant Name	Value	Description
MDPROPVAL_RR_NORANGEROWSET	1	The provider does not support range rowsets.
MDPROPVAL_RR_READONLY	2	The provider supports read-only range rowsets.
MDPROPVAL_RR_UPDATE	4	The provider supports updatable range rowsets.

MDTREEOP

Constant Name	Value	Description
MDTREEOP_ANCESTORS	32	Show only members that are ancestors of the selected member.
MDTREEOP_CHILDREN	1	Show only members that are children of the selected member.
MDTREEOP_SIBLINGS	2	Show only members that are siblings of the selected member.
MDTREEOP_PARENT	4	Show only members that are parents of the selected member.
MDTREEOP_SELF	8	Show the selected member in the list.
MDTREEOP_DESCENDANTS	16	Show only members that are descendants of the selected member.

ADOMD Properties Collection

The following table shows a list of all OLEDB properties for the Microsoft OLAP Provider.

The Connection Object's Properties

Property Name	Description	Type
Active Sessions	The maximum number of sessions allowable. Zero indicates no limit.	Long
Asynchable Abort	Whether transactions can be aborted asynchronously. Read-only.	Boolean
Asynchable Commit	Whether transactions can be committed asynchronously. Read-only.	Boolean
Asynchronous Initialization	Indicates the asynchronous initialization setting. This can only be DBPROPVAL_ASYNCH_INITIALIZE, from the ADO constants.	Long
Auto Synch Period	Identifies the time (in milliseconds) of the synchronization between the client and the server. The default value is 10,000 (10 seconds).	Long
Autocommit Isolation Levels	Indicates the transaction isolation level when in auto-commit mode. Can be one of the DBPROPVAL_TI constants from ADO.	Long
Cache Policy	Reserved for future use.	Long

Table Continued on Following Page

Property Name	Description	Type
Catalog Location	The position of the catalog name in a table name in a text command. The value can be on of the DBPROPVAL_CL constants from ADO.	Long
Catalog Term	The name the data source uses for a catalog, e.g. 'catalog' or 'database'. Read/Write.	String
Catalog Usage	Specifies how catalog names can be used in text commands. Can be zero or more of DBPROPVAL_CU constants from ADO.	Long
Client Cache Size	The amount of memory used by the cache on the client. A value of 0 means there is no limit on the client memory that can be used. A value of 1–99 indicates the percentage of virtual memory to use for the cache. A value above 100 indicates the amount in Kb that can be used by the cache.	Long
Column Definition	Defines the valid clauses for the definition of a column. Can be one of the DBPROPVAL_CD constants from ADO.	Long
CompareCaseNotSensitiveStringFlags	Identifies the type of comparison to perform for case-insensitive strings.	Long
CompareCaseSensitiveStringFlags	Identifies the type of comparison to perform for case-sensitive strings.	Long
Connect Timeout	The amount of time, in seconds, to wait for the initialization to complete. Read/Write.	Long
Connection Status	The status of the current connection. Can be one of the DBPROPVAL_CS constants from ADO.	Long
CREATECUBE	The statement used to create a cube.	String
Current Catalog	The name of the current catalog.	String
Data Source	The name of the data source to connect to.	String
Data Source Name	The name of the data source.	String
Data Source Object Threading Model	Specifies the threading models supported by the data source object.	Long
Data Source Type	The type of data source.	Long
DBMS Name	The name of the product accessed by the provider.	String
DBMS Version	The version of the product accessed by the provider.	String

Property Name	Description	Type
Default Isolation Mode	Identifies whether the isolation mode is 'isolated', or the mode requested by the rowset properties. Isolated mode will be used if this value starts with Y, T or a number other than 0.	String
Execution Location	Identifies whether the query is resolved. Values can be: 0, for automatic selection. This is the default. 1, for automatic selection. 2, to execute the query on the client 3, to execute the query on he server.	Long
Extended Properties	Contains provider specific, extended connection information.	String
Flattening Support	Indicates the level of support by the provider for flattening.	MDPROPVAL_FS
GROUP BY Support	The relationship between the columns in a GROUP BY clause and the non-aggregated columns in the select list. Can be one of the DBPROPVAL_GB constants from ADO.	Long
Heterogeneous Table Support	Specifies whether the provider can join tables from different catalogs or providers. Can be one of the DBPROPVAL_HT constants from ADO.	Long
Identifier Case Sensitivity	How identifiers treat case sensitivity. Can be one of the DBPROPVAL_IC constants from ADO.	Long
Initial Catalog	The name of the initial, or default, catalog to use when connecting to the data source. If the provider supports changing the catalog for an initialized data source, a different catalog name can be specified in the Current Catalog property.	String
INSERTINTO	The statement used for inserting data into a local cube.	String
Integrated Security	Contains the name of the authentication service used by the server to identify the user.	String

Table Continued on Following Page

Property Name	Description	Type
Isolation Levels	Identifies the supported transaction isolation levels. Can be one of the DBPROPVAL_TI constants from ADO	Long
Isolation Retention	Identifies the supported transaction isolation retention levels. Can be one of the DBPROPVAL_TR constants from ADO.	Long
Large Level Threshold	Defines the number of levels a Dimension can have before it is deemed to be a 'large' dimension. A large level Dimension will have the levels sent from the server in increments, rather than all at once.	Long
Locale Identifier	The locale ID of preference for the consumer.	Long
Location	The location of the data source to connect to. Typically this will be the server name	String
Maximum Index Size	The maximum number of bytes allowed in the combined columns of an index. This is 0 if there is no specified limit or the limit is unknown.	Long
Maximum Row Size	The maximum length of a single row in a table. This is 0 if there is no specified limit or the limit is unknown.	Long
Maximum Row Size Includes BLOB	Identifies whether Maximum Row Size includes the length for BLOB data.	Boolean
Maximum Tables in SELECT	The maximum number of tables allowed in the FROM clause of a SELECT statement. This is 0 if there is no specified limit or the limit is unknown.	Long
MDX DDL Extensions	Defines any DDL extensions supported by the provider.	Long
MDX USE Extensions	Defines the USE extensions supported by the provider, allowing creation of user defined functions.	Long
Mode	Specifies the access permissions. Can be one of the DB_MODE constants from ADO.	Long
Multiple Results	Identifies whether the provider supports multiple results objects and what restrictions it places on those objects.	Long
Multiple Storage Objects	Identifies whether the provider supports multiple, open storage objects at the same time.	Boolean

Property Name	Description	Type
Multi-Table Update	Identifies whether the provider can update rowsets derived from multiple tables.	Boolean
NULL Collation Order	Identifies where NULLs are sorted in a list.	Long
NULL Concatenation Behavior	How the data source handles concatenation of NULL-valued character data type columns with non-NULL valued character data type columns.	Long
Number of axes in the dataset	Maximum number of axes that the provider supports.	Long
OLE DB Services	Specifies the OLEDB services to enable.	Long
OLE DB Version	Specifies the version of OLEDB supported by the provider.	String
OLE Object Support	Specifies the way on which the provider supports access to BLOBs and OLE objects stored in columns.	Long
ORDER BY Columns in Select List	Identifies whether columns in an ORDER BY clause must be in the SELECT list.	Boolean
Output Parameter Availability	Identifies the time at which output parameter values become available. Can be one of the DBPROPVAL_AO constants in ADO.	Long
Pass By Ref Accessors	Whether the provider supports the DBACCESSOR_PASSBYREF flag.	Boolean
Password	The password to be used to connect to the data source.	String
Persist Security Info	Whether or not the consumer requires that the data source object persist sensitive authentication information, such as a password, in encrypted form.	Boolean
Persistent ID Type	Specifies the type of DBID that the provider uses when persisting DBIDs for tables, indexes and columns. Can be one of the DBPROPVAL_PT constants in ADO.	Long
Prepare Abort Behavior	Identifies how aborting a transaction affects prepared commands. Can be one of the DBPROPVAL_CB constants in ADO.	Long

Table Continued on Following Page

Property Name	Description	Type
Prepare Commit Behavior	Identifies how committing a transaction affects prepared commands. Can be one of the DBPROPVAL_CB constants in ADO.	Long
Procedure Term	Specifies the data source providers name for a procedure, e.g. 'database procedure' or 'stored procedure'.	String
Prompt	Specifies whether to prompt the user during initialization.	Integer
Provider Friendly Name	The friendly name of the provider.	String
Provider Name	The filename of the provider.	String
Provider Version	The version of the provider.	String
Provider's ability to qualify a cube name	Identifies how object names in a schema can be qualified in an MDX expression.	MDPROPVAL_MOQ
Quoted Identifier Sensitivity	Identifies how quoted identifiers treat case. Can be one of the DBPROPVAL_IC constants from ADO.	Long
Read Only Session	Reserved for future.	String
Read-Only Data Source	Whether or not the data source is read-only.	Boolean
Reset Datasource	Specifies the data source state to reset. Can be one of the DBPROPVAL_RD constants from ADO.	Long
Rowset Conversions on Command	Identifies whether callers can enquire on a command and about conversions supported by the command.	Boolean
Schema Usage	Identifies how schema names can be used in commands. Can be one of the DBPROPVAL_SU constants from ADO.	Long
Server Name	The name of the server.	String
SOURCE_DSNsa	The connection string for the source data store.	String

Property Name	Description	Type
SOURCE_DSN_SUFFIX	The suffix to append to the SOURCE_DSN property for a local cube.	String
SQL Support	Identifies the level of support for SQL. Can be one of the DBPROPVAL_SQL constants from ADO.	Long
Structured Storage	Identifies what interfaces the rowset supports on storage objects. Can be one of the DBPROPVAL_SS constants from ADO.	Long
Subquery Support	Identifies the predicates in text commands that support subqueries. Can be one of the DBPROPVAL_SQ constants from ADO.	Long
Support for cell updates	Indicates whether the provider supports updating of the cells.	MDPROPVAL_PR
Support for creation of named sets and calculated members	Indicates the level of support for named sets and calculated members.	MDPROPVAL_MF
Support for MDX case statements	The level of support for case statements.	MDPROPVAL_MC
Support for named levels	The level of support for named and/or numbered levels.	MDPROPVAL_NL
Support for outer reference in an MDX statement	The level of support for outer references.	MDPROPVAL_MO
Support for query joining multiple cubes	The level of support for joining multiple cubes.	MDPROPVAL_MJC
Support for querying by property values in an MDX statement	Indicates whether or not the provider supports the query of property statements.	Boolean
Support for string comparison operators other than equals and not-equals operators	The level of support for complex string comparison operators.	MDPROPVAL_MSC

Table Continued on Following Page

Property Name	Description	Type
Support for updating aggregated cells	The level of support for updating aggregated cells.	MDPROPVAL_AU
Support for various <desc_flag> values in the DESCENDANTS function	The level of support for flags when describing descendants.	MDPROPVAL_MD
Support for various member functions	The level of support for functions that act on members.	MDPROPVAL_MMF
Support for various numeric functions	The level of support for numeric functions.	MDPROPVAL_MNF
Support for various set functions	The level of support for set functions.	MDPROPVAL_MSF
Table Term	The name the data source uses for a table, e.g. 'table' or 'file'	String
The capabilities of the WHERE clause of an MDX statement	The WHERE clause support for tuples.	MDPROPVAL_MS
Transaction DDL	Indicates whether Data Definition Language (DDL) statements are supported in transactions. Can be one of the DBPROPVAL_TC constants from ADO.	Long
USEEXISTINGFILE	When using CREATE CUBE or INSERT INTO, indicates whether an existing local cube file is overwritten. If the value starts with Y, T or a number other than 0, the existing file is used. If the value starts with any other character the existing cube file is overwritten.	String
User ID	The User ID to be used when connecting to the data source.	String
User Name	The User Name used in a particular database.	String
Window Handle	The window handle to be used if the data source object needs to prompt for additional information.	Long
Writeback Timeout	The maximum amount of time (in seconds) to wait whilst committing changes back to the server.	Long

The CubeDef Object's Properties

Property Name	Description	Type
CATALOG_NAME	The name of the catalog to which the cube belongs.	String
CREATED_ON	The date the cube was created.	Date/Time
CUBE_GUID	The GUID of the cube.	GUID
CUBE_NAME	The cube name.	String
CUBE_TYPE	Will be CUBE for a standard cube and VIRTUAL CUBE for a virtual cube.	String
DATA_UPDATED_BY	The ID of the person who last update data in the cube.	String
DESCRIPTION	The cube description.	String
LAST_DATA_UPDATE	The date the cube data was last updated.	Date/Time
LAST_SCHEMA_UPDATE	The date the cube schema was last updated.	Date/Time
SCHEMA_NAME	The name of the schema to which this cube belongs.	String
SCHEMA_UPDATED_BY	The ID of the person who last updated the schema.	String

The Dimension Object's Properties

Property Name	Description	Type
CATALOG_NAME	The name of the Catalog to which this Dimension belongs.	String
CUBE_NAME	The name of the cube to which this Dimension belongs.	String
DEFAULT_HIERARCHY	The unique name of the default Hierarchy for this Dimension.	String
DESCRIPTION	The description of the Dimension.	String
DIMENSION_CAPTION	The caption of the Dimension.	String
DIMENSION_ CARDINALITY	The number of members in the Dimension. This figure is not guaranteed to be accurate.	Long
DIMENSION_GUID	The GUID of the Dimension, or Null if no GUID exists.	GUID

Table Continued on Following Page

Property Name	Description	Type
DIMENSION_NAME	The name of the Dimension.	String
DIMENSION_ORDINAL	The number or the ordinal of the Dimension. This is 0 based.	Long
DIMENSION_TYPE	The type of the Dimension.	MD_ DIMTYPE
DIMENSION_UNIQUE_ NAME	The unique name of the Dimension.	String
IS_VIRTUAL	Indicates whether or not the Dimension is a virtual dimension.	Boolean
SCHEMA_NAME	The schema name to which this Dimension belongs.	String

The Hierarchy Object's Properties

Property Name	Description	Type
ALL_MEMBER	The name of the default member if the first level is All, or Null if the first level is not All.	String
CATALOG_NAME	Catalog name in which the table is defined or Null if the provider does not support catalogs.	String
CUBE_NAME	The name of the Cube to which this Hierarchy belongs.	String
DEFAULT_MEMBER	The default Level for this Hierarchy, or Null if no default exists.	String
DESCRIPTION	The description of the Hierarchy.	String
DIMENSION_TYPE	The type of the dimension.	MD_ DIMTYPE
DIMENSION_UNIQUE_ NAME	The fully qualified name of the Dimension to which this Hierarchy belongs.	String
HIERARCHY_CAPTION	The caption of the Hierarchy.	String
HIERARCHY_CARDINALITY	The number of members in the Hierarchy. This figure is not guaranteed to be accurate.	Long
HIERARCHY_GUID	The GUID of the Hierarchy, or Null if no GUID exists.	GUID
HIERARCHY_NAME	The name of the Hierarchy.	String

Property Name	Description	Type
HIERARCHY_UNIQUE_NAME	The fully qualified name of the Hierarchy.	String
SCHEMA_NAME	Schema name in which the table is defined or Null if the provider does not support schemas.	String

The Level Object's Properties

Property Name	Description	Type
CATALOG_NAME	Catalog name, or Null if the provider does not support catalogs.	String
CUBE_NAME	The Cube name to which the level belongs.	String
DESCRIPTION	The description of the level.	String
DIMENSION_UNIQUE_NAME	The unique name of the Dimension to which the level belongs.	String
HIERARCHY_UNIQUE_NAME	The unique name of the Hierarchy to which the level belongs.	String
LEVEL_CAPTION	The Caption of the level.	String
LEVEL_CARDINALITY	The number of members in the level. This figure is not guaranteed to be accurate.	Long
LEVEL_GUID	The GUID of the level, or Null if no GUID exists.	GUID
LEVEL_NAME	The level name.	String
LEVEL_NUMBER	The index number of the level.	Long
LEVEL_TYPE	The Type of the level.	MDLEVEL_TYPE
LEVEL_UNIQUE_NAME	The unique level name.	String
SCHEMA_NAME	Schema name, or Null if the provider does not support schemas.	String

The Member Object's Properties

Property Name	Description	Type
EXPRESSION	The expression which underlies a calculated measure.	String

JRO Object Summary

Microsoft Jet and Replication Objects 2.1 Library Reference

JRO Objects

Name	Description
Filter	A Filter that limits replication.
Filters	A collection of `Filter` objects.
JetEngine	The Jet Database Engine.
Replica	A copy of a replicated database.

The Filter Object

Properties of the Filter Object	Return Type	Description
FilterCriteria	String	The filter criteria, which allows a record to be replicated. Read only
FilterType	FilterTypeEnum	The type of the filter. Can be one of the FilterTypeEnum constants, as discussed in Appendix O. Read only
TableName	String	The table to which the filter applies. Read only

The Filters Collection

Methods of the Filters Collection	Return Type	Description
Append		Adds a new `Filter` object to the collection.
Delete		Removes a `Filter` object from the collection.
Refresh		Refreshes the collection from the design master.

Properties of the Filters Collection	Return Type	Description
Count	Integer	The number of `Filter` objects in the collection. Read only
Item	Filter	The default property, which allows indexing into the collection. Read only

The JetEngine Object

Methods of the JetEngine Object	Return Type	Description
CompactDatabase		Compacts the requested database.
RefreshCache		Forces the memory cache to write changes to the MDB files, and then refreshes the memory with data from the MDB file.

The Replica Object

Methods of the Replica Object	Return Type	Description
CreateReplica		Creates a new replica of the current, replicable database.
GetObjectReplicability	Boolean	Identifies whether or not an object is local or replicable.
MakeReplicable		Make a database replicable.
PopulatePartial		Populates a partial replica with data from the full replica.
SetObjectReplicability		Sets whether an object is local or replicable.
Synchronize		Synchronizes two replicable databases.

Properties

Properties of the Replica Object	Return Type	Description
ActiveConnection	Object	An ADO connection object or string, to which the replica belongs.
ConflictFunction	String	The name of the custom function to use for conflict resolution.
ConflictTables	Recordset	A recordset that contains the tables and conflict tables for each table that had conflicts. Read only
DesignMasterId	Variant	The unique identifier of the design master in a replica set.
Priority	Integer	The relative priority of the replica, for use during conflict resolution. Read only
ReplicaId	Variant	The unique id of the replica database in the replica set. Read only
ReplicaType	ReplicaTypeEnum	The type of replica. Can be one of the ReplicaTypeEnum constants, as discussed in Appendix O. Read only
RetentionPeriod	Integer	How many days replication histories are kept for.
Visibility	VisibilityEnum	Indicates whether the replica is global, local, or anonymous. Can be one of the VisibilityEnum constants, as discussed in Appendix O. Read only

Collections of the Replica Object	Return Type	Description
Filters	Filters	A collection of `Filter` objects, which specify the criteria records must match to be replicated. Read only

Method Calls

Filters

Filters.Append(*TableName As String, FilterType As FilterTypeEnum, FilterCriteria As String*)
Filters.Delete(*Index As Variant*)
Filters.Refresh

JetEngine

JetEngine.CompactDatabase(*SourceConnection As String, Destconnection As String*)
JetEngine.RefreshCache(*Connection As Object*)

Replica

Replica.CreateReplica(*replicaName As String, description As String, ReplicaType As ReplicaTypeEnum, Visibility As VisibilityEnum, Priority As Integer, updatability As UpdatabilityEnum*)
Boolean = Replica.GetObjectReplicability(*objectName As String, objectType As String*)
Replica.MakeReplicable(*connectionString As String, columnTracking As Boolean*)
Replica.PopulatePartial(*FullReplica As String*)
Replica.SetObjectReplicability(*objectName As String, objectType As String, replicability As Boolean*)
Replica.Synchronize(*target As String, syncType As SyncTypeEnum, syncMode As SyncModeEnum*)

JRO Constants

FilterTypeEnum

Name	Value	Description
jrFilterTypeRelationship	2	The filter is based upon a relationship.
jrFilterTypeTable	1	The filter is based upon a table. This is the default.

ReplicaTypeEnum

Name	Value	Description
jrRepTypeDesignMaster	1	The replica is the design master.
jrRepTypeFull	2	The replica is a full replica.
jrRepTypeNotReplicable	0	The database is not replicable. This is the default.
jrRepTypePartial	3	The replica is a partial replica.

SyncModeEnum

Name	Value	Description
jrSyncModeDirect	2	Use direct synchronization.
jrSyncModeIndirect	1	Use indirect synchronization.
jrSyncModeInternet	3	Use Internet based synchronization.

SyncTypeEnum

Name	Value	Description
jrSyncTypeExport	1	Export changes to the target database.
jrSyncTypeImpExp	3	Import and export changes to and from the target database.
jrSyncTypeImport	2	Import databases from the target database.

UpdatabilityEnum

Name	Value	Description
jrRepUpdFull	0	The replica can be updated.
jrRepUpdReadOnly	2	The replica is read-only.

VisibilityEnum

Name	Value	Description
jrRepVisibilityAnon	4	The replica is anonymous.
jrRepVisibilityGlobal	1	The replica is global.
jrRepVisibilityLocal	2	The replica is local.

ADO Error Codes

The following table lists the standard errors than might get returned from ADO operations.

Constant name	Number	Description
adErrInvalidArgument	3001	The application is using arguments that are of the wrong type, are out of acceptable range, or are in conflict with one another.
adErrNoCurrentRecord	3021	Either BOF or EOF is True, or the current record has been deleted; the operation requested by the application requires a current record.
adErrIllegalOperation	3219	The operation requested by the application is not allowed in this context.
adErrInTransaction	3246	The application cannot explicitly close a Connection object while in the middle of a transaction.
adErrFeatureNotAvailable	3251	The operation requested by the application is not supported by the provider.
adErrItemNotFound	3265	ADO could not find the object in the collection corresponding to the name or ordinal reference requested by the application.
adErrObjectInCollection	3367	Can't append. The object is already in the collection.

Table Continued on Following Page

Constant name	Number	Description
adErrObjectNotSet	3420	The object referenced by the application no longer points to a valid object.
adErrDataConversion	3421	The application is using a value of the wrong type for the current operation.
adErrObjectClosed	3704	The operation requested by the application is not allowed if the object is closed.
adErrObjectOpen	3705	The operation requested by the application is not allowed if the object is open.
adErrProviderNotFound	3706	ADO could not find the specified provider.
adErrBoundToCommand	3707	The application cannot change the `ActiveConnection` property of a `Recordset` object with a `Command` object as its source.
adErrInvalidParamInfo	3708	The application has improperly defined a `Parameter` object.
adErrInvalidConnection	3709	The application requested an operation on an object with a reference to a closed or invalid `Connection` object.

The following table lists the extended ADO errors and their descriptions:

Error Number	Description
-2147483647	Not implemented.
-2147483646	Ran out of memory.
-2147483645	One or more arguments are invalid.
-2147483644	No such interface supported.
-2147483643	Invalid pointer.
-2147483642	Invalid handle.
-2147483641	Operation aborted.
-2147483640	Unspecified error.
-2147483639	General access denied error.

Error Number	Description
-2147483638	The data necessary to complete this operation is not yet available.
-2147467263	Not implemented.
-2147467262	No such interface supported.
-2147467261	Invalid pointer.
-2147467260	Operation aborted.
-2147467259	Unspecified error.
-2147467258	Thread local storage failure.
-2147467257	Get shared memory allocator failure.
-2147467256	Get memory allocator failure.
-2147467255	Unable to initialize class cache.
-2147467254	Unable to initialize RPC services.
-2147467253	Cannot set thread local storage channel control.
-2147467252	Could not allocate thread local storage channel control.
-2147467251	The user supplied memory allocator is unacceptable.
-2147467250	The OLE service mutex already exists.
-2147467249	The OLE service file mapping already exists.
-2147467248	Unable to map view of file for OLE service.
-2147467247	Failure attempting to launch OLE service.
-2147467246	There was an attempt to call CoInitialize a second time while single threaded.
-2147467245	A Remote activation was necessary but was not allowed.
-2147467244	A Remote activation was necessary but the server name provided was invalid.
-2147467243	The class is configured to run as a security id different from the caller.
-2147467242	Use of OLE1 services requiring DDE windows is disabled.
-2147467241	A RunAs specification must be <domain name>\<user name> or simply <user name>.
-2147467240	The server process could not be started. The pathname may be incorrect.

Table Continued on Following Page

Error Number	Description
-2147467239	The server process could not be started as the configured identity. The pathname may be incorrect or unavailable.
-2147467238	The server process could not be started because the configured identity is incorrect. Check the username and password.
-2147467237	The client is not allowed to launch this server.
-2147467236	The service providing this server could not be started.
-2147467235	This computer was unable to communicate with the computer providing the server.
-2147467234	The server did not respond after being launched.
-2147467233	The registration information for this server is inconsistent or incomplete.
-2147467232	The registration information for this interface is inconsistent or incomplete.
-2147467231	The operation attempted is not supported.
-2147418113	Catastrophic failure.
-2147024891	General access denied error.
-2147024890	Invalid handle.
-2147024882	Ran out of memory.
-2147024809	One or more arguments are invalid.

Listed below are the OLEDB errors, and whilst they might not be relevant for some of the ADO work, they are included for completeness:

Error Number	Description
-2147217920	Invalid accessor.
-2147217919	Creating another row would have exceeded the total number of active rows supported by the rowset.
-2147217918	Unable to write with a read-only accessor.
-2147217917	Given values violate the database schema.
-2147217916	Invalid row handle.
-2147217915	An object was open.
-2147217914	Invalid chapter.

Error Number	Description
-2147217913	A literal value in the command could not be converted to the correct type due to a reason other than data overflow.
-2147217912	Invalid binding info.
-2147217911	Permission denied.
-2147217910	Specified column does not contain bookmarks or chapters.
-2147217909	Some cost limits were rejected.
-2147217908	No command has been set for the command object.
-2147217907	Unable to find a query plan within the given cost limit.
-2147217906	Invalid bookmark.
-2147217905	Invalid lock mode.
-2147217904	No value given for one or more required parameters.
-2147217903	Invalid column ID.
-2147217902	Invalid ratio.
-2147217901	Invalid value.
-2147217900	The command contained one or more errors.
-2147217899	The executing command cannot be cancelled.
-2147217898	The provider does not support the specified dialect.
-2147217897	A data source with the specified name already exists.
-2147217896	The rowset was built over a live data feed and cannot be restarted.
-2147217895	No key matching the described characteristics could be found within the current range.
-2147217894	Ownership of this tree has been given to the provider.
-2147217893	The provider is unable to determine identity for newly inserted rows.
-2147217892	No non-zero weights specified for any goals supported, so goal was rejected; current goal was not changed.
-2147217891	Requested conversion is not supported.
-2147217890	lRowsOffset would position you past either end of the rowset, regardless of the cRows value specified; cRowsObtained is 0.

Table Continued on Following Page

Error Number	Description
-2147217889	Information was requested for a query, and the query was not set.
-2147217888	Provider called a method from IrowsetNotify in the consumer and the method has not yet returned.
-2147217887	Errors occurred.
-2147217886	A non-NULL controlling IUnknown was specified and the object being created does not support aggregation.
-2147217885	A given HROW referred to a hard- or soft- deleted row.
-2147217884	The rowset does not support fetching backwards.
-2147217883	All HROWs must be released before new ones can be obtained.
-2147217882	One of the specified storage flags was not supported.
-2147217881	Invalid comparison operator.
-2147217880	The specified status flag was neither DBCOLUMNSTATUS_OK nor DBCOLUMNSTATUS_ISNULL.
-2147217879	The rowset cannot scroll backwards.
-2147217878	Invalid region handle.
-2147217877	The specified set of rows was not contiguous to or overlapping the rows in the specified watch region.
-2147217876	A transition from ALL* to MOVE* or EXTEND* was specified.
-2147217875	The specified region is not a proper subregion of the region identified by the given watch region handle.
-2147217874	The provider does not support multi-statement commands.
-2147217873	A specified value violated the integrity constraints for a column or table.
-2147217872	The given type name was unrecognized.
-2147217871	Execution aborted because a resource limit has been reached; no results have been returned.
-2147217870	Cannot clone a command object whose command tree contains a rowset or rowsets.
-2147217869	Cannot represent the current tree as text.
-2147217868	The specified index already exists.

Error Number	Description
-2147217867	The specified index does not exist.
-2147217866	The specified index was in use.
-2147217865	The specified table does not exist.
-2147217864	The rowset was using optimistic concurrency and the value of a column has been changed since it was last read.
-2147217863	Errors were detected during the copy.
-2147217862	A specified precision was invalid.
-2147217861	A specified scale was invalid.
-2147217860	Invalid table ID.
-2147217859	A specified type was invalid.
-2147217858	A column ID occurred more than once in the specification.
-2147217857	The specified table already exists.
-2147217856	The specified table was in use.
-2147217855	The specified locale ID was not supported.
-2147217854	The specified record number is invalid.
-2147217853	Although the bookmark was validly formed, no row could be found to match it.
-2147217852	The value of a property was invalid.
-2147217851	The rowset was not chaptered.
-2147217850	Invalid accessor.
-2147217849	Invalid storage flags.
-2147217848	By-ref accessors are not supported by this provider.
-2147217847	Null accessors are not supported by this provider.
-2147217846	The command was not prepared.
-2147217845	The specified accessor was not a parameter accessor.
-2147217844	The given accessor was write-only.
-2147217843	Authentication failed.
-2147217842	The change was canceled during notification; no columns are changed.
-2147217841	The rowset was single-chaptered and the chapter was not released.

Table Continued on Following Page

Error Number	Description
-2147217840	Invalid source handle.
-2147217839	The provider cannot derive parameter info and SetParameterInfo has not been called.
-2147217838	The data source object is already initialized.
-2147217837	The provider does not support this method.
-2147217836	The number of rows with pending changes has exceeded the set limit.
-2147217835	The specified column did not exist.
-2147217834	There are pending changes on a row with a reference count of zero.
-2147217833	A literal value in the command overflowed the range of the type of the associated column.
-2147217832	The supplied HRESULT was invalid.
-2147217831	The supplied LookupID was invalid.
-2147217830	The supplied DynamicErrorID was invalid.
-2147217829	Unable to get visible data for a newly inserted row that has not yet been updated.
-2147217828	Invalid conversion flag.
-2147217827	The given parameter name was unrecognized.
-2147217826	Multiple storage objects cannot be opened simultaneously.
-2147217825	Cannot open requested filter.
-2147217824	Cannot open requested order.
-2147217823	Invalid tuple.
-2147217822	Invalid coordinate.
-2147217821	Invalid axis for this dataset.
-2147217820	One or more cell ordinals is invalid.
-2147217819	Invalid columnID.
-2147217817	Command does not have a DBID.
-2147217816	DBID already exists.
-2147217815	Maximum number of sessions supported by the provider already created. Consumer must release one or more currently held sessions before obtaining a new session object.

Error Number	Description
-2147217814	Invalid trustee value.
-2147217813	Trustee is not for the current data source.
-2147217812	Trustee does not support memberships/collections.
-2147217811	Object is invalid or unknown to the provider.
-2147217810	No owner exists for the object.
-2147217809	Invalid access entry list.
-2147217808	Trustee supplied as owner is invalid or unknown to the provider.
-2147217807	Invalid permission in the access entry list.
-2147217806	Invalid index ID.
-2147217805	Initialization string does not conform to specification.
-2147217804	OLE DB root enumerator did not return any providers that matched any requested SOURCES_TYPE.
-2147217803	Initialization string specifies a provider that does not match the currently active provider.
-2147217802	Invalid DBID.
-2147217801	ConstraintType is invalid or not supported by the provider.
-2147217800	ConstraintType is not DBCONSTRAINTTYPE_FOREIGNKEY and cForeignKeyColumns is not zero.
-2147217799	Deferrability is invalid or the value is not supported by the provider.
-2147217798	MatchType is invalid or the value is not supported by the provider.
-2147217782	UpdateRule or DeleteRule is invalid or the value is not supported by the provider.
-2147217781	pConstraintID does not exist in the data source.
-2147217780	Invalid dwFlags.
-2147217779	rguidColumnType points to a GUID that does not match the object type of this column, or this column was not set.
-2147217778	URL is out of scope.
-2147217776	Provider cannot drop the object.
-2147217775	No source row.

Table Continued on Following Page

Error Number	Description
-2147217774	OLE DB object represented by this URL is locked by one or more other processes.
-2147217773	Client requested an object type that is valid only for a collection.
-2147217772	Caller requested write access to a read-only object.
-2147217771	Provider does not support asynchronous binding.
-2147217770	Provider cannot connect to server for this object.
-2147217769	Attempt to bind to the object timed out.
-2147217768	Provider cannot create an object at this URL because an object named by this URL already exists.
-2147217767	Constraint already exists.
-2147217766	Provider cannot create an object at this URL because the server is out of physical storage.
-2147217765	Unsafe operation was attempted in safe mode. Provider denied this operation.
265920	Fetching requested number of rows would have exceeded total number of active rows supported by the rowset.
265921	One or more column types are incompatible; conversion errors will occur during copying.
265922	Parameter type information has been overridden by caller.
265923	Skipped bookmark for deleted or non-member row.
265924	Errors found in validating tree.
265925	There are no more rowsets.
265926	Reached start or end of rowset or chapter.
265927	The provider re-executed the command.
265928	Variable data buffer full.
265929	There are no more results.
265930	Server cannot release or downgrade a lock until the end of the transaction.
265931	Specified weight was not supported or exceeded the supported limit and was set to 0 or the supported limit.
265932	Consumer is uninterested in receiving further notification calls for this operation.

Error Number	Description
265933	Input dialect was ignored and text was returned in different dialect.
265934	Consumer is uninterested in receiving further notification calls for this phase.
265935	Consumer is uninterested in receiving further notification calls for this reason.
265936	Operation is being processed asynchronously.
265937	In order to reposition to the start of the rowset, the provider had to re-execute the query; either the order of the columns changed or columns were added to or removed from the rowset.
265938	The method had some errors; errors have been returned in the error array.
265939	Invalid row handle.
265940	A given HROW referred to a hard-deleted row.
265941	The provider was unable to keep track of all the changes; the client must re-fetch the data associated with the watch region using another method.
265942	Execution stopped because a resource limit has been reached; results obtained so far have been returned but execution cannot be resumed.
265943	Method requested a singleton result but multiple rows are selected by the command or rowset. First row is returned.
265944	A lock was upgraded from the value specified.
265945	One or more properties were changed as allowed by provider.
265946	Errors occurred.
265947	A specified parameter was invalid.
265948	Updating this row caused more than one row to be updated in the data source.
265948	Row has no row-specific columns.

Support and Errata

One of the most irritating things about any programming book is when you find that bit of code you've just spent an hour typing simply doesn't work. You check it a hundred times to see if you've set it up correctly and then you notice the spelling mistake in the variable name on the book page. Of course, you can blame the authors for not taking enough care and testing the code, the editors for not doing their job properly, or the proofreaders for not being eagle-eyed enough, but this doesn't get around the fact that mistakes do happen.

We try hard to ensure no mistakes sneak out into the real world, but we can't promise that this book is 100% error free. What we can do is offer the next best thing by providing you with immediate support and feedback from experts who have worked on the book and try to ensure that future editions eliminate these gremlins. The following section will take you step by step through the process of posting errata to our web site to get that help. The sections that follow, therefore, are:

> Wrox Developers Membership
>
> Finding a list of existing errata on the web site
>
> Adding your own errata to the existing list
>
> What happens to your errata once you've posted it (why doesn't it appear immediately)?

There is also a section covering how to e-mail a question for technical support. This comprises:

> What your e-mail should include
>
> What happens to your e-mail once it has been received by us

So that you only need view information relevant to yourself, we ask that you register as a Wrox Developer Member. This is a quick and easy process, that will save you time in the long-run. If you are already a member, just update membership to include this book.

Wrox Developer's Membership

To get your FREE Wrox Developer's Membership click on Membership in the navigation bar of our home site, at http://www.wrox.com.

This is shown in the following screenshot:

Then, on the next screen (not shown), click on **New User**. This will display a form. Fill in the details on the form and submit the details using the **Send Form** button at the bottom. Before you can say 'The best read books come in Wrox Red' you will get the following screen:

Finding an Errata on the Web Site

Before you send in a query, you might be able to save time by finding the answer to your problem on our web site – http://www.wrox.com.

Each book we publish has its own page and its own errata sheet. You can get to any book's page by clicking on Support from the left hand side navigation bar.

From this page you can locate any book's errata page on our site. Select your book from the pop-up menu and click on it.

Then click on Enter Book Errata. This will take you to the errata page for the book. Select the criteria by which you want to view the errata, and click the Apply criteria… button. This will provide you with links to specific errata. For an initial search, you are advised to view the errata by page numbers. If you have looked for an error previously, then you may wish to limit your search using dates. We update these pages daily to ensure that you have the latest information on bugs and errors.

Adding an Errata to the Sheet Yourself

It's always possible that you may find your error is not listed, in which case you can enter details of the fault yourself. It might be anything from a spelling mistake to a faulty piece of code in the book. Sometimes you'll find useful hints that aren't really errors on the listing. By entering errata you may save another reader hours of frustration, and of course, you will be helping us provide even higher quality information. We're very grateful for this sort of advice and feedback. You can enter errata using the 'ask a question' of our editors link at the bottom of the errata page. Click on this link and you will get a form on which to post your message.

Fill in the subject box, and then type your message in the space provided on the form. Once you have done this, click on the Post Now button at the bottom of the page. The message will be forwarded to our editors. They'll then test your submission and check that the error exists, and that the suggestions you make are valid. Then your submission, together with a solution, is posted on the site for public consumption. Obviously this stage of the process can take a day or two, but we will endeavor to get a fix up sooner than that.

E-mail Support

If you wish to directly query a problem in the book with an expert who knows the book in detail then e-mail support@wrox.com, with the title of the book and the last four numbers of the ISBN in the subject field of the e-mail. A typical email should include the following things:

We won't send you junk mail. We need the details to save your time and ours. If we need to replace a disk or CD we'll be able to get it to you straight away. When you send an e-mail it will go through the following chain of support:

Customer Support

Your message is delivered to one of our customer support staff who are the first people to read it. They have files on most frequently asked questions and will answer anything general immediately. They answer general questions about the book and the web site.

Editorial

Deeper queries are forwarded to the technical editor responsible for that book. They have experience with the programming language or particular product and are able to answer detailed technical questions on the subject. Once an issue has been resolved, the editor can post the errata to the web site.

The Authors

Finally, in the unlikely event that the editor can't answer your problem, s/he will forward the request to the author. We try to protect the author from any distractions from writing. However, we are quite happy to forward specific requests to them. All Wrox authors help with the support on their books. They'll mail the customer and the editor with their response, and again all readers should benefit.

What We Can't Answer

Obviously with an ever growing range of books and an ever-changing technology base, there is an increasing volume of data requiring support. While we endeavor to answer all questions about the book, we can't answer bugs in your own programs that you've adapted from our code. So, while you might have loved the help desk systems in our Active Server Pages book, don't expect too much sympathy if you cripple your company with a live adaptation you customized from Chapter 12. But do tell us if you're especially pleased with the routine you developed with our help.

How to Tell Us Exactly What You Think

We understand that errors can destroy the enjoyment of a book and can cause many wasted and frustrated hours, so we seek to minimize the distress that they can cause.

You might just wish to tell us how much you liked or loathed the book in question. Or you might have ideas about how this whole process could be improved. In which case you should e-mail feedback@wrox.com. You'll always find a sympathetic ear, no matter what the problem is. Above all you should remember that we do care about what you have to say and we will do our utmost to act upon it.

Index

Index

Index

Index

Index

Index

Index

Index

Index

The JRO Objects

JETENGINE

Methods
CompactDatabase   RefreshCache

REPLICA

Collections
Filters

Properties
ActiveConnection   Replicaid
ConflictFunction   ReplicaType
ConflictTables   RetentionPeriod
DesignMasterId   Visibility
Priority

Methods
CreateReplica   PopulatePartial
GetObjectReplicability SetObjectReplicability
MakeReplicable   Synchronize

FILTER

Properties
FilterCriteria
FilterType   TableName

The ADOMD Objects

CONNECTION

CATALOG
Collections
CubeDefs
Properties
ActiveConnection
Name
Methods
Events

CUBEDEF
Collections
Dimensions
Properties
Description
Name
Properties
Methods
Events

CELLSET
Collections
Axes
Properties
ActiveConnection
FilterAxis
Item
Source
State
Properties
Methods
Close
Open
Events

DIMENSION
Collections
Hierarchies
Properties
Description
Name
UniqueName
Properties
Methods
Events

AXIS
Collections
Positions
Properties
DimensionCount
Name
Properties
Methods
Events

CELL
Collections
Positions
Properties
FormattedValue
Ordinal
Value
Properties
Methods
Events

HIERARCHY
Collections
Levels
Properties
Description
Name
UniqueName
Properties
Methods
Events

POSITION
Collections
Members
Properties
Ordinal
Methods
Events

LEVEL
Collections
Members
Properties
Caption
Depth
Description
Name
UniqueName
Properties
Methods
Events

MEMBER
Collections
Children
Properties
Caption
ChildCount
Description
DrilledDown
LevelDepth
LevelName
Name
Parent
ParentSameAsPrev
Type
UniqueName
Properties
Methods
Events